914.29

ASK
6.95

Please return/renew this item by the last date above. You can renew on-line at
www.library.lbhf.gov.uk/
or by phone
020 8753 2400

h&f
putting residents first

Hammersmith & Fulham Libraries

Published by:

Travel Publishing Ltd

Airport Business Centre, 10 Thornbury Road,

Estover, Plymouth PL6 7PP

ISBN13   9781904434856

© Travel Publishing Ltd

Country Living is a registered trademark of The National
Magazine Company Limited.

PLEASE NOTE:

All advertisements in this publication have been accepted in good faith by Travel Publishing and
they have not necessarily been endorsed by *Country Living* Magazine.

All information is included by the publishers in good faith and is believed to be correct at the time
of going to press. No responsibility can be accepted for errors.

Editor:	Peter Long
Printing by:	Latimer Trend, Plymouth
Location Maps:	© Maps in Minutes ™ (2009) © Collins Bartholomews 2009 All rights reserved.
Walks:	Walks have been reproduced with kind permission of the internet walking site: www.walkingworld.com
Walk Maps:	Reproduced from Ordnance Survey mapping on behalf of the Controller of Her Majesty's Stationery Office, © Crown Copyright. Licence Number MC 100035812
Cover Design:	Lines & Words, Aldermaston
Cover Photo:	Dolbadarn Castle, Snowdonia National Park © www.picturesofbritain.co.uk
Text Photos:	Text photos have been kindly supplied by the Pictures of Britain photo library © www.picturesofbritain.co.uk and © Bob Brooks, Weston-super-Mare

Foreword

From a bracing walk across the hills and tarns of The Lake District to a relaxing weekend spent discovering the unspoilt hamlets of East Anglia, nothing quite matches getting off the beaten track and exploring Britain's areas of outstanding beauty.

Each month, *Country Living Magazine* celebrates the richness and diversity of our countryside with features on rural Britain and the traditions that have their roots there. So it is with great pleasure that I introduce you to the *Country Living Magazine Guide to Rural Wales*. Packed with information about unusual and unique aspects of our countryside, the guide will point both fair-weather and intrepid travellers in the right direction.

Each chapter provides a fascinating tour of Wales, with insights into local heritage and history and easy-to-read facts on a wealth of places to visit, stay, eat, drink and shop.

I hope that this guide will help make your visit a rewarding and stimulating experience and that you will return inspired, refreshed and ready to head off on your next countryside adventure.

Suzy Smith

Editor, Country Living magazine

PS To subscribe to *Country Living Magazine* each month, call 01858 438844

Introduction

This is the fourth edition of *The Country Living Guide to Rural Wales* and we are sure that it will be as popular as its predecessors. Peter Long, a very experienced travel writer has completely updated the contents of the guide and ensured that it is packed with vivid descriptions, historical stories, amusing anecdotes and interesting facts on hundreds of places in Wales. In the introduction to each village or town we have also summarized and categorized the main attractions to be found there, which makes it easy for readers to plan their visit.

The advertising panels within each chapter provide further information on places to see, stay, eat, drink and shop. We have also selected a number of walks from walkingworld.com (full details of this website may be found to the rear of the guide), which we highly recommend if you wish to appreciate fully the dramatic landscapes, rich cultural heritage and rural charm of this attractive Celtic country.

The guide however is not simply an 'armchair tour'. Its prime aim is to encourage the reader to visit the places described and discover much more about the wonderful towns, villages and countryside of Wales in person. In this respect we would like to thank all the Tourist Information Centres who helped us to provide you with up-to-date information. Whether you decide to explore this region by wheeled transport or on foot we are sure you will find it a very uplifting experience!

We are always interested in receiving comments on places covered (or not covered) in our guides so please do not hesitate to use the reader reaction forms provided at the rear of this guide to give us your considered comments. This will help us refine and improve the content of the next edition. We also welcome any general comments which will help improve the overall presentation of the guides themselves.

For more information on the full range of travel guides published by Travel Publishing please refer to the order form at the rear of this guide or log on to our website (see below).

Travel Publishing

Did you know that you can also search our website for details of thousands of places to see, stay, eat or drink throughout Britain and Ireland? Our site has become increasingly popular and now receives monthly over 160,000 visits. Try it!

website: www.travelpublishing.co.uk

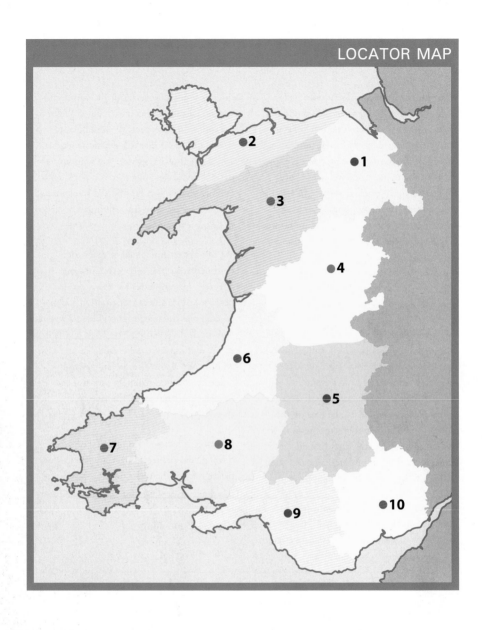

Contents

LOCATOR MAP

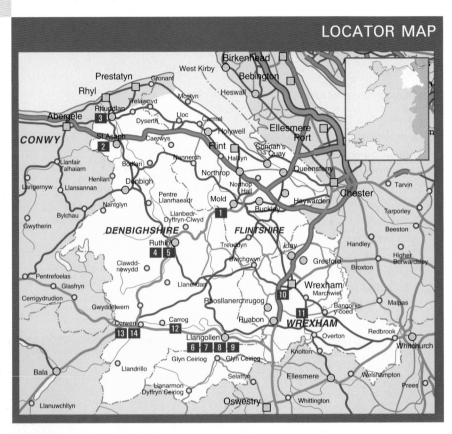

ADVERTISERS AND PLACES OF INTEREST

🏛 historic building   🏛 museum and heritage   🏛 historic site   ⚜ scenic attraction   🌿 flora and fauna

1 | North Wales Borderlands

This area of Wales can easily be overlooked by visitors as they speed westwards, but it is a mistake not to stop and explore the towns, villages and countryside as they are rich in history, heritage and scenic beauty. One of the best ways of seeing the countryside is by bicycle or, for a more testing challenge, by mountain bike. Each of the different areas has its own special character and scenery: the Clwydian Hills, a 22-mile long chain of heather-clad hills and a designated Area of Outstanding Natural Beauty; the Dee estuary; the broad, gentle sweep of the Vale of Clwyd with historic towns like Ruthin, St Asaph,

Denbigh and Rhuddlan; Wrexham, the largest town in North Wales, and its surrounds; The Maelor (once a detached portion of Flintshire), where the Cheshire Plains transform into the Welsh Hills; Chirk and the beautiful Ceiriog Valley. The Romans certainly forayed into the area from their major town of Chester and there is also evidence of Celtic settlements.

However, it was during the 13th century that Edward I, after his successful campaign against the Welsh, set about building his ambitious Iron Ring of huge fortresses along the Dee estuary and the North Wales coast.

Colwyn Bay, Clwyd

Each was built a day's march from its neighbours, and the first was begun at Flint in 1277. This was the cutting-edge military technology of its day and, though the great fortresses are now in ruins, the remains of the massive project – the largest seen in Europe – are still very much in evidence.

Plus, this area of Wales teems with wildlife. In fact, the land around the Dee estuary is home to a great number of waders and wildfowl, which feed on the mudflats left by the retreating tides.

Between the estuary and the Clwydian Range lie small, compact villages as well as the market towns of Mold and Holywell, a place of pilgrimage that became known as the Lourdes of Wales. The range, a grassy line of hills above the Vale of Clwyd, offers fabulous views and exhilarating walks; it is one of the eight designated Areas of Outstanding Natural Beauty in Wales.

Further south lie Llangollen and the Dee Valley. Llangollen is a delightful old town in a picturesque riverside setting, which is not only a charming place to visit, but is also the home of the annual International Music Eisteddfod (not the same as the National Eisteddfod). An eisteddfod was, originally, a meeting of bards where prizes were awarded for poetry reading and singing and, while local events still draw people from all over the country, the event at Llangollen has a true international flavour with such eminent figures as Luciano Pavarotti having graced its stage. The town is also famous for the Llangollen Railway, a re-opened section of the Barmouth–Ruabon line, which closed in 1960.

Though this northern gateway to the country is not a particularly large area, it boasts all but one of the Seven Wonders of Wales, wonders while not quite as spectacular as the more familiar Seven Wonders of the World are nonetheless all interesting in their own right and well worth a visit. They are listed in the famous 19th century rhyme:

> *Pistyll Rhaeadr and Wrexham Steeple,*
> *Snowdon's Mountain without its people,*
> *Overton Yew Trees, St Winefride's Well,*
> *Llangollen Bridge and Gresford Bells.*

The Borderlands offer an impressive variety of attractions, from castles and country houses to churches and museums, country parks and farm parks, lakes and canals, and leisure pursuits from walking, cycling and riding, to birdwatching and golf (more than 20 courses). There is also superb fishing for salmon and trout on the Rivers Dee and Clwyd, sea fishing in the Dee estuary and trout or coarse fishing at numerous lake fisheries. Festivals and other special events are staged throughout the year, and visitors are welcome to attend many rehearsals as well as performances by renowned Welsh choirs – a unique and moving experience that will long be remembered.

Mold

🏛 St Mary's Parish Church   🏛 Mold Museum

🏛 Bailey Hill   🌳 Loggerheads Country Park

🐦 Daniel Owen   🐦 Richard Wilson

🎨 Clwyd Theatr Cymru   🎨 Mold Carnival

Flintshire was one of the few counties in Britain to have detached portions. The largest was known as Maelor Saesneg, or Flintshire Detached. At one time it was part of Cheshire, but in 1536 was transferred to Wales by Richard II. In 1974 it became part of Wrexham Maelor District, which later became the County Burgh of Wrexham. To complicate matters, the burghs of Prestatyn, Rhyl and St Asaph were once in Flintshire as well, and there was another detached portion around Marford and Rossett.

Mold was Flintshire's county town, and is proud to claim the novelist, tailor and Methodist preacher **Daniel Owen** (1836–1895) as one of its own. He is often hailed as Wales' greatest novelist, and, writing only in Welsh, it was his honest accounts of ordinary life that were to make him one of the greatest 19th-century novelists and also to gain him the title the Welsh Dickens. His most famous books were *Rhys Lewis* and *Enoc Huws*. Owen's statue stands outside the town library, which is also the home of **Mold Museum**, where a room is dedicated to Owen's memory.

Though born in Montgomeryshire, Mold claims landscape painter **Richard Wilson** (1713-1782), as its own. After pursuing a career in London, he returned to his native Wales and settled in Mold to concentrate on the dramatic scenes of mountainous Welsh countryside that became his trademark. He died in Colomendy, and his grave and memorial can be found near the north entrance to **St Mary's Parish Church**. It was one of his descendants, Brian Wilson, who founded the American group The Beach Boys. Dating from the 15th century and built by Margaret Beaufort, Countess of Richmond, to celebrate her son Henry VII's victory at Bosworth in 1485, the church has some interesting stained-glass windows as well as some fine architectural ornamentation. A light and airy building, this church was constructed on the site of an earlier church whose original oak roof, carved with Tudor roses, has been retained in part.

The church stands at the foot of **Bailey Hill**, the site of a Norman motte and bailey fortification that was built at this strategic point overlooking the River Alyn by Robert de Montalt, who may have given the town its English name. First captured by the Welsh in 1157, and then again by Llywelyn the Great in 1199, ownership of the castle passed through many hands and today, not surprisingly, little remains of the fortress, as its site is now

Loggerheads Country Park, Mold

Loggerheads Country Park

Loggerheads, nr Mold, Denbighshire CH7 5LH
Tel: 01352 810586
wesbites: www.denbighshire.gov.uk
or www.loggerheads.biz or www.fresh-air.info

Loggerheads Country Park is a popular visitor
destination, attracting over 100,000 visitors every
year. The New Interactive Countryside Centre gives
visitors an insight in to the history and life within
the Park and provides necessary information and an
excellent learning opportunity. It has been described
as "interactive, vibrant and fun and aimed at people
of all ages, especially families."

This is an established Rural Country Park set in a
limestone valley in the Clwydian Range Area of
Outstanding Natural Beauty and encompasses a
mining and tourism history. The Park is also
managed for conservation, with SSSI (Site of
Special Scientific Interest) designation and rich and varied natural habitats. A Discovery
Trail gets visitors out and about in the park. They can see evidence of the history for
themselves, along with abundant wildlife. Visitors also get the chance to become a Trail
Detective and collect the secret symbols. New and improved bridges, signs, welcome
board, and free events all year round, add to the experience, providing a fantastic day out
for all the family.

marked by a bowling green. Bailey Hill may
have given the town its Welsh name of Yr
Wyddgrug, which means The Mound.

On the outskirts of Mold lies **Clwyd
Theatr Cymru**, which offers a wide range of
entertainment including theatre, music and
frequent exhibitions of art, sculpture and
photography. It has a bar, coffee shop,
bookshop, free covered parking and disabled
access. Every summer it hosts the **Mold
Carnival**. The composer Felix Mendelssohn
was said to have been inspired by the town's
surroundings when writing his opus *Rivulet*,
and the nearby limestone crags provide
panoramic views over the surrounding
countryside.

One such scenic area lies four miles west of
Mold on the A494 – **Loggerheads Country**

Park (see panel above), which is situated on the
edge of the Clwydian Range. Classified as an
Area of Outstanding Natural Beauty, this large
park is an ideal environment for all the family,
especially younger members, as there are
various trails that are each about one-and-a-half
miles long. The trails all start near the late18th-
century mill building that used water from the
River Alyn to drive a water wheel and two sets
of stones to grind corn from the local farms. A
regular bus service takes you to Loggerheads
from both Mold and Chester.

Around 200 years ago, Loggerheads was a
centre for lead mining, due to the plentiful
supply of ore-bearing limestone, and many
relics of those days can still be seen within the
quiet woodland. There is a fine selection of
local arts, crafts and souvenirs on display in

🏛 historic building 🏛 museum and heritage 🏚 historic site 🔱 scenic attraction 🌱 flora and fauna the Craft Shop at the **Loggerheads Countryside Centre**, where there is also a tearoom.

Around Mold

RHOSESMOR
3 miles N of Mold on the B5123

🏚 Parish Church of St Paul   🏛 Moel y Gaer

🏛 Wat's Dyke

Moel y Gaer, near this small village, was considered to be a fine example of an Iron Age hill fort until archaeological digs unearthed evidence that suggested this site had been inhabited from as far back as 3500BC.

To the west of the Rhosesmor lie the remains of a short section of **Wat's Dyke**, a much shorter dyke than Offa's, which is thought to have been built by the Mercian King Aethelbald in the 8th century. Just under 40 miles long, the dyke ran southwards from the Dee estuary to Oswestry.

The **Parish Church of St Paul** dates from 1876, when the parish of Caerfallwch, in which Rhosemor is situated, was formed. The village was once a centre of lead mining, and beneath it are natural and man-made tunnels.

Wat's Dyke, Rhosesmor

There is even said to be an underground lake, the largest in Europe.

HALKYN
4½ miles N of Mold on the B5123

🏚 Parish Church of St Mary   🏔 Halkyn Mountains

The village lies close to the long ridge of the **Halkyn Mountains,** which rise to some 964 feet at their highest point and are scarred by the remnants of ancient lead mines and quarries, some of which date back to Roman times. In the 17th century, Derbyshire lead miners were brought here to work in the newly opened mines. The medieval parish church was demolished in 1878, and the present **Parish Church of St Mary** was built some distance away in the same year.

FLINT
5 miles N of Mold on the A5119

🏚 Flint Castle   🐦 Ian Rush

Flint can boast two historical firsts: it was the first associated borough in Wales to receive a charter (in 1284) and it was also the site of the first of Edward I's Iron Ring fortresses. Dotted along the North Wales coast, a day's march apart, Edward I's ring of massive fortresses represented Europe's most ambitious and concentrated medieval building project, started after the Treaty of Aberconwy in 1277 and completed in 1284 by James of St George.

Flint Castle, now in ruins, stands on a low rock overlooking the coastal marshes of the Dee estuary and the Wirral peninsula. Originally surrounded by a water-filled moat, the remains of the Great Tower, or Donjon, are an impressive sight. Set apart from the main part of the castle, this tower, which is unique among British castles, was intended as a last retreat and, to this end, it was fully self-sufficient, even having its own well.

Flint Castle featured in the downfall of Richard II, when he was lured here in 1399 from the relative safety of Conwy Castle and was captured by Henry Bolingbroke, Duke of Lancaster and the future Henry IV. The imprisonment of Richard is remembered in Shakespeare's *Richard II*, where, in response to Bolingbroke's, "My gracious Lord, I come but for mine own," the defeated Richard replies, "Your own is yours, and I am yours, and all." At this point even the King's faithful greyhound is said to have deserted him.

During the Civil War, the town and castle remained in Royalist hands, under the leadership of Sir Roger Mostyn, until 1647, when both were taken by General Mytton, who was also responsible for dismantling the castle, thus creating the ruins we see today.

Ian Rush, the Welsh international footballer, though born in St Asaph, went to school in Flint.

HOLYWELL
7 miles N of Mold on the A5026

🏛 St Winefride's Chapel	🏛 St Winefride's Well
🏛 Parish Church of St James	🦜 Gutun Owain
🏛 Basingwerk Abbey	🦜 Gerard Manley Hopkins
🏛 Greenfield Valley Heritage and Country Park	

The town is well worth visiting solely on account of its fine town centre, which boasts over 60 listed buildings dating from Georgian and Victorian times. Thursday and Saturday are market days, when stalls crowd the main street. In the town lies one of the Seven Wonders of Wales, **St Winefride's Well**, which was once a place of pilgrimage and, at

one time, was referred to as the Lourdes of Wales. According to tradition, Winefride, the niece of St Beuno, was beheaded by Prince Caradoc after refusing his advances. It is claimed that a spring gushed from the place where her head fell and that she returned to life after her uncle had replaced her head. Winefride (Gwenfrewi in Welsh) went on to become an abbess at Gwytherin Convent near Llanrwst and, in 1138, her remains were given to Shrewsbury Cathedral. Caradoc was struck dead by lightning on the spot. Thought to have healing qualities, the well has been visited by pilgrims since the 7th century and still is, particularly on St Winefride's Day, the nearest Saturday to 22 June. The well, and the Vale of Clwyd, is beloved of the poet **Gerard Manley Hopkins**. He trained as a priest at St Beuno's College, Tremeirchion, and St Winefride's Well inspired him to write a verse tragedy, which

St Winefried's Well, Holywell

contains many beautiful, evocative lines:

The dry dene, now no longer dry nor dumb,
but moist and musical.
With the uproll and downcarol of day and night
delivering water.

On Wales in general he was equally lyrical:

Lovely the woods, water, meadows, combes, vales,
All the air things wear that build this
world of Wales.

St Winefride's Chapel was built by Margaret Beaufort (the mother of Henry VII) in around 1500 to enclose three sides of the well. The Victorian statue of St Winefride has a thin line round the neck showing where her head was cut off. Also here stands the **Parish Church of St James**, which was built in 1770 and probably stands on the site of the original chapel, which was constructed by St Beuno in the 7th century.

Basingwerk Abbey, to the east of Holywell, was built by Cistercian monks in 1132. The abbey functioned as a self-sufficient community, as the Cistercians lay great emphasis upon agricultural labour. Although this was an English house, Basingwerk absorbed Welsh culture and the Welsh bard, **Gutun Owain**, was associated with the abbey from where he wrote *The Chronicle of Princes*, which is also known as the *Black Book of Basingwerk*.

The abbey survived until the Dissolution of the Monasteries in the 16th century. In a tranquil setting that contrasts with the busy roads not far away, this magnificent ruin contains an arch, which, despite weather, beaten columns and faded 'message of love', is a fine example of Norman ecclesiastical architecture. In one of the buildings the remains of timber beams that once supported a roof can be seen.

Linking Holywell with the ruins of the abbey is the **Greenfield Valley Heritage and Country Park**, a 70-acre area of pleasant woodland and lakeside walks with a wealth of monuments and agricultural and industrial history. There are animals to feed, an adventure playground and picnic areas. In the 18th and 19th centuries this was a busy industrial area that concentrated on the newly established production processes for textiles, copper and brass.

NORTHOP
4 miles N of Mold on the A5119

🏛 Parish Church of St Peter and St Eurgain

🏛 Grammar School   🦜 William Parry

A church existed in Northop as early as the 6th century. The present **Parish Church of St Peter and St Eurgain** was extensively rebuilt in the mid 19th century, and much of the medieval fabric was lost. St Eurgain was the niece of St Asaph, the second bishop of St Asaph diocese. The church's tower is 98 feet high, and one of the landmarks of the area. The town's old **Grammar School**, dating from the 16th century, still stands in the churchyard.

The town was the birthplace (date unknown) of **William Parry**, a leading Catholic who was supposedly involved in a plot to assassinate Elizabeth I. He was the son of Harry ap David, and his real name was William ap Harry. He was eventually hanged in 1585, but present-day historians believe that he was innocent.

EWLOE
4 miles E of Mold on the B5125

🏛 Ewloe Castle

Ewloe (pronounced Yoo-low) was once famous for the manufacture of bricks and earthenware tiles. Hidden in a steeply wooded glen area are the remains of **Ewloe Castle**, a fortification built by the Welsh. It was founded by Llywelyn ap Gruffyd, known in English as Llywelyn the Last in 1257 after he had retaken this part of Wales from the English. Some 150 years later, a tower, two wards protected by a curtain wall, and an outer ditch were added, but the castle failed to live up to expectations, and by the late 13th century it ceased to have any military significance.

The town achieved temporary fame when the footballer Michael Owen bought a full street of houses here, called Austen Close, to house his family.

CONNAH'S QUAY
5 miles NE of Mold on the B5129

🐾 Wepre Country Park

This is the largest town in Flintshire, and is wholly industrial in nature, having three power stations and a steelworks. The town is said to get its name from the former landlord of an inn that stands near the docks. To the south of the town is the 160-acre **Wepre Country Park**, where there are ancient woodlands, walks, a fishing pool and a visitor centre.

HAWARDEN
5 miles E of Mold on the A550

🏛 Harwarden Castle

🏛 Parish Church of St Deiniol

🏛 Gladstone Memorial Chapel

🏛 St Deiniol's Residential Library   🏛 Castle Park

Mentioned in the *Domesday Book*, this small village close to the English border has two castles, one a ruin dating from the 13th century and another that was once the home of the Victorian Prime Minister, William

Gladstone. **Harwarden Castle**, Gladstone's home for some 60 years after his marriage to the daughter of Sir Stephen Glynne in 1839, was started in 1750 and enlarged and castellated by Sir Stephen in 1809. The remains of the older castle, chiefly the circular keep and the hall, still stand in **Castle Park**.

The **Parish Church of St Deiniol**, as well as having stained-glass windows by Burne-Jones, also houses the **Gladstone Memorial Chapel**, where marble effigies of the distinguished statesman and his wife, who are buried in Westminster Abbey, can be seen. The church was largely rebuilt after a deliberate fire in 1857, though records go back showing that one existed here in the 12th century. The parish was once a 'peculiar', which means that the rector was not answerable to any bishop. He therefore wielded considerable power, and had his own ecclesiastical court. He could also issue marriage licenses and prove wills.

The village's connections with Gladstone continue to this day as the former Prime Minister donated his collection of books to the famous **St Deiniol's Residential Library**, which lies adjacent to the church.

CAERGWRLE
6 miles SE of Mold on the A541

🏛 Caergwrle Castle   🐾 Waun-y-Llyn Country Park

🐾 Hope Mountain

Once occupied by the Romans as an outpost station for nearby Chester, **Caergwrle Castle**, which stands on a high ridge, probably started life as a Bronze Age hill fort. It was Dafydd, brother of Llewelyn the Last, who constructed the fortification in 1277 more or less in its present form, and it was from here, in 1282, that Dafydd launched his last Welsh attack on the English King, Edward I. He had

codified, could have been lost forever. A special monument, the **Translator's Memorial**, commemorates and names those who, under Morgan's guidance, assisted him in translating the Bible. Major restoration work on the cathedral was entrusted to Sir George Gilbert Scott, who also worked on the restoration of the cathedrals at Bangor and St David's as well as building many churches and houses throughout the United Kingdom. (The Scott dynasty takes a bit of sorting out: Sir George Gilbert Scott (1811–1878), the most prolific builder and restorer, had two architect sons, George Gilbert Scott Jr (1839–1897) and John Oldrid Scott (1842–1913). John Oldrid's son Sir Giles Gilbert Scott (1880–1960), was responsible for Liverpool Cathedral.)

In the centre of St Asaph is **Elwy Bridge**, which is believed to date from the 17th century although it was the fine renovation work by Joseph Turner in 1777 that allows it to carry today's heavy traffic. The River Elwy is linked with a particularly fishy tale about Bishop Asaph, after whom the town is named. One day, Queen Nest, the wife of Maelgwn Gwynedd, King of North Wales, lost a precious ring - the ancient and sacred ring of the Queens of the North - while bathing in the river. Upset and fearing her husband's anger, the Queen went to St Asaph to ask for his help in retrieving the ring. Comforting the lady, St Asaph invited the royal couple to dine with him the following

evening where he told Maelgwn about the loss of the ring. The king's terrible rage could only just be contained by St Asaph and he suggested they begin their meal. As the king cut into the locally-caught salmon that started the feast, the sacred ring fell out on to his plate!

However, Glasgow – where Kentigern founded that city's cathedral – claims the events took place there, though the circumstances are slightly different.

RHUDDLAN
8 miles N of Denbigh on the A525

🏰 Rhuddlan Castle   🏰 Parliament House

🏰 Gillot's Tower   🏰 Dominican Friary

🏰 Parish Church of St Mary   🏚 Twt Hill

📖 Statue of Rhuddlan

The site of an early Norman stronghold can be seen on **Twt Hill**. The stronghold dates from the 11th century, and was built by Robert of Rhuddlan, known as the Terror of North Wales. At one time it may have incorporated a stone tower, though nothing can now be seen of it. The place was

Rhuddlan Castle

abandoned in about 1277 when Edward I built **Rhuddlan Castle** nearby. One of the Iron Ring of fortresses built by Edward I, as one of the most massive and impenetrable of his defences, it was the king's headquarters during his campaign and it was from here that Edward issued the **Statute of Rhuddlan** (in March 1284) that united the Principality of Wales with the Kingdom of England. He also gave the town a Royal Charter when his sovereignty was confirmed. The statute, which lasted until the Act of Union in 1536, was enacted on the site now occupied by **Parliament House** (the old court house) and there is a commemoration tablet on the wall that is said to be from the original building. Although the castle, like many, was partially destroyed during the Civil War, the town is still sometimes referred to as the Cradle of Wales.

While the castle in its heyday was a magnificent example of medieval defensive building, the most impressive engineering feat in the area was the canalisation of the River Clwyd to give the castle access, by ship, to the sea some three miles away. The remains of the dockgate, **Gillot's Tower**, can still be seen. This was built by James of St George, who was also responsible for the interesting concentric plan of the castle that allowed archers, stationed on both the inner and outer walls, to fire their arrows simultaneously.

At one time a **Dominican Friary** stood close to Twt Hill, though the remains are now on private property. The **Parish Church of St Mary** was founded in the 13th century, with an extra nave being added 200 years later. However, the original church may have been built about 1080. At one time it was considered as the place to build a new cathedral for what is today the Diocese of St

Asaph. There is the tombstone of an archbishop in the church – but an unusual one. He was William de Freney, Archbishop of Edessa in Syria. It was originally part of the Dominican friary, but was brought to the church in 1536. It was de Freney's uncle who had been sent to England by the Pope to found the Dominican order in that country.

DYSERTH
10 miles N of Denbigh on the A5151

🏛 Parish Church of St Bridget   🏛 Bodrhyddan Hall

🏛 Merseyside Children's Holiday Camp

🏛 St Mary's Well   🗺 Dyserth Waterfall

Lying in the foothills of the Clwydian Range, below Craig Fawr's slopes, this village, in the scenic Vale of Clwyd, boasts a 60-foot waterfall known as the **Dyserth Waterfall**, as well as the charming **Parish Church of St Bridget**, which dates from the 13th century.

Just to the west of the village lies **Bodrhyddan Hall**, the impressive 17th-century manor house of the Conwy family who have had their home here since the early 15th century. The hall houses the Charter of Rhuddlan, and visitors can also see, around the fireplaces in the white drawing room, panels that came from the chapel of a Spanish Armada ship that foundered off the coast of Anglesey. For the more ghoulish, one of the rooms contains an Egyptian mummy. Other notable items include Hepplewhite chairs, suits of armour and ancient weapons, and a family portrait by Sir Joshua Reynolds. **Bodrhyddan Gardens** are also of interest, the main feature being a box-edged Victorian parterre designed by William Andrews Nesfield, father of the famous William Eden Nesfield, who remodelled the house in 1875. William E had a very varied life, being a soldier and a watercolour painter before taking up garden

DOWNSBY ANTIQUES

6 High Street, Rhuddlan, nr Rhyl,
Denbighshire LL18 2UB
Tel: 01745 390666

Rhuddlan is a town steeped in history, with its Norman stronghold, its castle, its parish church and its Parliament House. These, and other historic buildings bring visitors from near and far, but the town has other attractions. No visit is complete without looking in at **Downsby Antiques**, which was started by owner Phil Garratt in 2002. Phil has been buying and selling antiques at auction for almost 40 years, and browsers in his shop are certain to find something to enhance the home or to give as a gift for a friend or loved one to treasure. Among the constantly changing stock are Victorian, Edwardian and quality reproduction furniture, porcelain from the same periods, antique jewellery, watches, vintage teddies and other collectables and curios. Phil offers a framing service – he'll frame pictures and almost anything else, including photographs, embroidery, medals and trophies. He is also always interested in buying scrap gold. Downsby Antiques is open from 10 to Tuesday to Saturday.

design when he was over 40. He worked on well over 200 estates, among the most notable being the Royal Botanic Gardens at Kew. A much older part of the garden at Bodrhyddan is centred around a well house (bearing the inscription 'Inigo Jones 1612') containing a spring, **St Mary's Well**, that may once have had pagan significance.

In 1909, a man called Arthur Lee founded the **Merseyside Children's Holiday Camp** here, and for 75 years it provided holidays for poor children from Liverpool and Birkenhead. The site is now occupied by a hotel and country club.

BODELWYDDAN
8 miles N of Denbigh off the A55

🏛 Marble Church   🏛 Bodelwyddan Castle

St Margaret's Parish Church is known as the **Marble Church**, and was built between 1856

and 1860 by Lady Willoughby de Broke as a memorial to her husband. The landmark white spire is of local limestone, while inside is an arcade made of 14 different types of marble. In the churchyard are buried several Canadian soldiers from a nearby camp who were shot for mutiny in 1918.

Opposite the eye-catching church stands **Bodelwyddan Castle**, a Victorian country house and estate that occupies the site of a 15th-century house. The castle is the Welsh home of the National Portrait Gallery, and as well as the wonderful collection of Victorian portraits on display, visitors can see furniture on loan from the Victoria and Albert Museum and sculptures from the Royal Academy. Anyone tiring of the glorious pieces exhibited here can relax and play one of several hands-on Victorian games and inventions in the gallery, while outside are picnic tables, an adventure playground, maze, terrace café and secret woodland walk. A hands-on science centre is the latest attraction.

18th and 19th-century landscaped parkland surrounds the castle and here, too, is an Arts and Crafts walled garden originally planted by TH Mawson, with some redesign work undertaken by H Moggridge in 1980.

RUTHIN
7 miles SE of Denbigh on the A525

🏛 Parish Church of St Peter 　🏛 Old Courthouse

🏛 Old Grammar School 　🏛 Ruthin Gaol

🏛 Nant Clwyd House 　🏛 Ruthin Castle

🏚 St Peter's Square 　🏚 Maen Huail

This old market town lies in the Vale of Clwyd, more or less surrounded by a ring of hills, with a layout that appears to have changed little from medieval days. In fact, a description of Ruthin made in Elizabethan times, where it is described as "the grandest market town in all the Vale, full of inhabitants and well replenished with buildings", is as true today as it was then. **St Peter's Square** is a good place from which to view the town; it was here in 1679 that a Catholic priest was hung, drawn and quartered. Situated behind a magnificent set of 18th-century wrought iron gates stands the town's splendid **Parish Church of St Peter**. Founded in the late 13th century as a collegiate church, its notable features include an early 16th-century oak roof that consists of 408 carved panels. Behind the church there are some beautiful buildings in the collegiate close – 14th-century cloisters, the **Old Grammar School** of 1284 and 16th-century almshouses.

St Peter's Square itself is edged with many

MANORHAUS
10 Well Street, Ruthin,
Denbighshire LL15 1AH
Tel: 01824 704830 Fax: 01824 707333
e-mail: post@manorhaus.com
website: www.manorhaus.com

Boutique Rooms, Restaurant and Gallery

A Grade II-listed Georgian building in the heart of historic Ruthin underwent a major refurbishment in 2006 that combined many of the best original features with stylish modern interior design and up-to-the-minute facilities. The eight bedrooms in **Manorhaus** (the 'haus' is a nod of respect towards the Bauhaus school of design) range from cosy doubles with wet-room showers to a luxurious suite with a lounge area and roll-top bath; all have king-size beds, goose down bedding, Egyptian cotton sheets, flat-screen TV with DVD/CD player and free wi-fi high-speed internet access. Each room is individually designed in collaboration with artists who show their work in the rooms on a long-term basis. The owners have chosen the furniture, fabrics and colours to blend with the artwork, providing a high level of comfort combined with eye-catching style and elegance.

In the restaurant (booking recommended) à la carte dinners highlight the best of Welsh produce, including Salt Marsh lamb, Welsh Black beef and Menai mussels. Thoughtfully chosen wines accompany the fine food, and the bar also stocks a variety of bottled beers and a selection of single malts and Welsh spirits. The restaurant and lounge areas also act as a gallery space showcasing the work of contemporary Welsh artists.

🏛 historic building 　🏛 museum and heritage 　🏚 historic site 　🌄 scenic attraction 　🌿 flora and fauna

RUTHIN CRAFT CENTRE

Park Road, Ruthin, Denbighshire LL15 1BB
Tel: 01824 704774 Fax: 01824 702060
e-mail: thegallery@rccentre.org.uk
website: www.ruthincraftcentre.org.uk

The Centre for Applied Arts

Opened in July 2008, **Ruthin Craft Centre** is a stunning modern building dedicated to the work of contemporary artists from Wales and throughout the UK and beyond. Built of zinc and cast stone with reddish-pink tones, it blends well with its setting, conveying a sense of the spirit of Denbighshire, boldly contemporary yet respecting tradition, elegant with the suggestion of being hand-turned. Set against the backdrop of the Clwydian Hills (the undulating roofs echo the surrounding hills), it is a fitting home for one of Europe's leading contemporary craft institutions. It was transformed on the Centre's existing site with the aid of an Arts Council of Wales lottery grant that provided £3.1 million of the £4.3 million total cost. This amazing development was designed by architects Sergison Bates, who represented Britain at the Venice Architecture Biennale in 2008. The project was conceived to be both an internationally renowned venue for contemporary crafts and an important focus of educational and leisure facilities for the local community. Three new galleries facilitate the staging of large-scale exhibitions, working with leading museums and galleries around the world. Two of these display the best modern work by artists from Wales and beyond, the other is a space for collections and a retail outlet. The courtyard round which the Centre is set is a focal point, with outdoor furniture designed by Jim Partridge and Liz Walmsley. A café on the north

side of the courtyard has a south-facing terrace, and next to this are six studios that provide a stimulating working environment, an education room, two studios for artists in residence and a Tourist Information Centre/Cultural Gateway that looks at the culture of Wales through specially commissioned films by artists, along with information leaflets of Denbighshire and North Wales.

There is a changing programme of exhibitions in the three gallery spaces throughout the year showing the breadth of the applied arts and crafts including ceramics, textiles, jewellery, glass, metalwork, basketry plus much more; the exhibitions are programmed to show in the individual gallery space or at times a major exhibition will be on show through all the three galleries with exhibitors from Wales, the UK and also international makers work being shown in this internationally regarded centre for craft and the applied arts.

There is always something new and exciting at Ruthin Craft Centre, which is open every day from 10 to 5.30. Entry is free, with free on-site parking.

Old Court House, Ruthin

lovely buildings, including the particularly eye-catching 15th-century Myddleton Arms with its unusual Dutch style of architecture and its seven dormer windows that have been dubbed the Eyes of Ruthin. At one time there were around 60 inns and pubs in Ruthin – one for every 10 men in the town – and nine of these were to be found around the square. On the south side of St Peter's Square stands the impressive wattle-and-daub **Old Courthouse**, which dates from 1401 and was a temporary resting place for prisoners, who were kept in the cells below the magnificent beamed courtroom.

On Clwyd Street, a major new attraction opened in May 2002. This is **Ruthin Gaol**, through whose gates thousands of prisoners – men, women and children, the guilty and the innocent – passed between 1654 and 1916. Visitors (all volunteers these days!) can see how prisoners lived their daily lives: what they ate, how they worked, the punishments they suffered. The cells, including the punishment, 'dark' and condemned cell, can be explored, and there are hands-on activities for children. In Castle Street can be found one the oldest town houses in North Wales. **Nant Clwyd House** is a fine example of Elizabethan

architecture, although the present 16th-century building shows traces of an earlier house. During the reign of Elizabeth I it was the home of Dr Gabriel Goodman, an influential man who was the Dean of Westminster for 40 years. He established Ruthin School in 1595 and the town's almshouses. Ruthin is also renowned for **Maen Huail**, a stone that stands in the market place and which, according to legend, marks the place where Huail was beheaded by King Arthur because of rivalry in love.

Ruthin Castle, begun in 1277 by Edward I, was the home of Lord de Grey of Ruthin who, having proclaimed Owain Glyndwr a traitor to Henry IV, was given a large area of land originally held by the Welshman. After Glyndwr crowned himself Prince of Wales, de Grey was the first to suffer when Ruthin was attacked in 1400. Though the town was all but destroyed, the castle held out and survived the onslaught. During the Civil War, the castle again came under siege, this time surviving for 11 weeks in 1646 before eventually falling to General Mytton, who had the building destroyed. Partially restored and then owned by the Cornwallis-West family, Ruthin Castle played host, before and during World War I, to many famous and influential Edwardians including the Prince of Wales (later Edward VII), the actress Mrs Patrick Campbell, and Lady Randolph Churchill, the mother of Winston Churchill. Today, the castle, with its charming grounds and roaming peacocks, is a hotel that specialises in medieval banquets.

LLANARMON-YN IÂL
11 miles SE of Denbigh on the B5431

🏛 Parish Church of St Garmon

The capital of the Lâl region and occupying an attractive position on the banks of the

River Alun, at the southern end of the Clwydian Range, this small village is noted for the **Parish Church of St Garmon**. It has been considerably altered over the years, and now only one of the two naves is wholly medieval. The fine Llwd memorial dates from 1639, and there are two medieval effigies (one of a knight and one of a bishop) rescued from Valle Crucis Abbey (see also Llangollen). Up until Tudor times, pilgrims would flock to the shrine of St Garmon here.

LLANFIHANGEL GLYN MYFYR
11 miles SW of Denbigh on the B5103

🏛 Parish Church of St Michael   🏞 Llyn Brenig

🏞 Llyn Alwen   🌲 Clocaenog Forest

This sleepy village lies in the fertile vale through which the River Alwen runs. Just to the north lies the **Clocaenog Forest**, Wales' second largest commercial plantation, which covers much of the southern moorland between the vales of Clwyd and Conwy. Managed by the Forestry Commission, it has well-marked forest trails of varying lengths that lead walkers through the mixed plantations of larch, spruce, pine, beech, oak and ash.

On the edge of the forest lies **Llyn Brenig**, a massive man-made reservoir that was completed in 1976 to accompany the smaller **Llyn Alwen**, which dates from the early 1900s. Close to the dam, and reached along the B4501, is a Visitor Centre that explains the local history and ecology of this tranquil Welsh valley, as well as acting as a starting point for lakeside walks. By the lake, depending on the time of year, butterflies such as Orange Tip and Tortoiseshell can be seen and, along with water sports on the lake, fishing is also available.

The **Parish Church of St Michael** is basically medieval, though it was partially rebuilt in 1852 and restored in 1902

CERRIGYDRUDION
12½ miles SW of Denbigh on the B4501

🏛 Parish Church of St Mary Magdalene

🕮 Y Fuwch Frech

This village's name, often misspelt as 'Druidion', means 'Place of the Brave' and has no connection with Druids. There are many tales of fairy cattle to be found in Wales, creatures that are thought to have descended from the aurochs, the wild cattle that roamed Britain in prehistoric times. Cerrigydrudion has it own cow, **Y Fuwch Frech** (the freckled cow), who lived on nearby Hiraethog mountain. For years she supplied the area with milk and would always fill any receptacle brought to her. One day, a witch began to milk her into a sieve and continued until the cow went insane and drowned herself in Llyn Dau Ychen. The **Parish Church of St Mary Magdalene** is said to have been founded as early as 440 AD. The present building is medieval, and was mentioned in the Norwich Taxation documents of 1254. It was enlarged in 1503 and restored in 1874.

GWAENYNOG BACH
1½ miles W of Denbigh on the A543

🏛 Gwaenynog Hall

During the late 19th and early 20th centuries Beatrix Potter was a frequent visitor to the beautifully situated estate of **Gwaenynog Hall** (not open to the public), which was owned by her uncle Fred Burton. It is thought that her sketches, dating from a visit in 1909, of the kitchen garden (which has now been restored) were the basis for *The Tale of the Flopsy Bunnies* and also the working environment of the fictional Mr McGregor the gardener, who wanted to bake Peter Rabbit in a pie.

Llangollen

The town, which is in the Dee Valley, takes its name from its founder, a monk called St Collan, who set up his cell and monastery here in the 7th century. A legend says that he was instructed to ride a horse for one full day along a valley and then stop. At the place where he stopped, he was to mark out the boundaries of a monastery. This he did, and it soon became an important place. Another story tells of St Collan, after fighting with a giantess in a nearby mountain pass, washing off the blood in a well, known locally as **Ffynnon Collen** (St Collen's Well).

The **Parish Church of St Collen** is largely perpendicular, though there is an Early English doorway. It is, like many churches in this part of Wales, double-naved, and its chief glories are the two late medieval roofs.

The town nowadays draws visitors from all over the world who come here for the annual **International Musical Eisteddfod**, which has been held since 1947. For six days every July, musicians, choirs, folk singers and dancers from all over the world, many performing in their national costumes, converge on the town to take part in this wonderful cultural event that is centred around the **Royal International Pavilion**. Between 2,000 and 5,000 competitors take part, and, in a small town with only 3,000 inhabitants, crowds of around 120,000 people are not unknown. Dylan Thomas visited and wrote about the Eisteddfod, and Luciano Pavarotti, Tiri Te Kanawa and Placido Domingo have taken part. This event should not be confused with the **National Eisteddfod**, the annual Welsh language cultural festival whose venue alternates between the north and south of the country.

The first recorded eisteddfod was held at Cardigan Castle in 1176, and the modern eisteddfod began as a competition between bards at the Owain Glyndwr hotel in Corwen in 1789; it became a truly national event at Llangollen in 1858, when thousands of people

River Dee, Llangollen

PROACTIVE ADVENTURE HOLIDAYS

Tyn Dwr Hall Centre, Tyn Dwr Road, Llangollen,
Denbighshire LL20 8AR
Tel: 01588 630123 Fax: 01588 630323
e-mail: office@proactive-adventure.com
website: www.proactive-adventure.com

Proactive Adventure Holidays is a respected and experienced provider of Outdoor Education. The company has many years experience of providing residential outdoor breaks to families, schools and youth groups. The organization caters for age groups from 6 to 60 and all levels of ability. The centre has a range of accommodation varying from a Yurt camp to 3 star en-suite bedrooms.

With easy access from the motorway network and main services, the centre features on-site facilities including a full high ropes course, BMX track, climbing and abseiling tower, archery and orienteering course. Off-site in the local area canoeing and kayaking is offered, both on placid water or white water. There are exciting venues close by for climbing and abseiling and the surrounding mountains offer great guided mountain walks. For those who fancy something a little more exciting there is available caving and white water gorge walks. If you don't mind traveling for about an hour there is also coasteering which is great fun and very popular.

Unlike many large commercial providers who use "in house" trained instructors, Proactive Adventure Holidays only employ instructors who hold National Governing Body Awards and who have at least 3 years post qualifying experience. There is 24 hour cover by staff qualified in First Aid as well as 24 hour security to ensure the highest standards of welfare.

Scheduled activity programmes run for three or four days, or if you prefer the centre can tailor make one to suit your needs. For further information please visit the website on www.proactive-adventure.com or phone 01588 630123

📖 stories and anecdotes 🦜 famous people 🎨 art and craft 🎭 entertainment and sport 🚶 walks came to Llangollen from all over the country. Music, prose, drama and art are included in the festival, which culminates in the chairing and investiture of the winning poet.

Throughout the rest of the year there are many other attractions in Llangollen to keep visitors satisfied. The **Llangollen Motor Museum** (see panel below) features over 60 cars, motor bikes and even pedal cars from the earliest days of motoring to the present day.

Much later, in the 19th century, Llangollen was famous as the home for 50 years of the **Ladies of Llangollen**, Lady Eleanor Butler and Miss Sarah Ponsonby. These two Irish women ran away from their families in Ireland and set up home together in 1780 in a cottage

above the town. As well as devoting their lives to "friendship, celibacy and the knitting of blue stockings", the ladies also undertook a great deal of improvements and alterations that turned a small, unpretentious cottage into the splendid house – **Plas Newydd** – seen today. The marvellous 'gothicisation' of the house was completed in 1814 and some of the elaborate oak panels and the glorious stainedglass windows were donated to the couple by their famous visitors, who included Sir Walter Scott, William Wordsworth, the Duke of Gloucester and the Duke of Wellington. The ladies were both buried in the churchyard of St Collen, sharing a grave with their friend and housekeeper Mary Caryll.

Llangollen Motor Museum

Pentre Felin, Llangollen, Denbighshire LL20 8EE
Tel: 01798 860324
e-mail: llangollenmotormuseum@hotmail.com
website: www.llangollenmotormuseum.co.uk

The **Llangollen Motor Museum** is located near the town, nestling between the Llangollen Canal and the river. The building, dating back to the 1820s, was originally a slate dressing works and had many other uses before becoming a museum in 1985. The museum demonstrates in an informative , yet informal, way the charm and character of our motoring past, and the collection comprises more than 60 vehicles, from cars and motor bikes to invalid carriages and pedal cars. There is a recreation of a 1950s village garage complete with petrol pumps and the owners' living quarters. Included in the museum's collection are a Model T Ford, a splendid 1925 Vauxhall 38/93, a 1925 Citroën Boulangere from the vineyards of France and many of the cars that grandad used to drive. Among the motor bikes are great British names, including Norton, Triumph, Ariel, Sunbeam and BSA. The Museum is owned and run by the Owen family, headed by Gwylim, who was involved in the design and construction of cars at Vauxhall, his wife Ann and one of his sons, Geoffrey, who is a car restorer. For those who like to repair and restore their own vehicles, the Museum keeps a large stock of spares for classic cars, mainly from the 1960s.

The Museum also has a small exhibition showing the history and development of the British canal network and life on the canals through models, paintings, pottery and other memorabilia. School parties are welcome, and for car clubs a private field is available for picnics or overnight camping. The Llangollen Motor Museum, which has a refreshment and souvenir shop, is open Tuesday to Sunday March to October; winter opening by arrangement.

🏠 historic building   🏛 museum and heritage   🏚 historic site   🏞 scenic attraction   🌿 flora and fauna

Bersham Ironworks

North Wales, is now a busy place with plenty to offer the visitor. Growing and prospering around the commercial importance of its brick and tile manufacturing, brewing, steel and coal, today Wrexham still holds a variety of markets. An interesting experience for city dwellers is the cattle market held on Saturdays when farmers from the surrounding area come to socialise and oversee transactions and where visitors can wander around soaking up the rural atmosphere.

For those wishing to find out more about the town and its social, industrial and local history, then **Wrexham Museum**, housed in the County Buildings that were originally constructed as the militia barracks in 1857, is a good place to start. The discovery of a skeleton nearby – it became known as Brymbo Man - traces the town's history back as far as the Bronze Age, while the Romans are also known to have settled in the Wrexham area. Both Roundhead and Cavalier troops were garrisoned in the town during the Civil War and, in 1882, Britain's first lager brewery was built here. The suburb of Acton was the birthplace of **Judge Jeffreys**, the notoriously harsh lawman who was nicknamed 'Bloody' for his lack of compassion and his belief in swift justice.

Perhaps Wrexham's best known building, and one that's a particular favourite of American tourists, is the **Parish Church of St Giles** which dominates the town's skyline. It is famous for being the burial place of **Elihu Yale**, the benefactor of Yale University, who was laid to rest here on his death in 1721. His father had emigrated from Wrexham to North

of industrial interest. It passes through Plas Power and Nant Mill, woods that stretch along the River Clywedog between Bersham and Coedpoeth. A well preserved section of Offa's Dyke cuts through Plas Power (see Prestatyn). The village was established around 1670 and was the home of the **Davis Brothers**. The fine workmanship of these two famous iron masters can be seen in the beautiful gates at Chirk Park (see Chirk) and at St Giles' Church in Wrexham.

The master and owner of **Bersham Ironworks** from 1762, John 'Iron Mad' Wilkinson, was famous for the cannons he bored for use in the American War of Independence, and for the cylinders he produced for James Watt's steam engines. The ironworks are open in the summer, the Heritage Centre all year round.

WREXHAM
9½ miles NE of Llangollen off the A483

- 🏛 Parish Church of St Giles
- 🕊 Judge Jeffreys
- 🏛 Clywedog Valley and Trail
- 🕊 Elihu Yale
- 🏛 King's Mill
- 🏛 Wrexham Museum
- 🏛 Erddig
- ✎ Wrexham Science Festival

This once small market town, which is considered to be the unofficial capital of

America in 1637, and Elihu was born in Boston. In 1691 Elihu sent a cargo of books and Indian goods from Fort Madras where he was Governor. The sale of the books enabled him to initiate the University of Yale in 1692. The memorial quadrangle at Yale has a Wrexham Tower (see also Bryneglwys). Yale's tomb in St Giles was restored in 1968 by members of Yale University to mark the 250th anniversary of the benefaction and it can be found in the churchyard to the west of the tower. His tomb is inscribed:

Born in America, in Europe bred,
In Africa travelled and in Asia wed,
Where long he lived and thrived; in London dead.
Much good, some ill he did; so hope's all even,
And that his soul through mercy's gone to heaven.
You that survive and read his tale take care
For this most certain exit to prepare.
When blest in peace, the actions of the just
Small sweet and blossom in the silent dust.

The church itself is also well worth taking the time to look over; its 136-foot pinnacle tower is one of the Seven Wonders of Wales. Begun in 1506 and much restored, this Gothic tower still carries some of the original medieval carvings, in particular those of St Giles, which are recognisable by his attributes of an arrow and a deer. Elsewhere in the church are a colourful ceiling of flying musical angels, two very early eagle lecterns, a Burne Jones window and the Royal Welsh Fusiliers chapel.

Just to the south of Wrexham, and found in a glorious 2,000-acre estate and country park, is **Erddig** (see panel opposite), one of the most fascinating houses in Britain, with stunning state rooms, exhibitions of family memorabilia collected by the servants, restored outbuildings and exquisite grounds that include the National Ivy Collection.

Along with Erddig, which lies within the **Clywedog Valley and Trail**, is **King's Mill**, a restored mill that dates from 1769, although an older mill has been on the site since 1315.

Every year in early spring the town hosts the **Wrexham Science Festival**.

GRESFORD
13 miles NE of Llangollen on the B5445

🏛 Parish Church of All Saints 🏛 Gresford Bells

🏚 Gresford Colliery Disaster

This former coal mining town was the site of the **Gresford Colliery Disaster** in 1934 which killed 266 men. The colliery closed in 1973, but the wheel remains in memory of those who lost their lives in this terrible disaster. The town's **Parish Church of All Saints** is one of the finest in Wales, with notable medieval screens, stained glass, font and misericords, and a memorial to the mining disaster; it is also home to the famous **Gresford Bells**, one of the Seven Wonders of Wales, which are still rung every Tuesday evening and on Sundays.

HOLT
15 miles NE of Llangollen on the B5102

🏛 Holt Bridge 🏛 Holt Castle 🌿 H G Wells

🏛 Parish Church of St Chad

The River Dee, which marks the boundary between Wales and England, runs through this village and its importance as a crossing point can be seen in the attractive 15th-century **Holt Bridge**. The village of Holt was also the site of a Roman pottery and tile factory that provided material for the fort at nearby Chester. For a short while, the town had a very famous inhabitant – **H G Wells**, who was a teacher at the local school. There are scant remains of **Holt Castle**, or Castrum Leonis as

Erdigg

nr Wrexham LL13 0YT
Tel: 01978 355314

Two miles south of Wrexham, in a glorious 2,000-care estate and country park, **Erddig** is one of the most fascinating houses in Britain, not least because of the unusually close relationship that existed between the owners and their servants. This is movingly illustrated by the extraordinarily detailed exhibition of family

memorabilia collected by the servants and on show to visitors. The late 17th century mansion was begun by Joshua Edisbury, the High Sheriff of Denbighshire, who subsequently fled, unable to meet his debts. The house passed into the hands of the Meller family and to their descendants until finally coming under the ownership of the National Trust. The stunning state rooms display most of their original 18th and 19th century furniture and furnishings, including some exquisite Chinese wallpaper.

The outbuildings have been restored, including kitchen, laundry, bakehouse, stables, sawmill, smithy and joiner's shop, and visitors can wander around the country park and the dairy farm. The large walled garden has been restored to its 18th century formal design and incorporates Victorian additions, notably a parterre and yew walk, as well as a canal garden and fish pool; it also contains the National Ivy Collection, and a narcissus collection. Erddig is open to the public between late March and early November except Thursday and Friday. It has a plant sales area, a shop and a licensed restaurant. Video presentations are available, and conducted tours by prior arrangement.

it was called, built by John de Warren in the 13tth century. The **Parish Church of St Chad** originally dates from the late 14th century, though it was almost completely rebuilt between 1871 and 1873.

BANGOR-IS-Y-COED

11 miles E of Llangollen on the B5069

🏠 Parish Church of St Dunawd   ⚘ Racecourse

Bangor-is-y-coed (The Place of the Choir Below the Wood), also known as Bangor-on-Dee, is in the area known as the Maelor, where the Cheshire Plains meet the Welsh Hills. The **Parish Church of St Dunawd** dates from the early 14th century and later, and is named after a Welsh saint who founded a monastery here in about 560 AD. Due to its support of the Celtic peoples in their struggle against the

Anglo Saxons, it was destroyed in 607 AD by Ethelfrid of Northumbria in what turned out to be the last victory by the Saxons over Celtic Christianity. Apparently, 1,200 monks were laid to the sword as Ethelfrid considered praying against him was tantamount to fighting against him. Those fortunate enough to have survived are thought to have travelled to Bardsey Island. Local legend also suggests that Owain Glyndwr married Margaret Hanmer in the hamlet of Hanmer, just four miles away. The village is well known to race-goers as it is home to a picturesque **racecourse**, situated on the banks of the River Dee, which stages several national hunt meetings annually. The village itself has a charming 17th-century bridge said to have been built by Inigo Jones.

🎭 stories and anecdotes   🐦 famous people   🎨 art and craft   🎡 entertainment and sport   🚶 walks

OVERTON

10 miles E of Llangollen on the A539

🏛 Parish Church of St Mary   🌱 Overton Yew Trees

This substantial border village is home to another of the Seven Wonders of Wales – the **Overton Yew Trees**, 21 trees that stand in the churchyard of the **Parish Church of St Mary**. Dating from medieval times, these tall, dark and handsome trees have a preservation order placed upon them. Within the church itself there are some interesting artefacts from the 13th century.

CEFN-MAWR

4½ miles E of Llangollen on the B5605

🏛 Pontcysyllte Aqueduct

🌄 Ty Mawr Country Park

Towering some 126 feet above the River Dee and carrying the Llangollen branch of the Shropshire Union Canal, **Pontcysyllte Aqueduct** is a magnificent construction some 1,007 feet in length. Built in 1805 by Thomas Telford, this cast iron trough supported by 18 stone pillars was much scorned by people at the time, although today it is greatly admired and is still used regularly by pleasure boats. **Ty Mawr Country Park** is well worth a visit.

CHIRK

5½ miles SE of Llangollen on the B5070

🏛 Parish Church of St Mary   🏛 Chirk Castle

This attractive border town's origins lie in the 11th century castle of which, unfortunately, little remains except a small motte close to the town's **Parish Church of St Mary**. The church dates originally from Norman times, but it has been added to and restored over the years. It was originally dedicated to St Tysilio, the son of a Powys prince, but became St

Mary's in the 16th century. Today, Chirk is perhaps better known for the National Trust owned **Chirk Castle,** which lies a mile outside the town, and goes back almost 700 years. The magnificent iron gates were made and erected in 1701 by the Davis Brothers, and are one of the glories of the grounds (see also Bersham).

The Myddleton family of Chirk Castle have a red hand on their coat of arms that, legend has it, appears there as a reminder of the family's past misdeeds and could not be removed until a prisoner had survived 10 years in the castle dungeons. In the centre of Chirk is a war memorial designed by Eric Gill.

Just south of the town are two splendid constructions that span the Ceiriog valley: the first, an aqueduct built in 1801 by Thomas Telford, carries the Llangollen branch of the Shropshire Union Canal, while the other is a viaduct built in 1848 to carry the then new Chester to Shrewsbury railway line over the River Ceiriog.

GLYN CEIRIOG

2½ miles S of Llangollen off the B4500

🏛 Parish Church of St Ffraid ⚘ Ceiriog Forest

🏚 Chwarel Wynne Mine Museum

This former slate mining village is more properly called Llansantffraid Glyn Ceiriog, and is home to the **Chwarel Wynne Mine Museum,** which, as well as telling the story of the slate industry that used to support the village, gives visitors a guided tour of the caverns where the slate was mined. There is also a nature trail around the surrounding countryside. A narrow gauge tramway, the Glyn Valley Railway, once linked the Shropshire Union Canal at Gledrid with the quarries and mines at Glyn Ceiriog. Opened in 1873 and originally horse-drawn, it was later converted to steam and diverted through

Pontcysyllte Aqueduct

Chirk Castle estate to meet the Great Western Railway at Chirk station. It carried slate, silica, chinastone and dolerite downstream, and returned with coal, flour and other commodities. It also carried passengers, and though it closed in 1935, the bed of the tramway can still be seen here and there. The Glyn Valley Tramway Group was founded in 1974 to conserve evidence of the GVR and has little museums in the Glyn Valley Hotel at Glyn Ceiriog and the former waiting room at Pontafog station. A GVR Museum and Visitor Centre is to be established in the old locomotive shed and yard at Glyn Ceiriog.

The village lies in the secluded Vale of Ceiriog, and just to the west is the beautiful **Ceiriog Forest,** which offers surprisingly pastoral views and vistas along with forest walks and trails. The **Parish Church of St Ffraid** (another name for Bridget) was completely rebuilt in about 1790.

LLANARMON DYFFRYN CEIRIOG

6½ miles SW of Llangollen on the B4500

🏛 Parish Church of St Garmon 🏚 Tomen Garmon

⚘ Ceiriog ⚘ Ceiriog Trail

This peaceful village in the heart of the Vale of Ceiriog was the birthplace of the famous Welsh bard **Ceiriog,** whose real name was John Hughes (1832–1887). A collector of folk tales as well as a poet, he is sometimes called the Robert Burns of Wales. The 14-mile Upper **Ceiriog Trail** for walkers, mountain bikers and horse riders passes his home, Pen-y-Bryn. In the churchyard of the **Parish Church of St Garmon**, built in 1846, are yew trees, one of which may be over 1,000 years old. Also in the churchyard is a small tumulus, which may date from the Bronze Age. Local legend says it is **Tomen Garmon**, from which St Garmon preached and in which he was buried.

LLANTYSILIO

1 mile W of Llangollen off the A5

🏛 Parish Church of St Tysilio   🏚 Horseshoe Weir

🌿 Helena Faucit

Situated on the banks of the River Dee, and close to Thomas Telford's **Horseshoe Weir**, which was built in 1806 to supply water to the Llangollen Canal, lies the **Parish Church of St Tysilio**. A Norman building, it was here, in 1866, that Robert Browning worshipped, and a brass plaque placed by Lady Martin commemorates his visit. Lady Martin, also known as the actress **Helena Faucit**, lived in the house next to the church. She, too, is remembered at the church by a chapel that was built following her death in 1898. In 1885, she published a book called *On Some of Shakespeare's Female Characters*, which was popular in its day.

GLYNDYFRDWY

4 miles W of Llangollen on the A5

🏛 Parish Church of St Thomas   🌿 Eos Griffiths

🏚 Owain Glyndwr's Mound

Once within the estate of Owain Glyndwr, this village lies on the historic and important A5 and between the Berwyn and Llantysilio mountains. A mound by the road, known as

Owain Glyndwr's Mound, was once part of an impressive earthwork fortress that was later incorporated into part of the Welsh hero's manor house and estate. It was here, in 1400, that he declared himself to be Prince of Wales. Though it looks much older, the **Parish Church of St Thomas** dates only from 1858. Much more recently, Glyndyfrdwy has become known as the home of the Dutch Butterfly Man, **Eos Griffiths**, who is known worldwide for creating the bright and colourful ornamental butterflies that can be seen adorning homes from Scandinavia to Australia.

CORWEN

9 miles W of Llangollen on the A5

🏛 Parish Church of St Mael and St Sulien

🏛 Rug Chapel

🏛 Parish Church of All Saints, Llangar

🏚 Caer Derwen   🌿 Owain Glyndwr

This market town, in a pleasant setting between the Berwyn Mountains and the River Dee, has, for many years, been known as the Crossroads of North Wales. The town's origins can be traced back to the 6th century when the Breton-Welsh saints, Mael and Sulien, founded a religious community here. The **Parish Church of St Mael and St Sulien** still bears their name. This church was founded in the 12th century, though what can be seen nowadays dates mainly from the 13th to 15th century. It has an incised dagger in a lintel of the doorway that is known as **Glyndwr's Sword**. The mark was reputedly made by Glyndwr when he threw a dagger from the hill above the church in a fit of rage against the townsfolk. However, the dagger mark actually dates from the 7th to 9th century and there is another such mark on a 12th-century cross outside the southwest corner of the church.

The town was once the headquarters of

THE COTTAGE
BED & BREAKFAST

Carrog, nr Llangollen,
Denbighshire LL21 9AP
Tel: 01490 430644
e-mail: enquiries@thecottagecarrog.co.uk
website: www.thecottagecarrog.co.uk

Set in the heart of the Dee Valley, The
Cottage Bed & Breakfast is a former
farmhouse, parts of which date back some 400 years. It is possesses all the characteristics of
age, including low doors and differing floor levels. The owner does not regard the property as
suitable for young children as there is a large deep ornamental pond on the patio.

The accommodation comprises 1 double and 1 double/twin en suite bedroom, both equipped
with all the little touches you would expect from a four star B&B such as luxurious toiletries and
fluffy towels. Afternoon tea is served to guests on arrival. Breakfast offers guests a wide choice
of fresh, locally sourced produce. Coeliacs are especially welcome. Evening meals can be
enjoyed in the village pub or other eating-places or other eating-places around the area. If the
weather is fine, guests may use the BBQ area in the large garden.

Walking, cycling and most outdoor activities are available from this lovely village, whilst the
station at Carrog offers the opportunity to enjoy the scenic steam railway ride into Llangollen, the
small town beside the River Dee, which is renowned for its International Musical Eisteddfod held
every July.

Owain Glyndwr, who gathered his forces here
before entering into his various campaigns.
Owain Glyndwr (c1354–c1416), the self-styled
Prince of Wales, led the last major attempt to
shake off the yoke of the English. His status as
a national hero was reinforced with the rise of
Welsh Nationalism from the 18th century
onwards. Descended from the Princes of
Powys, he studied law in London and served
with Henry Bolingbroke, an opponent of
Richard II who was later to become Henry IV.
When Glyndwr returned to Wales, he
encouraged resentment against the oppressive
English rule. In September 1400, a year after
Bolingbroke had usurped the throne, Glyndwr
entered into a feud with a neighbour, Reynold,
Lord Grey of Ruthin, which sparked an
uprising in North Wales and a national struggle
for independence. Glyndwr formed an alliance
with King Henry's most influential and
powerful opponents and by 1404 controlled

most of Wales and embarked on a series of
campaigns. But by the next year he had twice
been defeated by Henry IV's son Prince Henry
(later Henry V), his English allies had been
eliminated and even help from the French was
fruitless.

By 1409 Glyndwr's main strongholds were in
English hands and his campaigns came to an
unsuccessful conclusion.

It was in the Owain Glyndwr Hotel in 1789
that a local man, Thomas Jones, organised a
bardic festival that laid the foundations for the
modern eisteddfod. Across the River Dee
from the town lies **Caer Derwyn**, a stone
rampart around a hill that dates from
Roman times.

To the west of Corwen, and set in pretty,
landscaped grounds, is the simple, stone-built
Rug Chapel. A rare example of a private chapel
that has changed little over the years, Rug was
founded in the 17th century by Old Blue

Stockings, Colonel William Salisbury, in collaboration with Bishop William Morgan (the first translator of the Bible into Welsh), and its plain exterior gives no clues to its exquisitely decorated interior. It is testimony to Salisbury's high church outlook, and is best described as a painted chapel. Few parts have been left unadorned and, as well as the beautifully carved rood screen (a Victorian addition) the ceiling beams are painted with rose motifs. However, not all the decoration here is exuberant; there is also a sombre wall painting of a skeleton as a reminder of mortality. The architect Sir Edwin Lutyens acknowledged that his work was influenced by this beautiful chapel and evidence of this can be seen in his most elaborate commission, the Viceroy's House, New Delhi, which was completed in 1930.

Another interesting religious building can be found just to the south of Rug, in the direction of Llandrillo. The **Parish Church of All Saints** at Llangar, overlooking the confluence of the Rivers Dee and Alwen, is medieval, and though it was superseded in the 19th century by a new church at Cynwyd, this small place still retains many of its original features. In particular, there are some extensive 15th-century wall paintings and a minstrels' gallery. Both Rug Chapel and Llangar church are now cared for by CADW – Welsh Historic Monuments.

LLANDRILLO
12 miles SW of Llangollen on the B4401

🏛 Parish Church of St Trillo   🜂 Craig Berwyn

🜲 Berwyn Mountains

The road to Llandrillo from the north, follows the Vale of Edeirion and the River Dee as it weaves its way below the northwest slopes of the **Berwyn Mountains**, another mountain range that is popular with walkers and visitors.

CORWEN MANOR

8 London Road, Corwen, Denbighshire LL21 0DR
Tel: 01490 413196
website: www.corwenmanor.com

Corwen Manor was originally the old union workhouse, which was built in 1837. It is now a thriving craft centre owned and run by the sayer family. The craft shop which has a good range of Welsh gifts and souvenirs also has a wool shop, which sells King Cole wool and haberdashery. The candle workshop is best known for its wide range of novelty candles, all made in Wales. So whether you collect cats, dogs, frogs, pigs, dragons, owls or teddy bears you're sure to find them here. For the budding candle maker they stock candle making supplies and craft kits. For that special occasion there is a range of personalised gifts from candles to love spoons, which can be personalised with names and dates of your choice in English of Welsh. For the fisherman Corwen Manor stocks a fine range of fishing tackle and baits. Most top brands stocked all at very competitve prices. Feeling hungry and need a snack? Corwen Manor has a delightful café selling snacks, drinks and homemade cakes.

🏛 historic building   🏛 museum and heritage   🏛 historic site   🜂 scenic attraction   🜲 flora and fauna

GLYNDWR PLANTS

Tafarn Bric, Corwen, Denbighshire LL21 9BU
Tel: 014904 413313/413688
Fax: 014904 413313
e-mail: stubbs@tafarnbric.co.uk
website: www.glyndwrplants.co.uk

Glyndwr Plants was developed on the site of Tafarn Bric which was an unlicensed tavern on one of the ancient drovers' routes between North Wales and London. 'Bric' is a derivative of 'Pric' which is the Welsh word for stick. Since the premises were unlicensed, money for ale could not change hands so sticks were purchased and notched, indicating how much the stick was worth. These sticks were then exchanged for ale or porter. The owners of Glyndwr Plants, John and Myfanwy Stubbs, hasten to point out that they no longer carry on this tradition!

Established in 1997, the company grows and sells hardy plants, (nearly all grown on their own site) for all types of gardens and gardeners, so whether you are a novice or connoisseur, you can be sure there will be something for you. Knowledgeable staff are available at all times to give advice and many customers return year after year to browse the new additions to the trees, shrubs, herbaceous perennials, or to discover what's new for their hanging baskets and patio tubs.

After browsing the plant centre, why not relax in the friendly Coffee Shop where you'll find a wide range of home made, freshly produced, tasty foods, along with freshly ground coffee, teas and cold drinks.

This small village is a good starting point for walks in the Berwyns and footpaths from the village lead towards **Craig Berwyn**, whose summit is over 2,100 feet above sea level. The name means 'church of St Trillo', and the successor of the church he founded here, the **Parish Church of St Trillo**, was built in the mid 19th century on a site that had been occupied by a place of worship for centuries. The east window is worth seeing.

BRYNEGLWYS
5 miles NW of Llangollen off the A5104

🏛 Parish Church of St Tysilio   🏛 Plas-Yn-Yale

Standing on the slopes of Llantysilio Mountain, the large 13th-century **Parish Church of St**

Tysilio in the heart of the village is, surprisingly, connected with the family who helped to found Yale University in the United States. Close to the village lies **Plas-Yn-Yale**, the former home of the Yale family and the birthplace of Elihu Yale's father. Elihu himself was born in 1647 in Boston, Massachusetts, and went on to become a governor of India before coming to England. Known for his philanthropy, Elihu was approached by an American College who, after receiving generous help, named their new college in Newhaven after him. In 1745, 24 years after his death, the whole establishment was named Yale University. Elihu Yale is buried in the Church of St Giles in Wrexham.

🎬 stories and anecdotes   🦜 famous people   🎨 art and craft   🎭 entertainment and sport   🐾 walks

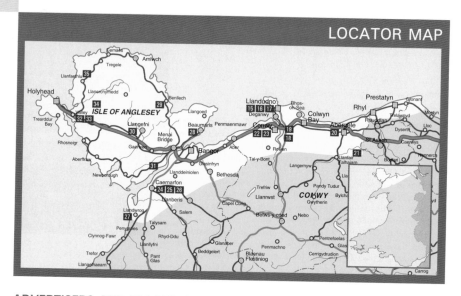

LOCATOR MAP

ADVERTISERS AND PLACES OF INTEREST

🏰 historic building 🏛 museum and heritage 🏚 historic site 🌳 scenic attraction 🌿 flora and fauna

2 | North Wales Coast & Anglesey

The coast of North Wales draws visitors in their thousands to its holiday resorts, but this very traditional region, where Welsh is still spoken on a daily basis, has many other treasures, both man-made and natural. The coastline from Prestatyn to Bangor was, before the coming of the railways, littered with small fishing villages. During the 19th century, as the hours of mill workers from the industrial towns of Lancashire and the Midlands were reduced, the concept of an annual holiday, albeit in some cases just the odd day at the seaside, became widespread. Served by the newly-built railway network, the fishing villages expanded to accommodate visitors. Boarding houses and hotels were built for society visitors coming to take the sea air,

and amusements and entertainment were soon a regular feature. Llandudno still retains much of its Victorian and Edwardian charm, while other resorts, such as Rhyl, have tried to counter the unsettled British summer weather with the creation of indoor complexes.

Prestatyn, to the east, lies at one end of Offa's Dyke (see Prestatyn). Built more as a line of demarcation rather than a fortification, the dyke runs from the coast southwards to Chepstow. Still substantially marking the border with England, many sections of the ancient earthwork are visible and can be seen from the waymarked footpath that runs the length of the dyke. It was also along the coast that Edward I built his Iron Ring of castles and while many are in ruins, two in particular

Llandudno Pier

Beaumaris Castle, Anglesey

are exceptional. Conwy Castle, now a World Heritage Site, was built in such a position that the surrounding land provides suitable protection from attack. Caernarfon Castle, as much a royal residence as a fortress, was the place where Edward, in 1301, crowned his son (later Edward II) as Prince of Wales. There were princes before this. In 1218 Llywelyn the Great and his descendents were given the title by his brother-in-law, Henry III of England. However, Edward II was the first heir to the English throne to have the title bestowed on him. Centuries later, in 1969, it was in the grounds of the splendid castle ruins that Queen Elizabeth invested the same title on her eldest son, Prince Charles.

Caernarfon and Bangor lie at opposite ends of the Menai Strait, the channel of water that separates mainland Wales from the Isle of Anglesey. It was not until the 19th-century that a bridge was constructed across the strait, and Thomas Telford's magnificent Menai Suspension Bridge of the 1820s was joined, some 30 years later, by Stephenson's Britannia Bridge. Two great monuments to 19th century engineering, the bridges still carry traffic, both road and rail.

The Isle of Anglesey, with its rolling hills, fertile farmland and miles of wild and craggy coastline, has attracted settlers from the Stone Age onwards and is littered with evidence of Neolithic, Bronze Age and Iron Age people. Anglesey has its impressive castle, Beaumaris, built by Edward I to repel invasion from its neighbours. Today's invaders are largely tourists and holidaymakers, attracted by the elegant seaside resorts, the fishing, the sailing and the walking.

Llandudno

🏚 Church of St Tudno	🏚 Deganwy Castle
🏔 Great Orme	🏛 Llandudno Museum
🏔 Promenade	🏯 Pier	🏯 White Rabbit Statue
🏯 Great Orme Tramway	🏯 Llandudno Cable Car
🏯 Great Orme Copper Mine	🐦 Bodafon Farm Park

Originally just a collection of fishermen's cottages, Llandudno – the Queen of Welsh resorts – was developed in the 1850s under the watchful eye of the Liverpool surveyor Owen Williams. A delightful place that is a wonderful example of Victorian architecture, Llandudno was planned around a pleasant layout of wide streets and, of course, a promenade, the essential feature of a resort from that age. The **Promenade** is now lined with renovated, redecorated and elegant hotels

and the wide boulevard gives it an air of the French Riviera. Off the Promenade towards the Little Orme by the fields, **Bodafon Farm Park** is a working farm and also home to the North Wales Bird Trust. Farm attractions include sheep shearing, ploughing, harvesting and collecting eggs. The Trust houses 1,000 birds, including eagle owls, falcons and tropical birds. A permanent Victorian puppet show can be watched on the promenade close to the **Pier**, which was opened in 1878 and has been popular with visitors ever since. Stretching 2,220 feet out to sea, it's the longest in Wales and one of the finest in the UK, with shops, cafés, bars and amusements. In 1914 the suffragettes attempted to burn it down. Later, Ringo Starr, of Beatles fame, worked on the pleasure streamers that docked at the pier. The North Shore has been voted one of the two best beaches in Wales.

VENUE CYMRU

The Promenade, Llandudno, Conwy LL30 1BB
Tel: 01492 879771
Fax: 01492 860790
e-mail: richard.p.jones@venuecymru.co.uk
website: www.venuecymru.co.uk

Originally known as the North Wales Theatre, Conference Centre and Arena, **Venue Cymru** received its new designation following a competition launched in a local newspaper to find a new, shorter and bilingual name. When the complex was officially opened in January 2007 it was described as the beginning of a new era for Entertainment, Conferencing and Events in Llandudno.

Throughout the year it hosts a wide range of entertainment featuring many household names. The 2009 season, for example, saw comedians such as Ken Dodd, classical music from the distinguished Prague Symphony Orchestra, straight plays such as *Billy Liar*, and musicals such as *Chicago* and *Jolson!* Verdi's epic opera *Aida*, the ballet version of *Wuthering Heights*, and circus from Le Grand Cirque Fantazie were also among the 169 different shows hosted by the venue.

A popular amenity at the Venue is the restaurant where pre-show diners can take in the spectacular views of the bay whilst enjoying the finest freshly prepared food. Showgoers can also relax and unwind in the café bar which, in addition to serving alcoholic drinks, also offers a selection of cakes, pastries and coffees.

🎭 stories and anecdotes 🐦 famous people 🎨 art and craft 🎵 entertainment and sport 🚶 walks

Along the seafront can be found the **White Rabbit Statue**, from Lewis Carroll's much loved story *Alice In Wonderland*. The tribute is to the real Alice - Alice Liddell - who came here on holiday with her family; it was also at Llandudno that her parents spent their honeymoon. Among the visitors to Dean Liddell's holiday home were such notable characters of the day as William Gladstone and Matthew Arnold, as well as Lewis Carroll. Though little is known today of Carroll's stay with the family, visitors can be certain that it was on the broad, sandy beaches at Llandudno that the Walrus and the Carpenter "wept like anything to see such quantities of sand" and it was the White Knight who considered "boiling it in wine" to prevent the Menai Bridge from rusting.

Although Llandudno is very much a product of the Victorian age, it earlier played host to Bronze Age miners and the Romans and, in the 6th century, St Tudno chose Great Orme as the site of the cell from where he preached. The saint was one of the seven sons of King Seithenyn, whose kingdom, it is said, sank beneath the waves of Cardigan Bay. The cell's successor is the **Church of St Tudno**, which was Llandudno's parish church when it was a fishing village, and which dates mainly from the 15th century. In 1852 it lost its 'parish church' status. One of its treasures is a roof boss depicting Christ's 'stigmata' - the wounds to his hands and feet where he was nailed to the cross and the wound in his side. At **Llandudno Museum** visitors are taken through the town's history, from ancient times to the present day, by a collection of interesting exhibits including a child's footprint imprinted on a tile from the Roman fort of Canovium (Caerhun), and objets d'art collected from all over the world by Francis Chardon.

POTS 2 COLOUR CERAMIC CAFÉ

11 Llewelyn Avenue, Llandudno,
Conwy County LL30 2ER
Tel: 01492 863108
website: www.pots2colour.co.uk

Based in its own custom studio in the centre of Llandudno, **Pots 2 Colour Ceramic Café** is a pottery painting studio which encourages artistic creativity within a colourful, caring, environment. Owner Angela provides everything you need for your pottery painting party, whether it is for you and your family, or a group of friends or a single painter.

"We are the only family friendly pottery activity in Llandudno" says Angela, "if you get stuck for ideas, we have lots of books to look to for inspiration, and our staff are very happy to help and inspire you towards your goal. What is amazing is that no two items come out looking the same - everything is totally unique."

Pots 2 Colour offer traditional glazing & firing or quick paint sessions, T shirt painting and soap & bath bomb making.

🏛 historic building 🏦 museum and heritage 🏚 historic site � scenic attraction 🌿 flora and fauna

THE GREAT ORME TRAMWAY

Llandudno, Conwy LL30 2NB
Tel: 01492 879306 Fax: 01492 574040
e-mail: tramwayenquiries@conwy.gov.uk
website: www.greatormetramway.co.uk

The Great Orme Tramway has been delighting visitors ever since it opened on July 31st, 1902. An engineering marvel of its age, it's still the only cable-hauled tramway still operating on British public roads. At the Halfway Station exhibition, visitors can discover the fascinating history of this unique funicular tramway and then enjoy the spectacular ride to the top. The whole tramway has been lovingly restored so that it's now possible to re-live the experience of travel as it was more than 100 years ago. Passengers travel in the original tramcars, each of which is named after a Saint and, following the restoration, ready for another century of service.

The Great Orme itself is a wonderland of nature and history. Look out for the two varieties of butterfly which are unique to the area, the wild Kashmir goats and the rare flowers. The view from the Great Orme's 679ft (207m) summit are breathtaking, stretching from Snowdonia and Anglesey, all the way to the Isle of Man, Blackpool and the Lake District. Other attractions include the headland's amazing Bronge Age copper mines and the 6th century St Tudno's Church.

As well as being the home of Llandudno's roots, the massive limestone headland of **Great Orme** still dominates the resort today and also separates the town's two beaches. Two miles long, one mile wide and 679 feet high, its name, Orme, is thought to have originated from an old Norse word for sea monster. In what is now a country park, there are prehistoric sites in the form of stone circles and burial sites, and the remains of Bronze Age mines. The summit can be reached by the **Great Orme Tramway**, a magnificent monument to Victorian engineering constructed in 1902 that is Britain's only cable hauled, public road tramway. Another way of reaching the summit is by the **Llandudno Cable Car**, the UK's longest. The **Great Orme Copper Mine** is the only Bronze Age copper mine in the world open to the public. Visitors can explore the 3,500-year-old

Great Orme Copper Mine, Llandudno

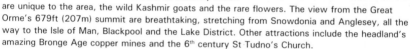
🖼 stories and anecdotes 🐦 famous people 🎨 art and craft 🎭 entertainment and sport 🚶 walks

SNOWDONIA NURSERIES

Llanrwst Road, Glan Conwy,
Colwyn Bay, Conwy LL28 5SR
Tel: 01492 580703
e-mail: info@snowdonianurseries.co.uk
website: www.snowdonianurseries.co.uk

Snowdonia Nurseries is a family owned and run traditional Garden Centre with a difference, offering a huge range of garden products, but focussing very much on its own nursery grown plants.

Snowdonia Nurseries have developed an enviable reputation for quality, established after more than twenty five-years of steady trading. They are conveniently situated at Glan Conwy, just off the A55; and in addition to offering spectacular views of the estuary, and a superb range of plants, also provide first class car parking for the disabled - and an excellent coffee shop.

Personal service and attention is high on the agenda for Snowdonia Nurseries. Richard, proprietor, who has a BSc honours degree in horticulture from Bath University, is vastly experienced, and readily available to offer friendly advice on all potential purchases or just to load up your car with a heavy bag of potting compost.

He is justifiably proud of all their goods and confirmed: "We don't just put anything on the shelves. We specialise in quality, and offer a comprehensive range of products." A key event in the Centres calendar is at Christmas when the displays are spectacular which automatically creates and enhances the true Christmas spirit. It has been described as a magical environment and the children can meet Father Christmas in an amazing grotto, each year all donations go to charity. Amongst just some of the items available at his wonderful Aladdin's cave of goodies during the festive season are decorative Christmas lights for both indoor and outdoor displays; very bright and long life LED lights; artificial Christmas trees; candles, table and giftware - plus real Christmas trees available from the first week in December.

In addition to their wide range of festive products, during the rest of the year they also have numerous soft fruit trees, bushes and vegetable plants displays, together with garden furniture, barbeques, gift ware and home accents.

And when all the shopping is completed, take some time to unwind and enjoy some light refreshments in the Olive Tree Coffee Shop; where home made cakes, tea, coffee, and snacks form an essential part of a varied menu.

🏠 historic building 🏛 museum and heritage 🏚 historic site 🏔 scenic attraction 🌿 flora and fauna

passages, see the great opencast mine workings, peer into the 470-foot shaft and discover how our ancestors turned rock into metal. The Visitor Centre is open to non-mine visitors, and also at the site are a tearoom serving Welsh cream teas and a shop selling a wide variety of books, minerals, fossils and other souvenirs. Great Orme is home to a herd of wild goats descended from a pair presented to Queen Victoria by the Shah of Persia.

Just south of Llandudno, on Conway Bay, lies Deganwy, a once thriving fishing village that shares the same stretch of coastline though it has now been taken over by its larger neighbour. Often mentioned in Welsh history, Deganwy was a strategically important stronghold and **Deganwy Castle** was the seat of Maelgwn Gwynedd as early as the 6th century. The first medieval castle was probably built here by Lupus, Earl of Chester, shortly after the Norman Conquest. The scant remains seen today are, however, of a castle built by one of the Earl's successors in 1211. Henry II was besieged here by the Welsh and Deganwy was finally destroyed by Llewelyn ap Gruffyd (Llewelyn the Last) in 1263.

Around Llandudno

LLANSANFFRAID GLAN CONWY
3 miles S of Llandudno off the A470

🏭 Felin Isaf   🏭 Parish Church of St Ffraid

In Garth Road **Felin Isaf** has two working watermills and a museum describing the history of the site and the various uses and types of mills. The **Parish Church of St Ffraid** is medieval in origin, though it was largely rebuilt in 1839.

BODNANT
6 miles S of Llandudno off the A470

🌾 Bodnant Gardens

Situated above the River Conwy and covering some 80 acres are the famous Edwardian **Bodnant Gardens**, laid out by the 2nd Lord Aberconwy in 1875 and presented to the National Trust in 1949.

Bodnant Gardens

🎭 stories and anecdotes 🕊 famous people 🎨 art and craft 🎟 entertainment and sport 🏃 walks

COFFEE JUNCTION

179 Conway Road, Llandudno Junction, Conwy LL31 9AY
Tel: 01492 581219

Owner Clare Lockwood offers home cooking at its best at **Coffee Junction**, a recently converted café with a neat, bright, practical modern interior and seats for 35. The day gets off to a flying start with a generous traditional cooked breakfast, and the menu, supplemented by daily specials, provides plenty of choice for appetites large and small. The top-quality meat, which comes from a high-class local butcher, is the basis of some of the favourite dishes, which include a steak pie made with Welsh Black beef and a satisfying plate of ham with eggs (free-range, of course) and chips. Old-fashioned syrup sponge pudding is a delicious way to end a meal, and there's always a tempting array of other home-baked goodies, among them carrot cake, Victoria sponge and chocolate brownies to compliment the freshly brewed coffee. A takeaway service is available for most of the items on the menu. Coffee Junction is open from 9 to 4 Monday to Friday and from 9 to 3 on Saturday. Clare has quickly built up a large and growing following among the locals, but her café is also popular with tourists, holidaymakers and motorists – it's just seconds from Junction 19 of the A55 coastal road.

Follow the Llandudno junction (A547) signs. It is just a short drive to the fringe of Snowdonia National Park, the nearest beach and Conwy Castle.

RHOS-ON-SEA
3½ miles E of Llandudno on the B5115

🏛 Bryn Eurin   ⛪ Rev W Venable Williams

🎭 Harlequin Puppet Theatre

This very sedate North Wales coastal resort has a breakwater to shelter the pleasure boats and, along the promenade, is the small Chapel of St Trillo. Though the chapel's age is unknown, it is said to have been built above an ancient holy well and also on the spot from where, reputedly, Owain Gwynedd set sail, in 1170, and eventually landed on the North American continent – some 322 years before Columbus made his historic voyage to the New World! It is said to be the smallest church in Britain, as it can only seat six people. Southwest of the town is **Bryn Eurin**, all that is left of a prehistoric fort.

On the promenade is a monument to the **Rev W Venable Williams**, He helped in the development of Rhos, but was in many ways a controversial figure He resisted the demands of local farmers to have their tithes reduced, and had his mission church in Colwyn Bay set on fire because of this. He also tried frantically to stop Colwyn Bay from splitting from his own parish of Llandrillo yn Rhos, taking his fight all the way to Parliament and even Queen Victoria.

The **Harlequin Puppet Theatre** can be found on the town's promenade. When built in 1958, it was Britain's first permanent theatre specially for puppet shows, and continues to present shows to this day.

COLWYN BAY
5 miles SE of Llandudno on the A55

🐾 Welsh Mountain Zoo   ⛪ Terry Jones

⛪ Timothy Dalron   ⛪ Bertrand Russell

A more genteel place than the resorts found to the east, Colwyn Bay was built largely during the 19th century to fill the gap along the coast between Rhos-on-Sea and the village of Old Colwyn. As a result, there are many fine Victorian buildings to be seen, and the beach is served by a promenade along which most of the town's attractions can be found. Colwyn Bay includes among its famous sons ex-Monty Python **Terry Jones** and a former James Bond, **Timothy Dalton**. The philosopher **Bertrand Russell** (1872–1970) was cremated with no ceremony at Colwyn Bay crematorium and his ashes scattered in the sea.

Although Colwyn Bay lies on the coast, it is also home to the **Welsh Mountain Zoo**, a conservation centre for rare and endangered species that is best known for the Chimp Encounter, its collection of British wildlife and its feeding of the sealions. The zoo's gardens, laid out by TH Mawson at the end of the 19th century, incorporate both formal terraces and informal woodlands, with paths offering superb views of Snowdonia as well as the Conwy estuary and the North Wales coast. The Tarzan Trail Adventure Playground is a surefire winner with young visitors.

LLISFAEN

7 miles off the A55 SE of Llandudno

🏛 Parish Church of St Cynfran

The **Parish Church of St Cynfran** was supposedly founded in 777 AD the by the saint of the same name. The present church has been heavily restored, though parts date from the 14th century, with incorporated masonry from an even earlier building. Cynfran himself is a shadowy figure, said to be the son of King Brychan of Brecknock, himself a saint. There is a holy well to the north of the church.

ABERGELE

10½ miles E of Llandudno on the A548

🏛 Gwrych Castle   🏛 Parish Church of St Michael

🔱 Cefn-Yr-Ogo   📖 Abergele Train Disaster

Along with Pensarn, its neighbour on the coast, Abergele is a resort, which, though more modest than such places as Rhyl, Prestatyn and Colwyn Bay, is justly popular with those looking for a quieter seaside holiday. Outside the town, on Tower Hill, is the mock-Norman **Gwrych Castle**, built in 1814 and formerly the seat of the Earl of Dundonald. It is now a holiday centre and among its many attractions are medieval jousts and banquets. The **Parish Church of St Michael** is medieval in origin, though it was heavily restored in the mid 19th century. Outside the church is a Penitential Stone. This was where people had to do penance for their sins by standing and asking the congregation for mercy as they left the church. Also in graveyard is the mass grave of those people killed in the **Abergele Train Disaster,** which took place on 20 August 1868, when the Irish mail train from London was hit by wagons that had rolled down an incline towards it. They were being shunted onto a side line at the time, and their brakes had not been applied. It would have been a simple collision had not two of the wagons contained 50 barrels of paraffin. On impact, the wagons exploded, causing the front carriages of the mail train to catch fire. Thirty three people were killed, making it, at that time, the worth rail disaster in British history.

On 30 June 1969, two members of the Mudiad Amddiffyn Cymru (Welsh Defence Movement), Alwyn Jones and George Taylor, were killed when a bomb they were planting on the line went off prematurely. The royal train was due to pass on its way to Caernarfon

THE BEE HOTEL

Market Street, Abergele, Conwy LL22 7AA
Tel: 01745 832300

Food, Drink, Accommodation, Hospitality...

The Bee Hotel is at the very heart of life in Abergele. It's a three-storey 18th century white-painted building on a prominent corner site in the centre of town, where the A 547 meets the A548, and a short drive from the A55 main coast road – leave at exit 23a or 24. The Bee has long been a favourite not only with the local community but also with the thousands of tourists who make the journey to the North Wales coast throughout the year. Queen Victoria once dropped in while her horses were being changed on a trip through Wales, and today's visitors are guaranteed a right royal welcome from host Neil Cooper and his team. The Bee's accommodation comprises seven nicely appointed en suite rooms with practical modern furnishings, TV and hot drinks tray. A single, a twin, two doubles and three family rooms make this an excellent base for a wide cross-section of guests, from single people on business to holidaying couples and families with children.

The proximity of beaches at Pensarn and Rhyl and the North Wales Coast Path make the Bee an excellent choice for a traditional seaside holiday. In the bar, with its handsome panelled service counter, a selection of award-winning real ales is on tap throughout the long opening hours, along with other draught and bottled beers, wines, spirits and non-alcoholic drinks. The large enclosed beer garden with its safe play area is a popular spot in the summer months, and the hotel has plenty of free parking for customers. Food is an important part of the Bee's business, starting with a multi-choice breakfast and including snacks, light meals, daily specials, a full à la carte menu, Sunday roasts and regular themed evenings. The resident chef makes fine use of seasonal Welsh produce, and main courses, including popular home-made pies, are served with super 'real' chips. A fine choice of some 40 wines accompanies a meal (no food on Wednesdays).

The Bee has long been at the heart of social life in Abergele, a veritable hive of activity. Thursday is quiz night, Friday sees karaoke and dancing and Saturday brings live entertainment from top local performers; a resident DJ presides on music nights. The Bee also fields pool and darts teams in the local leagues. Abergele, a joint resort with Pensarn, is a popular destination for a seaside holiday, quieter than its larger and better-known neighbours Colwyn Bay and Rhyl. And for anyone seeking a friendly, relaxed, well-run place to stay the Bee is definitely the place to head for.

🏛 historic building 🏛 museum and heritage 🏛 historic site ⚘ scenic attraction 🌱 flora and fauna

for the investiture of Prince Charles as Prince of Wales, and they wanted to stop it as a protest (see also Caenarfon)

Situated on higher ground behind the castle are the natural caverns of **Cefn-Yr-Ogo** whose summit commands magnificent views of the surrounding coastline.

RHYL

14 miles E of Llandudno on the A548

🏊 Sun Centre　🐟 SeaQuarium

🐦 Nerys Hughes

Once little more than a couple of fishermen's cottages until its development as a seaside resort from 1833, Rhyl used to be the destination for many workers and their families from the industrial towns and cities of Wales, the Midlands and the northwest of England. Though the heyday of this once elegant resort has long since passed, Rhyl still has a lot to offer the holiday maker.

As well as the full range of amusement arcades and seaside attractions, Rhyl is home to two large and exciting complexes: the **Sun Centre**, one of the first all-weather leisure attractions in the country, with indoor surfing and daredevil water slides and flumes; and **SeaQuarium**, where visitors can enjoy a seabed stroll surrounded by sharks, rays and other ocean creatures.

Nerys Hughes, the actress from the TV series *The Liver Birds* and *District Nurse*, was born in Rhyl, and **Carol Voderman**, though born in Bedford, attended school in the town when her family moved to North Wales.

To the southwest of the town lies the mouth of the River Clwyd, which is crossed by Foryd Bridge, and to the south lies Rhuddlan Marsh where, in 795 AD, Caradoc was defeated by Offa of Mercia.

PRESTATYN

16½ miles E of Llandudno on the A548

🏰 Prestatyn Castle　🏛 Offa's Dyke

🐦 John Prescott　🚶 Offa's Dyke National Trail

With three great beaches – Ffrith Beach, Central Beach and Barkby Beach – Prestatyn has proved a popular holiday destination over the years and, as expected, all types of entertainment are available, making the town an ideal centre for family holidays Although the town undoubtedly expanded with the opening of the Chester to Holyhead railway line in 1848, people were flocking here 50 years before that, lured by descriptions of the air being like wine and honey and the abundant sunshine being deemed excellent for the relief of arthritic conditions and nervous disorders.

However, Prestatyn's origins go back to prehistoric times, as excavated artefacts have shown. While the Roman's 20th legion was stationed at Chester, it is thought that an auxiliary unit was based at a fort on what is now Princes Avenue. The discovery in 1984 of a Roman bath house in Melyd Avenue would certainly seem to support this assumption.

The settlement is mentioned in the Domesday Book as Prestetone, from the Anglo-Saxon Preosta Tun (meaning a settlement in which two or more priests reside). It was Lord Robert Banastre who was responsible for building the Norman **Prestatyn Castle**. It was of a typical motte and bailey design, but all that remains of the fortification today is one stone pillar on the top of a raised mound that can be found close to Bodnant Bridge.

Prestatyn lies at one end of the massive 8th century earthwork **Offa's Dyke**. Although the true origins of the dyke have been lost in the mists of time, it is thought that the construction of this border defence between England and Wales was instigated by King Offa, one of the most powerful of the early Anglo-Saxon kings. From 757 AD until his death in 796 AD he ruled Mercia, which covers roughly the area of the West Midlands. He seized power in the period of civil strife that followed the murder of his cousin King Aethelbald and, ruthlessly suppressing many of the smaller kingdoms and princedoms, created a single settled state that covered most of England south of Yorkshire. His lasting memorial is the dyke, which he had built between Mercia and the Welsh lands. With an earthwork bank of anything up to 50 feet in height and a 12-foot ditch on the Welsh side, much of this massive feat of engineering is still visible today. The northern end of **Offa's Dyke National Trail** leads up the High Street, climbs the dramatic Prestatyn hillside and wanders through the Clwydian Range. This long-distance footpath of some 180 miles crosses the English-Welsh border 10 times and takes in some extraordinarily beautiful countryside. From the Clwydian Hills through the lush plains of England and the much fought over lands of the Welsh borders, the footpath not only covers some superb terrain but also allows those walking its route to see a great variety of flora and fauna as well as take in the traditional farming methods that have survived in the more remote areas of this region.

John Prescott, the labour politician, was born in Prestatyn in 1938.

LLANASA
20 miles E of Llandudno off the A548

🏛 Parish Church of St Asaph and St Cyndeyrn

🏛 Gyrn Castle

The **Parish Church of St Asaph and St**

Cyndeyrn largely dates from the 15th century, though there has been a church on the site since at least the 6th century. It incorporates some stained-glass windows from Basingwerk Abbey (see Holywell), which was dissolved by Henry III in 1536. Close by the village stands **Gyrn Castle,** which originates from the 1700s and was castellated in the 1820s. It now contains a large picture gallery, and its grounds offer some pleasant woodland walks.

TRELAWNYD
19 miles E of Llandudno on the A5151

🏛 Parish Church of St Michael   🏛 Gop Hill

🖋 Trelawnyd Male Voice Choir

Formerly called Newmarket, this village is well known for its Bronze Age cairn, **Gop Hill,** the biggest prehistoric monument in Wales, which marks the place where, traditionally, Offa's Dyke began, although the town of Prestatyn also claims this honour. The **Trelawnyd Male Voice Choir,** with over 100 members, is reckoned to be one of the best choirs in North Wales. The **Parish Church of St Michael,** which measures only 55 feet by 19 feet, was rebuilt in 1724, though a church has stood on the site for centuries.

MELIDEN
17 miles E of Llandudno on the A547

🏛 Parish Church of St Melyd   🌿 Craig Fawr

Meliden is a former mining village, and in the 19th century several hundred miners worked in the local mines. Just to the south of Meliden lies **Craig Fawr,** a limestone hill that supports a wide variety of flowers and butterflies, including the Brown Argus, a rare sight in North Wales, whose larvae feed on the Common Rockrose. Nature trails have been laid around the site that not only take in the myriad of wildlife and plants, but also an old quarry where the exposed limestone reveals a wealth of fossils left deposited here over 300 million years ago. The short walk to the summit is well worth the effort as there are panoramic views from the top over the Vale of Clwyd, the coastline and beyond to Snowdonia.

The **Parish Church of St Melyd** is mentioned in the Domesday Book, though the present church largely dates from the 13th century and later. It is the only church in Wales dedicated to that particular saint. The half-timbered south porch, which seems out of place tacked on to a stone building, was added in 1884. It also has a Devil's Door (now bricked up), which allowed the devil to leave the church when summoned to do so by the priest. When the churchyard wall was rebuilt some time ago, a surprising number of skeletons were unearthed. It is thought that these may have been people who were thought at the time to be in league with the devil, and who were not allowed to be buried in consecrated ground. The relatives got round this ecclesiastical edict by burying them half in and half out of the churchyard.

POINT OF AYR
21½ miles E of Llandudno off the A548

Marking the western tip of the Dee estuary and with views across the river mouth to Hilbre Island and the Wirral, this designated RSPB viewing point is an excellent place to observe the numerous birds that come to feed on the sands and mudflats left by the retreating tide.

LLANFAIR TALHAIARN
11½ miles SE of Llandudno off the A544

  Mynydd Bodran   John Jones

This village, the start of a walk to the Elwy

HAWK & BUCKLE INN

Llannefydd, nr Denbigh, Denbighshire LL16 5ED
Tel: 01745 540249
e-mail: enquiries@hawkandbuckleinn.com
website: www.hawkandbuckleinn.co.uk

At **The Hawk and Buckle** you will find an effective antidote to the pressures of modern day life. Complete with Inglenook fireplace, this lovingly restored 17th century coaching inn enjoys the benefit of all modern day conveniences- including ample car parking- and provides the perfect retreat for that long promised short break, or small business conference.

Guest bedrooms are toilet and bathroom en-suite and include hairdryers, colour television and beverage making facilities - and they are centrally heated. Naturally the bedroom is an essential element of your stay and all rooms have been designed with that in mind – they include everything that you could wish for and have the additional bonus of disabled access and some truly remarkable views.

The delightful licensed restaurant is perfect for either a leisurely lunch or as a place in which to relax at the end of a day of activity and sightseeing. The restaurant produces an impressive range of traditional, home cooked dishes (including a hugely popular Sunday roast lunch). Fresh, local produce is used wherever possible. The restaurant is easily divided to create spaces for both groups and individuals - and it is well worth enquiring about the price reductions usually available to early diners. Bar meals and snacks are also available.

---

  stories and anecdotes   famous people   art and craft   entertainment and sport   walks

Valley, is the burial place of **John Jones** (1810–1869), another poet who was acclaimed as the Welsh Robert Burns (see also Llanarmon Dyffryn Ceiriog). The waymarked walk is basically a circuit of **Mynydd Bodran**, which rises to nearly 950 feet above the Elwy and Aled Valleys and provides some spectacular views.

LLANGERNYW

10½ miles SE of Llandudno on the A548

🏛 Parish Church of St Digian

🏛 Sir Henry Jones Museum   🌿 Llangernyw Yew

This quiet Denbighshire village was the birthplace, in 1852, of Sir Henry Jones, who became known as "the cobbler philosopher". Born the son of a local shoemaker, Henry Jones left school at the age of 12 to become apprenticed to his father but, after the long working day, Henry continued his studies well into the evenings. His hard work paid off, and he won a scholarship to train as a teacher, and then went on to study philosophy before eventually becoming Professor of Moral Philosophy at Glasgow University. A well-known and highly regarded academic, and a widely acclaimed lecturer on social affairs and liberalism, Henry received his knighthood in 1912, and was made a Companion of Honour in 1922. He died in the same year. Though Sir Henry is buried in Glasgow, this village has not forgotten its local hero. In 1934, Jones' childhood home, Y Cwm, was purchased by a fund set up to honour his memory and his work. Today, the **Sir Henry Jones Museum** takes visitors on a tour through the family house – the tiny kitchen and bedroom where the family lived and shoemaker's workshop where Henry and his father worked.

The whitewashed **Parish Church of St Digian** dates from the 13th century, though it was much restored in the 1800s. In the churchyard is the **Llangernyw Yew**. The oldest known tree in Wales, and one of the oldest living things in the world, the yew is estimated to be over 3,000 years old. An old legend says that every Easter and 31 July the angel of death - known as the Angelystor in Welsh – appears beneath the tree's boughs and solemnly announces the names of the people of the parish who will die within the next six months. A story is told of one Shôn ap Robert, who mocked the legend while drinking in a local pub. His friends challenged him to visit the yew tree on the next 31 July, and he took up the challenge. The first name he heard as he approached the tree was his own, and though he declared jokingly that he was not yet ready to die, within six months he was being buried in the churchyard.

Conwy

🏛 Conwy Castle   Town Walls   🏛 Toll House

🏛 Suspension Bridge   🏛 Conway Mussel Centre

🏛 Plas Mawr   🏛 Aberconwy House

🐾 Conway River Festival

🏛 Britain's Smallest House   🏛 Conway Rail Bridge

🏛 Parish Church of St Mary and all Saints

Situated opposite Deganwy, on the south bank of the Conwy estuary, Conwy has in recent times returned to something of its former self with the completion of the tunnel that carries the A5 under the estuary. No longer harassed by heavy traffic, the town is a delight to wander around, its small streets steeped in history and the whole place dominated by another of Edward I's great castles. The ruins of what was one of the most picturesque of the many Welsh fortresses remain eye-catching to this day. **Conwy Castle** is situated on a

Conwy Castle

compared with some of Edward's castles, Conwy is of a relatively simple design which relies on its position rather than anything else to provide a defence against attack. The town was walled at the same time and today the **Town Walls** still encircle the vast majority of Conwy, stretching for three quarters of a mile and including 22 towers and three gateways. The

rock that overlooks the River Conwy and its estuary, from which it commands wonderful views of the whole area.

Begun in 1283, the castle's construction was largely finished by the autumn of 1287 and,

castle was also built to be a suitable royal residence and was used twice by Edward I: once on his way to Caernarfon where his son, the first English Prince of Wales was born; and again in 1294, when trying to put down

THE POTTERS' GALLERY

1 High Street, Conwy, Gwynedd LL32 8DB
Tel: 01492 593590
Open daily 10 am - 5 pm (Closed Wednesday - Winter)
website: www.thepottersgallery.co.uk

The Potters' Gallery is a co-operative gallery showing the ceramic work of selected members of The North Wales Potters Association. Domestic ware to rare collectors' items on display and for sale.

left-right work belongs to Sonja, Charmain, Pea

Charmain Poole has been a key member of the association and gallery since its inception six years ago. Her work reflects her fascination with the relationship between pot and food. She uses red earthenware clay, to create domestic ceramics that lift the ordinary meal to something special and memorable. Tel 07850 732 535, citronbleu32@hotmail.com

Pea Restall (M.A. Ceramics- Wolves, M.A. Design- MMU) Pea's majolica painted forms have a story to tell. Sculptural hands, figures, animals and thrown pieces are expressive, sometimes amusing and even disturbing. She is available for private tuition, teaches at universities and F.E colleges, and is one of the directors of the International Ceramics Festival- Aberystwyth. Tel 01745 832146, www.peajrestall.co.uk, potterypea@aol.com

Sonja Moss- Dolega's work is influenced by everyday observations of habits and expressive body language. Her unconventional pieces reflect her focus on form and balance, combining simplicity and ornament. She uses various types of clay, glazes and decorative materials in order to create unique, one-off figurative works, which provide highlights for home and garden. Tel 0151 3272822, sonja.mossdolega@talktalk.net.

🎞 stories and anecdotes 🐦 famous people 🎨 art and craft 🎭 entertainment and sport 🚶 walks

the rebellion of Madoc ap Llewelyn. Now a World Heritage Site, the castle not only offers visitors spectacular views from its battlements, but also the huge curtain walls and eight massive round towers, are still a stirring sight. In 1399, Richard II stayed at the Castle before being lured out and ambushed by the Earl of Northumberland's men on behalf of Henry Bolingbroke, the Duke of Lancaster, who later became Henry IV. Conwy attracted the attention of Owain Glyndwr during his rebellion, and his men burnt it to the ground.

As with other castles further east, Conwy was embroiled in the Civil War. A Conwy man, John Williams, became Archbishop of York and, as a Royalist, sought refuge in his home town. Repairing the crumbling fortifications at his own expense, Archbishop Williams finally changed sides after shabby treatment by Royalist leaders and helped the Parliamentary forces lay siege to the town and castle, which eventually fell to them in late 1646.

The town developed within the shadows of its now defunct fortress, and slate and coal extracted from the surrounding area were shipped up and down the coast from Conwy. Later, the town fathers approached Thomas Telford, who planned a causeway and bridge, as Conwy's trade and links grew with the outside world. Built in 1826, the elegant **Suspension Bridge** replaced the ferry that previously had been the only means of crossing the river so close to its estuary. The **Toll House** (NT) has been restored and furnished as it would have been over a century ago. This suspension road bridge, its design sympathetic to its surroundings, was soon followed by the construction of the railway. By the side of Telford's bridge stands the Robert Stephenson designed tubular **Conwy**

Rail Bridge of 1846. Both builders breached the town walls in styles that complemented the town's architecture and the two structures are still admired today.

Bridges, however, are not the only architectural gems Conwy has to offer. **Plas Mawr** (CADW), an Elizabethan town house on the High Street, is one of the best preserved buildings in Britain from that period. . Built for the influential merchant Robert Wynn between 1576 and 1585, the house has an interesting stone façade and over 50 windows. Plas Mawr (the name means Great Hall) is particularly noted for its fine and elaborate plasterwork, seen to striking effect in the decorated ceilings and friezes and in the glorious overmantel in the hall. The authentic period atmosphere is further enhanced by furnishings based on an

Plas Mawr, Conwy

BISTRO BACH

Chapel Street, Conwy, Gwynedd LL32 8BP
Tel: 01492 596326
e-mail: bistrobach@hotmail.co.uk

Rather unusually the building occupied by **Bistro Bach** was built using reclaimed wood from redundant churches and halls around the area. To the side of the establishment is a courtyard with a striking castle turret - this can be reached from the Castle Walk.

The bistro is owned by Gethin Jones who is also the head chef. His appetising menu is based on locally sourced ingredients with special prominence given to Welsh mountain lamb and gold-award-winning beef from the local butcher's. The menu changes according to the seasons while the Specials Board is regularly updated. To accompany your meal, there's an extensive choice of local wines, ales from the local Great Orme Brewery and a wide range of Welsh liqueurs.

If you are visiting this medieval walled town in late October, you can participate in the Conwy Feast, a weekend celebrating food and drink which features celebrity chefs, real ale celebration, wine tasting, a busking festival and food halls stacked with local produce.

inventory of the contents in 1665. The house came into the possession of the Mostyn family during the 18th century, and in 1991 was given to the nation by Lord Mostyn. Close by is **Aberconwy House** (NT), a delightful medieval merchant's home that dates from the 14th century. The rooms have been decorated and furnished to reflect various periods in the house's history.

Occupying part of the site of a 12th century Cistercian Abbey, founded by Llwelyn the Great in 1199 and then moved to Maenan by Edward I, is the **Parish Church of St Mary and all Saints**. Some interesting features still remain from that time though there have been many additions over the centuries. The 15th-century rood screen is particularly fine. This was the burial place of the Princes of Gwynedd, and Llwelyn himself.

It is not surprising that the town and the surrounding area have strong links with the sea and Conwy also has a traditional mermaid story. Washed ashore by a violent storm in Conwy Bay, a mermaid begged the local fishermen who found her to carry her back to the sea. The fishermen refused and, before she died, the mermaid cursed the people of the town, swearing that they would always be poor. In the 5th century, Conwy suffered a fish famine that caused many to avow that the curse was fulfilled.

St Brigid is connected to another fish famine story. Walking by the riverside carrying some rushes, she threw the rushes upon the water. A few days later the rushes had turned into fish and ever since they have been known as sparlings or, in Welsh, brwyniaid - both meaning rush-like. Fishermen still land their catches, on the quayside and from here pleasure boat trips set sail. Nearby can be found what is claimed to be **Britain's Smallest House**, measuring 10 by 6 feet. It seems that its last tenant was a fisherman who was 6ft i6in tall – he was presumably also a contortionist! Conwy was once a famous pearl fishing centre, and had a thriving mussel industry, whose history is told in the **Conwy Mussel Centre**, open daily from mid-May to September. The **Conway River Festival** takes place every year in August, and is the premier yachting occasion for the whole of the Irish Sea.

Around Conwy

ROWEN
4 miles S of Conwy off the B5106

🏛 Parish Church of St Celynin   🏚 Maen-y-Bardd

🏚 Caer Bach   🌿 Parc Mawr   🪨 Tal-y-fan

From this very pretty, quiet village a track, which was once a Roman road, skirts by the foot of **Tal-y-fan**, which reaches 2,000 feet at its peak. Roughly six miles in length, the path passes by **Maen-y-Bardd**, a Neolithic burial chamber, and eventually drops down towards the coast at Aber. Another, circular, walk of about five miles, one of several in the Conwy Valley devised by Active Snowdonia, passes many impressive cromlechs and standing stones. The route also takes in **Caer Bach**, where there are traces of a Neolithic settlement, the wonderfully unspoilt 14th-century **Parish Church of St Celynin** and the Woodlands Trust's **Parc Mawr** woods.

TREFRIW
8 miles S of Conwy on the B5106

🏛 Trefriw Woollen Mill   🏚 Fairy Falls

🦅 Taliesin

This village, nestling into the forested edge of Snowdonia in the beautiful Conwy valley, sits on an old Roman road. It was once one of the homes of Llywelyn the Great, and the Parish Church of St Mary stands on the site of a former church built by him to please his wife, who refused to climb to the church at Llanrhychyrn, above the village. Standing eight miles from the sea, it was once the biggest inland port in Wales. The village today has two main attractions, **Trefriw Woollen Mill** and the local chalybeate springs. The woollen mill has been in operation since the 1830s and is still owned by descendants of Thomas Williams, who purchased it in 1859. It is run by hydro-electric power generated from the two lakes – Crafnant and Geirionydd - which lie to the west of the village. While the source of power is modern, the tapestries and tweeds produced here from raw wool are very traditional.

A footpath above the woollen mill leads to **Fairy Falls** where, in the early 19th century, a forge was founded to make hammers and chisels for use in the slate quarries. It closed at the beginning of the 20th century. Sometime between 100 AD and 250 AD, while prospecting for minerals in this area, the Romans opened up a cave where they found a spring rich in iron (chalybeate). Covered in later years by a landslide, it was not until the 18th century that the spring was uncovered by Lord Willoughby de Eresby, owner of nearby Gwydir Castle, who went on to built a stone bathhouse. Taking the waters became so popular that by 1874 the original bathhouse was replaced with a pumphouse and bath, and the bottled water was exported worldwide. Following a decline during much of the 20th century, interest in the natural spring waters has been rekindled. Visitors can take the waters, view the museum artefacts in the tearoom and browse in the spa beauty shop.

Lake Geirionydd, to the south of the

village, was the supposed birthplace, in the 6th century, of the great bard **Taliesin**, to whom in 1850, Lord Willoughby erected a monument. Taliesin was possibly the earliest poet to write in the Welsh language. He was referred to as the "Chief Bard of Britain", and is said to have served at the court of at least three British kings. In 1863, a local poet, Gwilym Cowlyd, being dissatisfied with the National Eisteddfod, started an arwest, a poetical and musical event that was held in the shadow of the monument every year until 1922. The monument fell down in a storm in 1976, but was restored in 1994. It lies on one of Active Snowdonia's Conwy Valley walks, which also passes Fairy Falls and old mine workings. The walk skirts Lake Crafnant and provides memorable views at many points along its route.

LLANRWST

10 miles S of Conwy on the A470

- 🏛 Parish Church of St Grwst
- 🏛 Gwydir Uchaf Chapel 🏛 Gwydir Chapel
- 🏛 Llanrwst Almshouses 🏛 Old Bridge
- 🏛 Gwydir Castle 🏛 Tu Hwnt i'r Bont
- 🎬 Battle of Llanrwst

The market centre for the central Conwy Valley owes both its name and the dedication of its church to St Grwst (Restitutus), a 6th century missionary who was active in this area. The town lies in the middle of the Conwy Valley between rich agricultural hills to the east, and the imposing crags of Snowdonia to the west. The **Battle of Llanrwst** took place in 954 AD between armies from North and South Wales, resulting in the defeat of the army commanded by the sons of Howell the Good, king of Deheubarth, in southwest Wales.

Famous for its livestock fairs and the manufacture of grandfather clocks and Welsh harps, Llanrwst was also known for its woollen yarn and its sail-making industry. The **Parish Church of St Grwst** with its fine rood screen dates from 1470, though the tower and north aisle are 19th century. The 1470 building replaced a thatched church from 1170 that was destroyed in the fighting of 1468. Next to the church lies **Gwydir Chapel**, famous for its richly carved Renaissance interior. This was the private chapel of the Wynn family and among its treasures is an imposing stone sarcophagus of the Welsh prince Llewelyn the Great. This chapel should not be confused with **Gwydir Uchaf Chapel,** which

River Conwy, Llanrwst

lies on the opposite bank of the river Conwy and is particularly noted for its ceiling covered with paintings of angels. The **Llanrwst Almshouses** date from 1610, and were built by Sir John Wyn of Gwydir. They were closed in 1976, and now house a small museum.

Below the chapel lies **Gwydir Castle**, the Wynn family's Tudor mansion, which has, in its grounds, some fine cedars of Lebanon planted in 1625 in celebration of the marriage of Charles I to Henrietta Maria of France. Here, too, is an arch built to commemorate the end of the Wars of the Roses, while inside the much restored house is a secret room, once hidden by a wooden panel, which is home to the ghost of a monk said to have been trapped in the tunnel that leads the arch. A walk west from the town takes in these historic buildings, the remains of an old crushing mill and the site of the old Hafna Galena Mine. Gwydir Castle was the home of Catherine of Berain, Elizabeth I's cousin (see also Denbigh). Although called a castle, it is, in fact, a fine Tudor house.

Back in town, the **Old Bridge** is thought to have been designed by Inigo Jones; it was built in 1636 by Sir Richard Wynn. Next to it stands **Tu Hwnt i'r Bont** (the House over the Bridge), a 16th-century courthouse that has since been divided into two cottages and is now a tearoom. At one point the town was governed neither by the Welsh nor the English, giving rise to the saying Cymru, Lloegr a Llanrwst - Wales, England and Llanrwst. It even applied (tongue in cheek, it has to be said) for independent membership of the United Nations.

BETWS-Y-COED
12 miles S of Conwy on the A5

The Gateway to Snowdonia – see next chapter.

CAPEL CURIG
9 miles S of Conwy on the A5

🏛 Parish Church of St Julitta   🏞 Mount Siabod

🏛 Plas-y-Brenin

Situated at the junction of the mountain roads to Beddgelert, Llyn Ogwen and Betws-y-Coed, Capel Curig has the reputation of being the wettest place in Wales. However, it is popular with climbers as well as hill walkers and anglers, who use the village as a base. A walk south of the village passes by lonely Llyn y Foel and climbs the steep ridge of Daiar Ddu to the top of **Mount Siabod**. The reward for this expenditure of energy is the most spectacular panoramic view of many of Snowdonia's great peaks. **Plas-y-Brenin**, the National Mountain Centre, provides excellent facilities for climbing, canoeing, dry slope skiing and orienteering.

The former **Parish Church of St Julitta** was founded by St Curig, a 6th-century bishop. The smallest church in Snowdonia, it is being gradually restored by the Friends of St Julitta. It was deconsecrated in the 1970s. St Julitta was a wealthy Turkish widow who was the mother of Cyriacus, who was killed by the Roman governor of Seleucia when he was three years old. Julitta was martyred, and her son was also declared a martyr.

Bangor

🏛 Bangor Cathedral   🏛 Theatre Gwynedd

🏛 Gwynedd Museum and Art Gallery   🏞 Bryn Terfel

🏞 Aled Jones   🏛 Menai Suspension Bridge

🏛 Britannia Bridge   🏛 Victoria Pier

🏛 University College of North Wales

🏛 Penrhyn Castle   🏛 The Swellies

A cathedral and university city, Bangor incorporates a wide variety of architectural

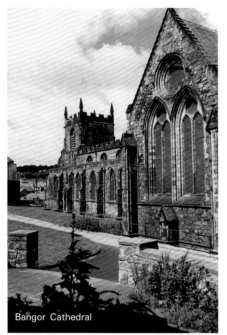

Bangor Cathedral

The main church of the oldest bishopric in Britain, **Bangor Cathedral** dates from the 13th century and has probably been in continuous use for longer than any other cathedral in Britain. During the Middle Ages, the cathedral became a centre of worship for the independent principality of Gwynedd, and the tomb of Owain Gwynedd, buried here after his death, became a starting point for pilgrims setting out on the arduous journey to Bardsey Island. Restored in 1866, the cathedral also contains a life-size carving of Christ dating from 1518 while, outside, there is a Biblical garden that contains plants which are associated with the Bible.

Until the slate boom of the 19th century, Bangor remained little more than a village, albeit with an impressive church. Its position on the Menai Strait, which separates Anglesey from the mainland, made this the ideal place for nearby Penrhyn Quarry to build its docks, and the town soon flourished as a commercial centre. Its importance increased further when the **University College of North Wales** was founded here in 1884. Improvements in the roads, and then the coming of the railways to the North Wales coast, also saw Bangor grow in both stature and importance. The **Menai Suspension Bridge** was built by Thomas Telford between 1819 and 1826 and was the first permanent crossing of the Menai Strait. Before its completion, the crossing was made by ferry, and cattle on their way to and from market would swim the channel. Another deciding factor in building the bridge was the treacherous currents to be found in the strait. The worst accident took place in 1785, when a ship carrying 55 people ran aground on a sandbar. Efforts to refloat it proved fruitless, and when it became swamped with water and keeled over only one person survived. Rocks

styles that remind the visitor that this is not only an interesting and stimulating place, but also one with a long history. A monastic community was founded here as early as 525 AD by St Deiniol, and the town's name is derived from the wattle fence that surrounded the saint's primitive enclosure – the term 'bangori' is still used in parts of Wales to describe the plaiting of twigs in a hedge. However, there were settlers in the area long before St Deiniol, including the Romans at nearby Segontium, and the **Gwynedd Museum and Art Gallery** is just the place to discover the area's 2,000 years of history, as well as to see the reconstructions of the domestic life of the past generations. The art gallery exhibits a range of work by artists from all ages. Close by in Deiniol Street is **Theatre Gwynedd**.

and reefs called **The Swellies** just beneath the surface between the two bridges also cause whirlpools. This was where HMS Conway was lost in 1953.

However, there was much local opposition to the construction, not only from the ferrymen but also from shipowners worried that the

Menai Suspension Bridge, Bangor

structure would impede the passage of their tall ships. As a result of this concern, the road bridge stands at a height of 100 feet. The **Britannia Bridge**, a mile further southwest from Telford's bridge, is a combined road and rail crossing and was built between 1846 and 1850 by Robert Stephenson. In 1970, a fire meant that it had to be rebuilt. The lions guarding the bridge are by John Thomas, who was responsible for much of the sculpture at the Houses of Parliament. Also jutting out into the Menai Strait from the town is the 1,500-foot long **Victoria Pier**, which was built in 1896. As well as being attractive, the pier is a pleasant place from which to view Snowdonia, the coast and the small boats passing by, and to admire the houses, some of them quite magnificent, which stand beside the water. Both pleasure and fishing trips can be taken from the pierhead. Bangor is a major centre of the mussel industry.

The town was the birthplace of two singers – **Bryn Terfel**, the international operatic tenor, and **Aled Jones**, singer of *Walking in the Air*. Surprisingly, on the sound track of the

film *The Snowman*, someone else sings the song.

To the west of the town and overlooking Beaumaris on the Isle of Anglesey lies **Penrhyn Castle** (NT), a dramatic neo-Norman construction built by Thomas Hopper between 1820 and 1845, and incorporating Doll and Railway Museums.

Around Bangor

ABERGWYNGREGYN
6 miles E of Bangor off the A55

🏛 The Cross   🞄 Rhaeadr Aber Falls

Well to the south of the village lie **Rhaeadr Aber Falls**, reached by taking a footpath through sheltered woodland, where the drop of the river is said to be among the steepest in Wales. Above the village is **The Cross**, a huge cross marked out by trees on the hillside. Some people claim it was planted as a memorial to the crew of a German bomber that crashed on the hillside. The reality is more mundane - it was planted by scientists from

Bangor University in the mid 1950s as an experiment in sheep management.

LLANFAIRFECHAN
8 miles E of Bangor on the A55

🏠 The Parish Church of St Mary and Christ

🦢 Traeth Lafan

An excellent base for energetic walks amid stunning scenery, Llanfairfechan also has a long stretch of sandy beach and a nature reserve at **Traeth Lafan**. The **Parish Church of St Mary and Christ** dates from 1864, and was built by local benefactor Colonel John Platt.

PENMAENMAWR
10 miles E of Bangor off the A55

🏠 Parc Plas Mawr   🏠 Cefn Coch

A tiny quarrying village before the arrival of the railway in 1848, this small holiday resort, with its sand and shingle beach, has changed little since William Gladstone holidayed here in the 19th century, and it still boasts many fine Victorian buildings. Gladstone was a frequent visitor, and there's a bust of him on a granite obelisk in Paradise Road. Penmaenmawr has a small industrial heritage park, **Parc Plas Mawr,** which features industrial heritage, as well as works of art such as sculpture and objects carved from wood. The foundations of a house owned by the Derbyshire family have been uncovered by archaeologists.

In the town's steep mountain-backed hinterland can be found many prehistoric sites, including one of Wales' best known Bronze Age stone circles, **Cefn Coch**. An urn was uncovered here containing the remains of a child as well as a bronze dagger said to be evidence that a ritual sacrifice once took place here.

BETHESDA
7 miles SE of Bangor on the A5

🏠 Penryn Slate Quarries   🦢 Nant Ffrancon Pass

🦢 Carneddau Estate

This old quarry town takes its name from the Nonconformist chapel that was built here and served many of the 2,300 men and their families who worked in the quarry at its peak in 1875. The gouged rock of the **Penrhyn Slate Quarries** forms a huge hillside amphitheatre; it was the largest opencast slate mine in the world and still produces high-quality slate 250 years after it was first worked.

From the town, the main road travels through the beautiful **Nant Ffrancon Pass**, which runs straight through and up the valley of the River Ogwen and into the Snowdonia National Park. Five miles south of Bethesda on the A5, Llyn Idwal is one of several lakes on the National Trust's **Carneddau Estate**. In 1954 it was declared the first National Nature Reserve in Wales.

Caernarfon

🏠 Caernarfon Castle   🏠 Parish Church of St Mary

🏠 Hanging Tower   🦅 David Lloyd George

🏛 Museum of the Royal Welsh Fusiliers

🏛 Caernarfon Air World

🏠 Welsh Highland Railway

🏠 Segontium Roman Fort and Museum

🦅 Sir Hugh Owen   🚶 Lôn Las Menai

Situated on the right bank of the River Seiont, near the southwest end of the Menai Strait, Caernarfon (the name means fort on the shore) is a town steeped in history as well as a bastion of the Welsh language and national pride. The history of Caernarfon goes back to Roman times. **Segontium Roman Fort and**

🎬 stories and anecdotes 🦅 famous people 🎨 art and craft 🎟 entertainment and sport 🚶 walks

Museum (see panel below), half a mile from the town centre on the road towards Beddgelert, is the only place in Wales where it is possible to see something of the internal layout of an auxiliary station. Built to defend the Roman Empire against attack from rebellious tribes, the fort dates back to 77 AD, when the Roman conquest was finally completed following the capture of Anglesey. Certainly this was one of the most important garrisons on the edge of the Roman Empire and, during its life, it was not only a military, but also an administrative centre for northwest Wales. It is believed that Constantine the Great was born here. Excavations of the site have revealed coins which show that the fort was garrisoned at least until AD 394 and this long occupation can be explained by its strategic position controlling the fertile lands and mineral rights of Anglesey and providing a defence against Irish pirates. The well-preserved site is managed by CADW and the Museum, which is run by the National Museum and Galleries of Wales, displays many items, including coins, pottery and weapons that have been uncovered during excavation work.

However, it is another great construction and symbol of military power – the impressive **Caernarfon Castle** – that still dominates the town today. The most famous of the numerous great fortresses in Wales, the castle was begun in 1283 by Henry de Elreton, who was also building Beaumaris Castle, under the

Segontium Roman Fort

Beddgelert Road, Caernarfon, Gwynedd LL55 2WG
Tel: 01286 675625
website: www.segontium.org.uk

The Segontium Roman fort was an auxiliary fort built by the Romans when they spread their conquest of Britain into Wales, and dates back to 77 AD. Although it was a remote outpost, it is one of the most well known Roman sites in Britain and attracts thousands of visitors each year. From records, it is clear that it held a regiment of up to 1,000 auxiliary soldiers until about 394 AD. These troops were non citizens who would be in the service of the Roman army for 25 years. It was a very strategic establishment, as it controlled access to Angelsey, and protected the Welsh coast from the sea bound Irish raiders. Apart from being of military use, Segontium was also the administrative centre for north west Wales.

Visiting the fort, it is apparent that you are encouraged to have a 'hands on' approach. The fort is active in that it allows visitors into the remains so that you can not only see the remains, but experience them too.

The museum tells the story of the conquest and occupation of Wales and contains fine examples of the finds excavated from the Segontium site. Here you can get a vivid idea of life in this part of occupied Britain.

The Segontium Roman Museum opened in 1924 vividly portrays the story of the conquest and occupation of Wales by the Romans and displays the finds from nearby auxillary fort of Segontium, one of the most famous in Britain. The site was one of the first Roman sites to be developed as a historical venue.

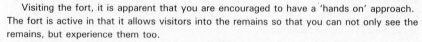

🏠 historic building 🏛 museum and heritage 🏛 historic site 🍃 scenic attraction 🌿 flora and fauna

stories and anecdotes 🚂 famous people 🎨 art and craft 🎭 entertainment and sport 🚶 walks

Caernarfon Castle

orders of Edward I. It took some 40 years to complete. Built not only as a defence but as a royal palace and a seat of government, the castle's majestic appearance was no accident, as it was designed to be a dream castle and is based around two oval-shaped courts divided by a wall. The outer defences are strengthened at intervals by towers and are, in places, up to 15 feet thick! Many attempts were made by the Welsh, over the years, to destroy the castle but their failure is confirmed by the presence today of this magnificent building. It was here that, in 1284, Edward I crowned his son the first English Prince of Wales, and the castle was once again used for such an investiture when, in 1969, the Queen crowned Prince Charles Prince of Wales. Many protests were planned about the investiture, but it passed off peacefully. However, two members of the Mudiad Amddiffyn Cymru (Welsh Defence Movement) were killed at Abergele the day before as they tried to plant a bomb on the line to stop the royal train (see also Abergele). Also at the castle, and housed in the Queen's Tower, is the **Museum of the Royal Welsh Fusiliers**, the country's oldest regiment.

GALERI

Doc Victoria, Caernarfon, Gwynedd LL55 1SQ
Tel: 01286 685252 Fax: 01286 678140
Box Office: 01286 685222
e-mail: post@galericaernarfon.com
website: www.galericaernarfon.com

Galeri is a £7.5m Creative Enterprise Centre located in Caernarfon's Victoria Dock area. It houses a flexible 400-seat theatre/cinema, DOC café bar, arts exhibition area, state of the art conference facilities, performance studios and 27 workspace units, which are occupied by 16 creative resident companies.

"Galeri is a really exciting venue, which is buzzing with life and activity throughout the day and during the evenings. Set in a clearly fantastic site, it is difficult to imagine any building in Wales with a better location." - Bryn Terfel, Patron.

The theatre is Galeri's main location for events and performances, both professional and amateur. The theatre also has a busy and exciting cinema programme, which offers the very best of the latest film releases as well as Art House and classic films. The arts exhibition area is no ordinary art gallery; the Art Space gives artists the opportunity to be less tied to the usual gallery practices. As well as featuring exhibitions by local and national artists, the aim here is to create a more experimental programme, with the artists working closely with the community on specific projects.

Set at Victoria Dock with the Menai in front and Snowdonia as a backdrop, it is difficult to imagine any building in Wales in a better location.

🏛 historic building 🏛 museum and heritage 🏛 historic site 🌳 scenic attraction 🌱 flora and fauna

The castle sits where the River Seiont meets the Menai Strait, the expanse of water that separates mainland Wales from the Isle of Anglesey. Close by, the old Slate Quay, from where slate was once shipped, is now the place from where fishing trips and pleasure cruises depart up the Strait to Beaumaris. Castle Square, on the landward side of the castle, holds markets and here, too, can be found statues of two famous Welshmen: the gesticulating, urging **David Lloyd George**, once a member of Parliament for the area, and **Sir Hugh Owen**, the founder of Further Education in Wales.

The Anglesey Hotel and the **Hanging Tower** stand by the castle walls and were a customs house until 1822. The last hanging to take place in the tower was in 1911 when an Irishman named Murphy was executed for murdering a maid. It is said that when he died the bell clapper in the **Parish Church of St Mary** fell off. The church itself was founded in 1307 and, though much of it has since been reconstructed, the arcades of the eastern and southern walls are part of the original 14th-century building.

Northgate Street is called, in Welsh, Stryd Pedwar a Chewch, meaning four and six street. Apparently it originates from the time when sailors flocked to this part of town looking for lodgings: four pence for a hammock and six pence for a bed!

From the town, walkers can enjoy a scenic footpath, the **Lôn Las Menai**, which follows the coastline along the Menai Strait towards the village of Y Felinheli and from which there are views across the water to the Isle of Anglesey. Caernarfon is the terminus of the **Welsh Highland Railway** (see panel on page 65), which is owned and operated by the Ffestiniog Railway, the oldest independent railway company in the world. In 2008, the West Highland was extended through the spectacular Aberglasyn Pass to Porthmadog and a link with the Ffestiniog Railway.

To the southwest of Caernarfon, and overlooking Caernarfon Bay, is **Caernarfon Air World**, located on the site of an RAF station that was built in 1940 and which is also the home of the first RAF mountain rescue team. As well as offering pleasure flights to visitors, there is the Aviation Museum, housed in one of the great hangars, which not only displays over 400 model aircraft, but also has various planes and helicopters on show and provides visitors with the opportunity to take the controls in a flight trainer.

Around Caernarfon

DINAS DINLLE
3 miles S of Caernarfon off the A499

🏰 Fort St David   🏰 Fort Williamsburg

🏰 Dinas Dinlle Fort

Dinas Dinlle is a seaside village at the mouth of the Menai Strait. With a shingle beach and cliffs overlooking Caernarfon Bay, there are many pleasant spots to picnic and enjoy the views down the Llyn Peninsula or across the bay to Anglesey. At the beach's northerly tip at Belan lies **Fort St David**, which was built in the 18th century along with **Fort Williamsburg** at Glynllivon. It was constructed by the first Lord Newborough, who felt concern over the threat of invasion by Napoleon; he also raised and equipped his own private army, The Royal Caernarfonshire Grenadiers, which, by the time of his death in 1807, had cost him a quarter of his fortune. **Dinas Dinlle Fort**, overlooking she shore, is much older, as it dates from the Iron Age.

CAE BERLLAN HOLIDAY COTTAGES

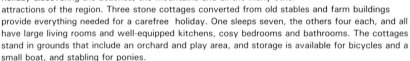

Tyn Lon, Llandwrog, nr Caernarfon, Gwynedd LL54 5SN
Tel: 01286 830818
e-mail: anncaeberllan@aol.com website: www.caeberllan.co.uk

Cae Berllan Holiday Cottages offer a secluded self-catering base for a holiday discovering the beaches, the mountains and all the many other attractions of the region. Three stone cottages converted from old stables and farm buildings provide everything needed for a carefree holiday. One sleeps seven, the others four each, and all have large living rooms and well-equipped kitchens, cosy bedrooms and bathrooms. The cottages stand in grounds that include an orchard and play area, and storage is available for bicycles and a small boat, and stabling for ponies.

LLANDWROG

4 miles S of Caernarfon off the A499

 Parish Church of St Tyrog

Llandwrog was built to serve the estate of Lord Newborough at Glynllifon Park, and memorials to the Newborough family may be seen in the **Parish Church of St Tyrog**.

CLYNNOG FAWR

10 miles SW of Caernarfon on the A499

🏚 Parish Church of St Beuno   🏚 St Beuno's Well

🏛 Bachwen

This typical Llyn Peninsula village on the Heritage Coast is famous for its remarkably large and beautiful **Parish Church of St Beuno**, which stands on the site of a chapel founded by the saint around 616 AD. One of the sons of the royal family of Morgannwg, St Beuno had great influence in North Wales, and he built his chapel on land that was presented to him by Cadwallon, King of Gwynedd. St Beuno's burial place and his shrine can be seen in this early 16th-century building, which lies on the Pilgrims' Route to Bardsey Island. For many years, his tomb was thought to have curative powers.

Nearby is **St Beuno's Well**, whose waters were also thought to cure all manner of illness and conditions, especially if the sufferer had

first visited the church. Close by, and virtually on the seafront, stands the capstone and three uprights of **Bachwen**, a Neolithic burial chamber.

Y FELINHELI

4 miles NE of Caernarfon off the A487

🔺 The Greenwood Centre   🔺 Glan Faenol

Situated south of this village is **The Greenwood Centre**, a forest heritage and adventure park. Opened in the early 1990s, this centre concentrates on exploring and explaining man's relationship with trees and how, by using conservation techniques, the loss of trees from the countryside can be halted whether in the equatorial rain forests or ancient temperate forests of Europe. The skills of ancient carpenters and joiners are also on show, particularly in the Great Hall, a building that was constructed entirely using medieval skills and knowledge and is held together by 500 oak pegs!

A couple of miles further east off the A487, bordering the Menai Strait, is **Glan Faenol** (NT), which includes parkland and farmland around Vaynol Hall, once one of the largest estates in North Wales. This is an important habitat for wildlife, and a pleasant walk leads to the sea and two viewing platforms. The estate has tracts of ancient woodland and several follies, including one built to rival the Marquess Column on Anglesey. The views of Snowdonia and across the strait are memorably depicted in one of Rex Whistler murals at Plas Newydd.

Isle of Anglesey

Menai Bridge

🏛 Menai Suspension Bridge   🏛 St Tysilio's Church

🌿 Pili Palas

Acting as a gateway to Anglesey, this largely Victorian town grew and developed after the construction of Thomas Telford's **Menai Suspension Bridge**, which connects the island to mainland Wales. The waterfront is a popular place for anglers and for those wishing to view the annual Regatta on the Menai Strait held every August, as well as for the promenade, known as the Belgian Promenade because it was built by refugees from Belgium who sought shelter here during World War I.

On Church Island, reached by a causeway from the town, there is the 14th-century **St Tysilio's Church**, built on the site of a foundation by St Tysilio in 630 AD. The site is thought to have been visited by Archbishop Baldwin and Giraldus when they may have landed here in 1188. It can be reached by a short causeway from the Belgian Promenade.

For a place with a difference, **Pili Palas** (Butterfly Palace) is an interesting and unusual attraction that will delight everyone. The vast collection of exotic butterflies and birds, from all over the world, can be seen in tropical environments, where visitors can marvel at the colourful creatures and see the wonderful tropical plants. There is also a Tropical Hide, an amazing Ant Avenue and a Snake House, and while adults relax in Pili Palas' café, children can let off steam in the adventure play area.

Around Menai Bridge

BEAUMARIS
4 miles NE of Menai Bridge of the A545

🏛 Beaumaris Castle   🏛 Courthouse

🏚 Museum of Childhood Memories

🏚 Beaumaris Lifeboat Station

🏛 Parish Church of St Mary and St Nicholas

🏛 Beaumaris Gaol   🌿 Menai Strait Regatta

An attractive and elegant town, Beaumaris was granted a charter by Edward I in 1294 and it adopted the Norman name beau marais, which translates as 'beautiful marsh'. The lawned seafront, now with its elegant Georgian and Victorian terraces, was once a marsh that protected the approaches to **Beaumaris Castle**. Often cited as the most technically perfect medieval castle in Britain, Beaumaris

Beaumaris

Castle was the last of Edward I's Iron Ring of fortresses built to stamp his authority on the Welsh. Begun in 1295, and designed by the king's military architect, James of St George, this was to be his largest and most ambitious project. Regarded as a pinnacle of military architecture of the time, with a concentric defence rather than the traditional keep and bailey, the outer walls contained 16 towers, while the inner walls were 43 feet high and up to 16 feet thick in places. It was never actually completed, as the money ran out before the fortifications reached their full planned height. Perhaps a measure of the castle's success was that, unlike other castles built by Edward I, it never experienced military action. Now a World Heritage Site and in the hands of CADW (Welsh Historic Monuments), Beaumaris Castle is still virtually surrounded by its original moat. There was also a tidal dock here for ships

coming in through a channel in the marshes - an iron ring where vessels of up to 40 tons once docked still hangs from the wall.

The **Parish Church of St Mary and St Nicholas** dates from the 14th century, and was originally the church for the castle garrison. It has noteworthy 16th century choir stalls and the stone coffin of Princess Joan, wife of Llywelyn the Great and illegitimate daughter of King John. For many years the coffin was used as a drinking trough for horses. The building has four clocks on its tower, and is said that someone who was about to be hanged in the old gaol nearby cursed the clock facing the gaol, saying that it would never tell the same time as the other three. It never did, until it was found out that the prevailing southwest winds were interfering with the hands. This was rectified and the clock has shown the correct time ever since.

ARIANDY

15 Castle Street, Beaumaris, Isle of Anglesey LL58 8AN
Tel: 07854 887792
e-mail: ariandy@rhiwlas.plus.com
website: www.ariandy.co.uk

Ariandy is an elegant Grade II listed Georgian town house located in the **very** centre of the attractive **historic** town of Beaumaris, close to the Castle, the Courthouse, the **gaol** and the parish church. Above what was formerly a bank, the property has recently been completely refurbished by owner Sian Davies, resulting in self catering accommodation of a very high standard, with everything needed for a short break or longer holiday in outstanding comfort for up to nine guests. On the first floor are fitted kitchen with a roomy breakfast area (all nine guests can eat together!), a large lounge with four inviting sofas and digital TV, a double bedroom and a bath/shower room with separate WC. On the floor above are three further bedrooms – a twin, a double with sea view and a spacious family room with double and single bed – a shower room and WC. To the rear of the property is a secluded sunny courtyard with a decking area – a delightful suntrap where guests can relax with a drink after a day's sightseeing. Ariandy, which is open all year round, is an ideal base for exploring the region **and the town with its numerous restaurants**. Attractions include lovely beaches, the coastal footpath, the hills and mountains, yachting and golf.

🏠 historic building 🏛 museum and heritage 🏚 historic site 🍃 scenic attraction 🌱 flora and fauna

Although Beaumarais saw little or no military action, the town briefly enjoyed notoriety as a haven for pirates, as well as being a busy trading port. With the advent of steam ships and paddle boats, the resort developed during Victorian times as visitors from Liverpool and elsewhere took the sea trip down to the town. It is now a popular place with the yachting fraternity due to its facilities and involvement in the annual **Menai Strait Regatta**. **Beaumaris Lifeboat Station** is one of seven stations operated by inshore boats funded by the Television programme *Blue Peter*. It has recently acquired a new weather station and can be visited between 10.30am and 4.30pm daily.

While having connections with both sea trade and developing as a holiday resort, Beaumaris was at one time also an administrative and legal centre for the island. The **Courthouse**, dating from 1614, is open to the public during the summer and, although it was renovated in the 19th century, much of its original Jacobean interior remains. It was here, in 1773, that Mary Hughes stood in the dock and was sentenced to transportation for seven years after she had been found guilty of stealing a bed gown valued at six pence!

Close by is **Beaumaris Gaol**, which was designed as a model prison by Hansom in 1829. In this monument to Victorian law and order, the last man to hang was Richard Rowlands, who cursed the church clock opposite as he climbed to the scaffold in 1862. Today's visitors can relive those days of harsh punishment as well as view the cells and the treadwheel and follow the route taken by the condemned men to their rendezvous with the hangman.

An equally interesting place for all the family to visit is the **Museum of Childhood Memories** in Castle Street. It is a treasure house of nostalgia with a collection of over 2,000 items in nine different rooms. Each one has its own theme, such as entertainment, pottery and glass, and clockwork tin-plate toys. Visitors can wander around and see the amazing variety of toys which illustrate the changing habits of the nation over the past 150 years.

LLANFAES
5 miles NE of Menai Bridge off the B5109

🏫 Parish Church of St Catherine

Now a quiet and sedate place, Llanfaes was a busy commercial village long before the establishment of Beaumaris as one of the island's major centres, and travellers from the mainland arrived here after crossing the Menai Strait from Aber and the Lavan Sands.

In 1237, Llywelyn the Great founded a monastery in the village over the tomb of Joan, his wife and the illegitimate daughter of King John. The tomb can now be seen in St Mary's Church, Beaumaris, where it was moved at the time of the Dissolution. In 1295, Edward I moved the inhabitants of Llanfaes to Newborough so that he could use the stone in the town to built Beaumaris Castle. During World War II, flying boats were built at a factory near the village. The **Parish Church of St Catherine** dates from 1845, and replaces an earlier church. It is an imposing, steepled building that seems much too large for the village.

LLANGOED
6 miles NE of Menai Bridge on the B5109

🏫 Castell Aberlleiniog 🏠 Haulfre Stables

In Edwardian times, this historic village was a popular resort with the lower middle classes who came here to relax in boarding houses by the sea. Llangoed's seaside charm is enhanced

CROMLECH MANOR FARM

Tyn-y-Gongl, Anglesey LL74 8SB
Tel: 01248 853489
e-mail: cromlech-manor-farm@hotmail.co.uk
website: www.angleseyhorseriding.co.uk

Cromlech Manor Farm is a family-run Stud Farm, Livery Stable, Riding School and Pony Club Centre set in some 35 acres of peaceful countryside, and boasting its own ancient monument - a cromlech or ancient stone burial chamber.

Drawing on more than 30 years experience, the Lomas family can cater for all your riding needs. They have a good selection of horses and ponies catering for varying capabilities, from novice to advanced horses and riders, and can provide for all ages. All lessons are taught in the outdoor menage. Lessons are group lessons, unless you specifically ask for a private lesson, and include half-hour, full hour and a 40 minute jumping lesson.

For the more experienced rider hacks out on the road of approximately 1 hour are available. And if you have always dreamt of riding on the beach, at Cromlech you can. They take experienced riders only on beach rides along beautiful Benllech Bay that last for approximately one and a half hours. Cromlech also offers a full livery service and if you would like to stay in this lovely corner of Anglesey, a caravan is available that can sleep up to 5 people, and parking for horse boxes to 'bring your pony on holiday'.

unfortunate and bizarre way via its lifeboat which, over the years, has been involved in many rescues, two of which are worthy of mention. Returning to Liverpool from Australia in October 1859, laden with cargo and passengers, including gold prospectors coming home after making their fortunes in the Australian Gold Rush, the **Royal Charter** sank.

A rigged iron vessel and the pride of the merchant fleet, the ship was all set to make the long passage in record time but, while sheltering from a hurricane in Moelfre Bay, she foundered with the loss of 450 passengers and crew. Only 39 people survived, and many believe that the gold still lies with the wreck out in the bay. Efforts have been made to recover the lost fortune with varying but not overwhelming degrees of success and it has been said that the larger houses around Moelfre were paid for with gold washed ashore from the wreck. This is despite customs officers swamping the village in an attempt to ensure that

Shingle Beach, Moelfre

🏚 historic building 🏛 museum and heritage 🏛 historic site 🔾 scenic attraction � flora and fauna

any salvaged gold ended in the Exchequer rather than in the hands of the locals. Charles Dickens visited the site on New Year's Eve 1859, and apparently based a story on the disaster in *The Uncommercial Traveller* (see also Pentraeth).

Din Lligwy Village, Moelfre

One hundred years later, almost to the day, in October 1959, the coaster *Hindlea*, struggling in foul weather, had eight crew members rescued by the Moelfre Lifeboat. The rescue earned Richard Evans, the lifeboat's coxswain, his second RNLI gold medal for gallantry. The **Lifeboat Station** can be visited between 9am and 4pm, with crew training at 7pm on Wednesdays.

At Llanallgo, between Moelfre and Dulas, is the mainly 15th-century **Parish Church of St Gallgo**, with its ancient bell, one of the oldest in the country. It was struck in the 13th century, and bears the inscription *Ave Maria Gracia Plena* (Hail Mary, Full of Grace), as well as the imprint of an Edward I coin struck in 1281. In the graveyard is a memorial to the victims of the *Royal Charter* tragedy. St Gallgo is famous as being the brother of Gildas, the 6th century historian of Britain, who wrote *De Excidio et Conquestu Britanniae*. He was born in the Kingdom of Strathclyde in Scotland, which at that time had strong ties with Wales, and even spoke the same language.

The **Seawatch Centre** has displays and exhibits about Anglesey's rich maritime heritage, including athe village's lifeboat. Beyond the station is a small outcrop of rocks, **Ynys Moelfre**, a favourite spot for seabirds and, occasionally, porpoises. About a mile inland from the village, off the narrow road, is the impressive **Lligwy Burial Chamber**, a Bronze Age tomb with a huge capstone supported by stone uprights, which lies half hidden in a pit dug out of the rock. Close by is **Din Lligwy Village**, the remains of a Romano British settlement that covers over half an acre. Certainly occupied around the 4th century AD, after the Roman garrison on Anglesey had been vacated, some of the stone walls of the buildings can still be seen and excavations of the site have unearthed pottery, coins and evidence of metal working from that period. Nearby are the ruins of the 14th century Capel Lligwy.

LLANDDYFNAN
5 miles NW of Menai Bridge on the B5109

🏛 Stone Science   🏚 Llanddyfnan Standing Stone

To the west of the village lies **Stone Science**, an unusual attraction that tells the story of the earth from its beginning to the present – a journey spanning 650 million years. The museum illustrates the science with displays of fossils, crystals and artefacts, and there are numerous and varied items for sale in the Stone Science shop. Nearly opposite is the

🏚 stories and anecdotes   🕊 famous people   🎨 art and craft   ✐ entertainment and sport   🚶 walks

eight-feet-high **Llanddyfnan Standing
Stone**.

LLANGEFNI
6 miles NW of Menai Bridge on the B5420

🏛 Oriel Ynys Môn

The island's main market and administrative
centre, Llangefni is also the home of **Oriel
Ynys Môn** (the Anglesey Heritage Centre), an
attractive art gallery and heritage centre, built
in 1991, which gives an insight into the history
of Anglesey. From prehistoric times to the
present day, the permanent exhibition covers a
series of themes including Stone Age Hunters,
Druids, Medieval Society and Legends.

Llyn Cefni Reservoir to the northwest of
the town is an important wildlife habitat and
nature reserve overlooked by a hide; it also
provides a pleasant picnic area. On the
northwest edge of town by the River Cefni,

The Dingle is a local nature reserve with
footpaths through mature woodland. The
A5114, which connects Llangefni to the A5, is
the shortest A road in the British Isles.

LLANFAIR PG
1 mile W of Menai Bridge off the A5

🏛 Railway Station   🏛 Llanfairpwllgwyngyll

💧 Marquess of Anglesey Column

Llanfairpwllgwyngyll, often called Llanfair
PG, is the village with the world's longest
place name. The full, tongue-twisting name is:
Llanfairpwllgwyngyllgogerychwyrn-
drobwyllllantysiliogogogch and the translation
is even longer - St Mary's Church in a hollow
of white hazel near to a rapid whirlpool and St
Tysilio's Church near the red cave. The name
is said to have been invented, in humorous
reference to the burgeoning tourist trade, by a
local man. Whether this is true or not, it has

SIOP ELENNA

*3 Church Street, Llangefni,
Anglesey LL77 7DU*
Tel: 01248 724594

Siop Elenna is just off the High Street in the
bustling market town of Llangefni, at the heart of
rural Anglesey. The building has been here for
over 100 years and there has been a fabric shop
based here for 20+ years. The current owner
came to the store to buy supplies and quite
literally, ended up buying the entire store and has
been here for the past 6 years.

Siop Elenna can supply all your craft and
haberdashery requirements. It is a veritable
emporium of crafts, inspiration and supplies, with
ribbons, needles/machine needles, sewing
threads, buttons, materials, quilting cottons,
curtain linings, knitting yarns, sewing and
knitting patterns and so much more to help you

create your own personal works of art, fashions
and gifts. Friendly staff are happy to offer helpful advice and tips based on their years of
experience. And if you don't find what you are looking for here, why not visit Siop Elenna's sister
shop Ylp Haberdashery Caernarfon, tel: 01286 678230.

🏛 historic building 🏛 museum and heritage 🏛 historic site 💧 scenic attraction 🌿 flora and fauna

Llanfair PG Station

is the modest building where, in 1915, the first Women's Institute in Britain was founded. The movement originated in Canada earlier in the same year.

However, the village's most famous building is its **Railway Station** – the often filmed station whose platform has the longest station sign and where the longest platform ticket in Britain could be purchased.

certainly done the trick, as many visitors stop by initially out of curiosity at the name.

The village, overlooking the Menai Strait, is where the Britannia Bridge crosses to the mainland. The **Marquess of Anglesey Column** looks out from here over to Snowdonia, and the quite splendid views from the top of the column are available to anyone wishing to negotiate the spiral staircase of some 115 steps. The column was finished two years after the battle of Waterloo, and the statue on top of the column was added, in 1860, after the death of Henry Paget, Earl of Uxbridge and 1st Marquess of Anglesey, whom it commemorates. Paget fought alongside the Duke of Wellington at Waterloo, where he lost a leg to one of the last shots of the battle. He lived to be 85, having twice been Lord-Lieutenant of Ireland after his military career ended(see also Plas Newydd).

The last public toll house, designed by Thomas Telford when he was working on the London-Holyhead road in the 1820s, stands in the village; it still displays the tolls charged in 1895, the year the toll house closed. Next door

Today, visitors can see a replica of the Victorian ticket office, examine some rare miniature steam trains and wander around the numerous craft and souvenir shops that can now be found here.

LLANGADWALADR

10½ miles W of Menai Bridge on the A4080

🏛 Parish Church of St Cadwaladr

Around the time that Aberffraw was the capital of Gwynedd, this small village was said to have been the burial place of the Welsh princes. The **Parish Church of St Cadwaladr** was founded in 615 AD as part of a royal monastery, and was probably built of wattle and daub – wattle walls covered in dried mud to provide stability and waterproofing – as the village's early name was Eglwys Ail, meaning 'wattle church'. The present building dates from the 12th century, and has a memorial stone to Cadfan, King of Gwynedd, who died in 625 AD. It is embedded in the church wall, and reads *King Cadfan, the Wisest and Most Renowned of All Kings Lies Here*. Cadwaladr was Cadfan's grandson, and he died in Rome in 682 AD. His body was brought here for burial.

ABERFFRAW

12½ miles W of Menai Bridge on the A4080

🏛 Parish Church of St Beuno

🏛 Church of St Cywfan   📷 Llys Llywelyn Museum

🏚 Din Dryfol Burial Chamber

🏚 Barclodiad y Gawres Burial Chamber

Though this was the capital of Gwynedd between the 7th and 13th centuries, and therefore one of the most important places in Wales, there remains little trace of those times. In fact, no one quite knows where the court buildings were situated. However, a Norman arch, set into the **Parish Church of St Beuno** is said to be from the chapel of the royal court. The church as we see it today dates largely from the 16th century. The **Llys Llywelyn Museum**, although modest, has exhibitions recounting the area's fascinating history.

On an island just offshore is the **Church of St Cywfan**. It dates originally from the 13th century, though what we see today mainly dates from the 14th and 15th centuries. At one time, the building was much bigger, but when erosion started to bite at the island, and old graves started to fall into the shoreline, parts of it were demolished. By 1891 it was roofless, but money was eventually raised to refurbish it.

Inland, the **Din Dryfol Burial Chamber** provides further evidence of Iron Age life on the island while, to the north of Aberffraw, on the cliff tops above Porth Trecastell, is the **Barclodiad y Gawres Burial Chamber**. Considered to be one of the finest of its kind, this burial chamber, along with Bryn Celli Ddu, contains some notable murals. This area is also known as Cable Bay, as it is here that a transatlantic cable came ashore.

PLAS NEWYDD

2 miles SW of Menai Bridge off the A4080

🏛 Plas Newydd   🏚 Bryn Celli Ddu

Bryn Celli Ddu, a wonderful example of a Bronze Age passage grave, lies up a narrow country road close to **Plas Newydd** (NT), which is situated on the banks of the Menai Strait. The splendid mansion house was designed by James Wyatt, and is surrounded by gardens and parkland laid out in the 18th century by Humphry Repton. Not only are there fabulous views over the water to Snowdonia from the lawns but there is a woodland walk, an Australian arboretum and a formal Italian style garden terrace.

As well as Britain's largest collection of works by Rex Whistler, the house contains a military museum. It is not to be confused with Plas Newydd near Llangollen.

BRYNSIENCYN

5 miles SW of Menai Bridge on the A4080

🏚 Tre-Drwy   🏚 Caer Leb

🏚 Bodowyr Burial Chamber

🏚 Castell Bryn Gwyn   🐦 Foel Farm Park

🐦 Anglesey Sea Zoo   🦋 Sir Ellis Jones Ellis-Griffith

Close to this village there was once an important centre of Druid worship, but no signs remain of the temple that stood at **Tre-Drwy**. There are, however, several other interesting remains in the area. Just to the west of the village lies **Caer Leb**, an Iron Age earthwork consisting of a pentagonal enclosure 200 feet by 160 feet encircled by banks and ditches, while, just a short distance away is **Bodowyr Burial Chamber**, a massive stone that is, seemingly, delicately perched upon three upright stones. To the south of the burial chamber, and just a mile west of Brynsiencyn, are the earthwork remains of **Castell Bryn**

HOOTON'S HOMEGROWN FARM SHOP AND BUTCHERS

Gwydryn Hir, Brynsiencyn, Anglesey LL61 6HQ
Tel: 01248 430344   Fax: 01248 430322
e-mail: farm@hootonshomegrown.com
website: www.hootonshomegrown.com

Recently championed by Gary Rhodes - **Hooton's Homegrown** has a farm shop, butchery and café overlooking the Snowdonia Mountains. The Hooton family has farmed at Gwydryn Hir, Brynsiencyn since 1964. Today, with two of their sons, Andrew and James, Michael and Rosalind provide their customers with delicious food straight from the farm. They rear outdoor pork, lamb, Welsh Black cattle, free-range chickens, ducks and guinea fowl. They also rear turkeys and geese for Christmas. They grow a wide variety of fruit and vegetables all for sale in the farm shop. They also have Pick Your Own in season. Their chefs bake an array of cakes, savouries and frozen ready meals. The café serves delicious homemade meals (using their own home grown ingredients) and Fairtrade tea and coffee.

The shop also stocks local bespoke delicacies suitable for gifts. They also have a farm shop in Fron Goch Garden Centre, Llanfaglan, Caernarfon.

Gwyn, a site that has been excavated and shows traces of having been used from as far back as the New Stone Age through to the time of the Roman occupation of Britain.

Back in the village, and found down the small road leading to the shore is **Foel Farm Park**, a real working farm that offers visitors the opportunity to bottle feed lambs and baby calves, cuddle rabbits, see and help with milking and enjoy the homemade ice cream. There are also covered areas for rainy days, which include an adventure play den and an indoor picnic room.

Also overlooking the Menai Strait is the **Anglesey Sea Zoo**, an award-winning attraction that takes visitors beneath the waves and into the underwater world of a wide variety of sea creatures. The imaginative and innovative displays allow visitors a unique view of these interesting beasts, which include sea horses, oysters, conger eels and rays.

In the graveyard of the Victorian parish church is a monument to the grandly named **Sir Ellis Jones Ellis-Griffith**, MP for Anglesey from 1895 until 1918. Though born in Birmingham, he was brought up in the village, and died in 1926.

DWYRAN
8 miles SW of Menai Bridge off the A4080

🐦 Bird World

Just outside the village lies **Bird World**, a wonderful family attraction set in extensive parkland, with views over to the Snowdonia mountain range, where visitors can admire the wide variety of birds on display as well as picnic in the beautiful surroundings of the lake. There is also a small animal farm and pet area for the children along with a huge indoor play barn.

🎞 stories and anecdotes 🦃 famous people 🎨 art and craft 🖌 entertainment and sport 🌲 walks

NEWBOROUGH
9 miles SW of Menai Bridge on the A4080

- 🏛 Church of St Dwynwen
- 🗺 Abermenai Point
- 🗺 Llanddwyn Island
- 🗺 Anglesey Model Village and Gardens
- 🌿 Newborough Warren
- 🖼 Charles Tunnicliffe

Founded in 1303 by the former inhabitants of Llanfaes, who had been moved here by Edward I, the village stands on the edge of a National Nature Reserve that covers 1,566 acres of dunes, coast and forest. Among the many footpaths through the reserve, there are several forest trails that show how the Forestry Commission is constantly trying to stabilise the dunes. **Newborough Warren** is so called because, before myxomatosis, about 80,000 rabbits were trapped here annually. There is a route through the warren to **Abermenai Point**, but the way can be dangerous and advice concerning tidal conditions should be sought before considering the walk.

Llanddwyn Island is also accessible on foot, but again, tidal conditions should be carefully studied before setting out. On the island stand the ruins of the early medieval **Church of St Dwynwen**. She is the Welsh equivalent of St Valentine, and even today St Dwynwen's Day is still celebrated in some parts of Wales. Though she is the patron saint of love, her own story was far from lovely. She was one of the 24 daughters of Brychan Brycheiniog, and said to be the prettiest. She fell in love with a man called Maelon, but when he discovered that she was already promised to someone else, he raped her and left her. She prayed to God to let Maelon truly repent, and asked for two further wishes. God obliged. The other two being that he protected the hopes and wishes of true loves and that she should never marry. Also on the island is a holy well, in which, it was once thought, a sacred fish swam that could predict the future.

Until the 1920s, marram grass, which has been grown for conservation purposes from Elizabethan times, was also a mainstay of the area, helping to sustain a cottage industry in the production of ropes, baskets, matting and thatching materials. A high embankment was built here in the 18th century by Thomas Telford to stop the sea, which had previously almost cut the island into two.

Charles Tunnicliffe, the renowned wildlife artist, had a studio on the island for over 30 years and Anglesey Council has purchased a collection of his marvellous work, which can be seen at the Oriel (Gallery) Ynys Môn in Llangefni. On the A4080 signposted from Newborough, Newborough Forest is a pine forest with rides, glades and miles of walks.

Situated between Newborough and Dwyran lies **Anglesey Model Village and Gardens**, a delightful place where visitors can wander through the attractive landscaped gardens and see many of the island's many landmarks – all built to one twelfth scale. There is a children's ride-on train, as well as the garden railway, and the gardens themselves are particularly beautiful, with many water features and a good collection of plants and trees.

Holyhead

- 🏛 Parish Church St Cybi
- 🏛 Eglwys Bedd
- 🏚 Lifeboat Station
- 🏛 Four Mile Bridge
- 🌿 Gogarth Bay
- 🏚 Salt Island
- 🏖 Trearddur Bay
- 🏚 Cytiau'r Gwyddelod
- 🏚 Trefignath
- 🌿 South Stack
- 🏖 Porth Dafarch
- 🌿 Ellin's Tower
- 🏖 Canolfan Ucheldre Centre
- 🏚 Caer y Twr
- ⚔ Breakwater Quarry Country Park

Holyhead Mountain (Mynydd Twr) rises to

720 feet behind this town, which is usually called the largest on Anglesey though it actually sits on another island off Anglesey's coast, Holy Island. A busy rail and ferry terminal, especially for travellers to and from Ireland, Holyhead has all the facilities needed to cater for visitors passing through. It is also, despite being something of an industrial and commercial centre, a seaside resort. Its origins lie back in the times of the Romans and the early Celtic Christians. Parts of the **Parish Church St Cybi** date from the 14th to the 17th century and it is situated within the partially surviving walls of the small Roman fort, Caer Gybi (the source of Holyhead's Welsh name), and on the site of a 6th-century chapel. St Cybi, who died in 554 AD, was the brother of St David, patron saint of Wales, and he came here at the end of his life. His friend was St Seiriol of Penmon (see also Penmon). The shrine and relics of St Cybi were removed to Dublin by Henry IV's army when it invaded Anglesey, but were lost at the Reformation. Close to the church is a smaller church, **Eglwys Bedd** (Church of the Grave), which reputedly contains the tomb of Seregri, an Irish warrior who was repelled by the Welsh chief, Caswallon Lawhir, in 550 AD. The town's triumphal arches, built in 1821, commemorate George IV's visit here as well as the end of the A5, the major road from London.

The interesting **Canolfan Ucheldre Centre** is housed in an old convent chapel. It is an arts centre for northwest Wales opened in 1991, and presents both film, music and drama events as well as holding all manner of

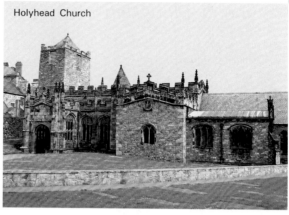

Holyhead Church

art and craft exhibitions and workshops. **Salt Island** (Ynys Halen), close to the town centre, is self-explanatory: a factory was built here to extract salt from the seawater. Rock salt was added to improve the sea salt's quality, and when an excise duty was charged, smuggling flourished, particularly between Four Mile Bridge and the Isle of Man, where salt was duty free.

While the town itself is not without interest, it is the immediate surrounding area that draws most visitors to Holyhead. **Four Mile Bridge** connects Holy Island to Anglesey, and was so called, not because it is four miles long, but because it it four miles from the ferry terminal in Holyhead. Its old name was Pont Rhyd Bont. **Breakwater Quarry Country Park**, just northwest of the town, incorporates Britain's largest breakwater. Designed by James Meadow and started in 1845, the structure, which shields an area of 667 acres, took 28 years to construct. From the country park there are many walks along the coast, including a route to **South Stack**. This is a reserve of cliffs and heath teeming with birdlife, including puffins, guillemots and razorbills. The RSPB visitor centre is open

Holyhead Mountain

Distance: *4.7 miles (7.5 kilometres)*
Typical time: *180 mins*
Height gain: *200 metres*
Map: *Explorer 262*
Walk: *www.walkingworld.com ID:860*
Contributor: *David and Chris Stewart*

ACCESS INFORMATION:

From Bangor keep on the A55 right across the island to Holyhead, about 25 minutes' drive. Follow the town centre sign on the first roundabout, then follow the signs for South Stack, passing the ferry terminal on your right. Keep following the signs for South Stack to your starting point for the walk, this is at the first car park on your left (free parking). If you have got to the car park with the cafe you have gone about 300yds too far.

DESCRIPTION:

A very interesting start with a visit to the Holyhead Mountain hut group, a hill fort on the summit, 360-degree views. There are two bird reserves in the area, one of which is Ellen's Tower, where the RSPB lend out binoculars for viewing the puffins, and finishes off with a walk on the cliffs. There are 263 species of wild plants in this area, a hermitage that dates from the 3rd century, some of the most demanding cliff climbs in the UK, and in Holyhead itself there is a Roman fort to visit.

FEATURES:

Hills or Fells, Mountains, Sea, Toilets, Birds, Flowers, Great Views, Food Shop, Good for Kids, Tea Shop, Woodland, Ancient Monument.

WALK DIRECTIONS:

1 | The entrance to the historic hut site is directly opposite the car park. If you want to leave this until later, turn left onto road and turn right onto access to Foel.

2 | As you aproach the house, take the dirt track to the right.

3 | Take the right-hand track that follows the line of the wall.

4 | Take the left-hand path of these two and head for the saddle. Carry on over the crossroads.

5 | Turn left at the crossroads.

6 | Turn left and start going uphill again. Take the left-hand path that follows the wall going uphill.

7 | After about 50 metres turn left and head steeply uphill.

8 | A few metres from the summit there is a wooden waymark for the path to South Stack. The path has been rebuilt with stone steps. Follow them down and bear left.

9 | Head for the radio dishes, keeping them to your right.

10 | Walk out to the headland for the view down to South Stack.

11 | After leaving the view of South Stack, carry on along the path until you come to a hole in the wall leading down to Ellin's Tower; this now belongs to the RSPB and they supply binoculars for you to look at the puffins etc.

12 | Take the path from the tower that runs back towards the car park.

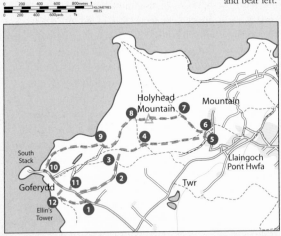

daily, the café daily in summer, and the lighthouse is open daily in summer for guided tours. The lighthouse, one of the most impressive in Wales, was built in 1809 and stands on a beautiful but dangerous site reached by a steep stone stairway of over 400 steps. Above the harbour

South Stack Cliffs, Holyhead

and breakwater, is a memorial to Captain Skinner, who drowned when his packet boat, *Escape*, was lost in 1832.

At the summit of Holyhead Mountain, from where, on a clear day, Snowdonia, the Isle of Man and the Mourne Mountains in Ireland can be seen, there is evidence of an ancient settlement. The remains of **Caer y Twr**, a hill fort, are visible and, close by, is **Cytiau'r Gwyddelod**, a hut settlement from the 2nd century.

Between South Stack and North Stack lies **Gogarth Bay**, where the RSPB sea bird centre includes a cavern, known as Parliament House Cave, which is used by a profusion of sea birds such as puffins, guillemots and even falcons. Visitors here can also watch the thousands of cliff-nesting birds via live television pictures, and enjoy the beautiful cliff top walks. **Ellin's Tower**, in the centre, is another spot favoured by ornithologists.

Aqua diving, windsurfing, water skiing and fishing are some of the many attractions of **Trearddur Bay**, a popular part of Anglesey's extensive coastline that lies just to the southwest of Holyhead. With large sandy

beaches, clear water and safe bathing, it is obviously popular. The Georgian house, Towyn Lodge, on the south side of the bay, played host to Thomas Telford while he was working on what is now the A5 road in the 19th century. A portion of the bay, **Porth Dafarch**, is owned by the National Trust. **Trefignath** is a chambered cairn with two tall pillars at each side of the entrance.

Down the years, the crew of Holyhead's lifeboats have won an amazing 70 awards. The **Lifeboat Station** can be visited on Sunday mornings, when crew training takes place at 10am.

Around Holyhead

RHOSCOLYN
4½ miles S of Holyhead off the B4545

🏛 Parish Church of St Gwenfaen 　 🏚 Bwa Gwyn

🏚 St Gwenfaen's Well 　 ⛰ Rhoscolyn Head

The name of this village means the moor of the column, the column in question thought to be a Roman one. It was once home to a thriving oyster industry that is now, sadly, in decline. China clay was also once quarried here, while the local marble was used in the construction of Worcester, Bristol and Peterborough Cathedrals.

The **Parish Church of St Gwenfaen** was originally founded in the 6th century by St Gwenfaen. **St Gwenfaen's Well** was said to have properties that cured, in particular, mental illness. **Rhoscolyn Head** is a superb headland ideal for cliff walking, and there are splendid views northwards over Trearddur Bay and, southwards, over Cymyran Bay. At **Bwa Gwyn** (White Arch) is a memorial to Tyger, a remarkable dog who, in 1817, led the four-man crew from a sinking ketch to safety. After dragging the cabin boy ashore and returning for the ship's captain, the dog collapsed and died from exhaustion.

VALLEY
3½ miles SE of Holyhead on the A5

🌿 Llyn Penrhyn

Valley sits on Anglesey, immediately opposite Holy Island. It was thought to have gained its name while Thomas Telford was cutting his road through the small hill here. Centuries earlier this was the home of Iron Age man whose weapons and horse trappings found in the area are now on display in the National Museum of Wales.

However, Valley is perhaps better known today for the nearby airfield established here during World War II as a fighter pilot base. In 1943, the American Air Force expanded the base's capability for use as an Atlantic terminal and now the RAF uses it for training flights

---

CIGYDD Y FALI BUTCHERS
The Old Court House, Station Road, Y Fali, Anglesey LL65 3EB
Tel: 01407 742391
e-mail: cigydyyfali@aol.com website: www.valleybutchers.co.uk

Cigydd Y Fali translates as The Valley Butchers and for many years Karl Jones and his team have been feeding the local population on the very best and succulent meats available - Karl achieving local acclaim when the shop won 11 Gold Awards for Excellence for their meat products.

Karl sells only meat reared on Anglesey that has been handpicked by himself, and specialises in tender lamb, tasty pork and well hung beef, with people travelling from all over the island - and even from the mainland - to buy his high-quality produce. It also sells award-winning pies and sausages, which are made on the premises, as well as locally produced eggs and cheeses. Its cooked meats are all produced on the premises, ensuring maximum flavour and freshness, and the shop sells to all the major hotels and restaurants in the area.

The shop is noted for its value-for-money prices, and also features a section selling fresh fruit and vegetables. This area of Anglesey is holiday country, with many self-catering cottages, campsites and caravan parks. So the shop is also popular with holidaymakers, who appreciate the immaculately clean premises, the friendly staff and the help and advice that is always given when

🏛 historic building 🏛 museum and heritage 🏚 historic site 🍃 scenic attraction 🌿 flora and fauna

CLEIFIOG UCHAF COUNTRY HOUSE

off Spencer Road, Valley, Anglesey LL65 3AB
Tel: 01407 741 888
e-mail: cleifioguchaf@btconnect.com
website: www.cleifioguchaf.co.uk

Standing at the end of a tree-lined driveway and set amidst 30 acres of grounds, **Cleifiog Uchaf Country House** is a lovingly restored and discreetly modernised 16th century longhouse. Inside, richly furnished lounges, sumptuous sofas, beautiful paintings and roaring fires all add to the charm and character of this wonderful country retreat. A major attraction here is Llywelyn's, an intimate bistro-style licensed restaurant serving a selective menu of dishes based on seasonal, locally sourced Anglesey produce. Llywelyn's Welsh chef trained at the world-famous Ballymaloe School in Ireland and he uses these fine ingredients to bring alive old classics, turning them into delicious 21st century dishes.

Cleifiog Uchaf offers guests the choice of either bed & breakfast, or self-catering accommodation. B&B guests stay in one of the delightfully varied rooms, all of which are individually styled and decorated and feature flat-screen TVs, DVD players, WiFi internet access and tea/coffee-making facilities. If you prefer self-catering, there are two converted cottages available, both with one bedroom and both beautifully furnished and decorated throughout, and with extra features such as Egyptian cotton towels and luxury toiletries.

ANGLESEY SHOOTING SCHOOL

Presaddfed Hall, Bodedern, Holyhead,
Isle of Anglesey LL65 3UE
Tel: 01407 740652 Fax: 01407 742702
e-mail: rosemary@presaddfedfreeserve.co.uk
website: www.presaddfed.co.uk

Set deep in the heart of stunning Welsh countryside at Presaddfed Hall, **Anglesey Shooting School** utilises the superb natural surroundings to provide both sport and relaxation. Whatever your experience, from absolute beginner to the expert Clay or Game Shot, the school has something for everyone. The layouts, set in 8 acres of picturesque countryside, are designed to simulate different types of shooting with high towers, doubles and flushes to add to the challenge. Instruction can be provided on an individual or group basis with all the required equipment provided, and simulated Game Days can also be arranged.

Light refreshments are available in the comfortable Club House with its log fire, and more formal catering arrangements can be made if required. Established in 1989, the School is open on Saturdays from March to mid-October from 12 noon until 5.30pm. There's a further session on Wednesday evenings from 6pm to 9pm, light permitting. The school will also open at other times for individuals, for parties (including corporate parties). And if you would like to stay nearby, just 5 minutes away is Presaddfed Hall, a handsome 17th century mansion with ten double bedrooms available.

stories and anecdotes famous people art and craft entertainment and sport walks

and for Air/Sea rescue. Opposite the barracks is **Llyn Penrhyn**, a complex of reed-fringed lakes with lots of wildfowl and dragonflies. Before the bridges to Holyhead were built, during the construction of the A5, the crossing to the town was made via Four Mile Bridge (see Holyhead).

RHOSNEIGR
7½ miles SE of Holyhead on the A4080

🏛 Parish Church of St Maelog   ⛲ Cymyran Bay

🌿 Tywyn Trewan Common   🏚 Norman Court

This small resort is situated in a quiet spot, close to the sandy beaches and rocky outcrops of **Cymyran Bay**. The River Crigyll, which runs into the sea by the town, was the haunt, in the 18th century, of the "Wreckers of Crigyll", who were famous for luring ships onto the rocks. Tried at Beaumaris in 1741, where the group of desperate men were found guilty and hanged, the wreckers became the subject of a ballad, *The Hanging of the Thieves of Crigyll*. In March 1883, the tea clipper the **Norman Court** ran aground off the coast near the village, though not as a result of wreckers. She was one of the fastest and best of the tea clippers of the day, and had become a famous name. She was carrying, not tea, but 1,000 tons of sugar for Greenock in Scotland. Twenty men were rescued from the ship, and two were lost. For over 24 hours the men had been clinging to the ship's rigging. For many years after, her wreckage could still be seen.

The **Parish Church of St Maelog** dates from 1848-49, though it looks much older. There has been a church on the site since at least the 6th century, when St Maelog chose this site to establish a church and monastery. He was the brother of Gildas and St Gallgo (see Moelfre), and died in Brittany.

The 1,400 acres of gorse and dunes at **Tywyn Trewan Common** is a paradise for botanists and ornithologists.

LLANFAIRYNGHORNWY
7 miles NE of Holyhead off the A5025

🏚 The Skerries   ⛲ Frances Williams

This village, on the approach to **Carmel Head**, has two claims to fame. It was here, in the 19th century, that **Frances Williams** founded the Anglesey Association for the Preservation of Life from Shipwreck. Along with her husband, who was the local rector, Frances raised funds for lifeboats on the island and, through her efforts, the first lifeboat station in the area was established. She was also noted as an artist, and some of her drawings are held by the University of Wales at Bangor.

Lying two miles offshore from the point at Carmel Head are **The Skerries**, a group of windswept islets whose Welsh name, Ynysoedd y Moelrhoniaid, means Island of Porpoises. On the islets stands the last lighthouse to be privately owned (ships had to pay a toll as they passed). When braziers stood there during the 18th century, they burnt approximately 100 tons of coal a night! Now automated and owned by Trinity House, its beam is rated at four million candles.

CEMAES
11 miles NE of Holyhead off the A5025

🏛 Parish Church of St Patrick Llanbadrig

🏚 Mynachdy   🏚 Ogof y March Glas

🏛 Wylfa Nuclear Power Station   ⛲ Cemaes Bay

🏛 Parish Church of St Mechell, Llanfechell

⛲ North Anglesey Heritage Coast

Boasting two glorious, safe, sandy beaches, **Cemaes Bay** is a popular place on the island

TRUE RETREATS

Tan Y Bryn, Rhyduyn, Church Bay,
Anglesey LL65 4EA
Tel: 01407 730589
e-mail: info@trueretreats.com
website: www.trueretreats.com

True Retreats is a holiday letting agency with a difference. Owners Andy and Emily Gearing offer a hand picked collection of stylish holiday accommodation in Anglesey and North Wales. They pride themselves on the quality of their properties and only feature 4 and 5 star graded accommodation. Each property has been selected for its unique features such as log-burning stoves, marble bathrooms, roll top baths, sea views, beach locations and even a hot tub!

Their selection provides the perfect 'get away' from the stress and strain of everyday life and the dramatic and diverse landscape and coastline of Anglesey make it an inspiring holiday destination for couples and families alike. Andy and Emily appreciate that 'Time Out' with friends and family is essential these days and they want to ensure they are 'True' to your needs and find the ideal 'Retreat' just for you. Their ethos is to provide a tailor made holiday that is unique to each customer. They understand that a holiday isn't just about the property; it's about the quality of experience and value for money - that's why they have a wealth of guests who return time and time again.

The True Retreats collection provides something for everyone, from baby friendly cottages to family favourites, romantic retreats, pet friendly properties and business breaks. They also have a Special Selection of properties that can be rented for stylish hen parties, cosy honeymoons, birthday parties, reunions and anniversaries. Whatever the occasion or number in your party, Andy and Emily are sure to find you your True Retreat!

Not only do they feature accommodation of the highest standards in some of the most breathtaking locations, they also have a range of activities available to you. These include private chefs, food delivery service, babysitting, spa pampering, horse riding, fishing, golfing, kite surfing, cycle hire.....the list is endless. They will happily book the activities for you prior to your arrival and even arrange transport to and

from your chosen destination to ensure that your every need is met and your holiday is truly something special.

They also appreciate that sometimes it can be the personal little touches that make all the difference so welcome hampers, flowers, bathrobes or luxury toiletries are provided to make your stay feel extra special.

🔲 stories and anecdotes 🐿 famous people 🎨 art and craft 🎭 entertainment and sport 🚶 walks

that was also once a favourite with smugglers. However, today, Cemaes is a quiet and picturesque fishing village, with a small tidal harbour with much to offer holidaymakers: wonderful walks, abundant wildlife, fishing, hotels, shops, pubs and also the opportunity to learn a little of the Welsh language. Cemaes sits in the middle of the **North Anglesey Heritage Coast**, and is the most northerly village in Wales.

Ogof y March Glas – Cave of the Blue Horse - on Cemaes Bay was named after an incident that took place over 200 years ago. Following a family dispute, a young man furiously galloped away from his house near the bay on his dappled grey horse. Blinded by rage, he galloped headlong over the cliff; only his hat was ever seen again, although the carcass of his horse was found washed up in the cave.

At Llanbadrig, north of the village, is the **Parish Church of St Patrick**. Badrig is Welsh for Patrick, and there are three churches in Wales dedicated to that particular saint. However, the one at Llanbadrig is the only one with a tangible connection to him. The original church dates from about 440 AD, and was founded by the great man himself after he was sent by Pope Celestine I to Ireland to spread Christianity. It is said he was shipwrecked on Yns Badrig, off the coast, but managed to get to land, where he took refuge in St Patrick's Cave on the shore close to where the church now stands. He

found a well there with fresh drinking water, and founded the church in gratitude. The present church dates from the 15th century, though there is a more modern church in the village as well. At Llanfechell, south of the village, is the **Parish Church of St Mechell**, the nave and part of the chancel of which dates from the 13th century.

Around the headland at the western edge of the bay lies **Wylfa Nuclear Power Station**. Its visitor centre is the starting point for a guided tour of the station and also contains a mass of information about the nature trail surrounding the plant. Cemlyn Bay, home to thousands of terns between April and July, is managed as a nature reserve by the North Wales Wildlife Trust. **Mynachdy** contains old settlement sites and the remains of some long disused copper mines.

AMLWCH
14 miles NE of Holyhead on the A5025

🖼 Amlwch Railway Museum   ⛏ Parys Mountain

South of this seaside town lies the pock-marked **Parys Mountain**, which has provided

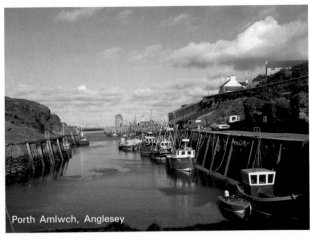
Porth Amlwch, Anglesey

copper for prospectors from as early as Roman times. In 1768 a copper boom helped make Anglesey the copper centre of the world, but by 1820 the rush was over as prices fell and the mineral deposits became exhausted. The harbour, which was built during more prosperous times, is now used mainly by pleasure craft. In its heyday, Amlwch had 6,000 inhabitants and 1,000 ale houses. The **Amlwch Railway Museum** has displays on trains and associated memorabilia.

DULAS
15 miles E of Holyhead off the A5025

🐦 Ynys Dulas

A once thriving village, Dulas was, in the early 19th century, home to both a brickworks and a shipbuilding industry. Standing at the head of the Dulas River, that runs into the bay, the village overlooks **Ynys Dulas**, a small island which lies a mile or so offshore and is the haunt of grey seals. On the island itself is a 19th century tower built as a beacon and a refuge for sailors; a former lady of Llysdulas manor house had food left there for stranded mariners.

LLANERCHYMEDD
11 miles E of Holyhead on the B5112

🏛 Parish Church of St Mary   🐟 Llyn Alaw

To the north of the village lies **Llyn Alaw**, Anglesey's largest lake, well known for its fine trout fishing as well as the abundant wildlife found around its shores. Covering some 770

acres, the lake is actually a man-made reservoir, produced by flooding marshland. It supplies most of the island's industrial and domestic needs. Some people actually believe that Llanerchymedd was the burial place of Mary, mother of Jesus. A book, *The Marian Conspiracy*, was even published claiming that the actual burial site is where the present **Parish Church of St Mary** now stands. This flies in the face of Roman Catholic dogma, which teaches that Mary bodily ascended to heaven.

LLANDDEUSANT
6½ miles E of Holyhead off the A5025

🏛 Llynnon Mill   🏛 Bedd Branwen

This village is home to Anglesey's only stone tower working windmill, built in 1775–76 at a total cost of £529 11s 0d. Four storeys high, with a boat-shaped cap, it ceased milling by wind power in 1924, but was restored and opened to the public in 1984. **Llynnon Mill** not only mills stoneground flour for sale (wind and conditions willing) but also has an attractive craft shop and a popular tearoom for visitors to enjoy.

Tradition has it that the green mound, **Bedd Branwen**, near the River Alaw, is the grave of Branwen, the heroine of the Welsh epic, *Mabinogion*. Opened in 1813, it later revealed a rough baked clay urn containing fragments of burnt bone and ashes. Since the discovery of more funeral urns in 1967, the site has become even more significant.

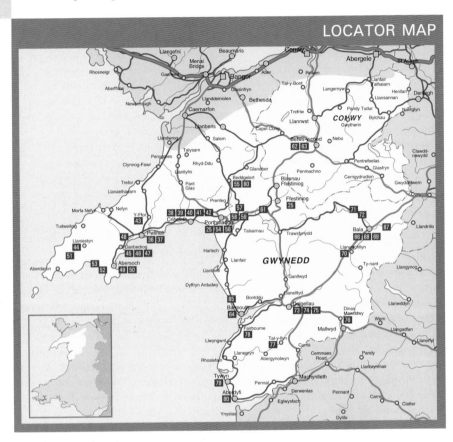

LOCATOR MAP

ADVERTISERS AND PLACES OF INTEREST

🏥 historic building 🏛 museum and heritage 🏚 historic site 🛋 scenic attraction 🌱 flora and fauna

3 | Snowdonia & Gwynedd Coast

To the south of Anglesey lies the Llyn (Lleyn) Peninsula, which forms the southern arm of the great curve of Caernarfon Bay. This is one of the most secluded and most beautiful parts of Wales, and over 100 miles of its shoreline are designated Areas of Outstanding Natural Beauty. During the Middle Ages, Bardsey Island, lying off the western tip of the peninsula, was a place of pilgrimage, and parts of the ancient route to Aberdaron, from where the pilgrims sailed to the island, can still be followed. Reminders of the area's early Christian past can be found throughout Llyn, along with more ancient monuments, such as hill forts, churches and standing stones. This region, like the northern coast and the Isle of

Anglesey, has been a favourite holiday destination since the coming of the railways in the mid 19th century.

The attractive Victorian resorts along the southern shore of the peninsula are sheltered and provide plenty of scope for sailing, swimming and fishing. Though born in Manchester, the place where David Lloyd George lived until he was 16 years old – Llanystumdwy – is a popular place to visit. However, the whole region is filled with splendid attractions to see and exciting things to do. Perhaps the most popular of all is the fantasy village of Portmeirion, built from the 1920s to the 1970s by Sir Clough Williams-Ellis, made famous by the TV series *The*

 stories and anecdotes famous people art and craft entertainment and sport walks

Cader Iris, Snowdonia

includes surviving tracts of the vast forests that once covered much of Wales. From the earliest times, this region was mined for its minerals. Gold was extracted here long before the Romans arrived and, as recently as the 19th century, there were mini-gold rushes in a belt that stretched from Bontddu along the line of the River Mawddach. Copper, lead and slate were also mined up until the start of the 20th century, and the scars left by those industries can still be seen today. Several of the mines have found new roles as visitor attractions, along with the little railways that once carried the minerals from the mines and quarries to the coast.

Prisoner in 1966 and 1967.

There are three National Parks in Wales, and Snowdonia, at some 840 square miles, is the largest and certainly the most dramatic. Set up in 1951, and embracing a number of mountain and hill ranges, Snowdonia National Park (Parc Cenedlaethol Eryri in Welsh) extends southwards from Snowdon as far as Aberdovey and Machynlleth, eastwards to Bala, and northwards to Conwy. In the west, the park borders the Llyn Peninsula and the Cambrian coast.

There are several routes up to the summit of Snowdon, beginning at various points around its base. Some call for more energy than others, but the least arduous ascent is by the Snowdon Mountain Railway that runs from Llanberis. The most popular walk follows the railway. In and around nearby Betws-y-Coed, the walking is gentler and

In the middle of the 19th century, the coastal villages and towns, many of them obscure, quiet fishing communities, were put on the map and changed radically in character with the arrival of the main railway network. As the fashion for sea air grew and communications were made easier, they became popular seaside resorts and, today, many of them still retain Victorian and Edwardian buildings constructed to cater for holidaymakers. The scenery throughout the region is truly inspirational, and few would disagree with the verdict of the 19th-century traveller and writer George Borrow:

"Perhaps in all the world there is no region more picturesquely beautiful."

The Llyn Peninsula

Pwllheli

🏚 Penarth Fawr   🛶 Lifeboat Station

Sitting on the south coast of the Lleyn Peninsula, Pwllheli is its chief town, and is often referred to as the "jewel" in the Welsh scenic crown. Like Nefyn, it was granted a charter in 1355. This was given by the Black Prince to Nigel de Loryng, the local lord of the manor, who had helped the Prince win the Battle of Poitiers. A popular holiday resort with all the usual amusements, this is also still a market town, though its once busy port,

BLODWELL SEAVIEW APARTMENTS

11 Westend Parade, Pwllheli, Gwynedd LL53 5PN
Tel: 01758 701695
e-mail: carrieabrahams@aol.com

Blodwell Seaview Apartments are located in a central position in Pwllheli, the chief town of the Lleyn Peninsula and a popular holiday resort. Behind a distinctive yellow-painted frontage three bedrooms – a single, a double and a twin – are well equipped for a self-catering base for exploring, with shower room, kitchen and dining/living room overlooking the sea and a little lawn at the front. The town centre and the marina are a short walk away, and also nearby is the lifeboat station, which is open every day for visitors.

PLAS BODEGROES RESTAURANT WITH ROOMS

Nefyn Road, Pwllheli, Gwynedd, Wales LL53 5TH
Tel: 01758 612363   Fax: 01758 701247
website: www.bodegroes.co.uk

Chris and Gunna Chown's Georgian Manor House has long been a destination for culinary pilgrims anxious to sample Chris's justly celebrated Michelin starred cooking. It's no surprise then to find that **Plas Bodegroes** styles itself as a "restaurant with room." Banish any thought though, that things outside the kitchen and restaurant might be something of an afterthought.

The 11 lovely rooms with their goose-down duvets, Egyptian cotton and views over the gardens are a delight in themselves. An avenue of two hundred year old beeches fronts the house, and wisterias and roses perfume the verandah.

It's impossible not to return to the food though. Chris's reputation is based on the modern interpretation of traditional dishes, with prime Welsh ingredients to the fore: laverbread, mussels, sea trout, sea bass, lobster, mountain lamb and Black beef, Carmarthen ham, Bara Brith & butter pudding with Welsh whisky ice cream.

The wines are as outstanding as the food, and Gunna supervises that the service runs smoothly and politely. The restaurant is open for dinner Tuesday to Saturday (also Sunday on Bank Holiday weekends) and for Sunday lunch. A truly great restaurant with really good rooms sums it up neatly.

🎭 stories and anecdotes 👤 famous people 🎨 art and craft 🎭 entertainment and sport 🚶 walks

SNOWDONIA AND GWYNEDD COAST

where wine was imported from the Continent, is now home to pleasure craft, with a 420-berth marina and an annual sailing regatta. Pwllheli's **Lifeboat Station** operates an all-weather carriage-launched Mersey Class boat and an inshore D craft. The station can be visited from 10am to 3pm daily. During the National Eisteddfod in 1925, three members of the Army of Welsh Home Rulers met with three members of the Welsh Movement at the town's Temperance Hotel and joined forces to form the political party, Plaid Cymru.

Just to the east of the town lies **Penarth Fawr**, an interesting 15th-century manor house.

Around Pwllheli

ABERERCH
2 miles E of Pwllheli off the A497

🏛 Parish Church of St Cawrdal

🐦 Robert ap Gwilym Ddu

The **Parish Church of St Cawrdal** was built in the 14th and 15th century on the foundations of a much older building. It was founded in the 6th century by Cawrdaf, who was the son of Prince Caradog Freichfras of Brecon. In the churchyard is the grave of

Robert ap Gwilym Ddu (Robert Williams) and his wife. He lived between 1776 and 1850, and was a poet and hymn writer.

CRICCIETH
8 miles E of Pwllheli on the A497

🏛 Criccieth Castle   🐦 Criccieth Festival

🏛 Parish Church of St Catherine

This small family resort lies near the northeast corner of Cardigan Bay and enjoys fine views down the Llyn coastline and northeastwards to Snowdonia. Unlike many of the other resorts on the peninsula, Criccieth is more reminiscent of a south coast seaside town than one set in North Wales.

An attractive Victorian town, it is dominated by **Criccieth Castle**, which stands on a rocky outcrop with commanding views over the sea. Built in the early 13th century by Llywelyn the Great as a stronghold of the native Welsh princes, it was captured in 1283 and extended by Edward I; but the core of the structure – the powerful twin towered gatehouse – still exists from the original fortification. Despite Edward's strengthening of the defences, in 1404 the castle was taken by Owain Glyndwr and burnt and the castle walls still bear the scorch marks. One of the best preserved of the 13th century castles to

MIN Y GAER B&B
Porthmadog Road, Criccieth, Gwynedd LL52 0HP
Tel: 01766 522151 Fax: 01766 523540
e-mail: info@minygaer.co.uk website: www.minygaer.co.uk

Just 2 minutes from the beach and some excellent local restaurants, **Min Y Gaer B&B** is a friendly family-run licensed guest house. An ideal base for touring Snowdonia, it has 10 en suite guest rooms, many of them enjoying stunning views of Cardigan Bay and of Criccieth Castle. Guests have the use of the front lounge which has TV, DVD and honesty bar. There's ample parking or, if you are arriving by train, owners Jan and Tim Davis will pick you up at the station.

🏛 historic building 🏛 museum and heritage 🏛 historic site 🔍 scenic attraction 🌢 flora and fauna

BRON EIFION
COUNTRY HOUSE HOTEL

Criccieth, Gwynedd LL52 0SA
Tel: 01766 522385 Fax: 01766 523796
e-mail: enquiries@broneifion.co.uk
website: www.broneifion.co.uk

Bron Eifion Country House Hotel is a Victorian residence upgraded by its owners to provide top-quality guest accommodation. John and Mary Heenan, who came here in 2006, have created a feeling of splendour and opulence with fine paintings, furniture and carpets that befit the property's Victorian pedigree and complement its panelled walls and magnificent main staircase. The accommodation in the Grade II listed stone and slate house comprises 19 spacious, luxurious en suite bedrooms, many of them commanding superb views over the terrace and the five-acre landscaped gardens on three levels, which include handsome box hedges, a mini-maze and a helicopter landing area next to a daffodil field. Restful lounges warmed in the cooler months by open log fires are perfect spots to relax after a day's sightseeing and to meet the other guests.

In the elegant Orangery Restaurant guests and non-residents enjoy exciting dishes based on the very best Welsh produce, including fish and shellfish from Pwllheli, beef and lamb from Caernarfon and the pick of the season's supplies from Anglesey. Excellent service and a well-chosen wine list set the seal on a memorable dining experience further enhanced by marvellous sunsets over the bay. The location, the gardens, the stylish accommodation, the delicious food and the experienced resident team make Bron Eifion the perfect choice for a private party, a wedding or any other celebration. The restaurant seats 65 and for larger groups (up to 300) a marquee can be set up in the garden.

The whole house and its bedrooms can be taken over for a special occasion. The hotel is perfectly placed for a golfing holiday: Criccieth Golf Course is on the doorstep and there are five other fine courses a short drive away – Abersoch, Porthmadog, Pwllheli, Nefyn & District and Royal St David's. It's also an ideal venue for meetings and conferences, with executive services and facilities and adaptable that includes a boardroom for up to 20 and a theatre for up to 50. Private guests should book for a minimum of two or three days to get the most of the many scenic, historic and sporting attractions of the coast and countryside around Bron Eifion, which is located half a mile west of Criccieth on the A497 road on the shores of Cardigan Bay.

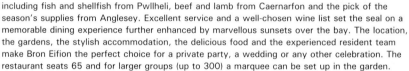
📖 stories and anecdotes 🐦 famous people 🎨 art and craft 🎭 entertainment and sport 🚶 walks

CADWALDERS ICE CREAM CAFÉ

Castle Street, Criccieth, Gwynedd LL52 0DP
Tel: 01766 523665
website: www.cadwaladersicecream.co.uk

Building on a reputation gained since 1927 for high quality ice cream - made in North Wales to a traditional secret recipe (which comprises 6lbs of "shan't tell you" and "a great deal of love and care") - **Cadwaladers Ice Cream Cafe** in the shadow of Criccieth Castle has long been a Sunday afternoon treat to savour. As well as delicious ice creams you can enjoy quality coffees, great chocolate drinks, teas, cold drinks, cakes, baguettes and pastries too.

Cadwalader's Ice Cream was started by husband and wife team David and Hannah when they built and opened the shop in Castle Street, Criccieth back in 1927. It has since become a mainstay of Criccieth's tourist attractions, but has stretched its wings to encompass its own chain of ice cream cafes and coffee shops, dotted around Wales and over the border. However it's this place that remains the true mecca for Cadwalader's devotees, with many still insisting vanilla remains the crème de la crème of its ice creams. But this doesn't mean there isn't plenty to choose from, including flavours like apricot & brandy, St Clementine, dragon's breath and chocolate pudding.

ANDREW KIME PHOTOGRAPHY

The Golden Eagle Gallery, 42 High Street, Criccieth,
Gwynedd LL52 0EY
Tel: 01766 522554
e-mail: info@imagesofsnowdonia.com
website: www.imagesofsnowdonia.com

Andrew Kime discovered his passion for landscape photography at the age of 7, a passion that has been with him ever since. Today, he travels frequently but appreciates above all North Wales, where he lives in the heart of Snowdonia National Park. This region, made up of lakes, peat bogs, deep forests and still-wild coasts, naturally offers him numerous opportunities to satisfy his passion. His images are the reflection of the profound respect that nature inspires in him and he hopes, in this way, to contribute to its protection. His photographs are frequently published in photo and nature magazines, calendars, cards and have been seen on ITV's 'Waterworld'.

You can now purchase a wide range of Andrew's work from his gallery, The Golden Eagle Gallery (the shop has been known as the Golden Eagle for at least four generations). All pictures are available as signed, high quality prints & canvases. It is also used as the base for Andrew's successful range of photography workshops. The Gallery is open 6 days a week, (3 days during the winter months of Jan - Mar, although Andrew will open by appointment at other times). If you need to confirm opening times or want to ensure Andrew will be at the gallery when visiting then please call ahead on the number shown above.

🏛 historic building 🏛 museum and heritage 🏛 historic site 🍃 scenic attraction 🌱 flora and fauna

be found in the North Wales countryside, the romantic ruins of Criccieth Castle have inspired many artists down the centuries including JMW Turner, who used it as the backdrop for a famous painting of storm-wrecked sailors. The annual **Criccieth Festival** is renowned for its traditional Celtic music and song.

The **Parish Church of St Catherine** was founded, on what is thought to be the site of a Celtic monastery, by Edward I when he captured the castle and gave Criccieth its royal charter in 1284. In about 1500 it was enlarged by the addition of a northern isle and arcade, and in the 19th century it was fully restored, with the aisle (which was in imminent danger of collapsing) being rebuilt.

LLANYSTUMDWY

6½ miles E of Pwllheli on the A497

🏠 Highgate   🏠 Parish Church of St John

🏛 Memorial Gates   🏛 Lloyd George Museum

🐿 David Lloyd George   🐇 Rabbit Farm& Farm Park

This peaceful little coastal village is best known as being the home of **David Lloyd George**, the Member of Parliament for Caernarfon for 55 years and the Prime Minister who, at the beginning of the 20th century, was responsible for social reform as well as seeing the country through the Armistice at the end of World War I. Though born in Manchester, Lloyd George grew up here, and his childhood home, **Highgate**, is now just as it would have been when the great statesman lived there. The **Lloyd George Museum** features a Victorian schoolroom and an exhibition of the life of this reforming Liberal politician. It is open Easter to October, and at other times by appointment. When Lloyd George died in 1945, he was buried beneath the boulder where he used to sit and think while young. It stands on the outskirts of the village, across the river from the **Parish Church of St John**. Opposite his grave is a set of **Memorial Gates** presented to the village by Pwllheli in 1952. They feature an elephant and a castle – elephants are part of the town's coat of arms.

He won this tribute in Parliament from Winston Churchill: "As a man of action, resource and creative energy he stood, when at his zenith, without a rival. His name is a household word throughout our

---

TYDDYN SIANEL HOLIDAY COTTAGES

Llanystumdwy, Criccieth, Gwynedd LL52 0LS
Tel: 01766 522738
e-mail: tyddynsianel@supanet.com
website: www.tyddynsianel.co.uk

Llanystumdwy is best known as the home of David Lloyd George, Prime Minister from 1916 to 1922, and visitors come from near and far to see his home, the museum dedicated to his life and his grave on the banks of the River Dwyfor. Pat Williams provides the ideal base for visitors and tourists in **Tyddyn Sianel Holiday Cottages**, three traditionally furnished cottages sleeping 2, 4 and 6. They are well appointed for a stress-free self-catering break and can be booked as one for larger families or groups of friends. The accommodation is open from April to October, with weekly bookings in summer and short breaks available in spring and autumn. The village stands half a mile from the coast near the A497 west of Criccieth.

📖 stories and anecdotes 🐿 famous people 🎨 art and craft 🎭 entertainment and sport 🚶 walks

Commonwealth of Nations. He was the greatest Welshman which that unconquerable race has produced since the age of the Tudors. Much of his work abides, some of it will grow greatly in the future, and those who come after us will find the pillars of his life's toil upstanding, massive and indestructible." Visitors to the **Rabbit Farm & Farm Park** at Llanystumdwy will meet rabbits of various breeds and other friendly animals including Shetland ponies, lambs and goats. Pony rides are available, and there's a café and a play area.

LLANGYBI

5 miles NE of Pwllheli off the B4354

🏛 St Cybi's Well   🏛 Garn Pentyrch

Just to the north of the village is **St Cybi's Well**, which was reputed to have curative properties for such diseases and illneses as warts, blindness, scurvy and rheumatism. The well was established in the 6th century when St Cybi was in the process of setting up religious cells and a monastery in Holyhead. It is sheltered by an unusual building with beehive vaulting, which is thought to be unique in Wales. Behind it is the Iron Age fort of **Garn Pentyrch**. A story tells of a boy who played with the fairies among the stones of Garn Pentrych, and who eventually disappeared for two years, though he looked no older when he came back. The Parish Church of Llangybi is medieval, and services are held here only five times a year.

GLASFRYN PARC FARMSHOP AND COTTAGES

Glasfryn Parc, Y Ffôr, nr Pwllheli, Gwynedd, North Wales LL53 6PG
Tel: 01766 810044
e-mail: info@glasfryn.co.uk
website: www.glasfryn.co.uk or www.glasfryncottages.co.uk

Glasfryn Parc is Wales' premier activity and adventure centre with numerous activities. Whether you decide to take the challenge of the go-kart circuit or try your hand at archery or ten pin bowling, the park provides everything for the ideal family day. Set within the 500 acre estate, in an area of Outstanding Natural Beauty, **Glasfryn Cottages** offer a great choice of self-catering accommodation, all with a 4 or 5-star rating from the Welsh Tourist Board. Also on site there is a cafe-diner selling home-made food, and a farm shop well stocked with Welsh-sourced products.

There are five delightful cottages available, sleeping 5-10 people, all have beamed ceilings, log fires, antique furniture, en-suite bathrooms and private gardens with picnic tables. The cottages while tranquil are but a short hop from the beaches of the Cardigan coast and the mountains of Snowdonia.

The **Glasfryn Farm Shop**, established in 2001, is gaining quite a reputation and has so much to offer. Choose from delicious Welsh Black Beef, Lamb and game reared here on the Glasfryn Estate. Quality Welsh produce, pickles preserves, gourmet foods and a wide range of cheeses. As well as

---

🏛 historic building 🏛 museum and heritage 🏛 historic site 🔱 scenic attraction 🌱 flora and fauna

NEFYN
12 miles NW of Pwllheli off the A499

🏛 Old St Mary's Church   🏛 Garn Boduan

🏛 Llyen Historical and Maritime Museum

Once a fishing village, this resort was granted a charter in 1355, along with Pwllheli, by the Black Prince. It was here in 1284 that Edward I celebrated his conquest over Wales. Housed in **Old St Mary's Church**, whose tower supports a sailing ship weathervane, is the **Lleyn Historical and Maritime Museum**, an excellent place to visit to find out more about this interesting and beautiful part of Wales. To the southwest of the village is **Garn Boduan**, an Iron Age hill fort where the foundations of over 100 buildings can still be seen. Three defensive walls surrounded the fort, though its position alone made it almost impregnable. It

can be accessed from the B4354, close to its junction with the A497.

TREFOR
8 miles NW of Pwllheli on the A499

🏛 Tre'r Ceiri   ⛰ Yr Eifl   ⛰ Gurn Ddu

⛰ Bwlch Mawr

This coastal former quarry village is dominated by **Yr Eifl** (The Rivals), which lies to the southwest and which, from its 1,850 foot summit, affords stunning views out over Caernarfon Bay to Anglesey and across the Llyn Peninsula. On the southeastern slopes of the hill is **Tre'r Ceiri** (Town of Giants), one of the finest Iron Age forts in the country. A stone wall surrounds this once heavily populated circle of 150 huts, some of it three feet high.

PEN-LLYN LUSITANO STUD & RIDING CENTRE
Llaniestyn, nr Pwllheli, Gwynedd LL53 8SW
Tel: 01341 730741
e-mail: penllynlusitanos@aol.com
website: www.lusitanocymru.co.uk

The Pendlebury family have been breeding and training horses at the **Pen-Llyn Lusitano Stud & Riding Centre** on the Lleyn Peninsula for some 35 years. It is recognised as one of the foremost studs in the land, holing the finest bloodlines. The mares here have been bred from three of the most famous Portuguese stallions of all time, starting in 1994 with the much loved and much missed Hilario. The centre offers riding breaks for all ages and skill levels, from beginners to the most experienced, in the lovely countryside, with treks along quiet country lanes or in the mountains and beach-and-pub rides, along with stable days that include a hack and lesson.

The riding centre also has pure- and part-bred Lusitanos for sale, and the unique way of training with patience and kindness means that many clients buy and keep their horses at the centre's livery stables. The beautifully even-tempered Lusitano horses are ideal for dressage, and the centre offers lessons in classical dressage. Janine Pendlebury was born into riding and gives wonderful displays and 'theatre' events all over the country. One of the stars at Pen-Llyn is Uivador do Broa, who returned to North Wales after two brilliant years in Portugal, where he was champion male at the 2008 International Festival of the Lusitano. The 2008 Breed Show was also a triumph, with the filly Bohemia, the mare Xacira and the part-bred Tessala (by Hilario) among the winners for Pen-Llyn. The centre is open all year, and accommodation is available locally.

🎭 stories and anecdotes 🎐 famous people 🎨 art and craft 🎪 entertainment and sport 🚶 walks

PLAS GLYN-Y-WEDDW GALLERY

Llanbedrog, nr Pwllheli, Gwynedd LL53 7TT
Tel: 01758 740763 Fax: 01758 740232
e-mail: enquiry@oriel.org.uk
website: www.oriel.org.uk

Oriel Plas Glyn-y-Weddw Gallery, the oldest art gallery in Wales, is located in a Grade II* listed Victorian Gothic mansion in picturesque grounds with views of Cardigan Bay and the mountains of Snowdonia. It first opened to the public in 1896 and enjoyed mixed fortunes down the years before Friends of the Gallery put it on a secure and successful footing in 1997 with lottery funding. Contemporary Welsh paintings form the core of the works in the Gallery, which hosts a varied programme of art exhibitions throughout the year and also has a permanent exhibition of Swansea and Nantgarw porcelain. Pictures, prints, jewellery, local crafts, postcards and greetings cards are on sale in the gift shop, and in the conservatory is a Taste of Wales accredited licensed tea room.

The Gallery is licensed for civil weddings and rooms can be hired for private functions, meetings and conferences. It also offers residential and non-residential arts-related courses, lectures and workshops for adults and children, musical concerts, craft fairs and retreats and pilgrimages in the Welsh Celtic tradition. Self-contained accommodation for up to 12 guests is in the rear wing of the building. The Gallery is open every day except Tuesdays (but open on Tuesdays in school holidays).

TREMFAN HALL

Llanbedrog, Pwllheli, Gwynedd, Wales LL53 7NN
Tel: 01758 740 169   Fax: 01758 740863
website: www.tremfanhall.com

Tremfan Hall is a majestic country house with views overlooking Llanbedrog Head, Cardigan Bay and the mountains of Snowdonia. The house was once the home of John Gwenogfryn Evans, a founder member of the National Library of Wales, and resident owner Sue Skinner has ensured that the décor and furnishing are totally in keeping with its history. She has made it into a very welcoming and civilised restaurant with friendly service, excellent food and drink and prestige accommodation.

The restaurant is open daily for dinner and for Sunday lunch. Head chef Nigel's menus highlight the fine local produce that is available, including Menai oysters, crab, and Welsh lamb and beef. The terrace is a delightful spot for morning coffee or a pre-dinner drink with the bonus of panoramic views of the coastline all around the bay to Harlech and beyond, with Snowdonia from Moel Hebog to Cader Idris forming a majestic backdrop.

The accommodation comprises four en suite doubles rooms and one twin, all furnished to a very high standard. Apart from relaxing at Tremfan Hall, the local area has plenty to offer all ages and tastes. Golf, shooting, watersports, quiet country walks or visits to secluded bays...are all within easy reach.

SIOP Y PLAS

Llanbedrog, Pwllheli, Gwynedd, Wales LL53 7TS
Tel: 01758 740654
email: sue@llanbedroggiftshop.co.uk
website: www.llanbedroggiftshop.co.uk

Siop-Y-Plas is located in Llanbedrog between Pwllheli and Abersoch, and must be your first stop if you are looking for the perfect gift for any occasion. The shop is stuffed to the rafters with fantastic gift ideas, specialising in light-hearted good quality in-door and outdoor gifts for all the family. Sue, proprietor, offers an excellent range of the coolest greetings cards, cushions, local paintings, tide clocks, gorgeous rugs and throws plus bright and beautiful beach bags galore!

She also stocks a wonderful range, from the Big Tomato Company, of kitchen and tableware featuring humorous slogans, such as the 'no use crying over spilt milk' milk jug, 'yummy mummy' & 'daddy cool' mugs and 'cat's whiskers' pet bowl.

Sue and her friendly staff ensure customers feel relaxed while choosing. You can sort out gifts for everyone with just one visit. Just don't forget to treat yourself to something special too.

The shop is opposite the National Trust Car Park on the way to the picturesque beach and Oriel Plas Glyn y Weddw.

The road between here and Clynnog Fawr passes by the **Gurn Ddu** and **Bwlch Mawr** hills, which sweep down towards the sandy beach.

LLANBEDROG

3½ miles SW of Pwllheli on the A499

🏛 Plas Glyn y Weddw

🏛 Parish Church of St Pedrog

🎞 Myndd Tir y Cwmwd   🎨 Tin Man

Named after the 6th century St Pedrog, Llanbedrog lies on the other side of **Mynydd Tir y Cwmwd** from Abersoch. The views from the summit are stunning. Don't miss the **Tin Man**, a modern sculpture made of beachcombed material. In Llanbedrog itself is **Plas Glyn y Weddw**, a neo-Gothic mansion that houses a collection of Welsh furniture

and holds various Welsh art exhibitions. The **Parish Church of St Pedrog** was founded in the 6th century by St Pedrog. The present church is mainly Victorian, though there are medieval fragments dating back to the 13th century.

ABERSOCH

6 miles SW of Pwllheli on the A499

🏛 Castellmarch   🌿 Tudwal's Islands

🎞 March Amheirchion

A popular family resort with safe beaches, Abersoch lies on each side of the estuary of the River Soch. Its sheltered harbour attracts a wide variety of pleasure craft. Just off the coast lie **St Tudwal's Islands** - named after the saint who founded a religious cell there in the 6th century. Both islands are now privately

🎞 stories and anecdotes   🐦 famous people   🎨 art and craft   🚲 entertainment and sport   🚶 walks

PERIOD PINE

FURNITURE AND HOME ACCESSORIES WAREHOUSE

Bron Y Berth, Penrhos, Pwllheli, Gwynedd LL53 7HL
Tel: 01758 614343 Fax: 01758 614100
e-mail: diane@periodpine.freeserve.co.uk
website: www.periodpine.net

Whatever your style Period Pine will have something for you. Be it shabby chic, New England, Country, Contemporary or Beach House. There is an extensive range of home accessories that include lamps, mirrors, pictures, tableware, linen, cushions decorative pieces and much more. Period Pine first built their reputation on selling antique French and German furniture that was hand picked, imported, restored and sold. They diversified a few years ago and are now renowned for their vast selection of painted, contemporary, antique, reclaimed and reproduction pieces in Oak, Pine, Elm and Beech.

The 15,000 sq ft showrooms have been skilfully and attractively converted into room settings that show off the products beautifully to give inspiration whatever your interior design project. Period Pine is the perfect choice and well worth a visit.

Period Pine is situated on the A499, 3 miles from Pwllheli on the Abersoch Road.

VENETIA RESTAURANT & ROOMS

Lon Sarn Bach, Abersoch, Gwynedd LL53 7EB
Tel: 01758 713354
e-mail: justask@venetiawales.com website: www.venetiawales.com

Venetia Restaurant and Rooms occupies a beautiful Victorian villa just minutes away from sheltered beaches and crystal clear waters in the magical seaside village of Abersoch. Owned and run by Marco Filippi and Jayne Edge, Venetia offers an irresistible combination of authentic Italian cuisine and 5-star luxurious accommodation.

Eating at Venetia is relaxed yet elegant, with a warm, friendly atmosphere in stylish surroundings that feature Italian designed and sourced furniture. Wherever possible Marco and his team source local produce, including obtaining fish/shellfish directly from local vessels - award-winning, sustainable Aberdaron crab, for example, or Cardigan Bay scallops. A varied menu is offered throughout the year reflecting the seasons. Marco who is a passionate fisherman, travelled to London as one of four finalists in the Seafish Seafood awards in the category of seafood chef of the year in 2007.

The accommodation at Venetia comprises 5 beautifully furnished and decorated rooms. There are Italian porcelain-tiled en suites with under floor heating, luxury Ginseng & Macadamia toiletries, refreshing powerful walk-in showers and Flare LED heated mirrors. Super comfy beds, Flos lighting designed by Philippe Starck, floor to ceiling bespoke mirrored wardrobes and wall mounted LCD TVs with DVD players all add to the appeal.

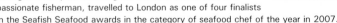

THE ABERSOCH CRAFTS CENTRE

Aberuchaf, Lon Garmon, Abersoch, Gwynedd LL53 7UG

The Abersoch Crafts Centre is located on the outskirts of the pretty seaside resort of Abersoch. As you approach the village from the north, just before entering the village itself turn right up the hill between the Spinnaker restaurant and Abersoch Land and Sea, and then follow the brown and white tourist signs marked 'Craft Workshops'. Amongst the craftspeople working here are an artist, a furniture maker, and a jeweller. There is also an art gallery.

THE ARTISTS STUDIO

Unit 4 The Craft Centre Tel: 01758 713307
mobile: 0781617068
e-mail: theartist@theartistsstudio.co.uk

The Artists Studio provides a showcase for the work of Neil Hopkins who completed his art education with the award of the Art Teacher's diploma and Art Teacher's Certificate. After a decade or so working as a designer for industry, he left his job in 1976 and painted his first watercolour in 1977. Since then his work has sold to all corners of the world and as one of North Wales' leading watercolourists, he regularly exhibits throughout Wales and into England. In recent years he has added chalk pastels to his output, and also a range of limited edition prints.

WILDWOOD FURNITURE

Unit 5 The Craft Centre Tel/Fax. 01758 712161
Mobile: 07967 704583
e-mail: jon@wildwooddesigns.co.uk
website: www.wildwooddesigns.co.uk

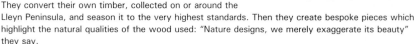

For the craftspeople working at **Wildwood Furniture** the declared aim is "to inspire individuality in peoples lives". This is reflected in every aspect of the creative process. They convert their own timber, collected on or around the Lleyn Peninsula, and season it to the very highest standards. Then they create bespoke pieces which highlight the natural qualities of the wood used: "Nature designs, we merely exaggerate its beauty" they say.

TURTLE PHOTOGRAPHIC GALLERY

Unit 6 The Craft Centre Tel: 01758 713641
website: www.turtlephotography.co.uk

Established in 1992 by Martin Turtle and his partner Margot Jones, **Turtle Photography** quickly established itself as one of the leading sources of marine and scenic photography in the area, and has had countless images published worldwide. Operating from converted farm buildings, Turtle Photography can now supply high quality Giclee prints mounted and framed to order as well as exhibition grade stretchered canvases in a variety of sizes, postcards, greetings cards, gift vouchers, and even inspirational abstract sculptures. All products are hand made on the premises by Martin Turtle.

---

stories and anecdotes famous people art and craft entertainment and sport walks

owned and are the home of bird sanctuaries.

The site of the 17th century mansion, **Castellmarch**, was said to be the home of **March Amheirchion**, one of King Arthur's Knights. Reputed to have the ears of a horse, March (the name is Welsh for horse) kept

them hidden and killed anyone who saw them – burying the bodies in a nearby reed bed. However, one day a man cut one of the reeds to make a pipe and, when it was played, it made no sound other than the words, 'March has horse's ears'. When March heard

---

CRUGERAN FARM HOLIDAYS

Sarn Meyllteyrn, nr Abersoch, Gwynedd LL53 8DT
Tel: 01758 730375
e-mail: post@crugeran.com
website: www.crugeran.com

Crugeran Farm Holidays is a well-run enterprise based on a working beef, sheep and cereal farm in a lovely peaceful setting in the heart of the Lleyn Peninsula. Three cottages close to the hamlet of Sarn Meyllteyrn, skilfully converted from barns and stables, are fully equipped for a self-catering holiday. With accommodation catering for numbers from 1 to 16 (the largest cottage sleeps 7 and is disabled friendly), they combine traditional and modern elements, and the lovely interiors are enhanced by handsome antique and auction furniture.

It's a great place for a family holiday, and children will spend many happy, busy hours in the gardens, which include swings, a trampoline, and a playhouse. Safe, sandy beaches, cliff walks and coastal paths are no more than four miles away, and the area is ideal for touring, walking, cycling (Crugeran has a lock-up for bikes) and golf.

Newly opened for 2009, a mile away near Botwnnog, Crugeran's owner Rhian Parry offers alternative and equally delightful self-catering accommodation in a large farmhouse with six bedrooms, three bathrooms, a superbly appointed living/dining area, an Aga-equipped kitchen, a utility room and an enclosed lawned garden, with a trampoline. Pets are welcome at this farmhouse only.

THE SUN INN

Llanengan, Abersoch, Gwynedd LL53 7LG
Tel: 01758 712660
e-mail: yrhaul@hotmail.com
website: www.thesuninn-llanengan.co.uk

The Sun is a cosy, traditional inn standing west of Abersoch on the tip of the lovely Lleyn Peninsula. Local couple John and Vivien Hughes are the most welcoming of hosts, and the convivial atmosphere is equally appealing to locals, families (dogs too!) and visitors from further afield. Robinsons of Stockport supply the cask ales, which can be enjoyed on their own or to accompany Vivien's excellent home cooking: favourites on her menu include fish pie, steak & ale pie, curries, lamb dishes and seasonal crab and scallops. The Sun's garden enjoys lovely views across to the surfing paradise of Hell's Mouth Bay. The inn is open lunchtime and evening, all day at the weekend and in the summer.

RHYDOLION SELF CATERING COTTAGES

Rhydolion, Llangian, Abersoch, Pwllheli,
Gwynedd, LL53 7LR
Tel: 01758 712342
e-mail: enquiries@rhydolion.co.uk
website: www.rhydolion.co.uk

Whether you are seeking a secluded rural retreat for peace and quiet or a convenient base to explore the surrounding area our 4 luxury cottages are in idyllic coastal and countryside location. Well known Abersoch, boating village only 2 1/2 miles away and surfing beach, 4 miles long at Porth Neigwl (Hell's Mouth) half a mile away.

Our cosy cottages are open all year and graded 5 stars by Visit Wales, 2 with open fire, 2 adapted for wheelchair guests. All sleep 27 with 2- 7 in 3 bedrooms per cottage. All prices include electricity, bed linen, Jacuzzi, four-poster and canopy beds, cot and high chair, barbecue, WI-FI connection and more. For the cottages there is a shared access to indoor games room, individual patio, enclosed garden, children play area, canoes and bicycles storage and ample parking area.

about this, he set off to kill the man for mocking him, but relented when he himself tried to play the pipe and got exactly the same words. Thereafter he made no attempt to hide his ears.

RHIW

11 miles SW of Pwllheli off the B4413

🏠 Plas yn Rhiw   🕊 RS Thomas

This hamlet lies in a miniature pass and overlooks Porth Neigwl (Hell's Mouth), a four mile sweep of beach so called because of its reputation for strong currents. It is now a favourite place for wind surfing.

Sheltered from strong gales by Mynydd Rhiw, **Plas yn Rhiw** is a small, part-medieval, part-Tudor, part-Georgian manor house that was given to the National Trust in 1952 by the unconventional Keating sisters from Nottingham. The three spinsters, Eileen, Lorna and Honora, purchased the property in 1938 and lovingly restored it after it had lain neglected for some 20 years. This they did with the help of their friend Sir Clough Williams-Ellis, the architect of Portmeirion.

The house is surrounded by glorious grounds, which were also restored by the sisters, providing fabulous views over Porth Neigwl. Visitors can wander through ornamental gardens and, in the spring, the bluebell and snowdrop woodlands. At one time the poet and clergyman **RS Thomas** (1913–2000) lived in one of the estate cottages, where he wrote some of his finest poetry (see also Eglwys Fach).

Plas yn Rhiw, Rhiw

🎭 stories and anecdotes 🕊 famous people 🎨 art and craft 🎟 entertainment and sport 🚶 walks

Aberdaron

ABERDARON

13½ miles SW of Pwllheli on the B4413

🏠 Parish Church of St Hywyn   🏛 Castel Odo

A small and delightful village, which is often busy in the height of summer. It was here, in 1405, that the Tripartite Indenture – the agreement to divide Britain with Wales becoming independent under the rule of Glyndwr – was signed. However, these plans were subsequently ruined by Henry IV and Henry V. Close to the sea, and originally dating from the 6th century, the **Parish Church of St Hywyn** is thought to have sheltered the 12th century Prince of Wales, Gryffydd ap Rhys, from marauding Saxons. During the Civil War, it once again proved a place of sanctuary as Cromwell's soldiers also sought refuge here. It was founded in the 6th century by St Hywyn. Its oldest parts date from the 12th century, though most of the building dates from an enlargement made

in 1417. It was closely associated with the abbey on Bardsey Island, and had the right of sanctuary.

One of Aberdaron's most famous native sons was Richard Robert Jones, the son of a local carpenter. A strange vagabond, known as Dic Aberdaron, this self-educated linguist is said to have spoken 35 languages and is renowned for having compiled dictionaries in Welsh, Greek and Hebrew. The great poet RS Thomas also hailed from Aberdaron. He wrote many inspired lines about his beloved country, summed up in this extract:

Every mountain and stream, every farm and little lane announces to the world that landscape is something different in Wales.

A mile or so from the village lies **Castel Odo**, an Iron Age fort providing evidence that there have been five different occupations of the peninsula dating back to the 4th century BC.

🏠 historic building 🏛 museum and heritage 🏛 historic site 🍀 scenic attraction 🌿 flora and fauna

UWCHMYNYDD

15 miles SW of Pwllheli off the B4413

🏛 Church of St Mary   🏚 Porth Oer

🌿 Mynydd Mawr   🌿 Braich-y-Pwll

Situated on the wild and beautiful tip of the Llyn Peninsula, it was from here that the first pilgrims set out across the two-mile wide Barsey Sound to Bardsey Island in the Middle Ages. On the summit of **Mynydd Mawr**, the National Trust has converted an old coastguard hut into a small information point. The National Trust is responsible for much of the land towards the tip of the Lleyn Peninsula, including the ecologically outstanding coastal heath of **Braich-y-Pwll**, where the ruins of the **Church of St Mary**, once used by the pilgrims, can still be seen. This heath is the spring and summer home of a variety of plant life and birds, including fulmars, kittiwakes, cormorants, guillemots and the rare chough. A similar variety has its home on the tiny islands of Dinas Fawr and Dinas Bach.

Five miles east of Aberdaron, on the south side of the Peninsula, Porth Ysgo and Penarfyndd cover 245 acres of beaches and cliffs, while two miles northwest of the village Mynydd Anelog is an 116-acre area of ancient commonland with the remains of prehistoric hut circles. Here, as in the other NT stretches of coastland on the Peninsula, is found our friend the chough, a relative of the crow with a distinctive red bill. Apart from here, this rare bird is usually found only in Pembrokeshire and on a part of the western coast of Scotland. The curiously named **Porth Oer** (Whistling Sands), located off the B4417 by Methlem, is worth a visit as at certain stages of the tide the sands seem literally to whistle when walked upon. The noise is caused by the rubbing together of minute quartz granules.

BARDSEY ISLAND

17 miles SW of Pwllheli off the B4413

🏛 Abbey of St Mary   🏛 Lord Newborough's Crypt

🏛 Lighthouse   🏚 Hermit's Cave

This wild, whale-shaped island in the Irish Sea has long been a place of pilgrimage, and has inspired many legends. One says that this is King Arthur's Avalon, another that his magician Merlin sleeps in a glass castle on the island. St Cadfan built an abbey here in the 6th century, though this would not have been an abbey as we know it today. It would have been an area of ground marked off with a low wall within which would have been chapels, churches, monks' cells and other buildings. On this site, in the 12th century, the Augustinian **Abbey of St Mary** was built. It was dissolved in 1537, and now only a few walls remain. St Dyfrig died here in 522 AD, and though his remains were later transferred to Llandaff Cathedral in Cardiff, it was from about this time that Bardsey became a place of pilgrimage. At one time it was considered that three pilgrimages to this holy island was equivalent to one to Rome.

Next to the abbey ruins is **Lord Newborough's Crypt**, where the once owner of the island is buried. There is also the **Hermit's Cave**, though it is doubtful if a hermit ever lived here, as it is too small. The **Lighthouse** on the south of the island was erected in 1821, and is the only square lighthouse maintained by Trinity House.

The island is now an important bird and field observatory. Bardsey is best known for its vast numbers of breeding shearwaters. A boat makes the 20-minute trip to the island from the hidden fishing cove of Porth Meudwy by Aberdaron.

The island's name is Norse in origin, and the Welsh name, Ynys Enlii, means Island of

Currents – a reference to the treacherous waters that separate Bardsey from the mainland.

Llanberis

🏠 Dolbadarn Castle   🏛 Welsh Slate Museum

🐦 Snowdon   🚂 Snowdon Mountain Railway

🚂 Llanberis Lake Railway   🚂 Electric Mountain

🚂 Dinorwig Power Station   🐦 Llyn Llydaw

🐦 Padarn Country Park   🐦 Glyder Fawr

🐦 Pass of Llanberis   🦅 Marged Ifan

🏃 Kingfisher Trail   🚴 Snowdon Race

🚴 Snowdon Marathon

🌿 Cwm Derwen Woodland and Wildlife Centre

This former slate-producing community has many attractions to keep the visitor occupied although it is, perhaps, best known for the nearby mountain, **Snowdon**. Rising to some

Summit of Snowdon

3,560 feet, this is the highest peak in Wales and the most climbed mountain in Britain. On a clear day, the view from the summit is breathtaking, with Ireland sometimes visible. However, before setting out for the summit it is worth remembering that the weather can change dramatically, and walkers and climbers should always be prepared. Many reach the summit the easy way, with the help of the **Snowdon Mountain Railway**, a rack and pinion system built in 1896 that has carried millions to the top of the mountain over the years. It is not surprising that this mountainous and inhospitable area is also steeped in legend and mystery. The eagles of Snowdon have long been regarded as oracles of peace and war, triumph and disaster, and Snowdon's peak is said to be a cairn erected over the grave of a giant who was killed by King Arthur. **Llyn Llydaw**, a lake just below Snowdon, is yet another contender for the *Lady of the Lake* story. Arthur himself is supposed to have been fatally wounded at the Battle of Camlann, which some people have identified with 'cwm-y-llan', or the 'valley of the lake'.

For those wanting another train ride, or are content with a more sedate journey, the **Llanberis Lake Railway** near Llanberis takes a short trip round Llyn Padarn, during which there are several different views of the mountain. The railway lies in **Padarn Country Park**, which gives access to 800 acres of Snowdonia's countryside and also includes Llyn (Lake) Padarn. The **Kingfisher Trail** is designed specifically for wheelchairs. By the side of the lake is **Cwm Derwen Woodland and Wildlife Centre**, with a woodland discovery trail and a timewalk exhibition with an audio-visual display. Here, too, is the **Welsh Slate Museum**, which tells

Snowdonia, Llanberis Pass

the story of the slate industry through a variety of exhibitions, a restored slate-carrying incline, a terrace of quarrymen's cottages, audio-visual shows and demonstrations. The De Winton waterwheel is the second largest in Britain and once provided all the power for slate mines.

Bus tours take visitors deep into the mountain tunnels and the machinery rooms of the **Electric Mountain**, which control the vast quantities of water used by **Dinorwig Power Station**. In Europe's largest man-made cavern the world's most powerful hydro-electric generators are in action.

In such a rugged setting, where life has always been harsh, it comes as no surprise to find that it is said that the strongest woman ever to have lived came from Llanberis. Born in 1696, **Marged Ifan** died at the ripe old age of 105. At 70, it was said, she could out-wrestle any man in Wales and could also catch as many foxes in one year as the local huntsmen in 10. After receiving many offers

of marriage, Marged is said to have chosen the smallest and most effeminate of her suitors. Tradition has it that she only beat her husband twice: after the first beating he married her and after the second he became an ardent churchgoer!

The **Snowdon Race** takes place every July, leaving from Llanberis, and finishing there as well. The mountain is five miles away, and is 3,560 feet high. The **Snowdon Marathon**, held every October, also starts and finishes at Llanberis.

The **Pass of Llanberis** (along the A4086) is one of the most desolate stretches of road in Wales and is dominated by Snowdon to the south and the curiously shaped **Glyder Fawr**, 3,279 feet to the north. Sheep graze beside the narrow road, which in some places is almost blocked by boulders and rocks.

Guarding the entrance to the pass and overlooking Llyn Padarn are the substantial remains of **Dolbadarn Castle,** which was built by Llywelyn the Great. After the battle of Bryn Derwin, where Llywelyn defeated his two brothers, hevictor held Owain ap Gryffydd prisoner here for some 22 years. The last stronghold of the independent princes of Gwynedd, it was from here, in 1283, that Dafydd ap Gryffydd fled from the English forces of Edward I. The exterior scenes for the film *Carry On Up The Khyber* were shot in and around Llanberis.

Snowdon Mountain Railway, Llanberis

Around Llanberis

NANT PERIS
2 miles SE of Llanberis on the A4086

🏛 Parish Church of St Peris   🏚 Well of Peris

Once known as Old Llanberis, the village lies at the opposite end of Llyn Peris from its larger namesake – Llanberis – and at the entrance to the Pass of Llanberis. The **Parish Church of St Peris** dates originally from the 12th century, and is worth visiting because of its 15th-century ceiling and chancel screen with a poor box having three locks. It stands on the site of St Peris's original church, and was founded in the 6th century. The Pass of Llanberis was once known as Nant y Mynach, or "valley of the monks", and it may refer to the foundation of the early church. The **Well of Peris**, which lies just north of the village centre, was, until relatively recently, much

visited for its healing powers, as well as for making wishes. A successful request was said to be signalled by the appearance of a sacred fish.

Porthmadog

🏛 Maritime Museum   🏛 Ffestiniog Railway
🏛 Welsh Highland Railway
🏛 Welsh Highland Heritage Railway

This is a busy town that can become even busier as holidaymakers take advantage of its many amenities. Out of the town, towards Tremadog and across The Cob, the scenery to the left is magical and, at low tide, cattle graze alongside herons and other seabirds and waders.

Seeing Porthmadog today it is hard to believe that this was once the busiest slate port in North Wales and, in fact, the town would never have existed had it not been for William Madocks, also responsible for neighbouring Tremadog. Member of Parliament for Boston, Lincolnshire, and a great entrepreneur, Madocks drained the mud flats that made up this estuary to create land for grazing cattle in the early 19th century. The Cob embankment, built to keep the tides at bay, enclosed some 7,000 acres of land and re-routed the River Glaslyn to produce a deep water channel that was ideal for the docks. Naming Porthmadog after himself (nearby Tremadog was named after his brother), he saw the beginning of the blossoming of the town in the 1820s. The history of the town and its waterfront is described in the **Maritime Museum** where, too, the importance of the trade in slate and Porthmadog's shipbuilding industry is told.

Porthmadog is also home to the **Ffestiniog Railway**, the world's oldest narrow track

WELSH HIGHLAND HERITAGE RAILWAY

Tremadog Road, Porthmadog, Gwynedd LL49 9DY
Tel: 01766 513402
e-mail: info@whr.co.uk website: www.whr.co.uk

Opposite the main line railway station in Porthmadog, the **Welsh Highland Heritage Railway** is a delightful attraction for all the family. Visitors to this friendly little self-contained branch line enjoy a ride in heritage carriages behind a steam or vintage diesel locomotive. Each 'railway experience – including the two foot gauge train ride, the miniature train ride, and the museum tour, lasts about 50 minutes: but you can ride all day on one ticket, if you like! The tour includes a guided, interactive educational tour of the engine sheds and museum, where children of all ages can climb on board the locomotives, blow the whistles and have great fun learning how everything works.

Refreshments can be enjoyed in the Russell Tea Room, which serves a good selection of teas and coffees, soup, sandwiches, cakes, snacks and meals. In the shop, enthusiasts and others will find a huge selection of railway-themed books, models, kits, tracks, paintings and memorabilia. Run almost entirely by volunteers, this charming little railway operates from 10.30 to 4 from April to the end of October, except for some Mondays and Fridays in October. Trains run every day from 10.30 to 4.00, between March 28th and November 1st, except for some Mondays and Fridays in October.

📽 stories and anecdotes 🦜 famous people 🎨 art and craft 🎭 entertainment and sport 🚶 walks

passenger carrying railway, and the **Welsh Highland Heritage Railway**. In 2010 it will also be the southern terminus of the **Welsh Highland Railway** running from Caernarfon.

Around Porthmadog

TREMADOG
2 miles N of Porthmadog on the A487

🏛 Peniel Methodist Chapel

🏛 Parish Church of St Mary   🍃 TE Lawrence

This village, developed, like its close neighbour Porthmadog, by William Alexander Madocks, is a wonderful example of early 19th-century town planning, and contains many fine Regency buildings. Madocks, who was the MP for Boston in Lincolnshire, bought the land in 1798 and built Tremadog on the reclaimed land in classical style, with

broad streets and a handsome market square with a backdrop of cliffs. He hoped that the town would be a key point on the intended main route from the south of England to Ireland, but his rivals in Parliament preferred the North Wales route, with Holyhead becoming the principal port. The little town of Tremadog, with its well-planned streets and fine buildings, remains as a memorial to Madocks, who died in Paris in 1828, where he is buried in the Père Lachaise cemetery (see also Porthmadog). **Peniel Methodist Chapel** is unusual, in that it is in the shape of a Greek temple, while the **Parish Church of St Mary** is a good example of a Gothic revival church. Inside is a plaque commemorating the Madocks family. The soldier and author **TE Lawrence** (of Arabia) was born in Tremadog in 1888, and the poet Shelley is known to have visited on several occasions.

THE GOLDEN FLEECE INN

Market Square, Tremadog, Porthmadog, Gwynedd LL49 9RB
Tel: 01766 512421
e-mail: info@goldenfleeceinn.com
website: www.goldenfleeceinn.com

Located in the historic market square of Tremadog, **The Golden Fleece Inn** is a truly traditional family-run hostelry that was originally a coaching inn. Owner Stuart Hallard, who has been here since 2000, not only offers his customers some outstanding real ales from a local brewery, a good selection of appetising food, but also a choice of accommodation. The intimate and comfortable bar is always welcoming with its coal fire and subdued lighting, and the Little Ivy Restaurant offers an interesting cuisine of British favourites with a Mediterranean influence. In addition to some of the best steaks in the area, you'll also find venison, kangaroo, ostrich, zebra and bison on the menu.

All bedrooms at The Golden Fleece Inn are individually designed with quality furnishings and high standards of décor, even featuring luxury high count Egyptian cotton bed linen. All rooms have en suite facilities, television with DVD player and tea making facilities. If you prefer self-catering, an apartment is available as well as a cottage sleeping 5 people which is adjacent to the inn. The Golden Fleece Inn is family friendly and welcomes children of all ages.

🏛 historic building 🏛 museum and heritage 🏛 historic site 🍃 scenic attraction 🌿 flora and fauna

PORTMEIRION

4 miles SE of Porthmadog off the A487

🏛 Plas Brondanw 🏛 Brondanw

🏺 Portmeirion Pottery

This very special village, in a wonderful setting on a wooded peninsula overlooking Traeth Bay, was conceived and created by the Welsh architect Sir Clough Williams-Ellis between 1925 and 1972. An inveterate campaigner against the spoiling of Britain's landscape, he set out to illustrate that building in a beautiful location did not mean spoiling the environment. In looks, this is the least Welsh place in Wales: the 50 or so buildings, some of which consist only of a façade, were inspired by a visit Williams-Ellis made to Sorrento and Portofino in Italy. The **Portmeirion Pottery** was established in 1960 by Clough's daughter Susan Williams-Ellis, and her husband, Euan. Susan had studied under Henry Moore and Graham Sutherland, and her classic designs include Botanic Garden (1972) and the recently relaunched Totem from the 1960s. Williams-Ellis' ancestral home, **Plas Brondanw**, lies some five miles away, up the A4085 northeast of Garreg, and the marvellous gardens here make the extra journey well worthwhile. Designed to please the eye, and also provide some fabulous views over the mountain scenery, there are, among the splendid plants, charming statues and elegant topiary terraces. Although less well known than the village and gardens at Portmeirion, the gardens at **Brondanw** are considered by some to be Clough Williams-Ellis' most important creation, and certainly

CAFFI'R IDDRAIS

Cromwell House, High Street, Penrhyndeudraeth, Portmeirion, Gwynedd LL48 6BC
Tel: 01766 304552
e-mail: stephen@sworley.orangehome.co.uk

A popular High Street café for many years, **Caffi'r Idrais** (Dragon's Den) offers a good choice of wholesome and appetising food at equally popular prices. The day starts with a selection of breakfasts, followed by lunches - salmon goujons perhaps, or omelette, salad, toasted sandwich or panini. At tea-time, there's an alluring choice of owner Sandra Worley's delicious home-made cakes which are freshly baked each day. Many of the items on the menu are also available to take away.

📖 stories and anecdotes 🐦 famous people 🎨 art and craft 🎭 entertainment and sport 🚶 walks

Portmeirion

Distance: *2.8 miles (4.5 kilometres)*
Typical time: *90 mins*
Height gain: *100 metres*
Map: *Explorer OL18*
Walk: *www.walkingworld.com ID:1952*
Contributor: *Pat Roberts*

ACCESS INFORMATION:

There is a large free car park at Portmeirion. From the A487 east of Porthmadoc, at Minffordd, follow signs for Portmeirion.

DESCRIPTION:

This easy walk can be coupled with a visit to Portmeirion. It has easy walking with one climb after Waymark 06 and the views are good. If you time your walk to coincide with the Ffestiniog Train timetable, there are opportunities for train-spotting.

FEATURES:

River, Wildlife, Birds, Flowers, Great Views, Mostly Flat, Woodland.

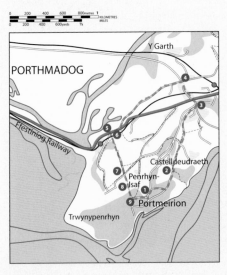

WALK DIRECTIONS:

1 | Wherever you are parked in the large car park, make for the entrance and walk back up the road you drove down.

2 | Take the bridleway off to the right. It passes a few houses and a three-fingered bridleway sign, where you go straight on. There are lovely views across to the mountains. After rising slowly, the track loses some height before reaching a road.

3 | At the road, turn left to the main A487. Cross with care and continue down the narrow road straight ahead. Cross the Ffestiniog Railway line, eventually to reach a T-junction.

4 | Here go left and walk this quiet minor road, eventually to reach the A487 again. Walk on the pavement, maintaining direction, towards Porthmadoc.

5 | Just after the warning signs for the tolls, but before the actual toll, cross the road to a footpath sign leading up to Boston Lodge Halt. You may be lucky to see one of the steam locomotives here. Walk a few metres left to a pedestrian crossing (just sleepers over the lines).

6 | Cross the line and go over the stile. The track swings right before swinging left and following the wall on your left. It then rises quite steeply between two walls, passing through a double gate before dropping slightly to another gate.

7 | Through the gate and across the gravel track, continue in the same direction down a green track with a wall on your left.

8 | Go through this gap in a high wall and the gate behind it, to pass through a similar gap in another high wall. Ignore a path off to your right, but continue ahead through another gate and down an enclosed path. Turn left as directed to reach a ladder-stile.

9 | DO NOT CROSS THIS STILE. Turn right down a narrow path to the car park.

D G DAVIES FAMILY BUTCHER

High Street, Penrhyndeudraeth, Gwynedd LL48 6BN
Tel: 01766 770239

In the same family for nearly 30 years, **D G Davies Family Butcher**
has built up a fine reputation for quality and service to its
customers. David and Medwyn set great store by prime Welsh
produce, including Conwy Valley and Salt Marsh lamb, Welsh Black
beef and pork from the Dee valley. Venison comes from Scotland,
and winter game mainly from Shropshire. This outstanding butcher cures its own bacon and sells a
variety of sausages (including gluten-free) and burgers, as well as bulk supplies for the home
freezer. Also on display in the cool cabinets or on the shelves are cooked meats, jams and
chutneys, mustards and sauces. D G Davies, easily identified on the High Street by its cheerful red
and green canopy, is open from 9 to 1 Monday and Thursday and from 8 to 5 Tuesday,

WENALLT GUEST HOUSE

Penrhyndeudraeth, nr Portmeirion, Gwynedd LL48 6PW
Tel/Fax: 01766 770321
e-mail: i.hartill@btinternet.com
website: www.wenalltguesthouse.co.uk

Wenallt Guest House is a substantial Edwardian property
standing on the A4085 close to a station on the Ffestiniog Railway. Hosts Sarah and Ian Hartill
have four large, well-appointed en suite guest bedrooms – two doubles, a twin and a single – with
central heating, digital TV and radio, alarm clock/radio, hospitality tray and comfortable seating.
The house has a pleasant patio and a terraced garden with views over the village to the mountains
above Harlech and the Dwyryd estuary. Wenallt is a convenient base for touring Snowdonia.
Wenallt is not suitable for young children or pets.

the most beautiful. Sir Clough continued
working up until his death at the age of 94
in 1978.

GOLAN

4 miles NW of Porthmadog off the A487

🏠 Brynkir Woollen Mill

Between the entrances to two wonderful
valleys, Cwm Pennant and Cwm Ystradllyn,
and a mile off the A487 Porthmadog to
Caernarfon road, lies **Brynkir Woollen Mill**.
Originally a corn mill, it was converted over
150 years ago for woollen cloth production
and, though now modernised (the River
Henwy is used to generate electricity although
the waterwheel still turns), visitors can still see
the various machines that are used in the

production process: Tenterhook Willey,
carders, spinning mules, doubling and hanking
machines, cheese and bobbin winder, warping
mill and looms.

FFESTINIOG

9 miles E of Porthmadog on the A470

🏛 Sarn Helen   🚶 Vale of Ffestiniog

🚶 Cynfal Falls

Situated above the **Vale of Ffestiniog**, there
is a delightful walk, beginning at the village
church, to **Cynfal Falls**, just below the village.
Above the falls stands a rock, known locally as
Pulpud Huw Llwyd, which recalls a local
mystic who preached from here. Three miles
to the northeast, Gamallt is a remote 300-acre
moorland that supports a variety of plant life

as well as water beetles, sandpipers, ring ousels, wheatears and meadow pipits. Archaeological remains include a large Iron Age settlement, and the important Roman road known as **Sarn Helen** crosses the property, which is in the care of the National Trust.

BLAENAU FFESTINIOG
12 miles NE of Porthmadog on the A470

- 🏛 Church of the Holy Protection
- 🏛 Pant-yr-ynn Mill 🏛 Ffestiniog Railway
- 🏛 Llechwedd Slate Caverns
- ⛲ Tan-y-Blwch County Park

This was once the slate capital of Wales. Stretching across from the feet of Manod towards the Moelwyn Mountains, the legacy of the slate industry is visible everywhere, from the orderly piles of quarried slate waste to the buildings in the town.

Today, the industry lives on in **Llechwedd**

Slate Caverns. Winners of many top tourism awards, they take visitors underground to explore the world of a Victorian slate miner and the man-made caverns of cathedral proportions, while, on the surface, there is a Victorian village to wander through. The Gloddfa Ganol mine, where digging began in 1818, was once the world's largest, and today slate is still being turned into commercial products. At the foot of Manod Bach, beside the waterfall at Bethania, **Pant-yr-ynn Mill** is the earliest surviving slate mill of the Diffwys Casson Quarry. Built in 1846, it later saw service as a school before being converted into a woollen mill in 1881. It worked until 1964, when it was closed down and the machinery scrapped. The original part of the building has been preserved and the waterwheel restored; it is now home to an exhibition dealing with Blaenau – the town, the communities, the landscape and the changes to it made by the 20 quarries in the

LYN'S CAFÉ

Church Street, Beddgelert, Gwynedd LL55 4YA
Tel/Fax: 01766 890374
e-mail: lindawheatley@btinternet.com
website: www.beddgelerttourism.com

Situated in the heart of Beddgelert in the foothills of Snowdon, **Lyn's café** is a very popular and welcoming establishment. Beddgelert, one of the most beautiful villages in Snowdonia, has long been renowned for the splendid hospitality it offers to visitors. This really is a pleasant little spot, ideal for those who wish to climb Snowdon – the highest mountain in Wales.

Some come to see the famous landmark, Gelert's Grave. Some to see Beddgelert in Bloom in the summer. Some to shop. Some just to stroll around this delightful village. Some for serious hiking and climbing.

The comfortable, light and airy interior is complemented by the delightful tea garden at the rear, where customers are treated to a menu perfect for walkers after exploring the local area. Choose from the popular Big Breakfast, sandwiches, soups, morning coffee, lunches, clotted cream teas and evening meals. The café holds a table License and is the perfect place for eating at any time of the day. Open throughout the day for most of the year.

🏛 historic building 🏛 museum and heritage 🏛 historic site ⛲ scenic attraction 🌿 flora and fauna

vicinity. The exhibition includes drawings and paintings by resident artist and industrial archaeologist Falcon D Hildred.

The town has one of the few Orthodox churches in Wales. The **Church of the Holy Protection** is in Manor Street, housed in a former shop. It was founded in 1981, though there has been Orthodox Christians here since the end of World War II, when Greek women who married Welsh soldiers came home with them. Over the years, many local people have joined the congregation. The church sees itself as the successor to the traditions and saints of the old Celtic Church, which disappeared when Roman Catholicism was introduced.

As well as having a mainline train service, Blaenau Ffestiniog is the end, or the starting point, of the narrow gauge **Ffestiniog Railway**, which runs through the vale to

Porthmadog. Built to carry slate down to the sea for shipping off around the world, the railway has since been renovated by enthusiasts and volunteers. There is a comprehensive service giving passengers the chance to admire the scenery of the vale on their journey to the coast. There are many stopping off points so walkers can take advantage, en route, of **Tan-y-Blwch County Park** and other beauty spots.

MAENTWROG
5 miles E of Porthmadog on the A496

🏠 Plas Tan-y-Bwlch

Lying in the Vale of Ffestiniog, this peaceful and attractive village is home to **Plas Tan-y-Bwlch**, built in the 19th century for the Oakley family. It is now owned by Snowdonia National Park, and is used as a residential centre for courses etc. The 19th-century

GRAPES HOTEL

Maentwrog, Blaenau Ffestiniog, Gwynedd LL41 4HN
Tel: 01766 590365 Fax: 01766 590654
e-mail: reception@grapes-hotel.co.uk
website: www.grapes-hotel.co.uk

The Grapes Hotel is one of the oldest and most famous coaching Inns in Wales. Found in the picturesque Village of Maentwrog, in the Vale of Ffestiniog, the Grapes Hotel is a 17th century Grade II listed coaching inn, with parts dating back as far as the early 13th century. Over 280 years the Grapes hotel has become renowned for its ales, home fare, hospitality and accommodation - a tradition that lives on today. This historic inn has a rich history of entertaining the famous of Wales. George Burrows wrote in 'Wild Wales' a masterpiece of its time, 'a magnificent parlour and partook of brandy and water'. Lloyd George and Lilly Langtry were also visitors.

Today the Grapes Hotel is a warm and comfortable traditional Inn, with real log fires, offering home cooked food made from the best local produce, a selection of local cask conditioned ale and some of the best accommodation anywhere in north Wales.

The Grapes Hotel warmly welcomes families, walkers and even the family dog (as long as they're well behaved!) to come and enjoy welsh hospitality at its best.

🎭 stories and anecdotes 🦜 famous people 🎨 art and craft 🎪 entertainment and sport 🚶 walks

GALERI BETWS-Y-COED

Ffordd Caergybi, Betws-y-Coed, Conwy LL24 0BW
Tel/Fax: 01690 710432
e-mail: info@galeribetwsycoed.co.uk
website: www.galeribetwsycoed.co.uk

Galeri Betws-y-Coed is an independent art gallery that displays pieces from many of the top Welsh artists. The shop is located in the heart of Snowdonia and is surrounded by some of the most spectacular scenery in the country. Providing the perfect venue to accompany the excellent artwork on show here.

Galeri Betws-y-Coed is an intimate and atmospheric art space; the warmth of centuries exudes from its knotted golden timbers; the whitewashed walls are gently illuminated from the spot-lit rafters and the natural light that pours in through the original 19th century windows. It is a building of endless creative possibilities; art and

literature go hand in hand, every corner has something to offer. There's a definite feel-good factor about the place, and it's apparent from the moment that you enter the building. The glowing glass cabinets overflow with hand-crafted wood sculpture, ceramics and jewellery. There is also and old-fashioned sweets shop – "Ffatri Fferins"- providing sweets just like you used to get as a child. It is widely recognised as one of the most exciting new galleries in North Wales.

TREM YR YNYS

Fford Caergybi, Betws-y-Coed, Conwy LL24 0BW
Tel/Fax: 01690 710432
e-mail: info@galeribetwsycoed.co.uk
website: www.self-catering-snowdonia.co.uk

Trem yr Ynys is located in the village of Betws-y-Coed, and offers quality self catering accommodation for up to 8 people over three floors. This holiday cottage is ideal for a family or group looking for a relaxing holiday in this beautiful part of North Wales.

On the ground floor there is a comfortable lounge with river views, a dining room, kitchen, and shower room with toilet and basin. On the first floor there are two bedrooms, one double bedroom and one twin bedroom. There is also a separate toilet and basin. On the second floor there are two bedrooms, one four-poster double bedroom (5ft bed) and one twin bedrooms. There is also a bathroom with shower over bath, toilet and basin.

Outside the cottage there is a good-sized garden that runs down to the river as well as a patio area with seating which is a great place to relax after a day spent exploring this beautiful part of Snowdonia.

There is also parking for 3 cars.

🏠 historic building 🏛 museum and heritage 🏚 historic site ꧁ scenic attraction 🌿 flora and fauna

terraced gardens provide glorious views of the surrounding area, and there are picturesque walks through woodland. Here, too, among the magnificent trees and rhododendrons, is an oak wood that provides a small reminder of the vast oak forests that once covered much of Wales.

Betws-y-Coed

🏛 Parish Church of St Michael   🏛 Waterloo Bridge

🏛 Pont-y-Pair   🏛 Ty Hyll   🏛 Motor Museum

🏛 Conwy Valley Railway Museum

💧 Swallow Falls   💧 Gwydyr Forest Park

💧 Conwy Falls   💧 Machno Falls

💧 Fairy Glen Ravine

A sizeable village at the confluence of four beautiful forested valleys, Betws-y-Coed lies on the edge of the **Gwydyr Forest Park** as well as in the Snowdonia National Park. The Forest Park offers horse riding, canoeing, mountain biking and over 20 miles of trails through mountain forests. The stone walls in the park were built by sailors after the defeat of the Spanish Armada to enclose game.

The village first came to prominence with the setting up in 1844 of an artists' colony by David Cox and other eminent Victorian countryside painters; their work inspired others, and the coming of the railway in 1868 brought the tourists to what soon became a busy holiday centre. The **Parish Church of St Michael**, near the railway station, has been in use since the 14th century and remained the town's major place of worship until the influx of visitors required a larger and more prestigious building. A major

attraction is the **Motor Museum**, whose unique collection of vintage and post-vintage cars includes a fabulous Bugatti Type 57. It evolved from the private collection of vehicles owned by the Houghton family, and is housed in an old farm. It is is open daily from 10.30am to 6pm from Easter to October.

As the village is close to the point where the Conwy, Lledr and Llugwy rivers meet, it seems natural that these waterways should play an important role in the development, building and beauty of Betws-y-Coed. Thomas Telford's **Waterloo Bridge**, a marvellous iron construction built in 1815, gracefully spans the River Conwy, and carried an inscription saying that it was built to commemorate the Battle of Waterloo, while the **Pont-y-Pair** (bridge of the cauldron), dating from around 1470, crosses the River Llugwy. Further downstream, an iron suspension footbridge spans the river by the church. However, the main attractions that draw people to this area are the waterfalls: the spectacular multi-level **Swallow Falls** on the River Llugwy, **Conwy Falls**, **Machno Falls** and **Fairy Glen Ravine**.

Next to the railway station is the **Conwy Valley Railway Museum** and shop, a popular place to visit in the summer. The village's most famous, and certainly most curious, attraction

Conwy Valley Railway Museum

Ty Hall, Betws-y-Coed

superstitious visitor, as there are two legends associated with the village inn. The first involves the daughter of an innkeeper, who fell in love with a local farmhand. One night the young man rode up on his white horse and the girl climbed down from her bedroom window and rode off with him, never to be seen again. The second legend concerns a friendly fair-haired lady who watches over all the events here. No one knows for sure whether the two stories are connected.

is **Ty Hyll**, the Ugly House (now the HQ of the Snowdonia Society), which stands close by the River Llugwy. Apparently this building, which looks as though it was literally thrown together from rough boulders, is an example of hurried assembly (possibly by two outlaw brothers) in order to obtain freehold on common land in the 15th century. The house was often used as an overnight stop by Irish drovers taking cattle to English markets. The scenery around Betws-y-Coed is truly magnificent, and within minutes of leaving the town centre there are numerous well-marked walks lasting anything from an hour to all day and suiting all energy levels.

Close by the village is the **Capel Garmon Burial Chamber**, which dates from around 1500BC. They are the remains of a long barrow with three burial chambers, one with its capstone still in position.

DOLWYDDELAN
6 miles SW of Bewts-y-Coed off the A470

🏠 Parish Church of St Gwydellan

🏠 Dolwyddelan Castle

The **Parish Church of St Gwydellan** dates from the 15th century. It was built by a man called Meredydd ab Ieuan, who lived in Cwn Penamnen. However, a band of brigands had taken over an old hospice once owned by the Knights of St John, and were terrorising the area. Rather than leave the place unattended when his household worshipped at the original parish church, some distance away, he had it pulled down, and erected this one nearer his

Around Betws-y-Coed

CAPEL GARMON
2 miles E of Betwys-y-Coed off the A5

🏛 Capel Garmon Burial Chamber

Surrounded by the spectacular scenery of the Snowdonia mountain range, this tiny village has an additional attraction for the

home, so that he could rush to defend it if it were were attacked. It contains St Gwyndellan's Bell, which dates from the 7th century, and was discovered in Victorian times on the site of the former church.

Here can be seen the stark remains of **Dolwyddelan Castle**, which is unusual among Welsh castles in that it was constructed by a native Welsh prince rather than by either the English or the Normans. Built between 1210 and 1240 by Llywelyn the Great (who was probably born here in 1173) to control a strategic pass through the mountainous region of his kingdom, the fortress fell to Edward I in 1283. In 1488, the place was acquired by Maredudd ap Levan, who built the village church that now houses his kneeling brass effigy. After Maredudd's death, the castle fell into ruin and the modern roof and battlements seen today were added in the

Dolwyddelan Castle

19th century when the core of the castle underwent restoration. However, the beauty of the castle is very much its lonely setting and from here there are stunning mountain views. The Castle is now looked after by CADW Welsh Historic Monuments. A walk starting at Dolwyddelan provides a succession of glorious views over the surrounding mountains, particularly Snowdon and Moel Siabod. The last part of the walk is along paths and lanes and across meadows by the River Lledr.

PENTREFOELAS
8 miles SE of Betws-y-Coed on the A5

🏠 Parish Church of Pentrefoelas

🏠 Watermill

The **Parish Church of Pentrefoelas** is one of the few in Wales that does not have a dedication. It is Victorian, and replaced a church built in 1760, which itself was built on the site of an old chapel. Once an upland estate village, Pentrefoelas is now becoming a focal point to mark the continuation and revival of crafts and skills that were used to maintain the estate; among the attractions is a working **Watermill**.

PENMACHNO
5 miles S of Betws-y-Coed on the B4406

🏠 Penmachno Woollen Mill   🏠 Penmachno Bridge

🏠 Ty Mawr Wybrnant   🏚 Ty'n y Coed Uchaf

This delightful village of picturesque stone cottages, set in a wooded valley, lies on the River Machno, from which it takes its name. Penmachno, surrounded by glorious countryside, situated within an area that is a stronghold of Welsh culture and here can be found the traditional **Penmachno Woollen Mill**. Visitors to the mill can see the working

🎞 stories and anecdotes 🐦 famous people 🎨 art and craft 🎭 entertainment and sport 👣 walks

Harlech Castle

power looms as they weave the cloth then browse through the shop among the finished articles and other Welsh craftwork on display. The sturdy **Penmachno Bridge** has five arches, and was built in 1785.

To the northwest of the village centre, and in the secluded Wybrnant valley, lies **Ty Mawr Wybrnant**, the birthplace of Bishop William Morgan (1545-1604) who was the first person to translate the Bible into Welsh (see also St Asaph). Now restored to how it probably appeared in the 16th and 17th centuries, the house (now in the ownership of the National Trust) includes a display of Welsh Bibles, including Morgan's of 1588. A pleasant one-mile walk starts at the house and takes in woodland and the surrounding fields.

To the northeast of the village and approached by a walk alongside the River Machno, lies **Ty'n y Coed Uchaf**, a small farm that gives visitors an insight into the traditional way of life of the Welsh-speaking community in this area.

HARLECH

🏛 Harlech Castle   🏛 Lasynys Fawr

🐿 Ellis Swynne   🏛 Parish Church of St Tanwyg

🌿 Morfa Harlech

Harlech means bold rock, and it is an apt description, as the town clings to the land at the foot of its spectacularly-sited castle. Another of Edward I's Iron Ring of Fortresses, which was begun in 1283, **Harlech Castle** is perched on a rocky outcrop for added strength and it is, today, a World Heritage Site in the hands of CADW. The castle's situation, close to the sea, has not only proved a great defence, but was also useful during its blockade by Madog and his men in 1294, when supplies transported in from Ireland enabled the 37 men inside to hold fast. If the use of power and strength to impress

🏛 historic building 🏛 museum and heritage 🏛 historic site 🌿 scenic attraction 🌿 flora and fauna

and intimidate an indigenous population was ever aided by architecture then Harlech is a prime example. Situated 200 feet above sea level, its concentric design, with lower outer walls, by the architect James of St George, used the natural defences of its site to emphasise its impregnability. However, in 1404, Owain Glyndwr managed to capture the castle and held it for five years while using the town of Harlech as his capital.

The song, *Men of Harlech*, has immortalised the siege during the War of the Roses when the castle was held for the Lancastrian side for seven years before it finally became the last stronghold to fall to the Yorkists in 1468. The last time Harlech saw action was 200 years later, during the Civil War, when it again withstood attack and was the last castle in Wales to fall to Cromwell's forces. The panoramic views from the castle's battlements take in both Tremadog Bay and the mountainous scenery behind the town.

Though not as imposing as the castle, **Lasynys Fawr** is another building worth a visit. The home of **Ellis Swynne** (1671–1734), a clergyman and one of Wales' most talented prose writers, famous for writing *Gweledigaetheu y Bardd Cwsc*, ("Visions of the Sleeping Bard"), regarded as one of the great works of Welsh literature (see also Llanfair). Dating from 1600, the house is an excellent example of its period. The **Parish**

Church of St Tanwyg dates from about 1840, and replaced an earlier church situated south of the town. St Tanwg came to Britanny from Wales in the 6th century.

Some of the scenes in the early James Bond film *From Russia With Love* were shot in Harlech. The famous Royal St David's golf course is just outside the town. Also outside the town, to the north, lies **Morfa Harlech**, a nature reserve with woodland trails that occupies the flat land between the town and Llanfihangel-y-Thaethau.

BONTDDU

9 miles SE of Harlech on the A496

Looking at this pleasant village it is hard to imagine that it was, over 100 years ago, a bustling centre of the Welsh gold mining industry. Apparently, there were 24 mines operating in the area around Bontddu, and it was one of these mines that provided the gold for the Royal wedding rings.

Afon Mawddach Estuary, Bontddu

🎭 stories and anecdotes 🐿 famous people 🎨 art and craft 🎭 entertainment and sport 🚶 walks

ORIEL GALLERY

2 Tyn-Y-Coed Buildings, High Street, Barmouth,
Gwynedd, Wales LL42 1DS
Tel: 01341 280285
e-mail: info@orielgallery.com website: www.orielgallery.co.uk

Barmouth lies on the West Coast overlooking Cardigan Bay, with the stunning backdrop of Cader Idris and also its picturesque harbour leading into the Mawddach Estuary, one of the most beautiful locations in Wales. The Mawddach Trail is a popular cycle route beside the river, along the old railway track to Dolgellau.

Valerie and Kevin McArdell opened Oriel/Gallery in 1992 specialising in local scenic and seaside views. The Gallery is situated in the High Street and has possibly one of the oldest original Victorian shop windows in the town.

The Gallery sells Valerie's originals and prints . Janet Bell's bright seaside images are always in stock as well as Keith Davies's original paintings and prints. Kevin likes to say that "we sell memories and dreams"; memories of holidays and dreams of summers to come.

Visitors to the Gallery often describe the selection of work as "lively", as the choice of images is constantly changing, and staying ahead of the latest trends. Valerie is one of the gallery's most prolific contributors. Her quirky interpretations of local scenes

LLWYNDU FARMHOUSE HOTEL

Llanaber, Barmouth, Gwynedd LL42 1RR
Tel: 01341 280144 Fax: 01341 281236
e-mail: intouch@llwyndu-farmhouse.co.uk
website: www.llwyndu-farmhouse.co.uk

Llwyndu Farmhouse Hotel is a fine old building at the base of the Rhinog Mountains, overlooking Cardigan Bay, with stunning views over the Lleyn Peninsula. Hosts Paula and Peter Thompson assure guests of the warmest of welcomes, making every visitor feel instantly at home. The exposed stone walls, sturdy old beams, mullion windows, inglenook fireplaces and spiral staircase paint a delightfully traditional scene, and the six en suite bedrooms combine individual character with abundant comfort. Three are in the farmhouse (two with four-posters), three in the converted granary and barn. Peter is a very talented chef, and his 2- or 3-course dinners set great store by top-quality local produce (sea bass, lobster, Welsh Black beef) on Mediterranean-influenced menus that combine traditional and modern elements. His breakfasts are equally unmissable, with prime bacon and sausages, free-range eggs, juicy kippers and naturally

🏛 historic building 🏛 museum and heritage 🏚 historic site 🐚 scenic attraction 🌿 flora and fauna

BARMOUTH
9 miles S of Harlech on the A496

🏠 Barmouth Bridge 🏠 Ty Gywn 🏞 Dinas Oleu

🏛 Lifeboat Station & Museum 🏞 Panorama Walk

Occupying a picturesque location by the mouth of the River Mawddach, Barmouth was once a small port with an equally small shipbuilding industry. As the fashion for seaside resorts grew in the 18th century, the character of Barmouth changed to accommodate visitors flocking here for the bracing sea air. Those suffering from scurvy were even fed seaweed, which is rich in vitamin C and grew in abundance in the estuary. However, the Barmouth seen today is, like many other resorts, a product of the railway age, and the Victorian architecture is still very much apparent. **Ty Gywn** is one of its older buildings, dating from the 15th century. The house, now the home to a Tudor exhibition, is said to have been built for Henry Tudor, Earl of Richmond, later Henry VII. It is thought to have been used as the meeting place where the plot to overthrow Richard III was hatched. The town is also home to a **Lifeboat Museum**. Its **Lifeboat Station**, which has seen service for 180 years, houses a Mersey Class and a D Class inshore. It is open

for visits every day from 10am to 4pm.

The town's harbour, host to a regular regatta, is overlooked by **Dinas Oleu**, a small hill that was the first property given to the newly formed National Trust in 1895. It was a gift from the local wealthy philanthropist, Mrs Fanny Talbot, who was a friend of two of the Trust's founding members. **Panorama Walk** is a scenic walk created as a tourist attraction at the turn of the 19th century. There are several viewpoints along its route, the best being the one from the promontory at the end of the path. Built in 1867, and half a mile in length, the **Barmouth Bridge** that carried the railway across the river mouth has a walkway from where there are magnificent views of the town, coast and estuary. The swing bridge section is nowadays only opened for maintenance purposes.

LLANABER
8 miles S of Harlech on the A496

🏠 Parish Church of St Mary

Found close to the cliff tops, the **Parish Church of St Mary** is said to have been used by smugglers, who hid their booty inside the tombs in the churchyard. Dating from the 13th century and later, this place of worship, which was once the parish church of Barmouth, has an interesting doorway that is one of the best examples of early English architecture. Some people still refer to the church by its ancient dedication, St Bonfan's.

DYFFRYN ARDUDWY
5 miles S of Harlech on the A496

🏚 Arthur's Quoit

Neolithic remains, as well as the remnants of Iron and Bronze Age

Dyffryn Ardudwy Burial Chamber

🎞 stories and anecdotes ⚜ famous people 🎨 art and craft 🎭 entertainment and sport 🚶 walks

settlements, abound in this area and in this village can be found two burial chambers. Perhaps the most interesting is **Arthur's Quoit**, the capstone of which is said to have been thrown from the summit of Moelfre by King Arthur.

LLANBEDR
3 miles S of Harlech on the A496

🏛 Parish Church of St Peter   🌿 Rhinog Fawr

🌿 Shell Island   🏛 Roman Steps

This village is an excellent starting point for walks along the lovely valleys of the Rivers Artro and Nant-col and into the Rhinog Mountains. At 2,360 feet, **Rhinog Fawr** may not be the highest local peak, but from its summit it commands superb views over the Coed y Brenin Forest to the Cambrian Mountains. The **Roman Steps** (see under Ganllwyd) are best reached from Llanbedr.

The **Parish Church of St Peter** (Bedr is welsh for Peter) is worth visiting to view the Llanbedr Stone, which was brought down to the church from an Iron Age hut circle above the village. It has an unusual spiral decoration.

More correctly described as a peninsula that is cut off at high tide, **Shell Island** is a treasure trove of seashells and wildlife, and the shoreline, a mixture of pebble beaches with rock pools and golden sands, is ideal for children to explore. Seals are often seen close by and there is plenty of birdlife – surprising, considering the fairly regular aircraft activity from the nearby Llanbedr airfield.

LLANFAIR
1½ miles S of Harlech on the A496

🏛 Parish Church of St Mary

🏛 Llanfair Slate Caverns

Between 1853 and 1906, Llanfair was a prosperous slate mining village and the old,

deep quarries, the **Llanfair Slate Caverns**, in use until 1906, are now open to the public, who can don a miner's helmet and set out on a self-guided tour. The caverns are accessed from the main tunnel, which opens out into a cathedral-like cavern. It was man-made, like all the tunnels in the complex. The tiny **Parish Church of St Mary**, among sand dunes, is Victorian, and in its churchyard Ellis Swynne (see also Harlech) is buried. Though the village is called Llanfair, the parish is called Llanfair juxta Harlech, meaning Llanfair next to Harlech, to differentiate it from other parishes in Wales called Llanfair.

Bala

🏛 Tomen y Bala   🌿 Llyn Tegid   🏠 Tegi

🐿 Rev Thomas Charles

This agreeable town is a good stopping-off point when exploring Snowdonia National Park. Roman and Norman remains have been found here, but the town was really founded in around 1310 by Roger de Mortimer, who was looking to tame the rebellious Penllyn district. The town was, by Tudor times, a small, and by all accounts not very successful, market town, but it later became an important centre for the knitted stocking industry that flourished in the 18th century before the Industrial Revolution put paid to it. Today, though tourism is certainly an important part of the town's economy, it has remained a central meeting point and a market place for the surrounding farming communities.

However, it is perhaps as a religious centre that Bala is better remembered. The **Rev Thomas Charles**, one of the founders of the Methodist movement in Wales in the 18th century, first visited Bala in 1778, and moved here in 1783 after marrying a local girl. Charles

Aran Ridge, Bala

Pennant). Notable sons of Bala include Thomas Edward Ellis, a Liberal Member of Parliament who worked hard for Welsh home rule, and Owen Morgan Edwards, who was a leading light in the Welsh educational system. There are statues to both these worthies in the town. The son of Owen Morgan Edwards, Sir Ifan ab Owen Edwards, established the Welsh Youth Movement, which has a camp at Bala Lake.

saw the great need for Welsh Bibles and other religious books, and he joined forces with a printer from Chester to produce a series of books and pamphlets. The story of Mary Jones, who walked some 25 miles from Llanfihangel-y-Pennant to buy a bible from Charles, was the inspiration for the foundation of the Bible Society (see also Llanfihangel-y-

Tomen y Bala is to the north east of the town, and is thought to be the motte of a Norman castle, which would have been built of wood. In the 17th and 18th centuries, the knitters of the town congregated here in fine weather to socialise as they worked. It was also used as a pulpit during open air religious

CIGYDD BALA BUTCHERS

69 High Street, Bala, Wales LL23 7AE
Tel: 01678 520422

Cigydd Bala Butchers is the number one choice butchers in Bala, and is owned by experience butcher, Mark Watkins.

Locals rave about the quality and service from this traditional butcher. Mark's old-fashioned principles like top quality local meat, careful maturing, generous cuts and a warm welcome are what make his meat so special and the service so different. From lamb cutlets to loin of pork, there's no better place to have confidence that you are buying affordable quality meat. The meats are locally reared and well hung for superb flavour and texture.

Mark has expanded and diversified his range to include Welsh yoghurt, free-range eggs, fresh fruit and vegetables plus a wide range of delicious hand made sausages and pies.

📖 stories and anecdotes 🐦 famous people 🎨 art and craft ✏ entertainment and sport 🚶 walks

THE BRYNTIRION INN

Llandderfel, nr Bala,
Gwynedd, Wales LL23 7RA
Tel: 01678 530205   Fax: 01678 530723
e-mail: thebryntirioninn@aol.com
website: www.bryntirioninn.co.uk

Set in stunning countryside in the village of Llandderfel, close to Bala Lake, **The Bryntirion Inn** is a delightful old hostelry that dates back to 1695. It is owned and run by the cheerful duo of Martin and Linda who met when they worked for the Landmark Trust on Lundy Island. The Trust administers the only pub on the island and the duo eventually decided to branch out on their own.

It was in 2003 that they took over the Bryntirion Inn which is just 4 miles from Bala on the B4401. Their main aim, they say, has been to create a welcoming atmosphere for everyone (including dogs!), whatever their reason for visiting. The happy combination of a friendly ambience, good food, well-kept ales, a log fire in the winter and a sunny courtyard in the summer has proved to be a great success.

Linda looks after the front of house, and also does the office work. Martin is a qualified chef with more than 20 years experience. His menu is predominantly based on fresh local produce with dishes such as Braised shoulder of Welsh lamb with rosemary gravy, and Welsh black beef, mushroom and ale casserole served in a 'Bryn Bara' featuring prominently on the menu. You'll also find Welsh beef and gammon steaks, as well as tasty fish, poultry and vegetarian dishes. Food is served from noon until 3pm, and from 6pm to 9pm, Monday to Saturday, and from noon until 8pm on Sunday. Booking is recommended on Saturday evenings. Meals can be enjoyed

throughout the inn, in the rear courtyard or at tables at the front which command a lovely view.

Dating back to 1695, 'The Bryn' serves real ales (including those local to the immediate area!), and from the award winning Purple Moose Brewery, a micro-brewery based in the historic harbour town of Porthmadog.

Even the car park is attractive at 'The Bryn', surrounded as it is by gardens and a wood. There is also a heated outdoor smoking area. High chairs are available for young children and further popular features here include monthly quiz and music nights.

If you are planning to stop over when visiting this picturesque Dee Valley region of north Wales, the inn boasts 1 Double/Twin and 1 Double room available, both with en suite facilities and a hearty breakfast is included in the tariff. Children are welcome and all major credit cards apart from American Express and Diners are accepted.

🏛 historic building 🏚 museum and heritage 🏛 historic site 🝊 scenic attraction 🍃 flora and fauna

AWEL YR ARAN RESTAURANT

81 High Street, Bala, Gwynedd LL23 7AE
Tel: 01678 520020
e-mail: laverne_16@hotmail.com
website: www.awelyraranbala.co.uk

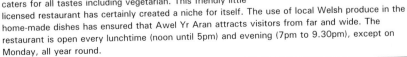

Opened in 2005 by Wendy Phillips, a college-trained chef, **Awel Yr Aran Restaurant** has steadily built up a reputation for providing a modern British menu which changes weekly and caters for all tastes including vegetarian. This friendly little licensed restaurant has certainly created a niche for itself. The use of local Welsh produce in the home-made dishes has ensured that Awel Yr Aran attracts visitors from far and wide. The restaurant is open every lunchtime (noon until 5pm) and evening (7pm to 9.30pm), except on Monday, all year round.

services. To the southwest of the town, **Llyn Tegid** (Bala Lake) is the largest natural lake in Wales and feeder of the River Dee. Four miles long, nearly three quarters of a mile wide and up to 150 feet deep, the lake is a popular centre for all manner of watersports; it is also the home of **Tegi**, the Welsh version of Scotland's Nessie. Formed during the Ice Age, the lake is an important site ecologically and has been designated a Site of Special Scientific Interest and a Ramsar site (Wetlands of International Importance). Many uncommon wetland plants flourish on its banks, and the birdlife includes coots, mallards, pochards, wigeons and great crested grebes. The fish life is interesting, too, and Bala is the only lake in Wales which is home to the gwyniad, a white-

scaled member of the herring family that feeds on plankton in the depths of the lake. Along the eastern bank runs the narrow gauge Bala Lake Railway, which provides the perfect opportunity to catch a glimpse of the Tegi (see under Llanuwchllyn).

Around Bala

FRONGOCH

2 miles N of Bala on the A4212

🏠 Chapel Celyn   🏛 Llyn Celyn   🏛 Arenig Fawr

Just to the northwest of the village lies the reservoir **Llyn Celyn** on whose banks is a memorial stone to a group of local Quakers who, centuries ago, emigrated to America to

PEN-ISA'R-LLAN ACCOMMODATION

Llanfor, Bala, Gwynedd LL23 7DW
Tel: 01678 520507 Mobile: 07818 444780
e-mail: thorpe.pennah@btinternet.com
website: www.pen-isar-llan.co.uk

Dating back more than 400 years and set in 7 acres of rolling farm land, **Pen-isa'r-llan** is a beautiful, traditional stone Welsh farmhouse with a Grade II listing. Located just a mile north of Bala town and the northern tip of lively Lake Bala, the house has been lovingly restored while preserving original features such as exposed beams and slate flooring. Owner Patricia Thorpe offers a variety of accommodation ranging from B&B in 5 charming and spacious en suite rooms, to a Bunk House and a self-catering cottage that can accommodate up to 8 people.

🎬 stories and anecdotes 🐦 famous people 🎨 art and craft 🎭 entertainment and sport 🥾 walks

THE NATIONAL WHITEWATER CENTRE

Canolfan Dŵr Gwyn Genedlaethol Tryweryn, Frongoch,
nr Bala, Gwynedd, LL23 7NU
Tel: 01678 521083
email:info@ukrafting.co.uk
website:www.ukrafting.co.uk

At **The National Whitewater Centre** we have been providing whitewater rafting for 25 years and the River Tryweryn is the best year-round whitewater facility in the UK. The Tryweryn is a steep, rocky mountain river with fast flowing rapids that offer an exhilarating and adrenalin fuelled trip. Because the Tryweryn is dam controlled we often have water when other rivers are dry!

Don't worry if you don't fancy adventure on the river: there are extensive riverside trails around the centre and picnic areas dotted around the site which give you the opportunity to take in the splendour of the surroundings. We are situated in the Snowdonia National Park and the breathtaking scenery offers a fantastic retreat, not only for the water sports enthusiast, but for everyone.

The National Whitewater Centre is centrally located in North Wales giving easy access to the attractions of Snowdonia and the coast. The nearby town of Bala caters for tourists all year round. We can be reached easily from all major towns and cities. The area has an excellent and diverse range of accommodation, places to eat and attractions to suit all tastes.

BALA LAKE RAILWAY

The Station, Llanuwchllyn, nr Bala,
Gwynedd LL23 7DD
Tel: 01678 540666
e-mail: balalake@btconnect.com
website: www.bala-lake-railway.co.uk

Run by the company and a team of voluntary helpers, the narrow-gauge **Bala Lake Railway** operates a four-times-a-day service between Easter and the end of September. Three steam and one diesel locomotive haul the trains from Llanuwchllyn to Bala, enjoying wonderful views along the lake shore on their 25-minute journey. The trains run on the track bed of what was once part of the standard gauge Great Western Railway line from Ruabon to Barmouth, a line that was closed under the Beeching proposals in the early 1960s.

The main station is at Llanuwchllyn ('the village above the lake'), where there is a buffet and souvenir shop. Here, visitors can see the engine being prepared for its journey to Bala and on most days can have a look in the loco shed. All trains stop at Llangower, the mid-point along the Lake, and at the other stops, Bryn Hynod and Pentrepiod, passengers can board by signalling to the driver and alight by telling the guard in advance. The trains all finish their day's work at Llanuwchllyn. Volunteers provide the train crews and fill other posts connected with the running and maintenance of the Bala Lake Railway, one of the Great Little Trains of Wales.

🏭 historic building 🏛 museum and heritage 🏚 historic site 🦢 scenic attraction 🌱 flora and fauna

HEN SIOP FRONGOCH CAFE

Frongoch, Bala, Gwynedd, Wales LL23 7NT
Tel: 01678 520285

Housed in the old post-office building, **Hen Siop Frongoch** is a café that offers a quiet, private atmosphere and welcomes anyone looking for a fine cup of coffee and an opportunity to have a pleasant chit-chat away from any crowds. It offers many home made dishes including lasagne, pies and pasties, with delicious crumbles and Bara Brith cakes for dessert.

escape persecution. The modern chapel close by, **Chapel Celyn**, that was built as a reminder of the rural hamlet was flooded when the reservoir was created in the 1960s. Overlooking Llyn Celyn is **Arenig Fawr**, which has, on its 2,800 foot summit, a memorial to the crew of a Flying Fortress that crashed here in 1943.

After the Easter Uprising of 1916 in Ireland, a former German prisoner of war camp near the village was used to hold 1,600 Irish prisoners, among them Michael Collins. It earned the nickname of the Sinn Féin University, as impromptu lessons were given by some of the prisoners on guerrilla tactics. When Lloyd George came to power in 1916 he closed it down. A plaque marks where it stood.

LLANUWCHLLYN
4 miles SW of Bala on the A494

🚶 Penllyn Forest   ⛰ Cwm Hirnant

⛰ Llyn Efyrnwy   🏛 Bala Lake Railway

This small village at the southern end of Bala Lake is a stop on the **Bala Lake Railway** (see panel opposite), which follows the lake for four miles with various stops where passengers can alight and enjoy a picnic or a walk. Spreading up from the eastern banks of

the lake is the **Penllyn Forest**, which can be reached and passed through via **Cwm Hirnant** on an unclassified road that weaves through the forest to moorland and eventually reaches **Llyn Efyrnwy** (Lake Vyrnwy).

Llanuwchllyn has long been a stronghold of Welsh tradition, and has statues to two eminent Welshmen, Sir Owen Morgan Edwards and his son Sir Ifan ab Owen Edwards, both closely involved in preserving Welsh language and culture.

Dolgellau

🏛 Dollgellau Bridge   🏛 Parish Church of St Mary

🏛 Quaker Heritage Centre   🏛 The Magic of Music

⛰ Cadair Idris   🐦 Dafydd Ionawr

🚶 Precipice Walk

Meaning meadow of the hazels, Dolgellau is the chief market town for this southern area of Snowdonia. Pleasantly situated beside the River Wnion, the town is very Welsh in custom, language and location. Owain Glyndwr held a Welsh parliament here in 1404, later signing an alliance with France's Charles VI. Now, the town's narrow streets can barely evoke those distant times and few early buildings remain. However, the seven-

Precipice Walk

Distance: *3.4 miles (5.4 kilometres)*
Typical time: *120 mins*
Height gain: *50 metres*
Map: *Explorer OL18*
Walk: *www.walkingworld.com ID:225*
Contributor: *Ian Morison*

ACCESS INFORMATION:

Car only. A National Park car park (no fee, toilets) is on the left-hand side of the minor road between Dolgellau and the village of Llanfachreth. Go north over the Afon Wnion bridge out of Dolgellau and turn right. After ½ mile fork left, signed Llanfachreth and Precipice Walk. The car park is two miles up the road.

DESCRIPTION:

After a short stretch in woodland, the path reaches open country and to the north, open views of the Coed y Brenin Forest appear. Turning southwest, the path runs high above the River Maddach. The ground drops steeply into the valley so that young children will need to be well supervised, but there are no sheer drops. The path is good, but occasionally rocky. At the end of this section, views open out, first to the sea at Barmouth and then over Dolgellau to the northern flanks of the Cader Idris range. Almost certainly one of the most beautiful panoramas in Wales. Finally, one returns following the banks of Llyn Cynwch until retracing the final few hundred yards back to the car park.

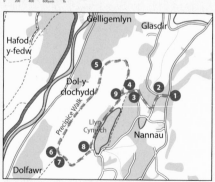

FEATURES:

Hills or Fells, Lake/Loch, Toilets, Wildlife, Birds, Great Views

WALK DIRECTIONS:

1 | Turn left out of the car park and follow the minor road for 100 yards.

2 | Turn left along the signposted track. Follow it round to the right where the track splits into two, keeping the open field to your left, then keep left as you pass a stone cottage.

3 | Cross a low ladder stile into woodland and turn right along the path.

4 | Cross the stile at the end of the wood into the open country. Follow the path round to the right – Llyn Cynwch is seen down the valley on the left. Turn right at the corner of the field following the signpost direction and cross the ladder stile. The village of Llanfachreth is seen in the valley to your right. As you follow the stony path round to the left, Coed y Brenin Forest stretches out in front of you.

5 | The narrow, but safe, path takes you along the flanks of Foel Cynwch through heather and bilberry. To the right lies the River Mawddach some 200m below. As you continue, the view opens out with the Mawddach Estuary becoming visible to the right with, ahead, distant views of Cader Idris.

6 | Here is the first superb spot for a picnic. To the west is seen the Mawddach Estuary, the viaduct carrying the railway into Barmouth and the sea beyond. In the valley to the south lies the town of Dolgellau with the northern flanks of the Cader Idris range beyond.

7 | Climb over the ladder stile and follow the path contouring round the hillside to the left. Cross a further ladder stile and follow a soft path of closely cropped grass down towards Llyn Cynwch.

8 | Follow round to the left and drop onto the path alongside the lake. Turn left. Follow the gentle, tree-lined, path beside the lake – another beautiful spot to have a break, particularly if it was windy out on the fellside.

9 | Rejoin the outward route and retrace your steps back towards the car park. Across the field on the right after the woodland you will see Nannau Hall, built in 1693.

arched **Dollgellau Bridge** over the river dates from the early 17th century and, before much of Dolgellau was built in an attempt to lure Victorian holidaymakers to the delights of Cadair Idris, there was a small rural Quaker community here. The **Quaker Heritage Centre** in Eldon Square tells the story of this community and also of the persecution that led them to emigrate to Pennsylvania. North of the town, the three-and-a-half-mile **Precipice Walk** offers superb views. The local gold mines provided the gold for the wedding rings of both Queen Elizabeth II (then Princess Elizabeth) and Diana, Princess of Wales. Two Siamas – **The Magic of Music** – is an award-winning attraction where visitors can see, hear and touch the music of Wales through film, interactive portals and hands-on instruments.

Within the **Parish Church of St Mary** there is an effigy of a knight, Meurig ab Ynvr Fychan, who lived in the 14th century. The church itself was built in 1716, and in the churchyard is a monument to **Dafydd Ionawr** (1751–1827 the Welsh poet.

To the southwest of Dolgellau is **Cadair Idris** (the chair of Idris) which rises to 2,927 feet and dominates the local scenery. On a clear day, a climb to the summit is rewarded with views that take in the Isle of Man and the Irish coast as well as, closer to home, the Mawddach estuary. Much of the area around the mountain became a national nature reserve in 1957. An old legend says that anyone who

ROYAL SHIP HOTEL

Queens Square, Dolgellau, Gwynedd LL40 1AR
Tel: 01341 422209   Fax: 01341 424693
e-mail: stay@royalshiphotel.co.uk
website: www.royalshiphotel.co.uk

The Royal Ship Hotel is an early 19th century Coaching Inn in the heart of the old Market Town of Dolgellau, ideally situated to explore the beauty of North & Mid Wales. Located in the Snowdonia National Park, one of the most picturesque countryside's imaginable, surrounded by mountains, rives & fishing lakes, only a few minutes drive to the Cambrian coastline, it is the perfect place for a relaxing holiday or short break.

A family run hotel, this historical building has been modernised and extended over the years. Behind its attractive ivy-clad facade, 23 individual furnished bedrooms, bar and restaurant are on offer and provides guests with the ideal atmosphere for a memorable stay. Choose from single, double, twin or family rooms of which 17 are en-suite, the remaining rooms have private bathrooms allocated, some have attractive views over the Town Square and the Cader Idris Mountain Range. All rooms are non-smoking and equipped with tea & coffee making facilities and television. Bathrobes and slippers are available at reception.

The Kitchen at the Hotel offers a wide selection of traditional Welsh & British as well as contemporary dishes, prepared with a continental touch. As previous winners of the Robinson's National Seafood Week Competition and emphasising healthy eating the Royal Ship Hotel serves a great choice of seafood.

stories and anecdotes famous people art and craft entertainment and sport walks

MEDI GIFTS AND HOMESTYLE

2-3 Heol-y-Bont, Dolgellau, Gwynedd LL40 1AU
Tel: 01341 421 755
e-mail: medi-hyb@tiscali.co.uk
website: www.medi-gifts.com

Medi Gifts and Homestyle is a quirky design-led gift shop offering *"a little piece of heaven at the foot of Cader Idris"*. Situated in a stunning oak-beamed listed building in the old market town of Dolgellau (in mid-Wales), this is the place to shop for high end products from Wales, Scandinavia and beyond. Medi offers something unique for all occasions with a wide range of shabby- chic, vintage, Shaker, enamel and local hand made goods for you and your home...' Stockist for Melin Tregwynt, Gisela Graham, InchBlue, Coach House and Contemporary Design Co, East of India, Maeleg, Miffy, Tom Gloster Pottery and many more. Owned and run by Nia Medi, actress, novelist and ex - designer on makeover programme Real Rooms for Pebble Mill.

And above the shop - the HYB Bunkhouse has four lovely rooms accommodating 16 people. Ideal for cycling in Coed y Brenin, walking, canoeing and Cader Idris. Free private car park at rear. Please ring or e-mail Medi for more information and availability.

GUINEVERE

Unit 3/4 Neuadd Idris, Eldon Square, Dolgellau,
Gwynedd LL40 1PY
Tel: 01341 422205

Based in the historic town of Dolgellau, **Guinevere** is a family run gift shop that was established over 20 years ago. The business has been developed with quality and service in mind with the customer as the number 1 priority.

This gift shop offers the best in retail therapy, with the accent firmly on those gifts and souvenirs that capture the wonder of Wales. Guinevere has a particular interest in jewellery and has been an outlet for Clogau Welsh Gold since its inception, each piece of Clogau Gold jewellery is of an original design and hand-crafted to a high standard. All designs have a deep sympathy for Welsh history and this is realised in many of the collections with particular motifs and gem arrangements associated with Welsh legend.

With a selection of original paintings and prints by local artists, lovespoons, picture frames, watches, miniature clocks, willow figurines, collectables and much more, Guinevere has gift ideas for every occasion.

sleeps on its slopes either wakes up mad or with the ability to write great poetry.

Around Dolgellau

LLANELLTYD
2 miles NW of Dolgellau on the A470

🏛 Cymer Abbey 🏛 Parish Church of St Elltyd

🜂 Kenric Stone

This is the point at which the Rivers Wen and Wnion, boosted by other waters further upland, meet to form the Mawddach estuary. Across the River Wen lie the serene ruins of **Cymer Abbey**, which was founded by Cistercian monks in 1198. This white-robed order was established in the late 11th century in Burgundy and they arrived in Britain in 1128 to seek out remote places where they could lead their austere lives. Cymer was one of two Cistercian abbeys created in the Snowdonia region during the Middle Ages – the other is Conwy Abbey – and Cymer held substantial lands in this area. Despite this, the abbey was poor and it also suffered badly during the fighting between England and Wales. In fact, by the time of the Dissolution in 1536 the abbey's income was just £51. Visitors to this CADW site can see the

remaining parts of the church, refectory and chapter house set in picturesque surroundings.

The **Parish Church of St Elltyd** is medieval, and has a curious stone within it called the **Kenric Stone**, which has a Latin inscription and the mark of a footprint.

LLANFACHRETH
3 miles N of Dolgellau off the A470

🏛 Nannau Hall 🏛 Parish Church of St Mackreth

Close to this beautifully located village is **Nannau Hall**, the ancient seat of the Vaughan family, who owned much of the land in this area. It is said that an earlier house on the site belonged to Howel Sele, a cousin of Owain Glyndwr, who, during a dispute with Glyndwr over Sele's Lancastrian sympathies, shot at but missed his cousin while out hunting. Glyndwr was so enraged that he killed Sele and hid his body in a hollow oak. This hiding place was later to receive a mention in Sir Walter Scott's *Marmion* as "the spirit's blasted tree". The **Parish Church of St Mackreth** is medieval, but was restored in the 1820s.

GANLLWYD
5 miles N of Dolgellau on the A470

🏛 Roman Steps 🜂 Dolmelynllyn 🜂 Rhaeadr Ddu

🜂 Coed y Brenin Forest Park

This hamlet gives its name to the attractive valley in which it is found and which is, in turn, surrounded by the **Coed y Brenin Forest Park**, an area of some 9,000 acres around the valleys of the Rivers Mawddach, Eden, Gain and Wen. Originally part of the Nannau Estate, founded by Cadougan, Prince of Powys, in 1100, the forest was acquired by the Forestry

Cymer Abbey, Llanelltyd

🎞 stories and anecdotes 🜂 famous people 🎨 art and craft 🎭 entertainment and sport 🜊 walks

Commission in 1922, when extensive planting of conifers took place. Ganllwyd was once a centre for gold mining and, during the 1880s, the nearby mine at Gwynfynydd was prosperous enough to attract some 250 miners. The mine had produced around 40,000 ounces of gold by the time it closed in 1917; it re-opened from 1981 to 1989. The mine is on the route of one of the four waymarked trails, that takes in waterfalls, forest nature trails and an old copper works. Orienteering is a good way to explore the park, and it offers some of the best mountain biking in the UK. Bikes can be hired at the visitor centre, which has a café, shop and exhibitions. There are also riverside picnic sites and a children's adventure play area.

Broadleaved woodlands once covered the land and some of these woodlands still survive at the National Trust's **Dolmelynllyn** estate. On the slopes of Y Garn, a path through this expanse of heath and oak woodland leads to **Rhaeadr Ddu** ('Black Waterfall'), one of the most spectacular waterfalls in Wales. Also in the heart of the forest, but reached from Llanbedr, can be found a series of hundreds of steps, known as the **Roman Steps**, which climb up through the rocks and heather of the wild Rhinog Mountains. In spite of their name they are certainly not Roman; they are thought to have been part of a late medieval trade route between the coastal region around Harlech and England.

TRAWSFYNYDD
10 miles N of Dolgellau off the A470

🏛 Trawsfynydd Nuclear Power Station

🔆 Llyn Trawsfynydd   🏛 Roman Amphitheatre

🕊 Hedd Wynn   🕊 St John Roberts

To the west of the village lies **Llyn**

Trawsfynydd, a man-made lake developed in the 1930s as part of a hydro-electric scheme. On its northern shores stands **Trawsfynydd Nuclear Power Station**, which opened in 1965 and was the country's first inland nuclear station, using the lake for cooling purposes.

Down a minor road close to the power station are the remains of a small **Roman Amphitheatre** that also served as a fort.

In the village centre is a statue in honour of **Hedd Wynn**, a poet and shepherd who was awarded the bardic chair at the 1917 Eisteddfod while he fought and died in the Flanders fields during World War I. The Parish Church of St Madryn was originally dedicated to St Mary, and then to the Holy Trinity before assuming its present dedication when the Church of Wales was disestablished. It was badly burnt in 1978 and rebuilt in 1981. It is connected to **St John Roberts**, who was born in the village to a Protestant family, but later converted to Roman Catholicism. He was hanged, drawn and quartered at Tyburn in London in 1610 and canonised in 1970 by Pope Paul VI as one of the 40 martyrs of England and Wales.

DINAS MAWDDWY
8½ miles E of Dolgellau on the A470

🏛 Pont Minllyn   🏛 Meirion Mill

🕊 Gwilliaid Cochion Maeddwy

During the Middle Ages, this now quiet village was a centre of local power, but the only surviving building from those days is a packhorse bridge, **Pont Minllyn**. A gateway to the upper Dyfi valley, it was once alive with quarries and mines, but all that today's visitors can see of past industry is the traditional weaving of cloth at **Meirion Mill**, where there is also a visitor centre, craft shop and café.

TY DERW

Dinas Mawddwy, nr Dolgellau,
Gwynedd SY20 9LR
Tel: 01650 531318
website: www.tyderw.co.uk

Ty Derw is a charming Victorian country house set in its own grounds in the beautiful Dyfi Valley at the gateway of the Snowdonia National Park. A stay of at least three days is recommended both to enjoy the fine hospitality extended by owners Nick and Mair Godley and to make the most of the glorious surroundings of lakes, hills and forests. Three ensuite double bedrooms (one ground floor) and one ensuite twin room provide ultimate calm and comfort. The guest sitting room has a good supply of maps and guide books, as well as TV, DVD and CD players. Food matters at Ty Derw! Nick prepares a splendid, hearty breakfast, and Mair works her magic to provide memorable dinners.

In the 15th and 16th centuries, the whole area surrounding the village was plagued by an 80-strong gang of band of bandits. They were know as the **Gwilliaid Cochion Maeddwy** (Red Bandits of Mawddwy). They stole cattle and sheep, robbed travellers and attacked farmsteads. Eventually, they were captured and executed in 1554, their burial place being a mound at Ros Goch ("Red Moor"),two miles from the village. The survivors exacted some revenge by murdering their prosecutor, Baron Lewis Owen.

CORRIS

6 miles S of Dolgellau on the A487

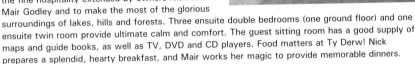

Railway Museum   King Arthur's Labyrinth

Corris Craft Centre

This small former slate-mining village, surrounded by the tree-covered slopes of the Cambrian Mountains, was home to the first narrow-gauge railway in Wales. It was constructed in 1859 as a horse-drawn railway, and steam locomotives were introduced in 1878 before the passenger service began in 1883. After closing in 1948, the Corris Railway Society opened a **Railway Museum**

that explains the railway's history and also the special relationship with the slate quarries through displays, exhibits and photographs. Part of the line reopened to passengers in 2003.

Industry of a different kind can be found at the **Corris Craft Centre**, which is home to a variety of working craftsmen and women. An excellent place to find a unique gift, the craft centre is also home to the fascinating **King Arthur's Labyrinth** – a maze of underground tunnels where visitors are taken by boat to see the spectacular caverns and re-live tales of the legendary King Arthur.

The legend of King Arthur is first told in *The Mabinogion*, a collection of stories that evolved over 1,000 years. Passed from generation to generation from the 4th century onwards, they were not written down in a surviving manuscript form until the 13th century. The *White Book of Rhydderch* and the *Red Book of Hergest* between them contain 11 stories, five of which centre round the exploits of King Arthur and his contemporaries. In these tales we meet Gwenhwyfar (Guinevere), Cei (Sir Kay), Bedwyr (Sir Bedivere), Myrddin (Merlin)

stories and anecdotes   famous people   art and craft   entertainment and sport   walks

and Gwalchmei (Sir Gawain). In the *History of the Britons*, written by the Welsh cleric Nennius around 830 AD, we first read of Arthur's battles, some at least of which took place in Wales, from about 515 AD onwards. The last great battle, against his nephew Mawdred and his Saxon allies, marked the end of a phase of Celtic resistance to the Saxons. This battle has been dated to 537 AD and is located by some historians on the Llyn Peninsula. In Welsh tradition, Merlin and the great bard Taliesin took the dying King Arthur to the magical Isle of Avalon, which recent research has identified as Bardsey Island, where St Cadfan established a monastery and where 1,000 Welsh saints are buried. The caverns of King Arthur's Labyrinth are the workings of the Braich Goch Slate Mine, which was operational between 1836 and 1970. At its peak, the

mine employed 250 men and produced 7,000 tons of roofing slate annually.

PANTPERTHOG
8 miles S of Dolgellau on A487

🏛 Centre for Alternative Technology

The **Centre for Alternative Technology** has exhibitions and displays on eco-friendly ways of generating power, greenhouse gases and pollution. You can see environmentally friendly ways of building, renewable energy schemes and energy efficiency. There is a visitor centre, a shop and a café.

TAL-Y-LLYN
5 miles S of Dolgellau on the B4405

🏛 Parish Church of St Mary   🔱 Tal-y-llyn Lake

This tiny hamlet lies at the southwestern end of the **Tal-y-llyn Lake**, which is overshadowed by the crags of Cadair Idris to

THE TYNYCORNEL HOTEL
Tal-y-Llyn, Tywyn, Gwynedd LL36 9AJ
Tel: 01654 782282
website: www.tynycornel.co.uk

A stunning location is just one of the delights that awaits visitors to the Tynycornel Hotel. t stands beside the 222-Acre Tal-y-Lyn Lake - a world-famous brown trout fishery - whose waters reflect the imposing Cadair Idris, the second tallest peak in Wales. Guests enjoy priority access to its prized waters.

The hotel's comfortably appointed bedrooms offer modern facilities while retaining their original charm, and most overlook the lake. All rooms are equipped with en suite bathrooms, free telephone and internet connection and modern TV's. The lounge and restaurant, which are open to residents and non-residents, provide the ideal environment for enjoying a light snack, a supper or a special celebration. The chefs source their ingredients from local suppliers and the menu features an excellent variety of dishes, from simple snacks to three-course meals. The bar is stocked with a selection of award-winning real ales produced by the hotel's sister company Evan-Evans Brewery in Llandeilo. The hotel is also a favourite base for walkers, cyclists, tourists and birdwatchers, or just for taking in the glorious scenery.

the north and is a great favourite with trout fishermen. The **Parish Church of St Mary** (at present closed), which some people think is one of the oldest churches in Wales, and has a plaque dating the original building to the 9th century. Some people claim it is even older. It has an unusual chancel ceiling of square panels decorated with carved roses. For the Tal-y-llyn Railway see Tywyn.

LLANFIHANGEL-Y-PENNANT
7 miles SW of Dolgellau off the B4405

🏠 Mary Jones's Cottage

🏠 Parish Church of St Michael   🏠 Castell y Bere

Just to the northeast of this small hamlet lie the ruins of **Mary Jones's Cottage**. After saving for six years for a Welsh Bible, Mary Jones, the 16-year-old daughter of a weaver, walked to Bala in 1800 to purchase a copy from Thomas Charles. As Charles had no copies of the Bible available, he gave her his own copy and the episode inspired the founding of the Bible Society (see also Bala). Mary lived to a ripe old age (88 years) and was buried at Bryncrug, while her Bible is preserved in the Society's headquarters in London. There is a memorial to her in the churchyard of the much-restored **Parish Church of St Michael**.

Close by lie the ruins of **Castell y Bere**, a hill top fortress begun by Llywelyn the Great in 1223. Taken by the Earl of Pembrokeshire, on behalf of Edward I, in 1283, the castle stayed in English hands for two years before being retaken by the Welsh and destroyed.

ARTHOG
6 miles SW of Dolgellau on the A493

🐾 Cregennan Lakes   🕊 Arthog RSP

🏠 Nature Reserve

Overlooking the Mawddach estuary, this elongated village is a starting point for walks into Cadair Idris. Beginning with a sheltered woodland path, the trail climbs up to the two **Cregennan Lakes** from where there are glorious mountain views. The lakes are fed by streams running off the mountains and they have created a valuable wetland habitat that is now in the care of the National Trust. Down by the river mouth, there is the **Arthog RSPB Nature Reserve** protecting the wealth of birdlife and wildlife found here.

FAIRBOURNE
8 miles SW of Dolgellau off the A493

🚂 Fairbourne Railway

This growing holiday resort lies on the opposite side of the Mawddach estuary from Barmouth and, from the ferry that carries passengers across the river mouth, runs the **Fairbourne Railway** (see panel on page 140). Originally a horse-drawn tramway, now steam-hauled, this 15in gauge railway runs from Fairbourne to the mouth of the Mawddach estuary. Its midway halt was given an invented name that outdoes the 59 letters of Llanfair PG by eight. Translated from the Welsh, it means Mawddach Station with its dragon's teeth on North Penrhyn Drive by the golden sands of Cardigan Bay. The dragon's teeth are anything but mystical: they are concrete tank traps left over from World War II.

LLWYNGWRIL
10 miles S of Dolgellau on the A493

🏠 Parish Church of St Celynin   🚂 Carstell-y-Gaer

The village is named after the giant Gwril, who was supreme in this part of the coast. He was said to be the lowland cousin of Idris, who ruled the mountains, and after who Cadair Idris is named. They spent most of their time throwing rocks at each other. A "llwyn" is a

🎭 stories and anecdotes 🐟 famous people 🎨 art and craft 🌿 entertainment and sport 🧍 walks bush or grove in Welsh, so the name means Gwril's grove. Above the village is **Castell-y-Gaer**, a prehistoric hill fort, and a mile south of the village is the wonderful 16th-century **Parish Church of St Celynin** at Llangelynin, over 600 years old and largely unrestored. Its treasures include wall texts, a rare set of pews named after local families, and the grave of Abram Wood, King of the Welsh gypsies.

TYWYN

14 miles SW of Dolgellau on the A493

🚂 Tal-y-llyn Railway   ⚜ Dolgoch Falls

⚘ National Trail

This coastal town and seaside resort on Cardigan Bay has long sandy beaches, dunes and a promenade, as well as being the start (or

the end) of the famous narrow-gauge (2 feet 3 inches) **Tal-y-llyn Railway**, which takes you as far as Abergynolwyn, seven-and-a-half miles inland. Like most narrow gauge railways in Wales, it was opened (in 1865) to bring slate from the quarries down to the coast. The original two steam engines are still in service.

The area around Tywyn is wonderful walking country, and marked walks include the new **National Trail** that runs between Machynlleth, Welshpool and Knighton. One of the stations on the line is Dolgoch, from which a walk takes in three sets of magnificent waterfalls, the **Dolgoch Falls**. Four walks of varying lengths and difficulty start at Nant Gwernol station and provide an opportunity to enjoy the lovely woodlands and to look at the remains of Bryn Eglwys quarry and the tramway that served it.

FAIRBOURNE RAILWAY

*Beach Road, Fairbourne,
Gwynedd, Wales LL38 2EX
Tel: 01341 250362   Fax: 01341 250240
e-mail: fairbourne.rail@btconnect.com
website: www.fairbournerailway.com*

Leave your car behind and truly relax! **The Fairbourne Railway** is fast becoming one of the UK's premier narrow gauge railways, offering a service second to none to the enthusiast, traveller and tourist in all seasons of the year. Laid in 1895 this train journey takes you from the old village of Fairbourne, between the golden beaches of Cardigan Bay and the magnificent Mawddach Estuary, under the mountains of Snowdonia, to the mouth of the Mawddach at Barmouth Ferry Station, where you can catch the ferry to the Harbour at the seaside resort of Barmouth. The full round trip takes 60 minutes and most trains are steam hauled. Return tickets are valid all day and passengers may break their journey at any of the four request stops.

Fairboune Station is home to the Railway and has attractions for all; a souvenir shop, pictorial museum tracing the Railway's history and the Rowen Centre, home to animals and fish, plus an ever-developing G scale model railway. The Railway also has its own station tea room and Harbour View café, both licensed, that sell everything from hot and cold drinks, light snacks to full meals.

🏛 historic building 🏛 museum and heritage 🏚 historic site ⚜ scenic attraction 🌿 flora and fauna

CRISS X STITCHES

The Old Print Shop, Red Lion Street,
Tywyn, Wales LL36 9DN
Tel/Fax: 01654 711466
e-mail: keithlathwell@hotmail.com
website: www.crissxstitch.co.uk

Both novice and expert stitchers will find a mine of
materials and advice in **Criss X Stitches** to help them get
the best results from their creative work. The shop enjoys
immense popularity with both local customers and stitchers further afield, keeping it named Wales
Retailer of the Year for three years running. Owners, Keith and Margaret Lathwell, have filled their
shop with a fine variety of patchwork materials, cross stitch kits, tapestries, threads, beads and a
wide selection of needlecraft accessories, including Daylight Company and DMC products. They also
host a number of expertly run courses on a variety of crafts throughout the summer months.

GILL'S PLAICE

16 Chapel Square, Aberdovey,
Gwynedd, Wales LL35 0EL
Tel: 01654 767875   Fax: 01654 767875

Situated in the peaceful seaside village of Aberdovey, **Gill's
Plaice** offers the perfect location to stop and buy fresh fish
and seafood as well as a stroll along the beach or harbour.
The passion and dedication of the staff create an inviting
and friendly atmosphere where customers can purchase
well-prepared haddock, sea bass, or plaice. Fully dressed crabs, lobsters and shrimps are also
available. The owner sources as much local fish as possible - this includes day-boat fish such as
mackerel, bass, bream, turbot, rock salmon and local trout according to seasonality and weather
conditions.

ABERDOVEY (ABERDYFI)

16 miles SW of Dolgellau on the A493

This resort at the mouth of the River Dovey
(or Dyfi) was once one of the most
important ports along the Welsh coast.
Shipbuilding flourished here, and records
show that on one particular occasion 180
ships were unloading or waiting for a berth.
The town has been attracting holiday-makers
since Edwardian times, when the railways
made such seaside trips possible for many
more people. It is a gentle, civilised spot,
with all the best attributes of a seaside resort
and none of the kiss-me-quick brashness of
many larger places. The Parish Church of St
Peter is a handsome building constructed in
1837, though the Victorian ballad, *The Bells of
Aberdovey*, has nothing to do with its peel of
10 carrillon bells, which were only installed in
1936. It recounts an old legend that the sea
drowned a great kingdom called Cantre'r
Gwaelod (Lowland Hundred) in Cardigan
Bay, and how on quiet summer evenings the
bells can be heard ringing out from beneath
the waves.

🏛 stories and anecdotes 🐦 famous people 🎨 art and craft 🎭 entertainment and sport 🚶 walks

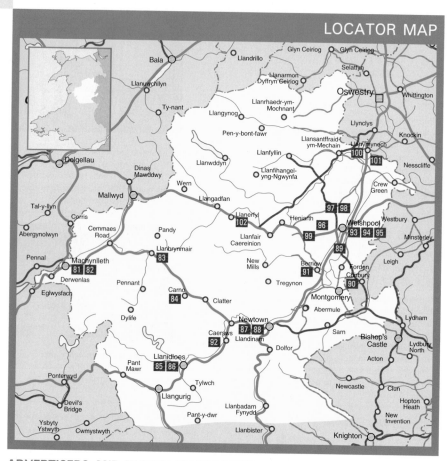

LOCATOR MAP

ADVERTISERS AND PLACES OF INTEREST

Accommodation, Food and Drink

83| Machinations Visitor Centre, Llanbrynmair   *pg 146*

84| Cledan Valley Tipi Holidays, Carno, Caersws *pg 147*

86| Mount Severn, Llanidloes   *pg 150*

90| The Herbert Arms, Chirbury, Montgomery   *pg 155*

91| Glansevern Hall Gardens, Berriew,
   Welshpool   *pg 156*

93| Cromwell's Restaurant, Welshpool   *pg 160*

94| The Raven Inn, Welshpool   *pg 160*

95| Revells Bistro & Restaurant, Welshpool   *pg 161*

97| Derwen Garden Centre & Farm Shop,
   Guilsfield, Welshpool   *pg 162*

98| Derwen House Apartments, Guilsfield,
   Welshpool   *pg 163*

99| Middle Sylfaen Farm, Golfa, nr Welshpool   *pg 163*

100| The Manse Bed & Breakfast, Llanymynech   *pg 164*

101| Rhandregynwen Hall, Four Crosses   *pg 164*

Activities

83| Machinations Visitor Centre, Llanbrynmair   *pg 146*

88| Penarth Vineyard, Newtown   *pg 152*

Arts and Crafts

81| Moma Wales - The Tabernacle, Machynlleth   *pg 144*

Fashions

85| L'Armoire Fashion House, Llanidloes   *pg 149*

🏛 historic building 🏚 museum and heritage 🏛 historic site ♙ scenic attraction ♣ flora and fauna

4 | North Powys

Once part of the old county of Montgomeryshire, this northern region of Powys is an area of varied landscape and small towns and villages. Situated between the high, rugged landscape of Snowdonia and the farmland of Shropshire, this is a gentle and pleasant region through which many rivers and streams flow. As well as being home to the highest waterfall outside Scotland, Pistyll Rhaeadr (one of the Seven Wonders of Wales), the region has another landmark in Lake Vyrnwy. Built in the 1880s to supply the expanding city of Liverpool with water, this large reservoir is a splendid feat of Victorian engineering that later found fame as a location for the film *The Dambusters*.

The major settlement here is Welshpool, a town situated on the banks of the River Severn and close to the English border. Originally known as Pool, the prefix was added to ensure that the dispute regarding its nationality was finalised once and for all. From the town, leisurely canal boat trips can be taken along the Montgomery Canal, but there is also a narrow gauge steam railway running westwards to Llanfair Caereinion. Near the town can be found the splendid Powis Castle, which is famous not only for the many treasures it houses, but also for its magnificent gardens.

Montgomery, a tiny anglicised town that gave its name to the county of Montgomeryshire, has a splendidly situated ruined borderland castle, is close to some of the best preserved sections of Offa's Dyke (see Prestatyn). Nearby, Newtown, which, despite its name, was founded in the 10th century, is another interesting and historic market town. Those who are interested in history, particularly social history, will find the Robert Owen Memorial Museum well worth a visit.

To the west and beyond the quaint town of Llanidloes lies Machynlleth, the home of Owain Glyndwr's parliament in the 15th-century. A visit to the Owen Glyndwyr Centre, which can be found in the part 15th century parliament house, tells the story of Glyndwr and his struggle against the English.

This is great walking country, which takes in some of the finest scenery in Wales. The many marked established trails and walks include a large part of Offa's Dyke Path and Glyndwr's Way, a 123-mile walk that follows a circular route across dramatic landscapes from Welshpool to Knighton by way of Machynlleth.

🎞 stories and anecdotes 🐦 famous people 🎭 art and craft 🎟 entertainment and sport 🚶 walks

Machynlleth

🏠 Parliament House   🏠 Plas Machynlleth

🏠 Parish Church of St Peter   🍂 Owain Glyndwr

🎨 MOMA WALES - The Tabernacle

This small town is a popular but not overcrowded holiday centre in the shadow of the Cambrian Mountains. It was here that **Owain Glyndwr** held one of his parliaments in around 1404 and, on the site today, stands **Parliament House**, a part 15th century building. It is home to the Owain Glyndwr Centre, which tells the story of the last native Prince of Wales and the rebellion he led against the English. The building also has a brass rubbing centre. Glyndwr's aims were independence for Wales, a church independent of Canterbury and the establishing of a Welsh university. After being refused redress when

Lord Grey of Ruthin seized some of his land, he laid waste the English settlements in northeast Wales and spent the next few years in skirmishes. He established other parliaments in Dolgellau and Harlech, and sought alliances with the Scots, the Irish and the French, and resisted many assaults by Henry IV's armies. Eventually Henry V seized Aberystwyth and Harlech, and Glyndwr soon disappeared from the scene, dying, it is thought, at the home of his daughter, Anne Scudamore. It was while presiding over the parliament that Owain was nearly killed by his brother-in-law Dafyd Gam. The plot failed, and Dafyd was captured. He was granted a pardon by Owain and later fought at the Battle of Agincourt.

Opposite the house is the entrance to **Plas Machynlleth**, an elegant mansion built in 1653, which was given to the town by Lord

---

MOMA WALES - THE TABERNACLE

Heol Penrallt, Machynlleth, Powys SY20 8AJ
Tel: 01654 703355 Fax: 01654 702160
e-mail: info@momawales.org.uk
website: www.momawales.org.uk

Converted in the mid-1980s from a Wesleyan chapel, **MOMA WALES - The Tabernacle** is now a highly successful gallery and centre for the performing arts. Since its opening MOMA WALES has expanded and now occupies four beautiful exhibition spaces alongside The Tabernacle. Throughout the year, MOMA (Museum of Modern Art) WALES shows modern Welsh art, featuring leading artists from Wales, works from the growing Tabernacle Collection, and in August selected entries from the Tabernacle Art Competition. Many of the works of art are for sale.

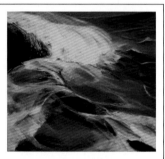

Andrea Kelland
(Tabernacle Collection)

The Auditorium of The Tabernacle has perfect acoustics and pitch-pine pews to seat 350 people. It is ideal for chamber and choral music, drama, lectures and conferences. A fine Steinway grand piano has been purchased and translation-booths, recording facilities and a cinema-screen have been installed. The oak-beamed Foyer has a bar and extensive access for the disabled has been made possible by a lift.

In late August every year the week-long **Machynlleth Festival** takes place in the Auditorium. Eminent performers take part in a wide range of events, from choral singing and jazz to chamber music and poetry readings.

🏠 historic building 🏛 museum and heritage 🏛 historic site 🐾 scenic attraction 🌿 flora and fauna

BLASAU DELICATESSEN

6 Penrallt Street, Machynlleth, Powys SY20 8AJ
Tel: 01654 700410
e-mail: merciahammond@yahoo.co.uk

Offering an extensive choice of top quality produce, **Blasau Delicatessen** puts a special emphasis on items sourced in Wales. You will find more than 20 varieties of Welsh cheeses, along with Welsh whiskey, beer, cider and wine. Owner Mercia Hammond bakes her own bread, as well as some delicious cakes. Sausage, pasties and pies are supplied by some of the best bakers and meat producers in Wales, and the jams and chutneys are also made locally. Hampers are available and most of the stock can be bought by mail order.

Londonderry, and which is surrounded by attractive gardens open to the public. This beautifully restored mansion was, up until 2006, home to Celtica, a museum and multi-media centre where the history and the legends of the Celts were displayed. The **Parish Church of St Peter** was originally dedicated to St Cybi, and was extensively rebuilt and enlarged in 1827, though the base of the tower is 15th century. At the centre of the town is an ornate Clock Tower dating from 1872, which was built by public subscription to mark the coming of age of Lord Castlereagh, heir to the Marquess of Londonderry. Alongside a converted Wesleyan chapel, The Tabernacle, is **MOMA WALES**, where several exhibition spaces are a showcase of the very best of modern Welsh art, with changing displays and exhibitions

throughout the year. The galleries (free admission) are open from 10am Monday to Saturday.

Around Machynlleth

CARNO

10 miles E of Machynlleth on the A470

🏠 Parish Church of St John the Baptist

🏭 Carno Wind Farm

The dress and interior designer Laura Ashley, who was born in Wales, and her husband moved to Machynlleth in 1963 and later settled at Carno, which became the site of the headquarters of the Laura Ashley empire. It was in the churchyard of the **Parish Church of St John the Baptist**, close to the factory, that she was buried after her death due to a

Windfarm, Carno

🎭 stories and anecdotes 🐦 famous people 🎨 art and craft 🎟 entertainment and sport 🚶 walks

MACHINATIONS VISITOR CENTRE

The Old Village Hall, Llanbrynmair,
nr Machynlleth, Powys SY19 7AA
Tel: 01650 521738 Fax: 01650 521635
e-mail: machinations@btconnect.com
website: www.machinationswales.com

Machinations Visitor Centre is a celebration of ingenuity, artistry and craftsmanship, a marvellous museum of mechanical magic in a lovely setting by the River Severn in the very heart of Wales. At the centre of the enterprise, which is housed in the extended Old Village Hall, is the only permanent exhibition of contemporary automata in the UK.

Automata are essentially moving figures, tableaux and sculptures that may be hand-turned, wind-driven or powered by electricity or clockwork, and visitors of all ages can watch fascinated as the models spin and whirl and bob, their mechanisms displaying a variety of cogs and cams and levers. The original models were collected and shown by Pat Osborne in Liverpool; later consigned to storage, they were brought to Llanbrynmair – and considerably added to – by Eric and Alison Williamson as an extension to their model making and design company.

Timberkits are a range of mechanical models and kits designed by Eric, who started in the 1970s making rocking horses and marionettes. The business expanded rapidly from small batch production here to mass production in China. The models – the range now extends to more than 20 – are still designed and prototyped here in Wales, and the shop at the centre sells them in kit form or assembled, with an option of electric operation. Timberkits also makes and sells a wide range of plywood puzzles based on animals, transport and buildings. The shop sells many other interesting toys and gifts with the emphasis on craft and creativity.

Machinations has several other attractions, including a fearsome moving red dragon in a glass tower, a bookshop and a café and riverside terrace where visitors can enjoy excellent home cooking. A great family favourite is Rabbit Village, still being developed on the mini-hills in front of the café; it is built largely in traditional style, with stone and slate, and the rabbits themselves are loved by one and all. Easter 2009 saw the opening of a play barn in the old manufacturing space at the back of the premises. Painting tables and a basket of toys are an additional attraction for children, and the centre can arrange parties for all occasions, with any of the resident facilities and

extras such as model-making workshops. The Centre, which is run by Eric and Alison's daughter Sarah, is open seven days a week, from 9.30 to 5 in summer and from 10 to 4.30 in winter.

🏠 historic building 🏛 museum and heritage 🏚 historic site 🐾 scenic attraction 🌿 flora and fauna

CLEDAN VALLEY TIPI HOLIDAYS

4 Bankhouses, Carno, nr Caersws, Powys SY17 5LR
Tel: 01686 420409
e-mail: tipis@cledanvalleytipi.co.uk
website: www.cledanvalleytipi.co.uk

Cledan Valley Tipi Holidays offers self-catering holidays with a difference in the peaceful, tranquil heart of mid-Wales, a million miles from the rush and routine of daily life, but easy to find signed off the A470 at Carno. From Easter to October eight American Indian-style tepees on a eight acre woodland site are available for hire, each positioned to maximise the special nature of the site. The smallest is for 2, the largest sleeps up to 8. They are provided with sheepskin rugs, throws, scatter cushions and futons, along with camping-style gas cookers, a cool box and a torch. The site has a shower/toilet block with its own solar lighting. This is a holiday for the outdoor enthusiast, with great walking, birdwatching and a host of other activities almost outside the tipi-flap.

fall in 1985. In the hills of Trannon Moor near the village is the National Wind Power's **Carno Wind Farm**, a site containing dozens of turbines that generate enough electricity to meet the needs of many thousand, homes. The plateau on which the farm is located is visited by over 30 bird species, including red kite, hen harrier, buzzard, red grouse, curlew and golden plover. The site access road is located off the A470 at the northern end of Carno village. Visitors can walk along the marked public footpaths that cross the site; there is an information board at the car park.

LLANBRYNMAIR

8½ miles E of Machynlleth on the B4518

🏛 Parish Church of St Mary   🏛 Machinations

🐾 Rev Samuel Roberts

On the banks of the River Twymyn, this village was the home for many years of the social reformer, **Rev Samuel Roberts**, who worked hard for the principles of social equality and was a leader of non-conformist opinion. He was also an advocate of free trade, Catholic emancipation and temperance, and in 1827 he advanced a plan for an inland penny postal service. Between 1857 and 1867

he was in America with his brother, Richard Roberts, preaching racial equality.

The **Parish Church of St Mary** is essentially 14th and 15th centuries, and stands on the site of an earlier building. It has an unusual bell turret supported by four wood uprights, and there are fragments of medieval glass in one of the windows.

In the village you will find **Machinations**, a museum dedicated to automata – figures driven by clockwork, electricity, wind or hand. These mechanical models are fascinating, and there are courses available, on constructing, painting and carving them.

DYLIFE

8½ miles SE of Machynlleth off the B4518

🏞 Dylife Gorge   🌿 Glaslyn Nature Reserve

Apart from an inn and a few houses, there is little left of this once prosperous lead mining community. A footpath from the settlement passes close to a grassy mound, which was once a Roman fort, built to guard the nearby lead mines. The path continues past more redundant lead mines that were last worked during the late 17th century, before it meanders through a woodland, following the

🎭 stories and anecdotes 🐦 famous people ⚘ art and craft 🎪 entertainment and sport 🏃 walks

banks of River Clywedog, and on towards Staylittle. The final part of the route lies close to Bronze Age tumuli, which suggest that mining occurred in the area even before the Roman occupation. Close to the village is **Glaslyn Nature Reserve**, a 540-acre tract of heather moorland that is the breeding site for the wheatear, golden plover, ring ousel and red grouse. **Dylife Gorge**, to the west of the village, was gouged from the landscape during the last Ice Age.

STAYLITTLE
11 miles SE of Machynlleth on the B4518

🏃 Hafren Forest   🏃 Plynlimon

A one-time lead mining village, Staylittle is said to have derived its name from the village's two blacksmiths who shoed horses so rapidly that their forge became known as Stay-a-Little. Situated in a remote area high in the Cambrian Mountains, Staylittle is on the edge of the **Hafren Forest**, which has several waymarked trails through the forest, along the banks of the upper River Severn and up to **Plynlimon**, which rises to 2,500 feet.

LLANIDLOES
16½ miles SE of Machynlleth on the A470

🏠 Market Hall   🏠 Llanidloes Castle

🏚 Van Lead Mine   🏠 Parish Church of St Idloes

🏛 Llanidloes Museum   🏚 Bryn Tail Lead Mine

🏞 Llyn Clywedog   🏞 Fan Hill

🎨 Minerva Arts Centre

🏃 Llyn Clywwedog Scenic Trail   🏃 Cascades Trail

🏃 Clywedog Gorge Trail   🏃 Aber Biga Wildlife Walk

This peaceful little market town, which sits at the exact centre of Wales, is certainly one of the area's most attractive, and its adaptability, from a rural village to a weaving town and now to a centre for craftspeople, has ensured that it is likely to remain so for many years to come. John Wesley preached here three times in the mid-1700s and the stone from which he addressed his audience can be seen outside the town's old **Market Hall**, which dates from 1609 and stands on wooden stilts. It was used by Quakers, Methodists and Baptists before those religious groups had their own premises, and has also been a courthouse, a library and a working men's institute. The upper floors now house the **Llanidloes Museum**, where there are displays and information on the textile and mining industries that thrived in the area during the 18th and 19th centuries. There is also a natural history exhibition and the red kite centre.

In 1839, the town was a focal point of the bitter Chartist Riots after the Reform Bill of 1832 had failed to meet

Llyn Clywedog Reservoir, Llanidloes

🏠 historic building 🏛 museum and heritage 🏚 historic site 🏞 scenic attraction 🌿 flora and fauna

L'ARMOIRE FASHION HOUSE

Plynlimon House, Llanidloes, Powys SY18 6EF
Tel: 01686 414803
e-mail: laura@larmoire.co.uk
website: www.larmoire.co.uk

A stylish recent addition to the attractions of Llanidloes is L'Armoire Fashion House, opened by Laura Thomas in March 2009.

In French, L'Armoire means 'The Wardrobe' and if you could fill your own wardrobe with a selection of the wonderful designer products on offer here, that would surely be sartorial heaven. Amongst the roll-call of famous names are Joseph Ribkoff, Oui Moments, Rouge and Betty Barclay. There are items from Catherine Andre, exclusive to Wales, along with pieces from Crea Concept and Gold.

To complement these elegant creations, L'Armoire also stocks jewellery by Barbara Easton, About Face, Jackie Brazil and Amber Moda, as well as hosiery from Cette and Gypsy. An aromatic collection of French soaps and perfumes is also available. Everything is displayed with great imagination and flair, making this a superb place to browse. But once you've seen the to-die-for fashion on show, you'll certainly want to do more than just browse! L'Armoire is open from 9.30am to 5pm, Monday to Saturday.

demands that included universal suffrage and social equality. Cheap labour, cheap wool and efficient new machinery had led to a boom in the wool and flannel trade in Llanidloes, as it had in Newtown, Machynlleth and Welshpool. Workmen flooded in, and in 1858 the population was more then 4,000. But the boom did not last, the factories closed, and unemployment inevitably ensued. Chartist propaganda reached the town and the Llanidloes unions adopted the charter. The crowds started to gather and to arm, the police moved in, and the Chartist leaders were arrested but were released by the crowd. The magistrates fled, and the Chartists ruled for a few days. Mills were re-opened and the prices of goods fixed. Then the Montgomeryshire Yeomanry came on the scene, 32 arrests were made and the Chartist ringleaders put on trial at Welshpool. Three were transported and the rest served terms of hard labour.

The Chartists originated in London in 1837, when a People's Charter was drawn up by the London Working Men's Association. Their six main demands were: equal electoral areas; universal suffrage; payment for MPs; no property qualifications for voters; vote by ballot; and annual parliaments. Support for the Charter spread quickly through Britain, with the Welsh miners especially vociferous. A petition with 1¼ million signatures was rejected by Parliament in 1839, and riots ensued in Lancashire, Yorkshire and Wales. In 1842, another petition, this one with 3½ million signatures, was rejected. The Chartist movement then went into something of a decline, and the repeal of the Corn Laws in 1846 helped to better the lot of the working classes.

The town has many arts and crafts shops and galleries featuring the work of local artists and craftspeople. **Minerva Arts Centre**, in

MOUNT SEVERN

Glan-y-Nant, Llanidloes, Powys SY18 6PQ
Tel: 01686 412344
e-mail: info@mountsevern.co.uk
website: www.mountsevern.co.uk

Few hotels offer a wider range of options than **Mount Severn**, a Grade II listed Georgian country house standing off the A470 a mile west of Llanidloes. Guests can choose anything from total rest and relaxation to non-stop action in and around this handsome, beautifully situated property. It nestles in 14 acres of woodland and grounds featuring superb trees, rhododendrons and azaleas. The grounds slope down to the banks of the River Severn, whose source is only ten miles away; the cool, clean waters are ideal for swimming or paddling, and a weir at this point facilitates canoeing and kayaking upstream. The ten en suite bedrooms are decorated and furnished to a very high standard: owner Joycelin Gray has two young children and is always pleased to welcome families with youngsters – two of the rooms interconnect. Day rooms include sitting rooms and a library, and a sumptuous breakfast using local produce ensures that the day gets off to a fine start. The area is full of things to see and do, from touring, walking and cycling to discovering the diverse wildlife and watching the red kites at their feeding stations. As well as being a great base for a leisurely holiday Mount Severn is also a popular conference and wedding venue and an activity centre that caters for anything from school trips to leadership courses, management development, organised trekking, water-borne sports and a host of other indoor and outdoor activities.

the High Street is the home of the Quilt Association and its unique collection of antique Welsh quilts. Exhibitions are held here, as are workshops and other events.

Llanidloes Castle has all but vanished, though there is a portion of the motte still standing. It was built by Owain de la Pole in 1280, when a charter for a weekly market was granted. The tower of the **Parish Church of St Idloes** dates from the 14th century, while the rest of the church is later. It is the only church in the country with a dedication to St Idloes, who was born in the 7th century, the son of Gwyddnabi ab Llawfronedd, described as a 'red-bearded knight'.

The Severn Way and Glyndwr's Way cross in Llanidloes, and an interesting marked five-mile walk covers sections of each. Five miles to the northwest of the town lies **Llyn Clywedog**, a reservoir that was developed in

the mid-1960s to regulate the flows of the Rivers Severn and Clywedog. Birds such as buzzards and red kite are frequently seen around the shores of the lake, as are occasional ospreys. Roads follow around both sides of the lake, with the B4518 curving round the slopes of the 1,580, foot **Fan Hill** where the chimneys of the now disused **Van Lead Mine** are still visible. It was once one of the most prosperous mines in this area of Wales, and it is recorded that in 1876, 6,850 tons of lead were produced. The deserted houses and chapels of the village that grew up around the mine add a sombre, evocative note.

There are a number of way-marked routes and walks in the area. The **Llyn Clyywedog Scenic Trail**, the **Clywedog Gorge Trail** and the **Aber Biga Wildlife Walk** on the lake's shores are short walks suitable for able-bodied families, whereas the **Cascades Trail** in the nearby Hafren Forest is suitable for wheelchairs. A booklet is available that explains cycle routes, including one round the lake. The remains of the **Bryn Tail Lead Mine** sit at the foot of the reservoir's dam, which rises to a height of 237 feet. The lake is well-stocked with rainbow and brown trout, and hosts fishing competitions.

Newtown

🏛 Parish Church of St Mary 🏛 Textile Museum

🏛 Robert Owen Memorial Museum

🏛 W H Smith Museum

📷 Pwll Penarth Nature Reserve

The name has not been appropriate for centuries, as Newtown's origins date from around 973 AD, though it only came to prominence after being granted a market charter by Edward I in 1279. This was a centre for textiles and weaving and, by the 19th century, was the home of the Welsh flannel industry that led it to be referred to as the "Leeds of Wales". Some of the brick buildings were built with a third or even fourth storey with large windows to let in light for the looms. One such building now houses the town's **Textile Museum**, which tells the story of this once important industry and also gives a very good impression of the working conditions of the people, which Newtown's

W H Smith Museum

24 High Street, Newtown, Powys SY16 2NP
Tel: 01686 626280

This Newtown shop and museum form a unique combination amoung W H Smith's many High Street branches. The shop has been restored to its original state at the time it was first opened in 1927, and on the first floor you will find the museum.

The museum houses displays, models and memorabilia which depict and engrossing chronicle of W H Smith from its beginnings as a humble news walk (paper round) started by Henry Walton Smith and Anna Smith in 1792, to the present day. The history tells how a small family-run business flourished over two centuries to become one of today's biggest British companies and a household name. The oak furniture in the museum all originated in W H Smith libraries. A stained and painted window, originally in the library at Worcester branch, depicts the arms of the See of Worcester, bordered by the images of Shakespeare and Bacon. This type of window was once a common feature in W H Smith shops, often portraying local coats of arms and literary figures.

The shop was restored to its original condition in 1975. Architects worked from the old blueprints and drawings and specialist craftsmen were engaged to recreate long-varnished fixtures and fittings. Modern peg-boarding and hessian was ripped from the walls to reveal beneath all the original mirrors and decorations which, miraculously, were in good condition.

The museum is open to the public during the shop's business hours; 9am - 5.30pm

PENARTH VINEYARD

Pool Road, Newtown, Montgomeryshire, Powys SY16 3AN
Tel: 01686 610383 (Visitor Centre) 01686 622550 (Shop)
e-mail: info@penarthvineyard.co.uk
website: www.penarthvineyard.co.uk

Penarth Vineyard is located two miles outside Newtown on the A483 towards Welshpool, in a lovely ten-acre site by the River Severn in the Montgomeryshire part of Powys. In the unique eco-climate of this part of Wales some varieties thought unsuited to the UK climate thrive, facing the elements and developing rich flavours and deep character.

Here they grow several grape varieties, notably Pinot Noir, Pinot Meunier and Chardonnay, along with some hybrid and experimental varieties.

The first vines were planted here in 1999, the next in the following year, and in 2002 the young vines had developed enough good fruit flavour for the first crop to be harvested. The first wine produced was a sparkling pink made with Pinot Noir and Pinot Meunier, with a soft berry fruit aroma and harmonious tannin that create an impressive depth of flavour in the mouth. Traditional methods are used: the wine spends two years in stainless steel tanks on lees, followed by 12 months bottle maturation that produces wines that can genuinely be judged the equal of French counterparts. The other main wines are Blanc de Blanc (Chardonnay), 'lees-led', with less fruit taste bit a fuller effect and a gooseberry finish, and the still Pinot Noir, full of fruit, with strawberry overtones that develop a cherry finish with age. The wines are actually produced at the renowned Three Choirs Vineyard in Newent under the expert care of master winemaker Martin Fawkes and his team, always with the involvement of the Penarth Vineyard management.

The wines are sold in restaurants in Wales and in London, in delis and farm shops throughout Wales, from an outlet at the entrance to the vineyard and online through the website. The farm shop on site sells a wide variety of home-grown vegetables and other top-quality Welsh produce, hampers, picnics and plants.

Visitors to Penarth get a real feel of the country as well the chance to tour the site, either making their own way round or on a pre-booked guided tour or evening wine tasting. Another attraction is the owners' string of straight Egyptian Arabian horses, wonderful creatures with a really lovely nature. Penarth Vineyard is open from 12 to 5, Easter to 1st January.

🏚 historic building 🏛 museum and heritage 🏛 historic site 🏞 scenic attraction 🌿 flora and fauna

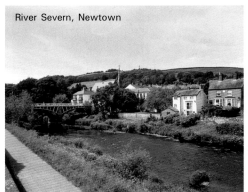

River Severn, Newtown

The former **Parish Church of St Mary** was abandoned in the 1840s due to flooding, and replaced by St David's Church. Its ruined nave originally had a south aisle, and the lower stages of the tower are 13th century. Its 15th-century screen was moved to St David's and can be seen there. In the churchyard is the grave of Robert Owen. The grave has magnificent Art Nouveau iron railings, and his monument depicts the man with his workers.

most famous son, Robert Owen, devoted much of his life to changing. Born in Newtown in 1771, Owen grew from a humble background to become a social reformer and the founder of the co-operative movement, who lobbied vigorously for an improvement in working conditions specifically within the textile industry. He is particularly associated with the New Lanark mills in Scotland, which he ran and partly owned. The workforce at New Lanark numbered 2,000, including 500 children, and Owen provided good housing, cheap goods and an infant's school. His remarkable life is told at the intimate **Robert Owen Memorial Museum**.

Another interesting visit to consider while in Newtown is to the **WH Smith Museum** (see panel on page 151), where the shop has been restored to its original 1927 layout, and devotes much of its space to the history of the booksellers from 1792 onwards. The people of Newtown must certainly be an enterprising lot as it was here that the first ever mail-order company was begun in 1859 by a man called Pryce-Jones. The business started in a small way with Welsh flannel, but expanded rapidly, and Pryce-Jones even obtained the Royal seal of approval by having Queen Victoria on his list.

Two miles east of Newtown is **Pwll Penarth Nature Reserve**, a feeding and nesting site for many species of wildfowl. The reserve has a nature walk and two hides, one accessible to wheelchairs.

Around Newtown

TREGYNON
4½ miles N of Newtown on the B4389

🌿 Gregynon Hall Gardens

Just to the south of the village lies **Gregynon Hall Gardens**, which are now part of the University of Wales, and where visitors can wander through the extensive woodlands on waymarked paths. Renowned for its spring bulbs, the sunken lawns before the house are associated with an unfinished design by William Emes. There is also a remarkable golden yew hedge. The hall is the setting for an annual music festival.

LLANFAIR CAEREINION
9 miles N of Newtown on the B4385

🚂 Welshpool and Llanfair Railway

🚂 Great Little Trains of Wales

This village is the western terminus of the **Welshpool and Llanfair Railway**. Passengers

🎭 stories and anecdotes 🦅 famous people 🎨 art and craft 🏃 entertainment and sport 🚶 walks

GOTTSCHALK STUDIOS

Penybryn, Manafon, Welshpool, Powys SY21 8BP
Tel: 01686 650678/ 01938 811724 Fax: 01938 811724
e-mail: gottschalkstudios@mac.com
website: web.me.com/gottschalkstudios/paulgottschalk

Working and living with his wife and seven children form his
home amidst the mid Wales hills and drawing on his 25 years
experience, Paul creates individual, one-off, contemporary sculpture, forge and metalwork pieces.
Should you want hooks upon which to hang your coats, a table at which to enjoy your meal,
unusual railings and gating with which to define your space or a stunning spatially enriching
sculpture, please contact Paul and Jenny. Visit strictly by appointment only.

at Llanfair can enjoy re-living the days of
steam, but also relax in the Edwardian style
tearooms at the station. The narrow-gauge
railway was originally opened to carry sheep,
cattle and goods, as well as passengers. It now
travels without the animals and goods but
with happy passengers, along the delightful
Banwy Valley, its carriages pulled by scaled-
down versions of steam locomotives from
Finland, Austria, Sierra Leone, Antigua and
Manchester. There are nine members of the
narrow-gauge **Great Little Trains of Wales**
(GLTOW): Bala Lake Railway; Brecon
Mountain Railway (Merthyr Tydfil); Ffestiniog
Railway (Porthmadog); Llanberis Lake
Railway; Rheilfford Eryri (Caernarfon);
Talyllin Railway (Tywyn); Vale of Rheidol
Railway (Aberystwyth); Welsh Highland
Railway (Caernarfon to Porthmadog); and the
Welshpool and Llanfair Railway.

MONTGOMERY

7 miles NE of Newtown on the B4385

🏠 Montgomery Castle   🗡 Robber's Grave

🏠 Parish Church of St Nicholas   🏛 Fridd Faldwyn

🏠 Hen Domen Castle   🏛 Old Bell Museum

Montgomery is an attractive market town with
a pleasant Georgian character, and also some
surviving Tudor and Jacobean buildings that
are worthy of note. Above the town, the ruins

of **Montgomery Castle** stand in affirmation
of this borderland region's turbulent history.
The first castle was built in around 1100 by
the Norman, Roger de Montgomery. Attacked
over the years by rebels, it was rebuilt in 1223
as a garrison when Henry III was attempting
to quell the Welsh, a consequence being that

Montgomery Castle

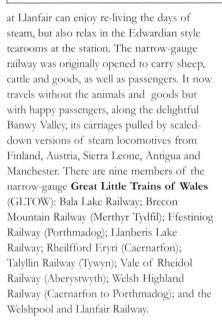

🏠 historic building 🏛 museum and heritage 🏛 historic site 🌱 scenic attraction 🌿 flora and fauna

the town received a charter from the king in 1227. During the Civil War, the castle surrendered to Parliamentary forces, but was demolished in 1649 in punishment for the then Lord Herbert's Royalist sympathies. The remains of the castle are open at all times and entrance is free. Access is up steep paths from the town, or by a level footpath from the car park, and the visit is worth it for the views alone. One mile from the town is the motte of yet another ancient castle – **Hen Domen**, again built by Roger de Montgomery.

Offa's Dyke (see Prestatyn) passes close by and is another reminder of the military significance that this area once held. In Arthur Street, the **Old Bell Museum** has 11 rooms of local history including features on civic and social life, Norman and medieval castles, the workhouse and the Cambrian Railway.

The 13th-century **Parish Church of St Nicholas** has some interesting features, including wooden carved angels, carved miserere seats, and the magnificent canopied tomb of Richard Herbert, Lord of Montgomery Castle. In the churchyard is the famous **Robber's Grave**. John Davis, hanged in public in 1821 for murder, proclaimed his innocence and swore that the grass would not grow above his grave for at least 100 years.

To the west of the town, the Iron Age hill fort of **Fridd Faldwyn** tops a 750-foot hill that also provides stunning views to Cadair Idris and eastwards into England.

THE HERBERT ARMS

Chirbury, Montgomery, Powys SY15 6BG
Tel: 01938 561216
website: www.herbertarmschirbury.co.uk

The Herbert Arms is a pleasant old inn located in the village of Chirbury, at the junction of the A490 and B4386 close to Montgomery on the border with Shropshire. Sisters Kathryn and Sarah acquired the premises in 2008, and with Sarah's partner Stéphane they have expanded its role from country local (a role it still fulfils admirably) to a destination dining pub that attracts lovers of good food from all over the region.

The interior is inviting and unpretentious, with cosy fires and quarry-tiled floor, and in the restaurant at the rear happy diners return time after time to savour a memorable culinary experience. 'The Frenchman and the Farmers' Daughters' wow the customers with classic-inspired cuisine bringing top-notch cooking (Stephane's CV includes 7 years at Michel Roux's Waterside Inn) based on the very best seasonal produce, sourced locally wherever possible. A typical evening menu, with about half a dozen choices for each course, might include homemade black pudding with caramelised apples and Madeira sauce; vintage cheddar cheese souffle with pickled beetroot salad; crisp pork belly, roasted pear & braising jus, roast lemon sole, crushed potato & bouillabaisse, dark chocolate & caramelised walnut delice and iced prune & armagnac parfait. Special dietary requirements can be catered for with a little notice.

The Herbert Arms is open for food lunch and dinner Wednesday to Saturday and lunch on Sundays.The bar is open Tuesday evening, Wednesday and Thursday lunchtime and evening and all day Friday to Sunday.

BERRIEW

7½ miles NE of Newtown on the B4390

🏛 Parish Church of St Beuno   🏛 Glansevern Hall

🏛 Maen Beuno

Over the years, this picturesque village of half-timbered houses beside the River Rhiw has been a frequent winner of Best Kept Village awards. Like a number of other places in Wales, Berriew is associated with St Beuno who apparently heard English voices while communing by the river here and warned the villagers of the imposing threat. A large glacial boulder, **Maen Beuno**, has been named after him. Berriew's **Parish Church of St Beuno** contains fine marble effigies of Arthur Price, Sheriff of Montgomeryshire in 1578, and his two wives, Bridget and Jane. The memorial cross of 1933 in the churchyard is by Sir Ninian Comper, whose work can be seen in churches all over Britain. Though there has

been a church on the site for centuries, the present church dates from 1802, with a complete refurbishment undertaken in 1875.

The Gardens at **Glansevern Hall** (see panel below), entered from the A483 by the bridge over the River Rhiew, were first laid out in 1801 and now cover 18 acres. Noted in particular for the unusual tree species, they also have lovely lawns, herbaceous beds, a walled garden, rose gardens, a lovely water garden and a rock garden complete with grotto. In the Old Stables are a tearoom, a garden shop and a gallery with regular exhibitions of paintings, sculpture and interior design. A wide variety of herbaceous plants, all grown at Glansevern, can be bought. Surrounding a very handsome Greek Revival house, the gardens are themselves set in parkland on the banks of the River Severn. Built for Arthur Davies Owen, Glansevern was the seat of the Owen family from 1800 until after World War II.

🏛 historic building 🏛 museum and heritage 🏛 historic site ⚜ scenic attraction 🌿 flora and fauna

CHURCH STOKE

10½ miles E of Newtown on the A489

🏚 Bacheldre Mill   🏚 Simon's Castle

🏚 Parish Church of St Nicholas

This attractive village, sometimes spelled as "Churchstoke" lies right on the Welsh-English border. Just to the west can be found some very visible and well preserved sections of Offa's Dyke (see Prestatyn). At Bacheldre, two miles along the A489, **Bacheldre Mill** is a fully restored watermill producing award-winning organic stoneground flour. Visitors can enjoy a guided tour and even mill their own flour. **Simon's Castle**, to the east of the village, is a motte and bailey site that was probably built in the 12th or 13th centuries. The **Parish Church of St Nicholas** is unusual, as it lies in England, while its parish is in Wales. Its tower is 13th century, and during the Civil War, when Royalist troops took refuge in the building, Parliamentarians set fire to the door to flush them out. The church was rebuilt in the early 19th century, and up until 1881 was dedicated to St Mary.

ABERMULE

4 miles NE of Newtown on the B4386

🏚 Dolforwyn Castle   🎞 Abermule Train Disaster

Across the Montgomery Canal and River Severn from this village, which is also known by its Welsh name Abermiwl, lie the scant remains of **Dolforwyn Castle**, which was built in 1273 by Llywelyn the Last (he was the last native ruler of Wales). This was the last castle to have been built by a native Welsh prince on his own soil, and Llywelyn also tried to establish a small town around the castle to rival that of nearby, and much anglicised, Welshpool. However, the castle was only a Welsh stronghold for four years before it was taken by the English and left to decay into the haunting ruins you see today. The **Abermule Train Disaster** took place in 1921, when 17 people were killed as two trains collided head on. Human error was found to be the cause. A double track was later laid, but curiously, as part of the Beeching cuts in the early 1960s, it reverted to single track.

KERRY

2½ miles SE of Newtown on the A489

🏚 Parish Church of St Michael and All Angels

Situated on the banks of the River Mule, a tributary of the River Severn, this village lies in the heart of sheep rearing country and has given its name to the Kerry Hills breed of sheep characterised by distinctive black spots on their faces and legs. Small, hornless and usually white apart from the markings, the Kerry Hills have very dense fleeces that are particularly suitable for dyeing in pastel shades for knitting yarns. This breed is one of several variants on the Welsh Mountain sheep. Others include Black Welsh Mountain, Badger-faced Welsh Mountain, Beulah Speckle Face, Lleyn and Llanwenog.

The **Parish Church of St Michael and All Angels** dates originally from 1176, though only the nave's north arcade survives from that time. The tower is 14th century, as is the chancel arcade. The rest dates from a rebuild in the 1880s. It has a chained Welsh Bible of 1690. There was, in former times, a custom at the church that the sexton would 'patrol' the congregation during services and ring a bell if he found anyone asleep.

LLANDINAM

5½ miles SW of Newtown on the A470

🏚 Parish Church of St Llonio   🐑 David Davies

This quiet village was the home of **David

🎞 stories and anecdotes 🐑 famous people 🎨 art and craft 🖋 entertainment and sport 🚶 walks

Davies, an industrialist who was instrumental in founding the docks at Barry in South Wales. Davies' bronze statue, made by the same Sir Alfred Gilbert who was responsible for Eros in Piccadilly, stands in the village. It has been awarded the title of the "Best Kept Village in Wales, Powys and Montgomeryshire" on a number of occasions. It is well worth visiting to view its black and white timbered buildings. During World War IIGordonstoun School was evacuated to here. Don't miss the **Parish Church of St Llonio.** Though largely rebuilt in the 19th century, it has a 13th-century tower, two old tomb recesses and a 17th-century reredos and carved choir stalls.

CAERSWS
4 miles W of Newtown on the A470

🌿 Llyn Mawr Reserve   🐿 John 'Ceiriog' Hughes

The village is built on the site of a 1st century Roman fort that was strategically positioned here by the Rivers Severn and Carno and, to the north, the remains of an earthwork fort can still be seen. In more recent times, Caersws was the home, for some 20 years, of the poet **John 'Ceiriog' Hughes,** who was then the manager of the local Van Railway. Born at Llan Dyffryn Ceiriog in 1833, when he was 17, he took employment on the railways in Manchester. In 1865, he became

stationmaster at Llanidloes and six years later took over at Caersws, managing the six-mile railway that ran to the Van lead mines. It is said that many people came to Caersws just for the delight of having a chat to the affable poet. Hughes lies buried in the graveyard at the nearby village of Llanwnog. Near Caersws, signposted off the A470 Machynlleth road, **Llyn Mawr Reserve** is a 20-acre lake with a wetland habitat noted for wetland birds such as the great crested grebe, tufted duck, snipe and curlew.

Welshpool

🏛 Strata Marcella   🏛 Cockpit

🏛 Powysland Museum   🏛 Grace Evans' Cottage

🏛 Montgomery Canal Centre   🌄 Long Mountain

🏚 Welshpool and Llanfair Railway

🌿 Severn Farm Pond Nature Reserve

This bustling market town, which was granted a charter in 1263 by the Prince of Powys, was, for a long time, known as Pool, - the Welsh prefix was added in 1835 to settle the long running dispute concerning its nationality, as it sits no more than four miles from the English border. As is typical with many places in the upper Severn Valley, Welshpool has numerous examples of picturesque, half-timbered

---

FEAST OF FOOD

2 Station Road, Caersws, Powys SY17 5EQ
Tel: 01686 689149

Lavinia Vaughan opened her shop **Feast of Food** in September 2007 with the intention of supporting local producers. So, amongst the extensive stock you'll find Welsh cheeses and beers, Shropshire bacon and sausages and locally produced cider and apple juice, meat pies, quiches, cakes, chocolates and organic vegetables. As Lavinia says "We don't stock local just for the sake of stocking local, or as a marketing gimmick, we stock what is right - real food, ethically produced and with low food miles whenever possible". Feast of Food is open from 10am to 6pm, Monday - Saturday.

🏛 historic building 🏛 museum and heritage 🏚 historic site 🌄 scenic attraction 🌿 flora and fauna

buildings, and that alone makes the place well worth visiting.

Housed in a former warehouse beside the Montgomery Canal is the **Powysland Museum**, which was founded in 1874 by Morris Jones. Earlier, many of the artefacts that formed the museum's original collection had been put together by the Powysland Club – a group of Victorian gentlemen who were interested in the history of mid-Wales. The museum covers various aspects of the region: the development of life in Montgomeryshire from the earliest times to the 20th century; local agriculture and farming equipment; and the building of the first canals and railways in the area.

Montgomery Canal, Welshpool

Along with the museum, the old warehouse is also home to the **Montgomery Canal Centre** where the story of this waterway is told. Completed in 1821, the canal carried coal and food from Welshpool to the upper reaches of the River Severn. Though, as with other canals, its decline came with the arrival of the railways, the section of the canal around Welshpool is once again open, and is now, used for pleasure cruises.

Near the town are the scant remains – no more than a few bumps in field – of **Strata Marcella**, the Cistercian abbey founded around 1170 by Owain Cyfeiliog, Prince of Powys. It was one of the largest Cistercian houses in Wales, with a church that was 273 feet long. When Henry VIII dissolved the abbeys in 1536, his men turned up at Strata Marcella to discover that it had already been dissolved by the monks themselves the year before. They had sold it to Lord Powis, who, by the time Henry's men turned up, had stripped it of everything that was of value. Lord Powis had even sold the stones from

which it was built, and they ended up in many churches and houses in the area.

The town is also home to two other interesting buildings, the **Cockpit** and **Grace Evans' Cottage**. The only surviving cockpit on its original site in Wales, this venue for the bloodthirsty sport was built in the 18th century and remained in use until the sport was banned in Britain in 1849. Grace Evans is certainly one of the town's best known citizens as she was instrumental in rescuing Lord Nithsdale (who was in disguise as a lady) from the Tower of London in 1716. As Lady Nithsdale's maid, Grace fled with the couple to France, but she returned to Welshpool in 1735 and lived at the cottage, which is said to have been given to her by a grateful Lord Nithsdale, until her death three years later.

At the southern edge of town on Severn Farm Industrial Estate is Severn Farm Pond, one of 13 nature reserves managed by the Montgomeryshire Wildlife Trust. This one is a particularly good site for dragonflies, damselflies and amphibia.

CROMWELL'S RESTAURANT

High Street, Welshpool, North Powys SY21 7JP
Tel: 01938 552658

With its striking 16th century Tudor frontage, **Cromwell's Restaurant** in Welshpool's High Street looks particularly inviting. Debbie Jandrell took over here in the autumn of 2006 and quickly established a reputation for serving wholesome and appetising food. Sunday lunches are a speciality but at other times you can enjoy dishes such as lasagne, chicken curry, Cheddar pie and an authentic Welsh Rarebit as well as vegetarian options. The home-made cakes and scones are especially popular. Cromwell's is licensed, is open every day and, in good weather, customers can enjoy their food at tables outside.

THE RAVEN INN

Raven Square, Welshpool, Powys SY21 7LT
Tel: 01938 553070
e-mail: steve.raveninn@btconnect.com
website: www.theraven-inn.co.uk

Located next to the eastern terminus of the Welshpool and Llanfair Light Railway, the **Raven Inn** has been known for a decade as one of the best places in the area for dining, thanks to award-winning Head Chef Stephen Griffiths. His menu is based on top quality local produce with Welsh beef and lamb featuring prominently along with fresh fish dishes of the day. Once a month, the Raven hosts a themed food evening and also has regular live music sessions. Children are welcome - they have their own menu and a play area in the eye-catching beer garden.

The **Severn Farm Pond Nature Reserve** sits in an industrial estate, however it attracts many birds, animals and insects, especially in the newly created ponds and wetland areas. **Long Mountain** stretches four miles along the Welsh side of the border east of Welshpool. It is crossed by Offa's Dyke (see Prestatyn) and on its highest point is an ancient hill fort known as Beacon Ring. It was on Long Mountain that Henry Tudor camped in 1485 before crossing the border, defeating Richard III at Bosworth Field and ascending the throne of England as Henry VII. Henry Tudor had a Red Dragon as his standard, and as king he incorporated the Welsh dragon into the Royal arms. There it stayed until James I displaced it with the Scottish unicorn. In 1901, the Red Dragon was officially recognised as the Royal Badge of Wales, and in 1959 the

Queen commanded that the Red Dragon on its green and white field should be the official Welsh flag.

Just to the southwest of the town lies one of the best known places in the area – **Powis Castle**. Inhabited for around 500 years, the various alterations that have taken place here over the years now cause the castle to look more like a mansion. The remains of a Norman motte and bailey are thought to be from the original castle, which is believed to have been built on this site in the early 12th century and was then destroyed during a dispute between Llywelyn the Great and Gruffydd ap Gwenwynwyn, a local landowner. Edward I granted the family a barony on condition that they renounced their Welsh title, which they subsequently did, and so the castle seen today was built. 2002 marked the 50th year

REVELLS BISTRO & RESTAURANT

Berriew Street, Welshpool, Powys SY21 7SQ
Tel: 01938 559000
e-mail: craig@revellsbistro.co.uk
website: www.revellsbistro.co.uk

Revells Bistro & Restaurant occupies a beautifully restored Art Deco cinema which originally opened in 1938. Craig and Rhian Humphreys took over here in 1991 and have firmly established Revells as one of the best places in the area to enjoy good food and good company. The restaurant has a very relaxed and welcoming atmosphere, with lots of antique furniture and vintage photographs of old Welshpool around the walls. At lunchtimes (from noon until 3pm) the menu offers an excellent choice that includes home-made lasagne, quiche and soup, as well as a wide selection of pasta dishes, char-grilled steaks, roasts, vegetarian options, paninis, baguettes and filled croissants. At other times, light snacks, freshly baked cakes and speciality coffees are all available. The evening menu, served from 6.30pm to 9.30pm, varies but includes quality dishes such as Welsh rack of lamb, pan seared Queen Scallops and home-made Gnocchi. Children are welcome at Revells (there are even toys for them to play with), and there are newspapers for the adults.

Every other weekend Revells hosts either a food themed evening - Italian, Spanish, French and Fresh Fish, for example - or live music by groups from around the world.

DINGLE NURSERIES & GARDEN

Welshpool, Powys SY21 9JD
Tel: 01938 555145 Fax: 01938 555778
e-mail: info@dinglenurseryandgarden.co.uk
website: www.dinglenurseryandgarden.co.uk

Set in the heart of rural Wales, 700 feet above sea level, **Dingle Nurseries & Garden** is a thriving family-run nursery with the added attraction of a quite superb garden. Barbara and Roy Joseph were the first to diversify the site into horticulture and their son, Andy and his family, now run a business that supplies plants all over the UK. The nursery has a specialist range of roses, along with herbaceous perennials, alpines, ornamental grasses and herbs, bare-rooted trees and hedging plants. Trees are the speciality, many of which are grown on site thus guaranteeing the highest quality.

A unique and glorious feature of the Dingle is the remarkable 4-acre garden, an inspiration to gardeners and lovers of gardens, and the subject of frequent TV programmes and articles in gardening publications. This beautiful secluded garden slopes away from the house on a south-facing site and contains a lake and woodland tracts.

The Dingle's opening hours are from 9am to 5pm, seven days a week (closed Christmas week).

📽 stories and anecdotes 🦜 famous people 🎨 art and craft 🎭 entertainment and sport 🚶 walks

Powis Castle, Welshpool

of the castle being in the hands of the National Trust, and the occasion was celebrated by a series of special events, all with a golden theme.

From the town, the narrow gauge **Welshpool and Llanfair Railway** takes passengers on a steam train journey through the Powis estates and the delightful Banwy valley to Llanfair Caereinion.

Around Welshpool

GUILSFIELD
2½ miles N of Welshpool on the B4392

🏛 Parish Church of St Aelhaiarn   🏛 Gaer Fawr

The large 15th-century **Parish Church of St Aelhaiarn** is well worth a second glance as, not only does it have an unusual upper chamber above the south porch, but there is also a splendid panelled roof from the same date and some fine 19th-century vaulting.

DERWEN GARDEN CENTRE & FARM SHOP

Guilsfield, Welshpool, Powys SY21 9PH
Tel: 01938 553015 Fax: 01938 556170
e-mail: info@derwengardencentre.co.uk
website: www.derwengardencentre.co.uk

The Derwen Garden Centre, lies just north of Welshpool off the B4392 and is a place to inspire gardeners and delight children. Here you can wander round fifteen show gardens each with its own theme from Gothic to Italian, Celtic to Seaside and more. The trees and shrubs, lush perennials, aquatic plants and climbers so beautifully displayed in the gardens can all be found in the Derwen's vast garden centre as can the statuary and pots that furnish the gardens.

Furnishings of a different kind can be found in what is an Aladin's cave of desirable objects from all over the world. Browsing is a great delight in a place like this and visitors can also pause to enjoy delicious home-cooked lunches, morning coffee, afternoon tea with cakes and pastries in the licensed restaurant which has a pretty patio dining area for alfresco eating. Evening bookings are also taken for groups of 25 to 50. Don't leave without visiting the farm shop which stocks a good range of local and organic produce including honey from nearby hives and delicious Welsh cakes.

The Derwen Garden Centre is open from 9.30am to 5.30pm, Monday to Saturday; and Sunday from 11am to 5pm.

🏛 historic building 🏛 museum and heritage 🏛 historic site 🌿 scenic attraction 🌿 flora and fauna

of King Brychan of Brycheiniog. The Parish Church of St Cynog was built in the late 18th century in fine Georgian style. Further up the wooded valley of the upper River Tanat, in the hamlet of **Pennant Melangell**, lies the **Parish Church of St Melangell**, where there can be seen two images that are said to be of a Welsh prince and the 7th-century St Melangell. The story goes that a hunted hare took refuge in the saint's cloak and thus she became the patron saint of hares. These creatures were once treated as sacred in this lonely area. A short distance further upstream is a small waterfall that marks the start of the valley.

LLANRHAEADR-YM-MOCHNANT
13 miles NW of Welshpool on the B4580

🏛 Parish Church of St Dogfan

💧 Pistyll Rhaeadr

Despite its relative isolation, this village attracts many visitors who pass through on their way to **Pistyll Rhaeadr** (see walk on page 168), which lies up a narrow road to the northwest of the village. This is one of the Seven Wonders of Wales and, with a drop of 240 feet, is the highest waterfall in Britain south of the Scottish Highlands. The English translation of the name is Spout Waterfall, an obvious name as the water drops vertically for 100 feet before running into a cauldron, and on through a natural tunnel in the rock before reappearing.

The **Parish Church of St Dogfan** dates originally from the 14th century, though the tower and parts of the main building are later. It was while vicar here in the late 16th century that Bishop William Morgan made his famous translation of the Bible into Welsh. He was granted permission to carry out this work by Queen Elizabeth I, her father Henry VIII having banned any official use of the Welsh language.

LLANFYLLIN
9 miles NW of Welshpool on the A490

🏛 Parish Church of St Myllin   🏛 Council House

🏛 Pendref Congregational Chapel

💧 St Myllin's Well

This charming and peaceful hillside town lies in the valley of the River Cain where it joins the Abel. It was granted its charter as a borough in 1293 by Llewelyn ap Gruffydd ap Gwenwynwyn, Lord of Mechain. Welshpool is the only other Welsh borough to have been granted its charter from a native Welsh ruler. To celebrate the 700th anniversary in 1993 of the granting of the charter a large tapestry of the town's historic buildings was created, which can now be seen in the **Parish Church of St Myllin**, a delightful redbrick building dating from 1706.

Overlooking the town is the beauty spot of **St Myllin's Well**. Water from the well has, from the 6th century onwards, been thought to cure all manner of ailments, and certainly the view over the town and to the Berwyn Mountains beyond, is uplifting. St Myllin, a 7th-century Celt, is traditionally alluded to as the first cleric to baptise by total immersion in his holy well. Opposite the church is the brick **Council House**, which has 13 wall paintings in an upstairs room. These were all done by a Napoleonic prisoner of war, one of several billeted in the town between 1812 and 1814. Ann Griffiths, the famous Welsh hymn writer, was baptised in **Pendref Congregational Chapel**, one of the oldest Non-Conformist places of worship in Wales, established in 1640 (see also Llanfihangel-Yng-Nowynfa). The present building dates from 1829.

Two miles southeast of Llanfyllin, off the A490, **Bryngwyn** is a handsome 18th-centry house by Robert Mylne, surrounded by 18th and early 19th-century parkland.

Pistyll Rhaeadr

Distance: *3.7 miles (5.9 kilometres)*
Typical time: *210 mins*
Height gain: *230 metres*
Map: *Explorer 255*
Walk: *www.walkingworld.com ID:1015*
Contributor: *Jim Grindle*

ACCESS INFORMATION:

The falls are a little remote and this is part of their charm. The easiest access is from the A483 just south of Oswestry. Turn off at the White Lion onto the A495. After a couple of miles this becomes the B4396 to Llanrhaeadr-yn-Mochnant. A well signposted but rather tight right turn in the village leads to a narrow road with passing places.

The falls are about four miles along this road. There is some roadside parking, but parking at the cafe, an old farm, is inexpensive. The cafe is not open on Mondays and is not always open in winter.

ADDITIONAL INFORMATION:

The falls are one of the Seven Wonders of Wales mentioned in a celebrated 18th-century verse:

Pistyll Rhaeadr and Wrexham Steeple,
Snowdon's Mountain without its people,
Overton Yew Trees, St Winefride's Well,
Llangollen Bridge and Gresford Bells.

DESCRIPTION:

The waterfall at Llanrhacadr is well known as one of the Seven Wonders of Wales and is the starting point of this walk. Leave the car park by the cafe at the foot of the falls and go through the gate to walk the 100m up to the bridge at the base of the falls. A right turn here takes you through a beech wood and two gates onto a large track. Almost at once you turn up on a steep rocky staircase built by volunteers and leading to another track.

Turn left and in a few minutes you will see a signpost indicating a ladder-stile and access to the top of the falls should you wish to visit them. The route continues up this quiet valley as far as a stream with a fence on the far side. Go down to where two streams meet and cross a gate at the junction of fences. At this point the route doubles back on itself towards some huge sheepfolds after which there is a gradual climb.

When the climb is over there are superb views of the main peaks of the Berwyns. Height is maintained for some 2km before a mine track leads down into the valley on the left.

The walk is level now and goes through woodland before once again reaching the bridge at the base of the falls.

Hills or Fells, Mountains, River, Toilets, Great Views, Food Shop, Moor, Tea Shop, Waterfall

WALK DIRECTIONS:

1 | To the right of the entrance to the cafe is a small wooden gate. Go through this and turn right. In 100m you will come to a little iron bridge at the foot of the falls.

2 | Don't cross the bridge when you have admired the falls, but turn right, into the wood. You pass one faint path leading off left and come to this gate. Go through and follow the path slightly left to a stile and gate at the edge of the wood. Beyond this gate is a stony track, which you follow for a few metres. You will see a signpost and some rocky steps on the left. Go up these steps to another track at the top.

3 | Turn left. Just over the brow of the hill look for a signpost on the left of the track. It is not very high.

4 | The signpost points towards a ladder stile by the trees on the extreme left of the picture. If you wish to see the top of the falls, then turn left, and return to continue the walk.   Further up the valley the path divides.

5 | You want the lower path, on the left. The path eventually peters out at a wide, reedy patch, just carry straight through it, picking the best way you can. You will reach a very straight and deep streambed (it sometimes has water in it). On the far side is a wire fence.

6 | Don't cross the stream or the fence but turn left, downhill to where the stream joins the main stream feeding the falls. You will have to cross this stream and the best way to do this is to turn left when you reach it so that you are going downstream. In about 100m you will reach a pebbly shore where the water is shallower. Once across, turn right and make for the corner where the two fences meet.

7 | In this corner are some low gates, the only place that you can get over the fence. Cross and turn left

– you have reached the furthest point of the walk in this direction and are now going back in the direction of the falls. Make for the stone walls of some sheep pens.

8 | Go to the left of the pens and then turn right, following a little stream uphill until you can cross it. The map shows a path here and you may find traces of it. You should aim for the group of conifers that you can just see on the skyline.

9 | When you reach the conifers, cross the gate and follow the fence on your left. There is a steady climb here. Eventually another fence comes in from the right and for a short distance you will be between the two. At the top of this first rise there is a gate on your left and good views of the Berwyns.

10 | Keep going with the fence over to your left. The ground drops, you cross a stream, and the grass gives way to a wide, stony track that climbs just a little more to the highest point of the walk. It then drops and takes a sharp turn left in the first of a series of bends into the valley on your left.

11 | The track goes left again before hugging the side of the hill. Just follow the track now until you come to another sharp bend – to the right – 800m away. At this bend, leave the track and keep ahead in the same direction as before, using sheep tracks to reach a path alongside a fence below you.

12 | Aim for the rowan tree - it is only a few minutes from the track. Now turn left and follow the path along the fence. Pass a stile on your right and you will come to another one leading into a wood. The path continues on the other side, almost immediately crossing a stream. Follow the path through woodland and some small clearings until you see some fencing below you on the right.

13 | Not too easy to spot, but you will be aware of people on the other side at this point. (If you go too far you will be right below the waterfall and know that you have to turn back.) Just out of sight is the iron bridge that you came to at the start of the walk. Cross it to get back to the gate and the cafe.

LOCATOR MAP

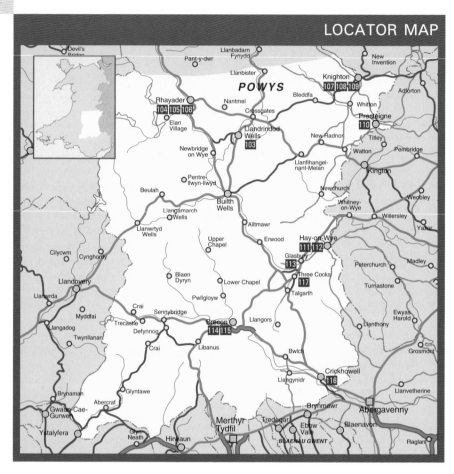

ADVERTISERS AND PLACES OF INTEREST

Accommodation, Food and Drink

104 | Gigrin Farm Red Kite Feeding Station & Cottages,
Rhayader   *pg 174*
106 | Liverpool House Guest House, Rhayader   *pg 177*
107 | Tower House Gallery & Coffee Shop,
Knighton   *pg 179*
108 | Mill at Lloyney, Lloyney, Knighton   *pg 179*
110 | The Radnorshire Arms Hotel, Presteigne   *pg 181*
112 | The Granary Café Restaurant, Hay-on-Wye   *pg 183*
113 | Black Mountain Lodge & Restaurant,
Glasbury, nr Hay on Wye   *pg 183*

115 | The George Hotel, Brecon   *pg 190*
116 | Askew's Family Bakery, Crickhowell   *pg 194*

Activities

103 | Llandrindod Wells Victorian Festival,
Llandrindod Wells   *pg 172*
104 | Gigrin Farm Red Kite Feeding Station & Cottages,
Rhayader   *pg 174*
109 | First 4 Yarns, Knighton   *pg 180*
111 | Paddles & Pedals, Hay-on-Wye   *pg 182*
117 | Black Mountain Activities, Three Cocks,
nr Brecon   *pg 197*

🏠 historic building 🏛 museum and heritage 🏚 historic site ⚘ scenic attraction 🌿 flora and fauna

5 | South Powys & Brecon Beacons

This southern region of the large county of Powys is steeped in history, and there is evidence aplenty of turbulent times past, from the Romans onwards. The Celtic standing stones and burial chambers and the ruined castles are among the many notable buildings and memorials left by past inhabitants.

In the heart of Wales (the northern part of this region) can be found the four spa towns of Llandrindod Wells, Builth Wells, Llangammarch Wells and Llanwrtyd Wells. Still popular tourist centres today, though no longer primarily spas, these places all grew and developed as a result of the arrival of the railways and the Victorians' interest in health. Although the architecture of these towns suggests that they date mainly from the 19th and early 20th century, there are the remains of a Roman fort (Castell Collen) close to Llandrindod Wells, and Builth Wells saw much fighting in medieval times. As well as the spa towns, the region also has the border settlements of Knighton and Presteigne, the second-hand book capital of the world Hay-on-Wye, and the ancient cathedral city of Brecon.

However, it is perhaps for its varied countryside that south Powys is better known. Close to Rhayader, in the Cambrian Mountains, are the spectacular reservoirs and dams that make up the Elan Valley. Built at the end of the 19th century to supply water to the West Midlands, not only are these a great feat of Victorian engineering, but also the surrounding countryside is home to one of Britain's rarest and most beautiful birds – the red kite.

Further south lies the Brecon Beacons National Park, which takes its name from the distinctively shaped sandstone mountains of the Brecon Beacons. However, there are two other ranges within the park's 519 square miles. To the east of the Brecon Beacons lie the interlocking peaks of the Black Mountains, which stretch to the English border, while to the west is Black Mountain, which, though its name is singular, refers to an unpopulated range of barren, smooth-humped peaks.

🎭 stories and anecdotes   👤 famous people   🎨 art and craft   🎵 entertainment and sport   🚶 walks

Llandrindod Wells

🏛 Old Parish Church of Llandrindod

🌱 Bailey Einion 🌱 Abercamlo Bog

🌿 Victorian Festival 🏞 Radnor Forest

🏛 Parish Church of the Holy Trinity

🖼 Radnorshire Museum

🖼 National Cycle Collection 🏚 Castell Collen

🏚 Heart of Wales Line 🏞 Rock Park

The most elegant of the spa towns of mid-Wales, Llandrindod Wells, though not primarily a spa today, is still a popular place that has retained its Victorian and Edwardian character and architecture. This was only a scattering of cottages and two churches until 1749, when the first hotel was built by a

Mr Grosvenor and, for a time, until that hotel closed in 1787, the town had a reputation as a haunt for gamblers and rakes.

Llandrindod Wells was, from 1880 up until local government reorganisation in 1974, the county town of the old county of Radnorshire. Despite its chiefly 19th and early 20th century architecture, however, it has ancient roots. To the northwest of the town lies **Castell Collen**, a Roman fort that was occupied from the 1st century through to the early 4th century and whose earthworks are clearly detectable today. The first castle was of turf and timber, put up by Frontinus in about 75 AD, with later versions being made of stone. It was the Romans who first understood the possible healing powers of the country's mineral rich waters, but it was with

Llandrindod Wells Victorian Festival

Victorian Festival Office, Wadham House, Middleton Street, Llandrindod Wells, Powys LD1 5DG
Tel: 01597 823441
e-mail : info@victorianfestival.co.uk website: www.vicfest.co.uk

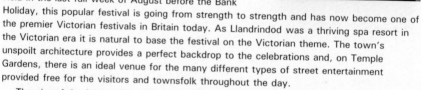

Each year Llandrindod Wells hosts a Victorian festival. Held in the last full week of August before the Bank Holiday, this popular festival is going from strength to strength and has now become one of the premier Victorian festivals in Britain today. As Llandrindod was a thriving spa resort in the Victorian era it is natural to base the festival on the Victorian theme. The town's unspoilt architecture provides a perfect backdrop to the celebrations and, on Temple Gardens, there is an ideal venue for the many different types of street entertainment provided free for the visitors and townsfolk throughout the day.

The aim of the festival is to provide a family fun festival and to cater for all ages and tastes, whilst keeping to a Victorian theme. Attracting some 40,000 visitors to a town that has a population of only 5,000 is no mean feat, but the apparent ease with which it is done is largely due to the transformation achieved in the town's reversion to the Victorian era. The effect of horses and carriages, Victorian window displays and the townspeople and some visitors sporting a whole range of appropriate costumes creates an atmosphere, the effect of which is nothing short of miraculous.

At the end of the nine days, the proceedings are closed in the grandest of manners with the moving torchlight procession and fireworks display over the lake - a spectacle not to be missed.

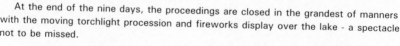

🏛 historic building 🖼 museum and heritage 🏚 historic site 🏞 scenic attraction 🌱 flora and fauna

the coming of the railway in 1867, along with the Victorians' enthusiasm for taking the waters, that Llandrindod Wells really developed into a spa town. People would flock here in their thousands (at its peak some 80,000 visitors a year) to take the waters in an

Castell Collen, Llandrindod Wells

attempt to obtain relief from ailments ranging from gout, rheumatism and anaemia to diabetes, dyspepsia and liver trouble. Special baths and heat and massage treatments were also available.

The most famous of the individual spas in Llandrindod during its heyday, **Rock Park** is a typically well laid out Victorian park where visitors coming to the town would take a walk between their treatments. With particularly fine tree planting and shrubbery, the park is still a very pleasant place, and here and elsewhere in town, visitors can still take the waters or experience some of the more modern therapies.

As well as the evidence of the town's popularity as a spa that is all around, today's visitors can find out more about its history at the **Radnorshire Museum** in Temple Street where there a collection of Victorian artefacts and a collection of relics excavated from Castell Collen. A splendid attraction in the Automobile Palace, a distinctive brick garage topped by rows of white lions, is the **National Cycle Collection**, an exhibition that covers more than 100 years of cycling

history, through an amazing collection of over 200 bicycles and tricycles that date back as far as 1818, and spans every development from the hobby horse and bone-shaker to the high-tech machines of today. Also here are old photographs and posters, historic replicas, the Dunlop tyre story and displays on cycling stars. Each year, Llandrindod Wells hosts a **Victorian Festival** (see panel opposite), swelling the population many times over and culminating in a torchlight procession and a fireworks display over the lake.

There are still two Anglican churches serving Llandrindod Wells. The **Old Parish Church of Llandrindod** ("The Church of the Holy Trinity"), just outside the town, is 13th-century, though its roof was later removed to encourage people to attend the new church in the town. It was rebuilt in 1894. The **Parish Church of the Holy Trinity** within the town was built in 1871, and is a much larger and grander affair.

Just outside Llandrindod Wells, off the A44 Rhayader road, there is free access to **Abercamlo Bog**, 12 acres of wet pasture that are home to water-loving plants, breeding birds such as the whinchat and reed bunting, and butterflies. Not far away, at Ithon gorge, is **Bailey Einion**, woodland home to lady fern, golden saxifrage, pied flycatchers, woodpeckers and cardinal beetles.

Wales is famous for its amazing little narrow-gauge railways, but it also has some full-size trains, too. One of the most popular tourist lines is the **Heart of Wales Line** that runs from Shrewsbury to Swansea, 'one line that visits two viaducts, three castles, four spa towns, five counties, six tunnels and seven bridges'. Dolau, six miles to the northeast of Llandrindod Wells, is the best starting point on the line to walk to the top of **Radnor Forest**, the highest point in the old county of Radnorshire. Llanbister Road and

Llangunllo are nearby request halts ideally placed for discovering the remoter scenic delights of the area.

Around Llandrindod Wells

ABBEY-CWM-HIR

6 miles N of Llandrindod Wells off the A483

🏛 Cwmhir Abbey

Cwmhir Abbey, founded by the Cistercians in 1143, is reputed to have been attacked by Owain Glyndwr in 1402 who thought that the monks were English sympathisers, while earlier it had been all but destroyed by

---

GIGRIN FARM RED KITE FEEDING STATION & COTTAGES

South Street, Rhayader, Powys LD6 5BL
Tel: *01597 810243*
e-mail: kites@gigrin.co.uk website: www.gigrin.co.uk

The red kite is one of the country's most beautiful birds, and at **Gigrin Farm Red Kite Feeding Station** visitors can see them feeding and wonder at their amazing grace, strength and manoeuvrability. Following a request from the RSPB, the station was founded in 1993 by Eithel Powell, who fed the birds which were roosting at the farm in the winter, and it I now owned and managed by Lena Powell and her son Chris. In 1993 about a dozen birds visited the farm; the numbers have risen steadily over the years and now up to 700 pairs can be seen in the area of the farm.

In conjunction with the Welsh kite Trust, Gigrin Farm also serves as a rehabilitation centre for red kites, receiving its first patients at the beginning of 2003. The Station opens at 1 o'clock every day and feeding takes place at 2pm in winter and 3pm in summer; it is one of the very best places to see these magnificent birds swoop down and take the meat aloft to find clear air space to enjoy their meal without being harried by other kites. Anything up to three quarters of a tonne of prime meat (so good that humans could eat it!) is bought in each week. The birds here are all natives to Wales, and tests have shown that they are all descended from a single female. Several hides are available at the Station, including some with wheelchair access and some designed for photography, and also on site are an interpretation centre with videos of kites and other wildlife, a waymarked trail, a shop and café, a picnic area, campsite and accommodation in two cottages sleeping 4 and 6.

🏛 historic building   🏛 museum and heritage   🏛 historic site   🏞 scenic attraction   🌿 flora and fauna

THE WILD SWAN WHOLEFOODS, FAIRTRADE FASHIONS & GIFTS

West Street, Rhayader, Powys LD6 5AB
Tel: 01597 811632
e-mail: shelagh@onetel.net
website: www.wild-swan.co.uk

No visit to Rhayader, often dubbed the Gateway to the Lakeland of Wales, is really complete without taking time to browse and buy at **The Wild Swan**. In one of the oldest buildings in the town, with many original features intact, Shelagh Owen's splendid shop offers quality and value for money over a wide range of products.

Upon entering, visitors will be overwhelmed by the tempting aromas of freshly ground coffee, spices and freshly baked bread. The food section presents a wide range of tasty produce such as organic eggs, freshly baked gluten free cakes, Welsh products, organic flour, a large selection of herbs and spices, freshly ground coffee and dietary goods. Beyond, shoppers will find natural remedies and supplements, and Shelagh is more than happy to offer help and advice on her products where needed. There is a large selection dedicated to hair care and hygiene products, handmade soaps, natural candles and health and diet books. Upstairs can be found a wide range of clothing including Fairtrade dresses, tops and scarves. Shelagh has also introduced a new range of natural clothing from Braintree Hemp

Shop hours are 9 to 5.30 Monday to Saturday, and flexible hours during the summer.

Henry III in 1231. It is a place of peace and tranquillity in the lonely Clywedog Valley that is well worth visiting; there is a memorial stone among the abbey ruins to Llywelyn the Last that marks, many believe, the grave of his headless body.

RHAYADER
6½ miles NW of Llandrindod Wells on the A44

- 🏠 Rhayader Castle 🌱 Gigrin Farm
- 🎭 Rebecca Riots ✍ Welsh Royal Crystal
- 🚶 Wye Valley Walk

Often referred to as the Gateway to the Lakeland of Wales, Rhayader lies at the entrance to the magnificent Elan Valley and the impressive collection of dams and reservoirs it contains. This town, whose name means "Waterfall of the Wye", dates back to

the 5th century, though the waterfall all but disappeared with the construction of a bridge over the river in 1780.

Little remains of **Rhayader Castle**, built here by Rhys ap Gryffydd in about 1177, except some defensive ditches. More recently, Rhayader was the scene of some of the **Rebecca Riots** protesting against toll gates (see also St Clears). The men, who dressed up as women and so earned themselves the nickname, Rebecca's Daughters, destroyed turnpikes in protest at the high toll charges. Many tall stories have grown up around these riots and some of them concern Rebecca herself, who is said to have appeared as an old blind woman at the toll gate and said, "My children, something is in my way."

The first gate to be destroyed was at Yr Efail Wen, where 'Rebecca' proved to be a

---

🎭 stories and anecdotes 🍽 famous people ✍ art and craft 🎵 entertainment and sport 🚶 walks

Nantmel

Distance: *3.0 miles (4.8 kilometres)*
Typical time: *120 mins*
Height gain: *210 metres*
Map: *Explorer 200*
Walk: *www.walkingworld.com ID:2440*
Contributor: *Pat Roberts*

ACCESS INFORMATION:

There is a free car park in Nantmel, near the telephone box. The village is reached by a slip road off the A44.

DESCRIPTION:

After visiting a lovely old church, walk near an unexpected viaduct, a relic of past times. The un-named mountain is only 355 metres high, but gives extensive views over a little know area of mid Wales.

FEATURES:

Hills or Fells, Church, Wildlife, Birds, Great Views, Butterflies, Public Transport.

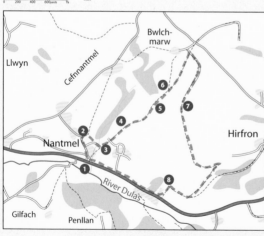

WALK DIRECTIONS:

1 | From opposite the car park walk up the hill signed 'Nantmel Church'. Walk through the church yard to a stile.

2 | Over the stile and walk right-ish towards the viaduct. Down into the valley to cross a stream and up the other side near to the viaduct. Do not walk through the gateway in front of you.

3 | Go left and uphill with the hedge on your right. Soon pass through a gate and ignore a gate on the right after about 30 metres. Continue up the field, with the fence on your right to reach a gate.

4 | Go through the gate to follow a faint track ahead, gradually edging nearer to the hedge line on your right.

5 | Reach this old stile and continue ahead with an old oak wood down to the left, and a fence on the right. Reach the corner of the field and gates in two directions.

6 | Go through the gate ahead and bear right to reach another gate near a small coppice. Go through the gate and bear right again to walk down the field, hedge line on your right, pass another small coppice and reach another gate.

7 | Go through this gate and straight ahead, aim for another gateway on the skyline. Through this gateway and ahead to another gate. (This was fenced when I walked it and I had to climb over). Turn left to walk down with the fence on your left. This track becomes wider and swings right to continue down, with a stream on the left. It is now more of a farm track and continues to swing right before going through another gate with a fence on the right.

8 | The track divides here but keep to the left fork, which swings left and down to the A44. Turn right to walk on the wide verge back to Nantmel.

LIVERPOOL HOUSE GUEST HOUSE

East Street, Rhayader, Powys LD6 5EA
Tel: 01597 810706 Fax: 01597 810964
e-mail: ann@liverpoolhouse.co.uk
website: www.liverpoolhouse.co.uk

A warm Welsh welcome from owner Ann Griffiths awaits guests at **Liverpool House**, her guest house a short walk from the centre of Rhayader. On two floors of adjacent Edwardian properties nine centrally heated bedrooms, each with its own character, seven with en suite showers, range from singles to family rooms. Two have four-posters, and all are equipped with TV, clock-radio, tea/coffee tray and hairdryer; an iron and board, fax facilities, a high chair, cot, toys and books are available on request. Rear rooms look across to the hills and the red kite feeding grounds. The main lounge has a 'computer corner' with free internet access. Ann sees that her guests start the day with a hearty breakfast, the perfect preparation for a day's walking or sightseeing. The house has secure private parking.

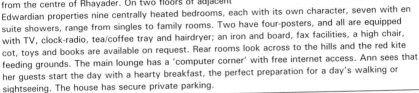

huge man called Thomas Rees. Many toll gates were demolished by the protesters until, in 1844, the remainder were removed legally.

Welsh Royal Crystal, a manufacturer of hand-crafted lead crystal tableware and gift items, is located in the town, and the factory takes visitors on a guided tour to watch the craftsmen at work. Rhayader is at one end of the beautiful **Wye Valley Walk**, which follows the river valley, criss-crossing the border, through Builth Wells and Hay-on-Wye to Hereford, Monmouth and Chepstow.

The area around Rhayader is still very rural, and on the outskirts of the town lies **Gigrin Farm**, where visitors can see red kites at close quarters as they are feeding.

ELAN VILLAGE
8 miles W of Llandrindod Wells off the B4518

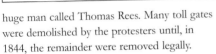

The village is close to the beautiful reservoirs of the **Elan Valley** – a string of five dammed lakes that are together around nine miles long and were constructed between 1892 and 1903. Formed to supply millions of gallons of water to Birmingham and the West Midlands, the first of the dams was opened in 1904 by

Edward VII and Queen Alexandra, and the final dam, the Claerwen Dam, was finished in 1952. Dubbed the Lakeland of Wales, the five man-made lakes are surrounded by magnificent scenery and this is a popular area

Garreg-ddu Reservoir, Elan Valley

🔝 stories and anecdotes   🐦 famous people   🎨 art and craft   ✏ entertainment and sport   🚶 walks

for walkers, cyclists and birdwatchers. The Elan Valley Visitor Centre, as well as incorporating a tourist information office, also has an exhibition telling the story of the building of the reservoirs and lots of information about the red kite.

Percy Bysshe Shelley visited his cousin Thomas Grove at Cwm Elan after being expelled from Oxford for writing a treatise supporting atheism. Soon after this visit he eloped with the schoolgirl Harriet Westbrook and married her in Scotland. They returned to Wales and for a brief spell in 1812 stayed at a house in the area called Nant Gwyllt. Like Thomas Grove's house, it is now submerged under the waters of **Caben Coch** reservoir, but when the water level is low the walls of the garden can still be seen. In 1814, Shelley left Harriet for Mary Godwin, and soon after Harriet drowned herself in the Serpentine. Shelley married Mary, who was later to write *Frankenstein*. In 1822, Shelley himself drowned off the Italian coast.

ST HARMON
8 miles NW of Llandrindod Wells on the B4518

🏛 Parish Church of St Harmon

🌱 Gilfach Nature Reserve

The **Parish Church of St Harmon** is famous for being the church where the diarist Francis Kilvert was vicar in 1876 and 1877 (see also Clyro). It was built in 1821, and is a simple affair with a very short chancel. Kilvert was born near Chippenham in 1840 and was educated at Wadham College, Oxford. He was curate to his father in Wiltshire before taking up a post at Clyro in 1865, where he started his famous diaries. They are detailed, vivid and very personal accounts of life in the remote Welsh countryside in mid-Victorian times. Back to England, then a year here, then back

to Bredwardine in Herefordshire, where he married. He died five weeks later of peritonitis, aged only 39.

To the southwest of the village lies **Gilfach Nature Reserve**, a Site of Special Scientific Interest, at the mouth of the Marteg Valley. Oak woodland, meadows and upland moorland support a rich diversity of wildlife, and in the ancient longhouse at the heart of the reserve there are exhibitions on the building's history and the surrounding wildlife.

Knighton

🏛 Spaceguard Centre   🏛 Offa's Dyke Centre

🏛 Pinners Hole   🌱 Kinsley Wood

🕊 Glyndwr's Way

Situated in the Teme Valley on the border of Powys and Shropshire, and half in Wales and half in England, Knighton lies on the path of Offa's Dyke (see Prestatyn). The Welsh name for the town is Tref-y-Clawdd, which means town of the dyke, and it is home to the **Offa's Dyke Centre,** where there is information about the long distance footpath that runs from Prestatyn to Chepstow. Here, too, visitors can find out more about the historic background to the 8th century dyke and the bloodshed caused by the battles that continued in the borderlands for hundreds of years.

Knighton and its near neighbour, the border town of Presteigne, saw many battles between the Anglo Saxons and the Celts. "It was customary for the English to cut off the ears of every Welshman who was found to the east of the Dyke (Offa's), and for the Welsh to hang every Englishman found to the west of it", wrote George Borrow in his 19th-century book, *Wild Wales.*

🏛 historic building 🏛 museum and heritage 🏛 historic site 🌄 scenic attraction 🌱 flora and fauna

THE GRANARY CAFÉ RESTAURANT

Broad Street, Hay-on-Wye, Powys HR3 5AE
Tel: 01497 820790

Opposite the town clock in Hay-on-Wye, **The Granary Cafe Restaurant** is one of the best-loved eating and meeting places in town. It was established more than 30 years ago, and the owners, sisters Caroline Pryce Mason and Jeannette Barker welcome customers into the traditional inviting surroundings with an open fire in the main ariea, hops decorating the beamed ceiling, a quiet anteroom and a spacious upstairs room.

On the premises they prepare food at very reasonable prices, from, usually three soups, interesting salads to generous main courses and handmade cakes and puddings. The daily choice of hot dishes might typically include authentic curries, spicy mediteranean pasta and meat dishes, fragrant North African tagines, or traditional pies made with shortcrust pastry and filled with beef, chicken or game. There are fish cakes, and smoked trout or salmon, all of which are sourced locally. Apple Strudel, lemon meringue pie, cheesecakes, pies and crumble are but a few of the puddings, with merringues, and scones usually available.

The opening hours are 9am-5.30pm, 7 days per week, longer hours including evening meals, during the Hay Festival, and during the summer holidays. Wifi internet is available.

THE BLACK MOUNTAIN LODGE & RESTAURANT

Glasbury, nr Hay-on-Wye, Powys HR3 5PT
Tel: 01497 847897 (accomm) 847779 (restaurant)
e-mail: info@blackmountain.co.uk
website: www.blackmountainlodge.co.uk

The Black Mountain Lodge & Restaurant occupies a lovely old building located close to the junction of the A438 and B4350 a short drive southwest of Hay-on-Wye. Owners Annette and Carl Durham have carefully modernised the property to provide up-to-date comfort and amenity while retaining original features like exposed stone walls and oak beams. The accommodation, open all year round, comprises ten excellent bedrooms, most of them en suite, including doubles, twins, triples and family rooms. Bunkhouse budget accommodation is also available.

The setting and the facilities make the Black Mountain Lodge a popular venue for business meetings and special occasions such as wedding receptions. It also has a fine restaurant serving evening meals based on prime Welsh produce. Typical main courses could include Welsh venison liver & port pâté with caramelised pear compote; fillet of Welsh beef with a smoked bacon, red wine and mushroom sauce; mango-stuffed Gressingham duck breast with an orange & rosemary reduction; and whole grilled John Dory. The owners run Black Mountain Activities at nearby Three Cocks.

corner of the Brecon Beacons National Park, grew up around **Hay Motte**, which still survives across the river from the main town centre. This castle was eventually replaced by **Hay Castle**, although this was all but destroyed in the early 1400s by Owain Glyndwr. However, a Jacobean manor house has been grafted on to part of the remaining walls and, close by, there are traces of a Roman fort.

Historic though this town may be, it is as the second-hand book capital of the world that Hay-on-Wye is best known. Among the town's many buildings can be found a plethora of book, antique, print and craft shops. The first second-hand bookshop was opened here in 1961 by Richard Booth, owner of Hay Castle, and since then they have sprung up all over the town – the old cinema, many houses, shops and even the old castle are now bookshops, at least 35 in all and with a stock of over a million books. The annual **Festival of Art and Literature**, held every May, draws thousands of visitors to the town.

The impressive **Hay-on-Wye Craft Centre** offers visitors a change from books as well as the opportunity to see craftspeople working at age-old skills, such as glass blowing, wood turning and pottery.

CLYRO
2 miles NW of Hay on the A438

🏛 Clyro Castle 🏛 Parish Church of St Michael

🌿 Cwm Byddog

Although little remains of the Roman station that was here, the remains of the motte and bailey of **Clyro Castle**, built by the fiendish William de Braose, can still be seen. The diarist Francis Kilvert was curate in the village between 1865 and 1872 and, in his journal, he describes both life in the village and the

surrounding area (see also St Harmon). There are Kilvert memorabilia in his former home, now a modern art gallery. The **Parish Church of St Michael**, where he was vicar, was founded in the 12th century. Apart from the tower, it was rebuilt in about 1853.

A little way north of Clyro, **Cwm Byddog** is a 15-acre ancient woodland with pollarded oaks, bluebells in spring, the remains of a motte and bailey castle and a variety of birds, including the blackcap and the garden warbler.

PAINSCASTLE
5 miles NW of Hay on the B4594

🏛 Castell Paen

🌿 Tawny Owl Animal Park and Craft Centre

Sometimes known as **Castell Paen**, the early castle built in 1130 by Payn FitzJohnon. A motte that still exists was later rebuilt in stone and, by the late 12th century, was in the hands of the notorious William de Braose. The cruelty of de Braose earned him a place in Welsh folklore and he was given the nickname the Ogre of Abergavenny. This was because he avenged the death of his uncle, the Earl of Hereford, by inviting several Welsh princes to Abergavenny Castle for a great feast. Instead of offering them hospitality, he had them all butchered. His name has also been given to several breeds of cattle in Wales, including the de Braose Maud and the de Braose David.

In 1198, the castle was attacked by Gwenwynwyn, Prince of Powys, but William and his English army slaughtered over 3,000 of Gwenwynwyn's men and the prince's dreams of a united Wales died along with them. However, de Braose met his match for cruelty in King John, who stripped him of his land. He escaped in disguise to France, where he died. After her husband's death, William's wife Maud suggested that John had also killed his nephew Prince Arthur and for this accusation both she and her youngest son were imprisoned in Corfe Castle with little food to keep them alive. So legend has it that when, some 11 days later, the dungeon door was opened, both prisoners were dead and, in an attempt to keep herself alive, Maud had half eaten the cheeks of her son.

Close to the castle remains is an altogether more pleasant place to visit, the **Tawny Owl Animal Park and Craft Centre**, which lies in the shelter of beautiful hills. Opened in 1998, the park is named after the wild owls that live in the broad-leafed woodlands surrounding the farm and, as well as the owls (which are not caged), visitors can also see a whole range of farm animals at close quarters. Along with the animals and the farm trails, there are also traditional country crafts on display and for sale that have been made using methods

passed down from generation to generation.

The **Parish Church of St Peter** is a simple building with a 14th century nave and a 15th century chancel, though there is plenty of evidence of a substantial restoration in the 19th century. Curiously, the chancel floor is about three feet lower than that of the nave.

Builth Wells

🏛 Parish Church of St Mary	🏰 Castle Mound
🏛 Cefn Carn Cafall	🎨 Wayside Arts Centre
🐾 Royal Welsh Show Ground	🚶 Groe Park

Another spa town of mid Wales, Builth Wells lies on the River Wye, which is spanned at this point by a six-arched bridge. The discovery of the saline springs in 1830 helped Builth Wells develop from a small market town into a fashionable spa that became more popular with the arrival of the railways towards the end of the 19th century. As a result, many of the town's original narrow streets are littered with Victorian and Edwardian buildings.

However, the town's history dates back much further than just a couple of hundred years. It grew up around a Norman castle that changed hands many times during the struggles with the English. The inhabitants of Builth Wells earned the nickname traitors of Bu-allt because of their

River Wye, Builth Wells

refusal to shelter Llywelyn the Last from the English in 1282 and, as a result, some 20 years later, Llywelyn partly destroyed the Norman stronghold. At the **Castle Mound** only the earthworks remain of the town's 13th-century castle that was built by Edward I on the site of the earlier motte and bailey structure. The earthworks can be reached by a footpath from the town centre. The **Parish Church of St Mary** was founded in Norman times, and has a 14th-century tower, the rest being Victorian. Above the south porch is a small room.

Since the 1963 opening of the **Royal Welsh Show Ground** at Llanelwedd, on the opposite bank of the Wye, the annual Royal Welsh Show, held in July, has gained a reputation as being the premier agricultural show in the country. Builth Wells is regarded as the centre for farming and agriculture in Wales and the show provides an opportunity for the farming communities to come together at what is considered to be one of the finest and most prestigious events of its kind.

Although spa treatments are no longer available here, Builth Wells remains a popular touring centre and base. As well as the many shops and the weekly market on Mondays, visitors can also enjoy the wide variety of arts and cultural events held at the **Wayside Arts Centre**, or take a pleasant riverside stroll through **Groe Park**.

On the summit of the nearby mountain, **Cefn Carn Cafall**, is a cairn that is said to have been built by King Arthur. The stone on top of the cairn bears the imprint of a dog's paw that, according to local legend, was left by King Arthur's dog, Cafall, while they were out hunting. Arthur built the cairn, placing the stone on top, and then named the peak. The story continues that if the stone is removed it will always return to this spot.

Around Builth Wells

ERWOOD
7 miles SE of Builth Wells on the A470

⚖ Erwood Station Crafft Centre and Gallery

Pronounced "Errod", the village's name is actually a corruption of the Welsh Y Rhyd (the ford), a name that harks back to the days when the shallow crossing of the River Wye here was used by drovers. The station at Erwood, closed in 1962, has been turned into the **Erwood Station Craft Centre and Gallery**.

GWENDDWR
5 miles S of Builth Wells off the A470

🏛 Parish Church of St Dubricius

The **Parish Church of St Dubricius** has some 14th-century features, though most of it dates from a Victorian refurbishment. At one time it was a small priory, attached to Abbey Dore in Herefordshire.

CILMERY
3 miles W of Builth Wells on the A483

🏛 Memorial to Llywelyn the Last

It was at this village (also called Cefn-y-Bedd) on the banks of the River Irfon, in 1282, that Llywelyn the Last, while escaping after the abortive Battle of Builth, was killed by the English. According to legend, the place where Llywelyn fell and died was once covered in broom, which then ceased to grow on the site - in mourning for the loss of the last native Prince of Wales. Thirteen trees have been planted here to represent the 13 counties of Wales. The rough hewn stone **Memorial to Llywelyn the Last** describes him as "ein llyw olaf" ("our last leader") while the English tablet beside the

🏛 historic building 📷 museum and heritage 🏛 historic site ⚖ scenic attraction 🌱 flora and fauna

monument calls him "our prince". Following his death, Llywelyn's head was taken to London and paraded victoriously through the city's streets. His death is still marked every year on 11 December at the memorial.

LLANWRTYD WELLS
13 miles W of Builth Wells on the A483

- 🏛 Cambrian Woollen Mill
- 🐟 Llyn Brianne
- 🐿 William Williams
- 🏊 World Bog Snorkelling Championship

Surrounded by rugged mountains, rolling hills and the remote moorland of Mynydd Epynt, it was here, in 1792, that the sulphur and chalybeate spring waters were discovered by a scurvy sufferer. As visitors came here in the 19th century to take the waters in relief of numerous complaints, the town developed. Today Llanwrtyd Wells is still a popular holiday centre, particularly with those who enjoy bird watching, fishing and walking. However, anyone visiting the town will be surprised that somewhere so small could have so many events and festivals throughout the year. It is the home of the 'Man versus Horse' race in May, a Folk Weekend in spring and a late autumn Beer Festival.

However the most unusual of all the events held here is undoubtedly the annual **World Bog Snorkelling Championship** that takes place each August. Competitors have to swim two lengths of a specially dug 180foot peat bog located a mile from the town. The swimmer's head must be submerged, and the use of the arms is forbidden. The latest variation is bog-snorkelling on mountain bikes!

In the 18th century, **William Williams,** the poet, hymn writer and one of the leaders of the Methodist revival, lived in the town (see also Llandovery), while another claim to fame

is that the Welsh rugby folk song, *Sosban Fach,* was written here in 1895. It translates into English as 'little saucepan'.

On the outskirts of the town lies the **Cambrian Woollen Mill**, which recalls the rich history of Wales' rural past. The first mill was founded in the 1820s, but its modern form dates from 1918, when it was opened by the Royal British Legion for the benefit of servicemen disabled in World War I. A tour of the mill allows visitors to see traditional cloths being woven while, in the factory shop, there is a wide choice of beautifully finished items to buy.

On high ground to the northwest of the town is **Llyn Brianne**, the latest of Wales' man-made lakes, which was opened in 1973. The dam that holds the water is the highest of its type in the country – at 300 feet – and the grand scale of the lake has to be seen to be believed.

LLANGAMMARCH WELLS
8 miles W of Builth Wells off the A483

- 🐿 John Perry
- 🐿 Theophilus Evans

Situated where the Rivers Irfon and Cammarch meet, Llangammarch Wells was the smallest of the Welsh spas and was renowned for its barium chloride carrying waters that were thought to be useful in the treatment of heart and rheumatic complaints. The old well and pumphouse are contained in the grounds of the Lake Country House Hotel. As well as being the birthplace in 1559 of **John Perry**, who was hanged in London in 1593 for treason, this now sleepy little town was also the home of the wonderfully named **Theophilus Evans**. He was vicar here, and also wrote a classical historical interpretation of the area entitled *View of the Primitive Age.*

🎭 stories and anecdotes   🐿 famous people   🎨 art and craft   🎵 entertainment and sport   🥾 walks

ABERGWESYN
12 miles W of Builth Wells off the B4358

⌖ Abergwesyn Pass

Situated in an isolated spot in the Irfon Valley, Abergwesyn lies on an old drovers' route that twists and climbs through the **Abergwesyn Pass**. Known as the roof of Wales, this is a beautiful pathway that, centuries ago, consisted of nothing more than dirt tracks, along which the drovers would shepherd cattle and other livestock from one market town to the next. A number of drovers' routes can still be followed, some in part by car. Many of the roads are narrow and, in the south, one such route begins at Llandovery and travels across the Epynt mountain and crosses the ford at Erwood.

NEWBRIDGE ON WYE
4 miles N of Builth Wells on the A470

🏛 Parish Church of All Saints　🗿 Drover's Statue

The **Parish Church of All Saints**, with its spire, was built in the decorated style in 1883 for the Venables family of nearby Llysdinam. The Rev. Francis Kilvert was chaplain to the Rev Richard Venables, who lived there. The **Drover's Statue** on the village green is a reminder that the village lies on an old drove road that ran from Tregaron and on into England. Droving – the driving of cattle, mainly to the English lowlands for fattening – was one of Wales's main industries until the Industrial Revolution. Drovers needed licenses to ply their trade, and had to be married, over 30 and a householder. This didn't stop them enjoying themselves in inns where they stopped overnight. Newbridge on Wye had 13 inns, and they usually put on dancing, singing, boxing and wrestling to entertain them.

Brecon

🏛 Brecon Castle　🗿 Heritage Centre

🏛 Captain's Walk　🗿 Brecknock Museum

🏛 Monmouthshire and Brecon Canal

🗿 South Wales Borderers Museum　🏛 Y Gaer

Famous for its ancient cathedral, Georgian architecture and annual Jazz Festival, Brecon lies on the banks of the River Usk, at the confluence of the Rivers Honddu and Tarrell in the heart of the National Park. The first evidence of a settlement in the area are the remains of the Roman fort **Y Gaer**, which lie two miles west of the town. First built in around 75 AD, the fort was rebuilt twice before it was finally abandoned in about 290 AD. A garrison for the 2nd Legion and the Vettonian Spanish cavalry, parts of the fort

Brecon Cathedral

Brecknock Wildlife trust

Lion House, Bethel Square, Brecon,
Powys LD3 7AY
Tel: 01874 625708. Fax: 01874 610552
e-mail: brecknockwtgcix.co.uk
website: www.wildlifetrust.org.uk

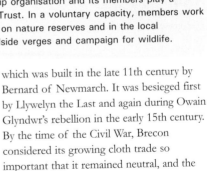

The Brecknock Wildlife Trust is part of the UK wide movement of county based Wildlife trusts. It is a registered charity operating in the county of old Breconshire, now the southern portion of Powys. To achieve its objectives of protecting wildlife and the habitats required for wildlife to thrive, the Trust owns and manages 18 nature reserves, provides advice to planners, landowners and farmers, operates species projects and promotes a greater understanding of wildlife and the environment through lifelong learning opportunities for adults and children.

The Brecknock Wildlife Trust is a membership organisation and its members play a significant role in carrying out the work of the Trust. In a voluntary capacity, members work with local schools, undertake practical projects on nature reserves and in the local community, carry out surveys, adopt local roadside verges and campaign for wildlife.

were excavated by Sir Mortimer Wheeler in 1924, and sections of the outer wall – in places 10 feet high – and traces of gates can be seen.

In the 5th century, the daughter of the local ruler was sent to Ireland to marry a local prince. They had a son, whom they named Brychan, and he was sent back to Wales to live with his grandfather. It is from him that the name of the town and the county is derived. Brychan's daughter was Tudful, and she eventually became a holy woman who was killed by Irish invaders in 480 AD. It is from her that the town of Mertyr Tydfil, 20 miles to the south, gets its name, 'merthyr' being Welsh for martyr.

A walk along the promenade beside the River Usk leads to the remains of medieval **Brecon Castle,** which can be found partly in the Bishop's Garden and partly at the Castle Hotel. The town grew up around this castle,

which was built in the late 11th century by Bernard of Newmarch. It was besieged first by Llywelyn the Last and again during Owain Glyndwr's rebellion in the early 15th century. By the time of the Civil War, Brecon considered its growing cloth trade so important that it remained neutral, and the townsfolk began dismantling the castle.

Close by stands Brecon Cathedral, an impressive and magnificent building that originated from an 11th century priory colonised by Benedictine monks from Battle in Sussex. It was founded by the Norman knight Bernard of Newmarch, who had been granted the lands by William the Conquerer. At the Dissolution of the Monasteries it became Brecon's parish church, called the Priory Church of St John the Evangelist, and was eventually elevated to a cathedral in 1923 when the new diocese of Swansea and Brecon was created. At one time chapels dedicated to

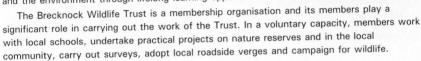 stories and anecdotes 🐟 famous people 🎨 art and craft 🌿 entertainment and sport 🚶 walks

THE GEORGE HOTEL

George Street, Brecon, Powys LD3 7LD
Tel: 01874 623421   Fax: 01874 611579
website: www.george-hotel.com

Set in the town of Brecon, at the heart of the magnificent Brecon Beacons National Park, this traditional hotel, run by a family-owned brewery, offers comfortable accommodation with a friendly, personal service.

The George Hotel enjoys an unrivalled reputation in the area for providing guests with superb hospitality and modern luxury whilst maintaining elements of the traditional styling for which it has always been known. The George Hotel specialises in weddings – both service and reception - and private functions and conferences. For that special event The Regency Suite can comfortably seat 120 guests. It is self-contained with its own bar facilities, the beautiful decor providing the perfect setting for any occasion.

There is an attractive variety of dishes carefully prepared with fresh local ingredients and available in the a la carte restaurant or bar and conservatory. The emphasis is on local produce, with a wide variety of speciality local dishes. The bar has a selection of excellent local cask conditioned ales produced by the hotel's sister company. It also has a fine selection of wines from around the world. Whether you want formality or a hearty dinner, the menus cater for everyone's taste. Delicious home-cooked food, excellent cask conditioned ales, a banqueting hall and a honeymoon suite make this a luxurious setting for a wedding, a conference, or just a delightful weekend away.

craftsmen filled the aisles, but only that to the corvisors (shoemakers) remains. Housed in a 16th-century tithe barn is the cathedral's imaginative **Heritage Centre.**

Some of the town's old walls survive, and one section, known as **Captain's Walk,** recalls the fact that Napoleonic soldiers were held prisoner here, with the officers being allowed to exercise along part of the walls. Found in another of the town's old buildings, the elegant former Old Shire Hall, is the **Brecknock Museum** where visitors can see the old assize court, as well as take in the extensive collection of artefacts and other items from past centuries, including the museum's large collection of Welsh love spoons.

The town's second museum is equally fascinating, and the **South Wales Borderers Museum** features memorabilia of the regiment's famous defence of Rorke's Drift. Over 300 years of military history are recorded here through various displays that include armoury, uniforms and medals. The regiment has taken part in every major campaign and war and has won 29 Victoria Crosses and over 100 Battle Honours. However, though its history is long and varied, it is the regiment's participation in the Zulu wars that is best remembered, and which was immortalised in the film *Zulu* starring Michael Caine. It recalls the heroic defence of Rorke's Drift in 1879, when 141 men from the regiment were attacked by 4,000 Zulus. Nine VCs were awarded here in a single day.

As well as having the River Usk flowing through the town, Brecon is also home to the **Monmouthshire and Brecon Canal,** a beautiful Welsh waterway that used to bring coal and limestone into the town. Work

🏠 historic building 🏛 museum and heritage 🏛 historic site 🏞 scenic attraction 🌱 flora and fauna

started on the canal in 1797, and a superb viaduct carries it across the River Usk just outside the town. There are attractive walks along the canal towpath, as well as pleasure cruises on both motorised and horse-drawn barges. The canal basin in the town has been reconstructed and is now proving to be an attraction in its own right.

Well-known natives of Brecon include Dr Hugh Price, founder of Jesus College, Oxford, and the actress Sarah Siddons.

Around Brecon

LLANFRYNACH
2 miles S of Brecon on the B4458

🏛 Parish Church of St Brynach

The **Parish Church of St Brynach** is Victorian, though it has a medieval tower. St Brynach was Irish, and came to Wales in the 6th century to preach and spread Christianity. On arriving in what is now Pembrokeshire, he caught the eye of the daughter of a local chieftain. He resisted her advances, and was then attacked and beaten for doing so.

LIBANUS
4 miles SW of Brecon on the A470

🏛 Brecon Beacons Mountain Centre

🏛 Twyn y Gaer   ⛰ Corn Du   ⛰ Pen y Fan

🏛 Bedd Illtyd   ⛰ Brecon Beacons National Park

To the northwest of this attractive hamlet, on Mynydd Illtyd common, lies the **Brecon Beacons Mountain Centre**, where visitors can find out about the **Brecon Beacons National Park** from displays and presentations; there are also some interesting remains to be seen in the area. **Twyn y Gaer**, a Bronze Age burial chamber, and **Bedd Illtyd**, a more modest ancient monument said

to be the grave of St Illtyd, the founder of the monastery at Llantwit Major. The Brecon Beacons are a small part of the National Park, and were given to the National Trust in 1965. This included the sandstone peaks of **Pen y Fan** (at 2,906 feet, the highest point in southern Britain) and **Corn Du**, and it has become one of the most popular parts of the UK with walkers. The area is also important for sub-alpine plants and is designated a Site of Special Scientific Interest. But the very popularity of the Beacons with walkers has caused great problems, exacerbated by military manoeuvres and the sheep that have grazed here since Tudor times. Erosion is the biggest problem, and the National Trust has put in place an ambitious programme of footpath and erosion repair.

PENCELLI
4 miles SE of Brecon on the B4558

🏛 Parish Church of St Meugan   🏛 Pencelli Castle

The **Parish Church of St Meugan**, which is actually in Llanfeugan, some way out of the village, was built by Ralph de Mortimer of Pencelli Castle in 1272. It is a handsome building with a sturdy tower. Much of the building you see nowadays dates from the 14th century. **Pencelli Castle**, of which there are now only scant remains, was built in the late 11th century by Ralph Baskerville, a Norman knight.

YSTRADFELLTE
12 miles SW of Brecon off the A4059

🏛 Parish Church of St Mary   🏛 Maen Madog

⛰ Fan Lia   ⛰ Fan Nedd   ⛰ Porth-yr-Ogof

The **Parish Church of St Mary** is mainly 16th century, and has a font of the same date. The church is supposed to have been founded by Cistercian monks. The village is a

🏛 stories and anecdotes   🦜 famous people   🎨 art and craft   🎭 entertainment and sport   🚶 walks

Maen Madog, Ystradfellte

recognised hiking centre and the area of classic limestone countryside around it is one of the most impressive in the British Isles. The narrow road heading north from the village climbs sharply and squeezes its way along a narrow valley between the 2,074-feet high **Fan Llia** on the east side, and the 2,176 feet high **Fan Nedd** on the west. The **Maen Madog** is a nine-foot high standing stone with a Latin inscription proclaiming that Dervacius, son of Justus, lies here.

To the south of Ystradfellte is **Porth-yr-Ogof**, a delightful area with a collection of dramatic waterfalls as the River Melte descends through woodland.

YSTRADGYNLAIS
18½ miles SW of Brecon on the B4599

🎭 Y Garn Goch

Situated at the top end of the Tawe Valley,

which stretches down to the city of Swansea, and close to the boundary of the Brecon Beacon National Park, is Ystradgynlais, a former mining community. A place rich in industrial heritage, iron was produced here as far back as the early 17th century and the legacy of this industrious past can still be seen, although the area surrounding the village is known as waterfall country and is popular with walkers, ramblers and cavers.

A local legend tells of three cauldrons, filled with gold, that are buried beneath **Y Garn Goch** – the red cairn – on the summit of Mynydd y Drum, to the east of the town. The story goes that one day a young girl will come to claim the treasure, which, until then, is protected by demons. To prevent anyone trying to take the gold, the legend also tells of a wizard and his apprentice who attempted to overcome the demons with their magic. While the elements raged, a spirit on a wheel of fire swept the apprentice out of the protective circle he had made and gave him a lighted candle, saying that as long as the candle burned his life would last. As soon as the candle was spent the apprentice died and the wizard, terrified, fled from the mountain.

CRAIG-Y-NOS
15½ miles SW of Brecon on the A4067

🏛 Craig-y-Nos Castle   📷 Dinosaur Park

📷 Mr Morgan's Farm   🌿 Craig-y-Nos Country Park

🌿 National Showcaves Centre for Wales

📷 Iron Age Farm

The **National Showcaves Centre for Wales** is centred on the largest complex of caverns in northern Europe, and lies to the north of this village. Discovered in 1912, the caverns have taken 315 million years to create and they include both the longest and the largest showcaves in Britain. The Cathedral Cave, as its name suggests, is like the interior of a great cathedral, and modern lighting and music accentuate the atmosphere. Near the entrance is a display on cave dwellers of the past. Dan-yr-Ogof has a series of lakes connected by passages, which you can explore as well. Within Bone Cave 42 human skeletons have been discovered, many of them dating back over 3,000 years to the Bronze Age. Deer bones over 7,000 years old have also been discovered.

Exploring the underground caverns is only one aspect of this interesting attraction, as there is also an award-winning **Dinosaur Park**, where life-size replicas of the creatures that roamed the earth during Jurassic times can be seen, and **Mr Morgan's Farm**, where Welsh cobs, the wagons they pulled and other farm animals are on show. The replica **Iron Age Farm** gives a realistic idea of how the farmers lived in that era.

To the east of the village lies **Craig-y-Nos Country Park**, where visitors can enjoy the unspoilt countryside and the landscaped country parkland of the upper Tawe Valley. The mansion in the country park, known as **Craig-y-Nos Castle**, was once the home of the 19th-century opera singer Madame Adelina Patti, She bought the estate in 1878 as a home for her and her second husband, the tenor Ernesto Nicolini. She installed an aviary, a little theatre modelled on Drury Lane, and a winter garden that was subsequently moved to Swansea's Victoria Park. Patti was born in Madrid in 1843, the daughter of a Sicilian tenor, and achieved fame in New York at an early age. Her first husband was the Marquis de Caux, her second Ernesto Nicolini, and her third the Swedish Baron Cedarström, whom she married in the Roman Catholic church at Brecon in 1898. The castle is now a hotel.

SENNYBRIDGE
7½ miles W of Brecon on the A40

🏚 Castell Ddu   📷 Disgwylfa Conservation Centre

Situated along the southern edge of the Mynydd Epynt and on the northern border of the Brecon Beacons National Park, this village is very much a product of the industrial age, as it only began to develop after the railways arrived here in 1872, when it became a centre for livestock trading. However, the remains of **Castell Ddu**, just to the west of the village, provides evidence of life here from an earlier time. Dating from the 14th century and believed to stand on the site of an 11th century manor house, this was the home of Sir Reginald Aubrey, trusted friend of Bernard of Newmarch, a Norman knight who was granted tracts of land in the area in the 11th-century, and who founded Brecon Priory. Two new waymarked walks have been opened on the Sennybridge army training area, beginning at **Disgwylfa Conservation Centre** on the B4519. The centre has an interactive learning centre and military and conservation displays. One of the walks is accessible to disabled visitors.

Crickhowell

🏚 Crickhowell Castle
🏚 Parish Church of St Edmund
🏚 Crickhowell Bridge   🏛 Crug Hywell
🌿 Pwll-y-Wrach Nature Reserve

Situated in the beautiful valley of the River Usk, and in the shadow of the Black Mountains that lie to the north, Crickhowell is a charming little town with a long history. The town takes its name from the Iron Age fort, **Crug Hywell** (Howell's Fort) that lies on the flat-topped hill above the town that is aptly

ASKEW'S FAMILY BAKERY

15 High Street, Crickhowell,
Powys NP8 1BD
Tel: 01873 810345
e-mail: stephen@stephenaskew.wanadoo.co.uk

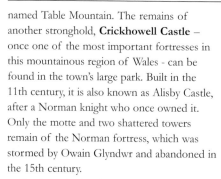

For more than 40 years **Askew's Family Bakery** has been a familiar and much-loved fixture on Crickhowell's High Street, just two minutes' walk from the River Usk. Stephen and Jenny Askew and his staff bake a wide range, cakes and pastries fresh each morning, with 30 or 40 varieties usually available.

Among the favourites are Danish pastries (pecan & maple, custard crown apple crown, cinnamon whirl), custard creams, iced buns, fruit pies, bara brith, Battenberg and lemon meringue pie, and, of course, the classics for special times of the year such as Easter and Christmas. Bread also comes in many varieties: large and small loaves, rolls, baps, baguettes, white, wholemeal, oatmeal, malted, granary. Morning goods include croissants, doughnuts, scones, teacakes, Chelsea buns, custard slices, pain au chocolat and pain aux raisins.

All the items can be eaten at the neat pine tables or to take away. Hot breakfasts, from individual items to traditional full English, are served until 11 o'clock. Askew's is open from 8.30 to 5 Monday to Saturday (half-day Wednesday).

named Table Mountain. The remains of another stronghold, **Crickhowell Castle** – once one of the most important fortresses in this mountainous region of Wales - can be found in the town's large park. Built in the 11th century, it is also known as Alisby Castle, after a Norman knight who once owned it. Only the motte and two shattered towers remain of the Norman fortress, which was stormed by Owain Glyndwr and abandoned in the 15th century.

The imposing **Parish Church of St Edmund** was founded in the 12th century by Lady Sybil Pauncefote, whose father Sir Hugh Turberville, owned the castle. Effigies of Sybil and her husband, the wonderfully named Sir Grimbald, can be seen in the sanctuary.

The picturesque and famous **Crickhowell Bridge**, which dates from the 16th century, spans the River Usk in the heart of the town. Still carrying traffic today, the bridge is unique

in that it has 13 arches on one side and only 12 on the other! The town, with its fine Georgian architecture, is popular with those looking for outdoor activities, such as walking, due to its close proximity to the Black Mountains and the National Park. Close by is **Pwll-y-Wrach Nature Reserve** in a steep-sided valley. Owned by the Brecknock Wildlife Trust, this woodland reserve has a waterfall and also a great variety of flora, for which it has been designated a Site of Special Scientific Interest.

Around Crickhowell

TRETOWER
2½ miles NW of Crickhowell on the A479

🏛 Tretower Court and Gardens 🏛 Tretower Castle

This quiet village in the Usk Valley is the home of two impressive medieval buildings –

Tretower Castle

Tretower Court and Gardens and **Tretower Castle** (both in the hands of CADW). The elder of these historic sites is the castle, though all that remains on the site of the original Norman motte is a stark keep that dates from the 13th century. The castle was built in this valley to discourage Welsh rebellion but, nevertheless, it was besieged by Llywelyn the Last and almost destroyed by Owain Glyndwr in 1403.

Adjacent to the castle remains lies the Court, a magnificent 15th century fortified manor house that served as a very desirable domestic residence particularly during the less turbulent years following Glyndwr's rebellion. While the 15th-century woodwork here and the wall walk, with its 17th-century roof and windows, are outstanding, it is the Court's gardens that are particularly interesting. The

original late 15th-century layout of the gardens has been re-created in such a manner that the owner of the time, Sir Roger Vaughan, would still recognise them. Among the many delightful features there are a tunnel arbour planted with vines and white roses (Sir Roger was a Yorkist), an enclosed arbour and a chequerboard garden. They are all best seen in the early summer.

TALYBONT-ON-USK
7 miles NW of Crickhowell on the B4558

Talybont Reservoir

Just beyond this attractive village, which won the Powys Village of the Year Award in 2003, the Monmouthshire and Brecon Canal passes through the 375-yard long Ashford Tunnel while, further south, lies the **Talybont Reservoir**. In this narrow wooded valley on the southeast slopes of the Brecons there are several forest trails starting from the car park at the far end of the reservoir.

LLANGORS
8 miles NW of Crickhowell on the B4560

Parish Church of St Paulinus

Llangors Lake   Rope Centre

The **Parish Church of St Paulinus**, dates from the 15th century, though there was much rebuilding in Victorian times. It may have been built on the site of a monastery that was founded in the 7th century and continued up until the 11th century. To the south of the village, which is sometimes spelled Llangorse, lies the largest natural lake in South Wales - **Llangors Lake** (Llyn Syfaddan). Around four miles in circumference and following its way round a low contour in the Brecon Beacons, the waters of this lake were, in medieval times, thought to have miraculous properties. Today, the lake attracts numerous visitors looking to

stories and anecdotes   famous people   art and craft   entertainment and sport   walks

enjoy not only the setting, but also the wide variety of sporting and leisure activities, such as fishing, horse riding and sailing, that can be found here. There is also a **Rope Centre**, with climbing, abseiling, potholing, log climbing and a high-level rope course.

Naturally, the lake is associated with a legend and local stories suggest that the land beneath the lake once belonged to a cruel and greedy princess. Though her lover was poor, she agreed to marry him only if he brought her great riches. So the lover set out to accomplish his task and in so doing robbed and murdered a wealthy merchant, giving the riches to his princess. However, the merchant's ghost returned to warn the happy couple that their crime would be avenged, not on them, but on the ninth generation of their family. One night, years later, a great flood burst from the hills, drowning the surrounding land and

its inhabitants. It is still said today that a city can be seen beneath the water.

TALGARTH
10½ miles N of Crickhowell on the A479

🏛 Parish Church of St Gwendoline

🏛 Bronllys Castle   🎋 Hywell Harris

Lying in the foothills of the Black Mountains, Talgarth is an attractive market town with narrow streets that boasts many historic associations as well as some fine architecture. The 15th-century **Parish Church of St Gwendoline** is the burial place of **Hywell Harris** (1714–73), an influential figure in the establishment of Welsh Methodism. Harris was also instrumental in establishing a religious community, "The Connexion", which was organised on both religious and industrial lines.

Although this is now a quiet and charming place, Talgarth once stood against the Norman drive into Wales. Some of the defensive structures can still be seen today – the tower of the church and another tower that is now incorporated into a house - though it has also served time as the jail.

On the outskirts of Talgarth lies **Bronllys Castle,** a well-preserved centuries old keep built by the Norman baron Bernard of Newmarch. Originally a motte and bailey castle, it was later replaced with a stone edifice and it now is a lone tower standing on a steep mound that is in the hands of CADW (Welsh Historic Monuments).

Llangors Lake

BLACK MOUNTAIN ACTIVITIES

Three Cocks, nr Brecon, South Powys LD3 0SD
Tel: 01497 847897
e-mail: info@blackmountain.co.uk website: www.blackmountain.co.uk

Established in 1992 by Annette and Carl Durham, **Black Mountain Activities** caters for all ages and skills, and all levels of action and adventure. Experienced instructors oversee a range of activities that includes water-borne (white water rafting, kayaking on the River Wye, raft building and canoeing fun days) and land-borne (walking on the Brecon Beacons, rock climbing and abseiling, caving, archery), and the gorge adventure that mixes both – scaling rock walls, jumping across boulders, scrambling up cascades, crawling behind waterfalls and exploring deep, dark holes in the ground. Transport is available to and from most of the venues, and accommodation is available at the nearby Black Mountain Lodge.

LLANGYNIDR
4 miles W of Crickhowell on the B4558

🏛 Chartists' Cave

To the south of this riverside village, on the open moorland of Mynydd Llangynidr, lies the **Chartists' Cave**, where members of the movement stored ammunition during their active years in the mid 19th century.

LLANGATTOCK
1 mile SW of Crickhowell off the A4077

🏛 Parish Church of St Catwg

🌱 Craig-y-Cilau Nature Reserve

The **Parish Church of St Catwg**, which was founded sometime during the early 6th century, is dedicated to one of Wales' most honoured saints. Born in around 497 AD, by the end of his life, in around 577 AD, he had become a bishop and taken the name Sophias. The church's large tower is from the 16th century, while the rest of the building dates from the 14th century and later. It was restored in Victorian times, but most of the medieval features can still be seen.

To the southwest of the village, towards the boundary of the Brecon Beacons National Park lies the **Craig-y-Cilau Nature Reserve**. With over 250 plant species and over 50 kinds of birds breeding within the area, this is one of the richest reserves in the National Park.

🎭 stories and anecdotes　🐦 famous people　🎨 art and craft　🎭 entertainment and sport　🚶 walks

LOCATOR MAP

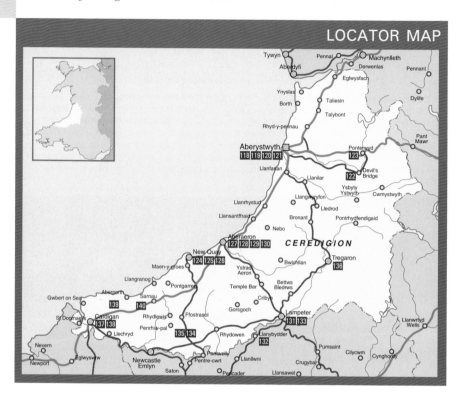

ADVERTISERS AND PLACES OF INTEREST

🏛 historic building   🏛 museum and heritage   🏛 historic site   🏞 scenic attraction   🌿 flora and fauna

6 | Ceredigion

Ceredigion's countryside features some of the most beautiful landscapes in Wales, and also attracts many rare species of birds, animals and plants. In particular, it is home to the graceful red kite, and keen birdwatchers are well served by nature reserves around the Teifi and Dyfi estuaries and at Llangranog, New Quay and Cors Caron. The new Ceredigion Coast Path is a 60-mile route between Cardigan on the Teifi estuary and Ynys Las on the Dyfi estuary. The path links towns and villages dotted along the spectacular coastline, and walkers will discover a wealth of wild flowers, seabirds and wildlife.

Ceredigion means the land of Ceredig, son of the Celtic chieftain Cunedda. Dating from around 415 AD, the region is steeped in history and tradition. It is renowned for its unique brand of Welshness and, within Wales, its inhabitants are affectionately known as "Cardis", as Ceredigion encompasses most of the former county of Cardiganshire. The patron saint of Wales, St David, was born in Ceredigion and many famous Welsh princes are buried in the ruins of Strata Florida Abbey. The region is not as well endowed with castles as the counties further north, but Aberystwyth and Cardigan castles both saw fighting before they were left in ruins, and Cardigan is credited with being the venue for the first recorded eisteddfod in 1176.

Perhaps, though, this county is best known for its coastline on the great sweep of Cardigan Bay. Many of the one-time fishing villages have now become genteel resorts, but few seem to have attained the great degree of brashness that is associated with other seaside holiday destinations. In the north of the county and close to the mouth of the River Dyfi is the great expanse of sand at Borth while, further south, the coastline gives way to cliffs and coves – once the haunt of smugglers.

Much of Ceredigion can be classed as very Welsh and very rural, and it is also an important area of learning. St David's College at Lampeter, a world-renowned ecclesiastical establishment, is now, as University College, part of the University of Wales, while Aberystwyth is home not only to the first university in Wales, founded in 1872, but also to the National Library of Wales.

🎦 stories and anecdotes 🐦 famous people 🎨 art and craft 🎭 entertainment and sport 🚶 walks

Aberystwyth

🏛 Aberystwyth Castle   🏛 War Memorial

🏛 Pier   🏛 Old College   🏛 Ceredigion Museum

🏛 Welsh Christian Heritage Centre   🏛 Cliff Railway

🏛 National Library of Wales

🏛 Aberystwyth Camera Obscura

🏛 Aberystwyth Harbour and Marina

Aberystwyth is the largest town on Cardigan Bay, the seat of local government and the home of the University of Wales Aberystwyth and the National Library of Wales. It is not only the unofficial capital of mid Wales but also a cosmopolitan coastal resort that, at its peak, attracted many thousands of tourists each year. Although there is evidence that the town is older, Aberystwyth as we know it can certainly be traced back to the late 13th century when, in 1277, Edward I began building **Aberystwyth Castle** and granted a

charter that made the settlement around the new fortification a free borough with a ditch and wall, a guild of merchants, a market and two fairs. Constructed to subdue the Welsh, the castle withstood a siege in 1282, but in 1404 it fell to Owain Glyndwr during fighting that destroyed the surrounding town. Glyndwr made the castle his base for four years and it became an important seat of government until, in 1408, it was recaptured by Prince Henry (who went on to become Henry V). In 1637, Thomas Bushell was given permission to set up a mint within the castle, and during the Civil War the silver coins minted here for Charles I were used to pay the Royalist soldiers, as Cromwell had taken control of the mints in London. However, the castle finally fell to the Parliamentarians in 1646 and Cromwell destroyed the building some three years later. Today, the ruins, standing on the rocky headland, remain an impressive sight. Also on Castle Point can be

GUSTO

7 Terrace Road, Aberystwyth,
Ceredigion SY23 1NY
Tel: 01970 612555

'For something unique'

If you don't want to be seen in the same clothes as everyone else, ditch the high street and head to **Gusto Clothing**, a small but perfectly formed independent clothing boutique based in the centre of Aberystwyth.

Owned by Becky Pope, Gusto has been well established for 10 years, as an independent boutique that sells clothes, which help you retain your individual style.

The boutique is stacked to the rafters with ethical fashions - Komodo, vintage fashions - Motel, womenswear from Great Plains, Insight 51, footwear and accessories. It is a perfect illustration of what makes small independent stores so special. It is filled with things they love and things you maybe wouldn't find anywhere else. The ethos is to offer distinctiveness and an honest friendly service.

found the town's **War Memorial**, a splendid monument that was commissioned the year after World War I ended. It is the work of the Italian sculptor Mario Rutelli.

In the years following the turmoil of the Civil War, and before the arrival of the railways, Aberystwyth remained essentially a fishing town, but with a growing shipbuilding industry. Although much of this industry has now ceased, **Aberystwyth Harbour and Marina** is still a bustling place that can accommodate over 100 vessels and, at the town quay, all manner of fish and seafood are landed.

The arrival of the railways in the 1860s saw the town expand rapidly as first the Victorians and then the Edwardians made their way here to enjoy the sea air and the beauty of the great sweep of Cardigan Bay. The town's 700 foot long **Pier** was constructed in 1864, and the Pavilion at the end was added in 1896 to provide a capacious venue for light entertainment. Great Victorian and Edwardian villas were built along the seafront, which still exist, converted now to hotels and guest houses. Just to the north, along the coast from the town centre, lies the longest electric **Cliff Railway** in Britain. It was opened in 1896, when it was powered by an ingenious water balance system. In 1921, it was converted to electricity, and it still carries passengers up the slope of Constitution Hill at a sedate four miles an hour. From the summit there are panoramic views over the bay and, inland, to the Cambrian Mountains. Also on the summit is the **Aberystwyth Camera Obscura**, housed in an octagonal tower. A faithful reconstruction of a popular Victorian amusement, the huge 14-inch lens - the biggest in the world – gives visitors an even better view from this excellent vantage point. It was originally built in 1880 within

Aberystwyth Cliff Railway

Aberystwyth Castle, and rebuilt on Constitution Hill in 1896, the year the Cliff Railway opened. However, by the 1920s it had gone. The present camera was built in 1985.

While the town today certainly seems to cater to holidaymakers' every need, Aberystwyth is also a seat of learning. The **Old College** was originally built to JP Seddon's design in the 1870s as a hotel designed to accommodate the influx of Victorian visitors. However, the venture failed, and in 1872 the high Gothic building was sold, becoming the first university in Wales and now home to the departments of Welsh, Education and Theatre, Film and Television. The great crowds of holidaymakers may have gone, but the town still has over 7,000 students living in it during term-time, adding greatly to its economy.

🎬 stories and anecdotes 🎭 famous people 🎨 art and craft 🎪 entertainment and sport 🚶 walks

HER DANDY WOLF

32 Eastgate, Aberystwyth, Wales SY23 2AR
Tel: 01970 625900
e-mail: herdandywolf@btconnect.com

If the high street doesn't cater to your taste, go off the beaten track and take to the side-streets. And where better to start than at **Her Dandy Wolf** - an independent boutique selling men's and women's clothes where accessories, gifts and shoes are displayed in vintage cabinets or hanging from reclaimed antlers. From the inviting pot of fresh flowers on the doorstep the aim is to create a welcoming relaxed environment in which to browse and be delighted. The shop is refreshingly light owing to huge double fronted windows where the displays take on the look of an art installation exuding charm and originality.

Stylishly combining contemporary clothing from smaller independent labels with vintage finds to create a unique look. Brands such as Loreak Mondian, Duck and Cover, Emily and Fin and Jovonna sit together in a space that covers two floors.

Her Dandy Wolf, founded by a mother and daughter partnership also showcases original and applied arts from across the UK which are available to buy. This is a shop that aims to inspire, provide quality and service with individuality and stimulate your senses.

TOKO

20 Eastgate, Aberystwyth, Ceredigion SY23 2AR
Tel: 01970 626633
website: www.tokocrafts.co.uk

A stroll through the side streets of Aberystwyth will bring you to Toko, at Eastgate, (in the original welsh "Y Porth Bach"- "the little gateway") which was opened by sisters Gwenda, and Janet. Their shared vision of a space in which local artists could exhibit and sell their paintings and craft works, as well as providing a creative space in which some of these skills could be passed on, was inaugurated in April 2002, with the opening of the shop and it's associated basement gallery. Since then there have been numerous exhibitions in varying media, by both established, and rising visiting artists, as well as an ongoing rotation of wares by six regularly affiliated artisans. They also attempt to give precedence to fairly traded and sourced crafts from the wider world, as well

as a large range of gifts and cards for all tastes and occasions. As you browse through the shop itself you will find a variety of traditional and contemporary gifts including; hand-wrought silver jewellery, and jewellery crafted from recovered and recycled sourced materials, candles, lanterns, glassware and ceramics, textiles including hand made cushions, a variety of bags, hats and scarves, patchwork quilts and rag rugs. We also carry a small range of quilting materials, threads and a small selection of haberdashery – buttons etc.

So please call in and treat yourselves there's a little bit of something for everybody.

🏭 historic building 🏛 museum and heritage 🏚 historic site 🏞 scenic attraction 🌱 flora and fauna

With such an intellectual heritage it is not surprising that the town is also the home of the **National Library of Wales**, one of only six copyright libraries in Great Britain, and the keeper of the majority of materials that relate to the Welsh people and their culture. Founded in 1909, the foundation stone of the building was laid by George V in 1911. In 1916, the librarians and books moved in, and in 1937, it was officially opened by George VI, though work on the building didn't officially finish until 1955. The library holds many early Welsh and Celtic manuscripts, among which is the *Black Book of Carmarthen*, a 12th-century manuscript that is the oldest written in Welsh. An enhanced visitor centre and other new facilities opened in 2002. Housed in a beautifully restored Edwardian music hall, right in the centre of the town, on Terrace Road, is the **Ceredigion Museum**, opened in 1982. It is housed in a former theatre, and has been described as "probably the most beautiful museum interior in Britain". It tells the history of Cardiganshire through an interesting collection of materials: the history of seafaring, agriculture, and silver and lead mining are all well chronicled. Within the Victorian Parish Church of St Michael, you will find the **Welsh Christian Heritage Centre**, with displays and artefacts that illustrate the history of Christianity in Wales.

Around Aberystwyth

DEVIL'S BRIDGE
10 miles SE of Aberystwyth on the A4120

🏛 Hafod Arch   🏛 Vale of Rheidol Railway

🌀 Devil's Bridge Waterfalls   🚶 Pwllpeiran Trail

The eastern terminus of the **Vale of Rheidol Railway**, the narrow gauge railway that runs from Aberystwyth through the Rheidol valley,

Devil's Bridge Waterfalls

Devil's Bridge attracts many people who come here to see the splendid **Devil's Bridge Waterfalls** that drop some 300 feet through this breathtaking gorge. While the scenery is marvellous, there are also three interesting bridges here – dating from the 11th, 18th and 20th century – which were built one on top of the other. An iron bridge built in 1901 straddles the top of the falls and, just below it, there is a stone bridge of 1708 while, further down stream again, lies the original **Pont-y-gwr-Drwg** (Bridge of the Devil), thought to have been built by the monks of Strata Florida Abbey. Local legend suggests, however, that the bridge was built by the Devil and that he would claim the first soul to cross to the other side. However, an old woman, wanting to retrieve her stray cow, outwitted the Devil by throwing a crust across the bridge, which her dog chased after. The Devil had to make do with the soul of the dog and the old lady

🎬 stories and anecdotes   🐦 famous people   🎨 art and craft   🎭 entertainment and sport   🚶 walks

MAES-Y-MOR

25 Bath Street, Aberystywth, Ceredigion SY23 2NN
Tel: 01970 639270
e-mail: bookings@maesymor.co.uk
website: www.maesymor.co.uk

Croeso Cymraeg Cynnes i bawb /
A warm Welsh welcome to all!

Maes-y-Mor offers superior self-catering accommodation at a budget price. Ideally situated near Aberystwyth's town centre, 80m from the beach and 40m from the bus station. It is an ideal base for both North and South Wales.

Accommodation at the hostel is room-only. Guests have full use of catering facilities, dining room, launderette, car park at the rear and secure shed for bikes. There is a large kitchen diner with fridge freezer, hob oven, microwave and toaster for your convenience.

All rooms have TV and tea/coffee making facilities and beds of a superior quality to ensure a good nights sleep. Towels and linen are provided. Halls and landings are themed in welsh history pictures.

Aberystwyth is nestled between three hills and two beaches, and hosts some castle ruins, a pier and a harbour. Visit Devil's Bridge with its dramatic waterfalls or Vale of Rheidol narrow gauge railway, it is also a university town so there is plenty of nightlife.

---

safely retrieved her cow. The legend goes on to say, however, that if you cross the bridge by night, the devil is likely to push you off in a fit of pique for being denied the old woman's soul.

Along with the footpaths and nature trails that descend the 94 steps of Jacob's Ladder to view the falls, other paths lead to another vantage point, the **Hafod Arch**. It was erected by Thomas Johnes, the squire of Hafod, in 1810 to honour the Golden Jubilee of George III, the farmer king. Johnes also transformed the area with forestation, planting the surrounding countryside with over four million trees, as if in anticipation of the Forestry Commission who now own the land. The Arch, which marks the highest point on the former Hafod Estate, is one of many points of interest on the **Pwllpeiran Trail**, a four-mile trail that affords exciting views over

Hafod and the Upper Ystwyth Valley, and provides information on the agriculture, forestry, wildlife and history to be seen along its route. One section of the walk joins the Cambrian Way Long Distance Path through Myherin Forest. On its way it passes through Gelmast farmyard, which was Thomas Johnes' original experimental farm. Elsewhere on the trail, below some new oak woodland, is the **Bwlch yr Oerfa**. The remains – no more than some bumps in the ground nowadays – are thought to be part of the former Cwmystwyth Grange of the Old Cistercian Abbey at Strata Florida, possibly a raised garden.

YSBYTY CYNFYN

10½ miles E of Aberystwyth on the A4120

🏤 Parish Church of St John

Found in the circular wall of the Victorian **Parish Church of St John**, are five stones

---

🏤 historic building 🏛 museum and heritage 🏚 historic site ⬥ scenic attraction 🌱 flora and fauna

LLOYDS OF PENLANLAS

Penlanlas, Rhydyfelin, nr Aberystwyth,
Ceredigion SY23 4RE
Tel: 01970 625319
e-mail: info@penlanlas.co.uk
website: www.penlanlas.co.uk

Golf Course   Club House   Fruit Farm   Nature Trail

In beautiful countryside signposted off the A487 in Rhydyfelin, **Lloyds of Penlanlas** provides visitors of all ages and a variety of interests with a wonderful day out. Owners Mark and Suzanne Lloyd established the Golf Course in 1993 in one of the most spectacular locations in Wales, with glorious views of the countryside in all directions. The undulating 9-hole course (par 62) is suitable for golfers of all abilities, and the pleasure and interest of a round are increased by numerous water features and established tree plantings of natural species. The peace and beauty are further added to by the wildlife, including the amazing red kites. The course is available from 8am till dark in the summer and from 10 to 4 in the winter; a range of equipment is sold in the club shop. Once a year the course plays host to one of the local societies and their friends, making money for local charities and good causes.

The very smart modern Club House has a licensed bar and upstairs function room that is available for golf societies and corporate days, wedding receptions, private parties, conferences and meetings. The Club House is open from 10 to 6 from March to September for teas and coffees, home-made cakes, light snacks and main meals, highlighting local or home-grown produce and their own chickens.

Penanlas Farm grows a wide variety of fruit and vegetables. It started in a modest way as a strawberry farm and now, with the aid of polytunnels, produces strawberries, raspberries, black, white and redcurrants, gooseberries, potatoes, carrots, green beans and broad beans. Pick Your Own is available in the summer. Fruit from the Farm is the basis of the wonderful Cegin Suzanne preserves made in small batches to a traditional family recipe; varieties include strawberry & champagne, gooseberry & mint, blackcurrant & port and marmalades.

Mark and Suzanne have created a Nature Trail that leads up to a superb viewpoint looking towards Snowdon and the Preseli Hills. Beside the trail is a strip of natural ground cover – a mix of kale, quinoa, linseed and wheat – that provides a habitat and source of food for a variety of wildlife. This unique opportunity to enjoy nature and glorious views is open to the public and to local educational groups.

📖 stories and anecdotes 🐦 famous people 🎨 art and craft 🖌 entertainment and sport 🚶 walks

Comisiwn Coedwigaeth Cymru
Forestry Commission Wales

Bwlch Nant yr Arian

Mae Nant yr Arian yn cynnig dewis perffaith o weithgareddau coedwig, o dawelwch llwybrau cerdded i rai o lwybrau beicio mynydd gorau.

Bwydo'r Barcud, Canolfan Ymwelwyr a Chaffi ar agor 11yb - 3yp Gaeaf, 10yb - 5yp Haf. Dim ond 10 milltir i'r dwyrain o Aberystwyth ar yr A44

01970 890453
www.forestry.gov.uk/cymru

From tranquil walks to premier mountain bike trails, Nant yr Arian offers the complete woodland experience.

Daily Red Kite Feeding, Visitor Centre & Restaurant. Open Daily from 11am - 3pm Winter, 10am - 5pm Summer time. Just 10 miles east of Aberystwyth on A44

01970 890453
www.forestry.gov.uk/wales

from a Bronze Age stone circle. Only one of the stones is now in its original position, and two of them have been used as gateposts at the entrance to the churchyard. This is an excellent example of the early Celtic church 'Christianising' pagan sites.

PONTERWYD

10 miles E of Aberystwyth on the A44

🐿 George Borrow   🐦 Kite Country Centre

🐦 Nant yr Arian Visitor Centre

An inn called the Borrow Arms remembers **George Borrow**, who came here to dry out after falling into a peat bog. Norfolk-born, Borrow was a noted philologist and linguist who travelled widely overseas, acting for a time as an agent for the British and Foreign Bible Society. Later, he tramped around England and Wales, sometimes with his step-daughter, and in 1862 published his

best-known work *Wild Wales*. Close by is the **Nant yr Arian Visitor Centre**, a Forest Enterprise centre with forest walks and trails, a mountain bike trail, orienteering course, tearoom, local crafts and picnic and play areas.

Here, too, is the **Kite Country Centre** and feeding station. Designated the Bird of the Century in 1999, the red kite was a fairly common bird in the Middle Ages, seen even in London scavenging in the streets. It was at that time considered useful and was even protected by the Crown, but with the passing of the Enclosures Act in the 16th century, this impressive bird was among many species thought to be a threat to agriculture. Persecuted as vermin, they disappeared entirely from England and Scotland, but a few pairs remained in mid Wales. With care and conservation efforts from individuals and organisations, the numbers gradually increased, so that now there are more than

300 breeding pairs. At 2pm each afternoon throughout the year, the kites swoop down to be fed, joined by other species looking for an easy meal, including crows, buzzards and ravens. Other red kite feeding stations in Wales are at Gigrin Farm near Rhayader, Powys, and Tregaron in Ceredigion, the latter feeding in winter only.

LLYWERNOG
9 miles E of Aberystwyth on the A44

🏛 Llywernog Lead & Silver Mine

Just to the north of the village lies the **Llywernog Lead & Silver Mine**, a museum that covers the history of this major rural industry in mid Wales. This mine opened in 1740 and had its most prosperous period between 1850 and 1879. In the slump that followed most of the mines closed for good,

Celtic Cross, Llanbadarn Fawr

but Llywernog refused to die and was briefly reopened in 1903 as a zinc prospect. It was saved in 1973 by the present owners.

LLANBADARN FAWR
1 mile E of Aberystwyth on the A44

🏛 Parish Church of St Padarn

Although this village has now become a suburb of Aberystwyth, it was once a town in its own right and, in the 6th century, St Padarn established a small monastery here. For over 600 years, the monastery and the church were dominant despite the merging of the bishopric at Llanbadarn – the oldest in Wales – with that of St David in the 8th century. The present **Parish Church of St Padarn** dates from a rebuild of 1257 after a fire destroyed the older church, and two Celtic crosses that are associated with St Samson, Padarn's brother.

PENRHYNCOCH
4 miles NE of Aberystwyth off the A487

🖋 Penrhyncoch Lakes

This is another village associated with one of Wales' great poets: Dafydd ap Gwilym, who was born just a short distance from Penrhyncoch (see also Pontrhydfendigai). Although little remains of Gwilym's house except a small pile of stones, his medieval poetry lives on. Situated above the village is a series of five lakes known as the **Penrhyncoch Lakes** that offer fishing.

TRE TALIESIN
7½ miles NE of Aberystwyth on the A487

🏛 Bedd Taliesin

This village was the home, in the 6th century, of one of the earliest recorded British poets, Taliesin. The standing stone behind the village, **Bedd Taliesin** ('Taliesin's Grave'), actually dates from the Bronze Age (around 15000BC)

🖼 stories and anecdotes 🐦 famous people 🖋 art and craft 🖊 entertainment and sport 🥾 walks

and while it marks a burial chamber, it is unlikely to be that of the poet. An old legend says that if anyone is to sleep on his grave for one night, he or she will waken up either a poet or a fool.

TRE'R-DDOL
8 miles NE of Aberystwyth on the A487

🏚 Lodge Park

The former medieval deer park, **Lodge Park**, is now managed by Forest Enterprise, which has restored this semi-natural woodland and has also preserved its northern boundary that comprised a ditch and bank. The Wesleyan chapel in Tre'r-ddol was bought, in 1961, by a Mr RJ Thomas to house his folk object collection. He left this collection to the National Museum of Wales and it is now administered by Aberystwyth's Ceredigion Museum.

FURNACE
10½ miles NE of Aberystwyth on the A487

🏚 Dyfi Furnace   🍃 Cwm Einion

This quaint old village was, in the 18th century, home to an iron ore smelting foundry and, today, **Dyfi Furnace** is an important early industrial site that has one of the country's best preserved charcoal burning blast furnaces. The bellows that pumped the air into the furnace were powered by a huge waterwheel driven by the River Einion and visitors here can see the wheel (now restored to working order) as well as tour this industrial heritage site and museum.

The road opposite Dyfi Furnace leads up the **Cwm Einion** – Artists' Valley – which is so called because it was once a favourite haunt of 19th-century watercolourists. As well as seeing the remains of a silver lead mine, walkers climbing up the valley will find

pleasant woodland trails and picturesque picnic spots.

EGLWYS FACH
11 miles NE of Aberystwyth on the A487

🐦 Ynyshir RSP Nature Reserve

Found in the sheltered waters of the Dovey estuary, the **Ynyshir RSPB Nature Reserve** is the home of a great many species of birds, in particular waders. It has an extensive network of walks, with bird watching hides, where visitors in winter can observe the reserve's unique flock of Whitefronted Geese from Greenland and the smaller flock of Barnacle Geese. It is the most important breeding site in Wales for lapwings and redshanks. The nature reserve's visitor centre has much information on the various species of birds found here.

The poet RS Thomas was the vicar of St Michael's Parish Church from 1954 until 1967 (see also Rhiw).

BORTH
5½ miles N of Aberystwyth on the B4353

🐦 Animalarium   🐦 Borth Bog
🏯 Cantre'r Gwaelod

The original settlement of this now popular seaside resort lies on the slopes of Rhiw Fawr and it is there that some of the older fishermen's and farmers' cottages can still be seen. The growth of the village began with the arrival of the railway linking it with Aberystwyth in the 1860s and its long, safe, sandy beach (recently voted one of the two best in Wales), along with the spectacular views out over Cardigan Bay and inland to the mountains, have ensured that it is still a much used holiday destination. Within Borth is the **Animalarium**, a collection of animals that includes wild animals, endangered species,

🏚 historic building 🏛 museum and heritage 🏚 historic site 🍃 scenic attraction 🐦 flora and fauna

Animalarium, Borth

YNYSLAS
7½ miles N of Aberystwyth off the B4353

🔍 Ynyslas Sand Dunes and Visitor Centre

Situated at the northern end of Borth beach, Ynyslas – the name means Green Island – extends to the Dovey (Dyfi) estuary, where there are broad expanses of sand, particularly at low tide, although the swimming is unsafe. The **Ynyslas Sand Dunes and Visitor Centre** explains the natural beauty of the Dovey in wildlife displays and slide shows. There is also a conservation shop selling books, stationery and 'green' pocket money gifts. From the centre there are glorious views over the river mouth to Aberdovey.

domestic animals and farm varieties.

At a very low tide it is possible to see the remains of a submerged forest that, according to local legend, once formed part of the dynasty of **Cantre'r Gwaelod** (the Lower Dynasty), which extended out into the bay and was protected by a huge sea wall. It was ruled by King Gwyddno Garanhir, and flourished in the 6th century. It was said to be very fertile, and that one acre of land in Cantre'r Gwaelod grew as much as four acres anywhere else.

One night the gatekeeper is said to have had too much to drink and forgot to close the gates against the rising tide so that, with the help of a storm, it drowned the forest and the dynasty.

To the east of the village lies **Borth Bog** (Cors Fochno), an important area of raised coastal peat mire (one of only two such areas in Europe) that supports an abundance of wildlife.

New Quay

🏛 New Quay Heritage Centre   🏛 Lifeboat Station

🔍 New Quay Head   🔍 Cei Bach

🐦 Bird and Wildlife Hospital   🔍 Treath Gwyn

🐦 Bird Rock   🖋 New Quay Yacht Club

🐦 Cardigan Bay Marine Wildlife Centre

This small yet busy resort, whose harbour now boasts more yachts than fishing boats, built its economy on fishing, smuggling, shipbuilding and coastal trading. However, although these traditional ways of life declined in the 19th century as the rail links developed, New Quay has retained much of its maritime charm. The first vessel to be built here was the 24ton sloop *William and Mary*, launched in 1779, and the subsequent shipping boom brought a great deal of employment to the area, causing the population to rise to 2,000. Hand in hand with

ABERARTH CRAFTS AT SMOCKLES

Old Sheffield House, Margaret Street, New Quay,
Ceredigion SA45 9QJ
Tel/Fax: 01545 560133
e-mail: aberarthcrafts@globalnet.co.uk
website: www.lovespoons.biz or www.smockles.co.uk

The legend of the lovespoon is lost in the mists of
time, but the tradition of giving carved wooden spoons
to symbolise affection is very much alive. Foremost
among the makers of lovespoons is Roy John Phillips,
who has been working in wood for more than 30 years. The lovespoons he
makes at **Aberarth Crafts** in New Quay are sold throughout the UK and far
beyond, providing treasured mementoes of special occasions and tokens of
affection for loved ones. They mainly range in size from 1.5 to11 inches, but
Roy will undertake commissions for almost any size. The spoons are made in
a variety of woods, including maple, lime, hornbeam, cherry, plum, yew,
walnut, oak and mahogany. They are also made in sterling silver or 9-carat
gold, and as pendants, earrings, brooches, bookmarks, key rings and
Christmas tree decorations.

Visitors to Roy's shop can watch him at work carving his lovespoons as
well as taking time to browse and buy among all the other lovely items on sale. These range from
folk art to ceramics, pewter gifts, handmade boxes, haberdashery, fleece hats, beeswax candles,
handmade soaps, photo frames, books, greetings cards and a wide variety of other craft items.

MYRTLE HILL GUEST HOUSE

Llandysul Road, New Quay,
Ceredigion SA45 9RP
Tel/Fax: 01545 560399
e-mail: myrtlehill@hotmail.com
website: www.myrtlehill-guesthouse.co.uk

Myrtle Hill is a large, white-painted Victorian
house in a peaceful location by the A486, a
short walk from the harbour, the beaches and
the coastal paths. Combining many handsome
original features with up-to-the-minute
comfort and amenities, the house offers
versatile accommodation for singles, couples
and families. Log fires keep things cosy in the cooler months, and when the sun shines the
peaceful walled garden is a pleasant place for a stroll.

An excellent breakfast starts the day, and packed lunches can be provided for guests setting
out to discover the scenic delights that are all around. An evening meal is also available with
notice, featuring fish freshly landed in the harbour and always a choice for vegetarians. Myrtle Hill
is an ideal base for walkers, cyclists, sailors and fishermen, and the dramatic coastline offers
breathtaking views. For motorists, the house is well placed for touring the West Wales coast and
the mountains of North and Mid Wales. Closer by, attractions in New Quay include the Beach
Heritage Centre, the Marine Wildlife Centre overlooking the harbour, the Yacht Club and the sea
birds gathering at Bird Rock, reached from New Quay Head.

🏠 historic building 🏛 museum and heritage 🏚 historic site ⌘ scenic attraction 🌿 flora and fauna

the shipbuilding and fishing industry, smuggling was also rife and, in 1795, New Quay was described as a place of "infamous notoriety", and the headland was reputedly riddled with a network of caves where contraband was stored. New Quay's **Lifeboat Station**, established 140 years ago, can be visited between 2pm and 4.30pm. One of its crew, Hanna Nuuttila, is the RNLI Photgrapher of the Year for 2008, her wining entry showing Pwllheli's Mersey class lifeboat aiding a yacht in trouble in force 8 conditions in September 2008.

New Quay's natural surroundings as a port and harbour of refuge led to its being considered, at one time, as a suitable place from which direct sailings could be made to Wicklow and Dublin. Today's visitors will find charter boats operating out of the harbour offering a wide range of trips including deep sea and inshore fishing outings. The **New**

Quay Heritage Centre has displays on the town's history, including local characters, shipbuilding, smuggling and fishing. It also details what is being done to protect the area's bottlenose dolphins, grey seals and porpoises.

The sands and boating facilities at New Quay have long been an attraction for holidaymakers and the **New Quay Yacht Club** welcomes all visitors. The north beach leads to the rocky headland, **New Quay Head**, where an invigorating path follows the line of the sheer cliffs to **Bird Rock**, the home of many sea birds. Inland, lies the **Bird and Wildlife Hospital**, which treats and returns to the wild any birds or mammals needing veterinarian treatment, particularly birds involved in oil spillages. The **Cardigan Bay Marine Wildlife Centre**, overlooking the harbour, has interpretive displays on marine life in Cardigan Bay, especially the bottlenose dolphins.

THE HUNGRY TROUT

2 South John Street, New Quay, Ceredigion SA45 9NG
Tel/Fax: 01545 560680
e-mail: thehungrytrout@hotmail.co.uk
website: www.thehungrytrout.co.uk

Overlooking the beautiful harbour of New Quay, The Hungry Trout is a regionally renowned seafood restaurant specialising in locally sourced ingredients from the sea and land around Cardigan Bay.

Chef & owner Tim Dutnell and his team of chefs offer a menu that fuses creativity, classical simplicity and natural local foods, all cooked & prepared, from appetisers, main courses through to our famous puddings with large choices including vegetarian options, dietary requirements are catered for, fresh fish & shellfish our speciality.

The restaurant sits 40 coverts comfortably, serving breakfasts, morning coffee, lunches & evening a'la carte with fully licensed bar and extensive wine list, with friendly staff to welcome you to a warm, inviting atmosphere and a outside terrace with commanding views over the bay. The Hungry Trout is a truly satisfying experience.

The Hungry Trout offers Bed and Breakfast with two double rooms, one being en-suite, both overlooking the harbour for information & rates please visit our website.

KAROB

Aberaeron Craft Centre, Aberaeron,
Ceredigion SA46 0DX
Tel: 01974 272026
e-mail: karob@welshcrafts.co.uk
website: www.welshcrafts.co.uk

All things Welsh and Wonderful, the craftsmen made them all. An ever-changing array of gifts for sale here, all hand made by skilled craftsman in Wales. Many of the crafts found here reflect centuries of tradition, though each craftsman has given their own unique touch to their craft.

OLD BARN HOBBIES

Unit 18, Aberaeron Craft Centre, Aberaeron,
Ceredigion SA46 0DX
Tel: 01545 571634
website: www.oldbarnhobbies.co.uk

The **Old Barn Hobbies** business is located in the Aberaeron craft centre and features wonderful arrays of model materials for hobbies such as miniature railways, dollhouses and model cars and bikes. The dollhouses available to buy here are spectacular and include a large Georgian style cottage and Boston house. You will also find materials for furniture and accessories. Model planes are also popular here and all tools and materials can be purchased. The Old Barn Hobbies is a toy dream world, selling everything you could possibly imagine.

TRIBAL DRAGON

Unit 14, Aberaeron Craft Centre, Aberaeron,
Ceredigion SA46 0DX
Tel: 01545 571140

Within the Aberaeron craft centre is the **Tribal Dragon**. A tattooist, who follows traditions from the days of the blue men of Wales, offers Celtic tribal markings, along with body piercing to locals and visitors alike. With a full license, the Tribal Dragon tattoo studio is truly Welsh, providing spectacular artwork for the body. Opening times are 7 days a week from 10.30 am till late, Thursdays are open until 2.30pm during term times and Sundays are open for bookings only.

BUTTONS & BOWS

Unit 16, Aberaeron Craft Centre, Aberaeron,
Ceredigion SA46 0DX
Tel: 01545570002
e-mail: lesleyfudge@aol.com

Located in Aberaeron craft centre, **Buttons & Bows** supplies threads and yarns for all your sewing and knitting requirements. The shop is brightly coloured with all the hundreds of varieties to choose from and there are many different buttons, bows, fringing and ribbons to choose from to finish off your splendid designs. The shop has exposed brickwork and is proud to be Welsh, with a flag standing tall outside of the store.

🏛 historic building 🏛 museum and heritage 🏚 historic site 🛆 scenic attraction 🌱 flora and fauna

The coast to the south of New Quay is best described as rugged, and there is a Heritage Coastal path that threads its way along the clifftops down through Cwmtudu to Llangranog and beyond. Whilst, to the northwest of the town are the long sandy beaches of **Treath Gwyn** (White Beach) and **Cei Bach** (Little Quay) that were once a hive of shipbuilding activity and are now peaceful and secluded places.

New Quay Beach

Along with Laugharne in Carmarthenshire, New Quay lays claim to being the original Llareggub in Dylan Thomas' *Under Milk Wood*. Thomas had an ambiguous relationship with New Quay: it is said that he was disliked in the town, not least for his failure to pay his bills. It would seem he had his revenge, however, as Llareggub reveals its true meaning when spelled backwards!

Around New Quay

LLANINA
1 mile E of New Quay off the A486

 Parish Church of St Ina    Cerrig Ina

 King Ina

This tiny village, with a long tradition of fishing, is also associated with the legend of **King Ina**, king of the West Saxons, who succeeded to the throne in 688 AD. One day, in the early 8th century, a ship was wrecked on the rocks close to the village during a violent storm, and a local fisherman and his wife and daughter, having seen the disaster, rowed out to rescue the stricken sailors. Once safe, the family, unable to understand the language

spoken by the shipwrecked strangers, sent for a monk who told them that they had saved King Ina. In thanksgiving, the king built a church from which the present **Parish Church of St Ina**, built in 1850, takes its name. **Cerrig Ina** (Ina's Stones) can be seen offshore and mark the spot where the original church stood.

ABERAERON
4½ miles NE of New Quay on the A487

 Alban Square    Aberaeron Wildlife Park

 Craft Centre

Situated at the mouth of the River Aeron, this is a delightful small town with charming Georgian houses, particularly around **Alban Square**. These are the result of astute town planning initiated in the early 19th century by the Reverend Alban Gwynne, who was happy to spend his wife's inheritance on dredging the Aeron estuary and creating this new port. He was thus instrumental in turning the settlement from a small fishing hamlet into a

 stories and anecdotes    famous people    art and craft    entertainment and sport    walks

bustling port that also became famous for its shipbuilding.

Just inland from the town lies **Aberaeron Wildlife Park**, the home of llamas, red deer, parrots, owls and Jimmy, who is believed to be the world's only albino crow and who starred in the television series *Gormenghast*. As well as the animals at the park, there are natural trails, a miniature railway and plenty of other activities to keep all the family amused.

Although animals, birds and fish abound in this area, Aberaeron also has a **Craft Centre**, housed in traditional farm buildings, where visitors can not only see the beautiful products being handmade but have the opportunity to buy a unique reminder of their time in the town.

LLYSWEN
4½ miles NE of New Quay on the A482

🏠 Llanerchaeron

Llanerchaeron sits to the east of the village, and is a small 18th-century estate and house, now owned by the National Trust that was typical of that owned by minor Welsh gentry. The house was designed by John Nash and built between 1794 and 1796. In the courtyard you can see a brewery, laundry, dairy and salting house. It was bequeathed to the National Trust in 1989 by JP Ponsonby Lewes.

ABERARTH
6 miles NE of New Quay on the A487

🏠 Parish Church of St David   🏠 Deinerth Castle

This former shipbuilding village is often bypassed because of the charm of its more illustrious neighbour Aberaeron, but it is a picturesque village overlooked by the **Parish Church of St David**. Founded in the 6th century, the church was rebuilt in 1860, but still contains three early Christian inscribed

stones from the 9th and 10th century. The scant remains of **Deinerth Castle** can be seen a little way inland from the village. It was probably built by Richard de la Mare in about 1110, though it was later destroyed by Gruffydd ap Rhys in 1116. It was then substantially rebuilt, only to be razed to the ground again by Owaibn Gwynedd 20 years later, when it was finally abandoned. It was rebuilt yet again, but was finally abandoned in about 1202.

LLANRHYSTUD
11½ miles NE of New Quay on the A487

🏠 Caer Penrhos   🏛 Castell Bach

🏛 Castell Mawr

To the south of the village, which lies near the confluence of the Rivers Wyre and Carrog, are the two former hill forts of **Castell Bach** and **Castell Mawr,** which are separated by a vale known as "the dell of slaughter" – a reference to an ancient battle. More remains can be found to the east, this time of **Caer Penrhos**. Built in around 1150 by Cadwaladr ap Gryffydd, the castle was razed to the ground some 50 years later to avoid it falling into a rival's hands.

PENNANT
4 miles NE of New Quay on the B4577

🌾 Mari Berllan Piter

In the 19th century, this village was the home of a recluse named **Mari Berllan Piter** (Mary of Peter's Orchard). Supposedly granted magical powers, her exploits were legendary. When a miller refused to grind her corn, she made his mill wheel turn the wrong way, a young girl who stole an apple from Mari's orchard was forced to walk home backwards and sometimes, it is said, Mari turned herself into a hare. The ruins of Mari's cottage, known

🏠 historic building 🏛 museum and heritage 🏛 historic site 🌿 scenic attraction 🌾 flora and fauna

locally as The Witch's Cottage, can still be seen surrounded by her now overgrown orchard.

LLANARTH

2½ miles E of New Quay on the A487

🏛 Parish Church of Llanarth 🪦 Cross of Girhiret

The **Parish Church of Llanarth** was built between 1870 and 1872 on the site of a much older building. Within it is an old stone inscribed with a cross, known as the **Cross of Girhiret**, named after an Irish nobleman of the 9th century. A local story tells that one night the Devil tried to steal the bell from the former church. However, he made such a noise that he woke the vicar who, armed with a bell, a book and a candle, climbed up into the belfry to investigate. By solemnly repeating the name of Christ, the vicar managed to drive the Devil to the top of the tower and forced him to jump off. In the graveyard is a

Parish Church of Llanarth

strangely scarred gravestone that is said to bear the marks made by the Devil when he landed.

CROSS INN

2 miles S of New Quay on the A486

🐝 New Quay Honey Farm

To the south of the village lies **New Quay Honey Farm**, the largest honey farm in Wales, housed in an old chapel.

Lampeter

🏛 University of Wales, Lampeter 📷 Elen Lloyd

Lampeter, with a population of just over 1,900, has long been the centre of this part of the Teifi Valley and an important meeting place for drovers. It was given its royal charter in 1284 by Edward I, and today is best known as being the home of a college of the University of Wales. Founded in 1822 by Bishop Thomas Burgess of St David's, St David's College, as it was first known, was Wales' first institution to award degrees, and only the third in England and Wales. It now predominantly teaches the liberal arts and theology. The main university buildings include CB Cockerell's original buildings round a stuccoed quadrangle dating from 1827, which were designed to mimic an Oxbridge College and, underneath these buildings, lies the town's old castle motte. Since 1971, the college has been integrated with the University of Wales – hence its new name **University of Wales, Lampeter** – although the campus still retains its own unique atmosphere.

While the 1,500 students add a certain bohemian flavour to Lampeter during term time, this is essentially a genteel and very Welsh town with a pleasant mixture of

📷 stories and anecdotes 🦅 famous people 🎨 art and craft 🏊 entertainment and sport 🚶 walks

CREATIVE COVE

40A High Street, Lampeter, Ceredigion   SA48 7BB
Tel: 01570 421985
e-mail: charlotte_mellor@hotmail.co.uk

Creative Cove is an adorable craft shop on Lampeter high street that believes your shopping experience should be as enjoyable as the time you spend using the products to create beautiful cards, wedding invitations and scrapbooks.

Creative Cove started life in the only way a craft shop really should – a passion for crafting. Charlotte Mellor, owner, has always been an avid craft enthusiast and had dreamed of starting her own business. She opened the shop three years ago and in store you'll find everything you'll ever need to be creative as well as friendly advice, suggestions and guidance on projects. Charlotte stocks plenty of great quality art supplies and specialist craft materials for children and adults including Winsor & Newton supplies, canvasses, modelling materials, jewellery making kits, glass, ceramic and fabric painting supplies plus greeting cards (many of which are of local scenes)...her customers

describe the shop as a treasure trove and are overwhelmed by the sheer choice and variety of items, so much so that one should allow plenty of time to browse.

JEN JONES WELSH QUILT & BLANKETS

Pontbrendu, Llanybydder, Ceredigion   SA40 9UJ
Tel: 01570 480610   Fax: 01570 481298
e-mail: quilts@jen-jones.com

For over twenty five years Jen Jones Welsh Quilts has been the destination for lovers of old textiles. She has specialised in antique Welsh quilts & blankets and in her 1735 listed cottage there are always over three hundred vintage quilts and a comparable number of vintage blankets to be found.

THE JEN JONES WELSH QUILT CENTRE

The Old Town Hall, High Street, Lampeter, Ceredigion   SA48 7BB
Tel: 01570 480610   Fax: 01570 481298
e-mail: quilts@jen-jones.com

A long term goal to open a gallery for Welsh Quilts is finally being realised. In late summer in the historic Old Town Hall, Lampeter, the doors will open on the inaugural exhibition featuring some of the spectacular quilts in Jen Jones' renowned private collection. Jen is also running a programme with a women's' group in Ethiopia to reproduce beautiful handmade replicas of early flannel geometric patchworks found in her collection.

These will be for sale in the Quilt Centre's Gallery Shop. For up-to-date information, check the website: www.jen-jones.com

Calico Kate

36 High Street, Lampeter, Ceredigion SA48 7BB
Tel: 01570 422866
e-mail: kate@calicokate.co.uk
website: www.calicokate.co.uk

Established in 2002, **Calico Kate** has gained a reputation as a 'treasure trove of textiles' for patchworkers, dressmakers, knitters and many related crafts.

In a building full of charm and character, you can wander through the eight rooms of fabric, haberdashery and yarn, in a relaxed and homely atmosphere.

Calico Kate is in Lampeter's High Street, between the handsome Town Hall and the NatWest bank. The shop is open Monday to Friday 10am - 5pm, Saturday 10am - 4pm (closed Wednesday and Sunday).

Georgian and Victorian buildings. Back in the 17th century, on what is now Maesyfelin Street, stood the home of the Lloyds of Maesyfelin. When the only daughter of the family, **Elen Lloyd**, became engaged to Samuel Pritchard, the son of a poet priest from Llandovery, her four brothers, fearing the loss of their inheritance, tied her lover underneath a horse and galloped him from Lampeter to Llandovery. Samuel died of his injuries and the brothers threw his body in the nearby River Teifi. On hearing what had happened, Elen was driven mad with sorrow and died soon afterwards. Samuel's father, Rhys, put a curse on the family and, just a short while later, their family house caught fire and burnt to the ground. The eldest brother, out of remorse, or perhaps due to the curse, killed his brothers and then himself.

Around Lampeter

LLANDYSUL
11 miles SW of Lampeter on the A486

🌿 Cnapan Folk Festival 🐦 Christmas Evans

Set in the deep and picturesque valley of the River Teifi, this traditional little Welsh town was another centre of the woollen industry, and also the birthplace, in the early 19th century, of the wonderfully-named **Christmas Evans**, a Baptist minister who was famed for his fiery, emotional sermons. The son of a cobbler, he was orphaned early in life, and became a Baptist minister instead of a Presbyterian minister because the Presbyterians required qualifications that he did not have. Today, this tranquil little town is renowned for its outstanding scenic views,

📖 stories and anecdotes 🐦 famous people 🎨 art and craft 🌿 entertainment and sport 🥾 walks

NANTGWYNFAEN ORGANIC FARM

Penrhiwllan Road, Croeslan, Llandysul, Ceredigion, SA44 4SR
Tel: 01239 851 914
email: amanda@organicfarmwales.co.uk
website: www.organicfarmwales.co.uk

Nantgwynfaen Organic Farm is a working farm of 62 acres in beautiful West Wales, near beaches, castles & cliff top walks. We produce free-range organic eggs, which we serve in our **bed and breakfast** and sell in our well-stocked **Farm Shop**. Meat is sourced from local organic farmers. We make our own organic speciality sausages and grow our own vegetables. Bread and jam is homemade. We have 3 en-suite bedrooms and a living room with log burner for guests to enjoy. Families are very welcome. Our bespoke wooden furniture can be seen throughout the farmhouse and in production in the workshop.

PENBEILI MAWR FARM COTTAGES

Penbeili Mawr, Coed y Bryn, Llandysul,
Ceredigion SA44 5NA
Tel: 01239 851059
e-mail: penbeilicottages@hotmail.co.uk
website: www.penbeilicottages.co.uk

'Coast and Country on your Doorstep'

Penbeili Mawr comprises three lovely holiday cottages, sympathetically converted from 200-year-old stone farm buildings, providing quiet, comfortable accommodation in a delightful country setting. Cowshed Cottage, sleeps two guests, Stable Cottage four and Dairy Cottage six. Combining handsome original features with all the expected modern amenities, they all have an open-plan living room, oven, hob, microwave, fridge-freezer, washing machine, plasma TV and DVD and CD player; a cot and high chair are available on request. Each has access to a large, enclosed, private garden with garden furniture and a barbecue.

The 87-acre farm on which the cottages are located includes 30 acres of broadleaf woodland that offer scenic walks and the chance to spot a wide variety of flowers, plants, birds and animals. Penbeili Mawr is situated near the junction of the B4334 and B4571 northeast of Newcastle Emlyn, and attractions within an easy drive include golf courses, fishing and canoeing on the River Teifi, the Teifi Valley Steam Railway, the National Botanical Garden of Wales and the Ceredigion Heritage Coast.

---

fishing and white water canoeing as well as for the delights of its Victorian town centre.

A few miles up the A486, Ffostrasol is the setting for the annual **Cnapan Folk Festival**, the largest Celtic folk music event on the British mainland.

CAPEL DEWI

8½ miles SW of Lampeter on the B4459

🏠 Rock Mills Woollen Mill

Close to the village lies **Rock Mills Woollen Mill**, which was established in 1890 by John Morgan, whose descendants still weave here

---

🏠 historic building 🏛 museum and heritage ⛫ historic site ♨ scenic attraction 🌱 flora and fauna

today. The machinery is powered by a waterwheel that also drives a small alternator to provide lighting, and the mill once provided power to the neighbouring church. From pure new wool, the mill produces all manner of woollen goods, including bedspreads, blankets and rugs, and it is one of the last traditional mills where the entire process, from fleece to fabric, may be viewed.

LLANDDEWI BREFI

7 miles NE of Lampeter on the B4343

🏯 Parish Church of St David   🏯 Llanfair Clydogau

This traditional country village was host, in 519 AD, to a synod was attended by St David. The meeting was called to debate the Pelagian heresy, a doctrine advocating freedom of thought rather than the Biblical version of original sin that determined the morality of the time. The **Parish Church of St David** stands on a mound said to have risen up as St David preached during the synod. The church itself dates from the 13th century and contains some old inscribed stones. One is known as St David's Staff and another has an inscription in the obscure Ogham language thought to commemorate a heretic of the type that St David was denouncing.

Close by are the sites of several hill forts including **Llanfair Clydogau**, where the Romans mined for silver, and which sit beside the Sarn Helen, a military road that once connected a gold mine in the south, at Dolaucothi, with a fort at Bremia in the north.

TREGARON

9 miles NE of Lampeter on the A485

🏛 Tregaron Kite Centre and Museum

🏯 Cors Caron   🕊 Henry Richard

🏛 Rhiannon Welsh Gold Centre

🏇 Festival of Harness Racing   🚶 Old Railway Walk

This small market town - a meeting place for 19th century drovers - still serves the remote farming communities in the Teifi valley. The surrounding land is sheep country and Tregaron became famous for its woollen industry and, in particular, its hand-knitted woollen socks, which many of were transported to the mining communities of South Wales. David Davies, an engineer from Llandinam, found another use for the wool - he used it to form a stable bed on which to lay the railway across Cors Caron bog. In the town's main square stands a statue of **Henry Richard** (1812–1888), the Liberal MP and son of Tregaron, who was a vociferous supporter of disarmament and an advocate of arbitration in international disputes; he became known as the Apostle of Peace.

Housed in the Old National School, which

View from Mountain Road, Tregaron

RHIANNON JEWELLERY

Main Square, Tregaron, Ceredigion SY25 6JL
Tel: 01974 298415 Fax: 01974 298690
e-mail: post@rhiannon.co.uk
website: www.rhiannon.co.uk

Welsh Jewellers since 1971

On the main square of Tregaron, **Rhiannon Jewellery** offers the widest choice of Welsh and Celtic jewellery and craftware in the world. Rhiannon Evans established the craft shop and gallery in 1971 in this charming early Victorian building, where many original features add to the pleasure of browsing and buying in this unique place. Rhiannon added Celtic jewellery in 1976, and the products of Rhiannon Welsh Gold and Rhiannon Celtic Jewellery have gained a reputation that has spread round the world. Rhiannon does all the designing and is responsible for most of the production, making everything on site by hand, with no imported or machine-made jewellery. Visitors can watch Rhiannon and her team of in-house trained, Welsh speaking goldsmiths at work on pendants, brooches, earrings, cufflinks, lovespoons and other pieces in a dedicated display workshop that has changed little since 1976.

The centre also showcases the work of some of Wales' best designer-makers. These vary from Brian Eburah, a fellow jeweller who specialises in combining precious metals with vibrant Titanium and Niobium, to Simant Bostock, a sculptor who uses Crystacast and Cold-Cast Bronze Resins to create fascinating figurines.

In what is one of the premier craft outlets in the whole of Wales, the displays in the light, spacious rooms include bronzes, ceramics, glassware, decanters, paperweights, lovespoons, textiles, woodwork, fruit bowls, toys and games, chess sets, piggy banks, red dragons, Welsh teddies, sheepskin rugs, books, CDs and DVDs of Welsh music....and much more. Other gift ideas include single malts and cream liqueur from Welsh Whisky and an amazing range of honey products: elderflower, fudge, mustard, ginger in honey, walnuts in honey, mead, honeyed marmalade. There's also a nice little tea room on the premises.

Rhiannon Jewellery, which is a truely traditional Welsh family company, is open from 10 to 5 Monday to Saturday, also on Sunday in July, August and December.

opened in 1873, the **Tregaron Kite Centre and Museum** is an interesting and informative place, dedicated to the red kite. With the dual aims of providing people with a better understanding of these beautiful birds of prey, and with ensuring their survival in this part of mid Wales, visitors to the centre can also see the kites being fed daily during the winter months. Also at the museum are artefacts from Ceredigion Museum that relate specifically to Tregaron and the surrounding area.

Although Tregaron is chiefly associated with sheep and wool, it is also the location of the **Rhiannon Welsh Gold Centre**, which is in the centre of the town. And in August each year the popular **Festival of Harness Racing** is held at the Tregaron Trotting Club grounds at Neuadd Brenigg

To the north of the town lies **Cors Caron**, an ancient bog that is home to rare flora and fauna. The land was originally covered by a glacier that, at the end of the last Ice Age, melted to create a natural lake which, gradually filled with sediment and vegetation. The peat grew in thickness, creating three distinctive domes above the original lake bed level. The **Old Railway Walk**, along the track bed of the old Manchester-Milford Haven railway, provides visitors with the chance to observe some of the over 170 species of birds recorded here, including red kites, buzzards and sparrow hawks. The walk starts from the car park near Maesllyn Farm on the B4343, two miles north of Tregaron.

PONTRHYDFENDIGAID
15 miles NE of Lampeter off the B4343

🏛 Strata Florida Abbey

Just a short distance from this village, the name of which translates as the "bridge across the blessed ford", lies **Strata Florida Abbey**, a Cistercian house founded in 1164 by Robert Fitzstephen. This austere order was renowned for seeking out remote and isolated sites for its religious establishments and Strata Florida - the vale of Flowers - is one such site. Even though the abbey is in ruins today, it is still an evocative place. Just two years after its foundation, the abbey's lands were overrun by Rhys ap Gryffyd but, in 1184, he refounded the abbey, and most of the buildings date from this time. During the 12th and 13th century, Strata Florida became not only one of the most important religious centres in Wales, but also a place that influenced Welsh culture, as it was patronised by

Stata Florida Abbey, Pontrhydfendigaid

🎞 stories and anecdotes 🐦 famous people 🎨 art and craft 🎭 entertainment and sport 🚶 walks

both royalty and poets. Some of the last native princes and princesses of Wales were buried here, as was Dafydd ap Gwilym, probably the most famous of all Welsh medieval poets, who was born near Aberystwyth (see also Penrhyncoch). In 1238, the Welsh princes swore their allegiance to Llywelyn the Great's son, Dafydd, at the abbey. This was also the time when the abbey became very wealthy, mainly through wool from the sheep that grazed its vast lands.

After the Dissolution in the 16th century, the abbey and its lands passed through various hands and the ruins today, which are now in the ownership of CADW, consist mainly of the cloister, the chapter house and the church. In the north transept stands a memorial to the poet Dafydd ap Gwilym. The yew tree that stands amidst the abbey's remains is thought to mark his grave. One legend associated with

the abbey suggests that the Holy Grail, which was given to the monks at Glastonbury by Joseph of Arimathea, later ended up at Strata Florida. When the abbey, which formed part of the Nanteos estate, was left to fall into ruins, the cup, which had pieces bitten out of its sides by pilgrims convinced of its healing powers, was stored at Nanteos mansion.

Cardigan

🏛 Cardigan Castle   🏛 Shire Hall

🏛 County Gaol   🏛 Parish Church of St Mary

🏛 Teifi Bridge   🏚 Cardigan Heritage Centre

🌿 Welsh Wildlife Centre   ✒ Theatr Mwldan

Once the busiest port in Wales, Cardigan is an ancient borough that received its first charter in 1199, and was, in the 12th century, a power base of Lord Rhys, one of the last Welsh

---

PENDRE ART

35 Pendre, Aberteifi, Cardigan, Ceredigion SA43 1JS
Tel: 01239 615151
e-mail: pendreart@hotmail.co.uk
website: www.pendreart.co.uk

Providing a window on the world of contemporary art in West Wales, **Pendre Art** is a stylish and well-presented gallery and café, which amazingly, was once a Post Office garage. It is owned and run by Liz and Andy Hickling-Baker both actors who have always been involved in the art world. In addition to showcasing the work of artists such as David Beattie, Eloise Govier and Iwan Dafis, and photographers Eric Lees and Michael Jackson, their gallery displays the work of local craftspeople working in jewellery, pottery, woodwork and sculpture. They hold regular exhibitions and workshops, for example, Batik with renowned batik artist, Wendy Evans. They also offer a picture framing service.

Set in the attractive and relaxing interior of the gallery the Coffee Shop serves high quality breakfasts, light lunches and cakes, along with freshly brewed Ferrari coffee, teas, soft and alcoholic drinks. Open-air seating is available at the front of the gallery. The Coffee shop and Gallery is open from 9.30am to 5pm, (extended opening hours in peak season) Monday to Saturday.

🏛 historic building 🏚 museum and heritage 🏛 historic site 🌿 scenic attraction 🌿 flora and fauna

THE CUSTOM HOUSE SHOP AND GALLERY

44 & 45 St Mary Street, Cardigan,
Ceredigion SA43 1HA
Tel: 01239 615541 Fax: 01239 615310
e-mail: info@customhousecardigan.com
website: www.customhousecardigan.com

Cardigan is a town steeped in history, and visitors should allow plenty of time to visit landmarks such as the Castle, Shire Hall, County Gaol, St Mary's Church and the Heritage centre, and also to enjoy a stroll along the banks of the River Teifi. History comes alive in the buildings, but one old building has found a new and fascinating cultural role.

Cardigan's original **Custom House** is now home to an amazing range of work by designers and makers based in Wales, along with an exclusive collection of creative home and lifestyle accessories. Among the many talented artists whose work can be seen and bought here are Catrin Howell, who specialises in ceramic sculpture, Sally James (mixed media paintings), Fran Evans (illustrator) and John Knapp-Fisher (prints).

The various rooms with their atmospheric stone walls and wooden floors provide a wonderful setting for these and other artists and for a wide variety of exclusive, original, stylish and very desirable items large and small. These include furniture, ironware, lamps and lighting accessories, designer knitwear, bags, shawls and scarves by Zoe Gealy, one-off designer necklaces, bracelets and brooches.....and a great deal more. A notable product in the garden section is the Servicue, a high-tech and very stylish permanent sculptural barbecue designed and manufactured in the UK.

The Custom House has also gained a wide-ranging reputation for its design commissions (including beautifully crafted oak pieces) and interior renovation projects.

The shop and gallery are open from 10 to 5 Monday to Saturday. Customers who can't visit the shop in person can access the excellent website, where 200 + items can be viewed and purchased online and delivered to the shopper's door. Gift tokens are also available.

In addition there is also a lovely, spacious, self-catering holiday apartment above the Custom House. For details please contact the shop.

 stories and anecdotes famous people art and craft entertainment and sport walks

Teifi Bridge, Cardigan

as the chapel of a Benedictine priory. It now dates mainly from the 19th century, and was once a place of pilgrimage, as it housed a fine statute of Our Lady that was destroyed at the Reformation.

The River Teifi, which provides Cardigan with its Welsh name Aberteifi, continues to be fished for trout and some still use the traditional coracle. Dating from pre-Christian times, coracles were once common on many of Britain's rivers and they have changed little over the centuries. The silting up of the Teifi estuary, along with the arrival of the railway, were the main causes of Cardigan's decline as a major port, which had, at one time, over 300 ships registered there.

However, while the river is no longer at the centre of the town's economy, it is still a place of charm enhanced by the six-arched **Teifi Bridge**, an ancient structure that was rebuilt in 1726. Housed in a warehouse built in 1745 on Teifi Wharf, the **Cardigan Heritage Centre** tells the story of this former county town, from prehistoric times through to the present day. From its origins in the medieval age to its heyday in the 18th and 19th centuries, the port, in particular, is explored through the eyes of those who lived here. In addition to the permanent exhibitions, there is a programme of

princes to rule an independent principality. The few remains of **Cardigan Castle**, which stand beside the river, conceal a turbulent history. The first castle was built in the 11th century, then rebuilt by Gilbert Fitzrichard in the early 1100s. Gryffydd ap Rhys took the castle in 1156 and rebuilt and strengthened it. It then passed into the hands of the Earl of Pembroke in 1240. Thought to be the site of the first eisteddfod in 1176, the castle fell to Parliament in 1645 during the Civil War.

The **Shire Hall** was built in 1763, and housed the courtroom and council chamber, which has previously been within the castle. In the 19th century these functions passed to the newly-built Guildhall. Prisoners who had been convicted at the Shire Hall were paraded through the street to the County Gaol, being pelted with rotten fruit and eggs as they went. The **County Gaol** itself still stands, and was built in 1793 to the designs of John Nash. In 1881, it was converted into a police station and private house. The **Parish Church of St Mary** was originally built in the 12th century

temporary exhibitions covering a range of topics. Those looking for performing arts and other cultural events will also not be disappointed as the **Theatr Mwldan**, in the town, is one of Wales' leading theatrical venues.

Beside the river, just outside the town, lies the **Welsh Wildlife Centre**, a nature reserve that provides a variety of habitats, including reed beds, woodland and meadow. As well as an extensive network of footpaths and, being home to a surprisingly wide variety of flora and fauna, the reserve also has an excellent visitor centre.

The cardigan as an item of clothing was named after the 7th Earl of Cardigan, John Thomas Brudenell (1797–1868), who commanded the Light Brigade during the Crimean War. He did not invent the cardigan (they had been around in the 17th century) but he did popularise it.

Around Cardigan

FELINWYNT
3½ miles NE of Cardigan off the A487

🦋 Felinwynt Rainforest and Butterfly Centre

This village is home to the **Felinwynt Rainforest and Butterfly Centre** (see panel below) where, in a large tropical house, visitors are transported to the jungle to see the beautiful free-flying butterflies that live amidst the exotic plants. There is also a rainforest exhibition, that explains the delicate ecology of this interesting habitat, a tea room and a gift shop.

ABERPORTH
6 miles NE of Cardigan on the B4333

🦋 Penbryn

The original village of Aberporth consisted of small, single-storeyed cottages with thick mud

The Felinwynt Rainforest Centre

Rhosmaen, Felinwynt, Cardigan, Dyfed SA43 1RT
Tel: 01239 810882
website: www.butterflycentre.co.uk

Felinwynt Rainforest Centre has become one of Ceredigion's chief attractions with thousands of visitors every year. The highlight of any visit is the Mini-Rainforest created by owner John Devereux. Wander through a jungle among tropical plants, exotic butterflies, waterfalls, pools and fish, with the soothing sounds of the Peruvian Rainforest.

The Video room show films of rainforests and butterflies. The Visitor Centre houses the gift shop with an extensive range of gifts for everyone, the café where you can have fresh cooked meals and snacks all day including Dorothy's homemade cakes and the exhibition based on the Tambopata region of Peru.

All the facilities are suitable for disabled. Entrance charge to Tropical House only.

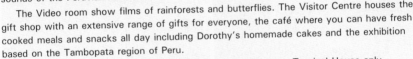

📽 stories and anecdotes 🐿 famous people 🎨 art and craft 🎭 entertainment and sport 🚶 walks

POTTERY & PAINTINGS

Aberporth Road, Tanygroes, Cardigan SA43 2HR
Tel: 01239 810265 Mob:07964454306
e-mail: joe.finch@virgin.net
website: www.potteryandpaintings.co.uk or www.TrudiFinch.co.uk

Come and browse in the large showroom and gallery where there is an extensive range of hand made pottery by master craftsman Joe Finch and beautiful pictures by, world renowned artist, Trudi Finch.

The studio and gallery, which have been awarded the 'Quality Assured Attraction' are situated in a beautifully converted stone farm building just 200 meters down a drive off the road between Tanygroes and Aberporth. (Just 1 mile from the lovely sandy beaches of Aberporth.)

Joe makes pots for every day use: dishes, bowls, jugs and plates, pots for cooking and serving food as well as some individual pieces. Practical, unassuming, wood-fired stoneware ceramics that he hopes people will find desirable and affordable.

Trudi's artwork covers many techniques, mediums and subject matter. She is best known for her fantasy fairies but also paints detailed flower, animal, children and landscapes images.

Watch the potter working, demonstrations and admission free. Open most days but please phone before making a special journey.

Llangranog

Distance: *2.8 miles (4.5 kilometres)*
Typical time: *90 mins*
Height gain: *100 metres*
Map: *Explorer 198*
Walk: *www.walkingworld.com ID:1451*
Contributor: *Pat Roberts*

ACCESS INFORMATION:

There is a free car park at the top of the hill down to Llangranog. It is signed left at the post office. There is parking at the cafe and pub down at the coast if you are using these facilities. For Llangranog, follow signs from the A487 from New Quay to Cardigan.

DESCRIPTION:

Not a long walk, but it can be rewarding if you wish to see dolphins and choughs. However, like all wildlife they do not appear to order. The spectacular views are always available.

FEATURES:

Sea, National Trust/NTS, Wildlife, Birds, Flowers, Great Views, Butterflies

1 | From the car park, walk left down to the post office and at the junction go left for about 150 metres. Look over the wall on the left to see a magnificent waterfall and, if you are lucky, some dippers.

2 | Just as the road starts to descend to the sea, take the 'No Through Road'on the right. There are wnderful views of the coast on the left.

3 | Where the road divides, take the left or lower path to contour around the mound ahead. The return is through the upper gate.

4 | When you reach the farmhouse of Lochtyn, take this gate to the right of the buildings; there is a footpath sign on it.

5 | After about 40 metres the path is signed to the left to follow the coast. After a while, it is joined by the coast path coming up from the left.

6 | Take the left, lower path to walk down to the headland of Ynys-Lochtyn, usually the home of the choughs, but return to this point to continue on the top path, which is the coast path, for views on up the coast towards Cwmtudu.

7 | The path ahead is the coast path, but leave it here to climb up to the ridge to the right.

8 | At the top, join a tarmac track. If you wish to climb to the top, walk right and up. Otherwise, go left through the kissing-gate and follow the track down to rejoin the outward route at Waymark 3. Walk down the road to the more main road where you turn left, and at the post office right, up to the car park.

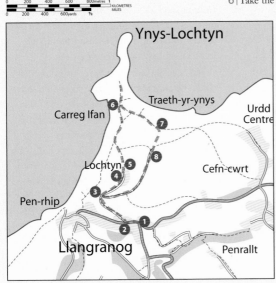

walls and thatched roofs that reflected the simple and hard lives of those living in this fishing and farming community. At one time Aberporth became famous for its herring industry as great shoals of the fish came to feed and spawn in the shallow waters of this sheltered part of the Cardigan Bay coast. Today, and particularly in the summer months, the village is a small yet thriving resort that is popular with yachtsmen.

A little way up the coast is the National Trust's beach at **Penbryn**, an SSSI, part of the Ceredigion Heritage Coast and a good spot for insect, bird and dolphin spotting.

The approach to this popular, sandy beach is by way of Hoffnant Valley from the Trust's car park at Llanborth Farm, where a shop, café and toilets are open in season. The valley is known locally as Cwm Lladron, Robbers Valley, probably because of past smuggling connections.

LLANGRANOG
9½ miles NE of Cardigan on the B4334

🏛 Parish Church of St Caranog   🎞 Carreg Bica

🐾 Sarah Jane Rees

Lying in a narrow valley and rather reminiscent of a Cornish fishing village, Llangranog (sometimes spelled Llangrannog) is not only one of the most attractive villages along the Ceredigion coast, but also one of the most popular resorts in the area. The headland and cliffs to the north of the village (now the property of the National Trust) offer excellent walks and dramatic scenery. The sheltered coves around Llangranog once helped to sustain a thriving shipbuilding industry, but they also proved perfect landing and hiding places for contraband and the area was rife with smuggling activity. On the beach there is a rock known as **Carreg Bica** ("Bica's

Rock"). Legend says it is the tooth of the giant Bica, who spat it out when he had toothache. The **Parish Church of St Caranog** is dedicated to a saint who was the grandson of Ceredig, from which Ceredigion gets its name. The church was founded in the 6th century, though the persent building dates from 1885. In the churchyard is the grave of **Sarah Jane Rees** (1839–1916), master mariner and poet. She was the daughter of a ship's captain, and taught navigation and mathematics in her native Wales, as well as in Liverpool and London. She was also a leading member of the Band of Hope and a supporter of the Temperance Movement.

MWNT
3½ miles N of Cardigan off the A487

🏛 Parish Church of the Holy Cross

This beauty spot was on the Pilgrims' Route to Bardsey Island off the Lleyn Peninsula. The tiny **Parish Church of the Holy Cross** dates from around 1400 and stands on the site of a much earlier Celtic church, originally built in a hollow to hide it from view and protect it from possible raiders coming by sea.

Much of the coastline here, including the cliffs, the rocky headland and the safe family beach, is owned by the National Trust. This area is a geological SSSI (Site of Special Scientific Interest) and is part of the Ceredigion Heritage Coast; it is especially rich in maritime flora. The bay was the site of a battle in 1155, when Fleming invaders were repelled by the local forces.

GWBERT-ON-SEA
2½ miles NW of Cardigan on the B4548

🌳 Cardigan Island

🐦 Cardigan Island Coastal Farm Park

This small resort on the eastern banks of the

River Teifi estuary is an excellent place for cliff walking and for looking out over the estuary and observing its wildlife. To the north of the village, and lying some 200 yards offshore, is **Cardigan Island**, a nature reserve to which there is no unauthorised access and which is inhabited by a flock of wild Soay sheep.

Back on the mainland, **Cardigan Island Coastal Farm Park** is an ideal place from which to look out over the island from the headland and also to observe the rare choughs and colony of seals, and some lucky visitors may also spot Cardigan Bay's bottlenose dolphins. The farm is also home to friendly farm animals, including goats, sheep, pigs, ponies and ducks, as well as a llama, a wallaby and rare breed cows.

HENLLAN
11½ miles SE of Cardigan on the B4334

🚂 Teifi Valley Railway

This village is home to the **Teifi Valley Railway**, another of Wales' famous little trains. This narrow gauge railway, which originally served the slate quarries, was created from a section of the Great Western Railway (also known as God's Wonderful Railway) that served the rural areas of West Wales. Today's passengers can enjoy a 40-minute steam train journey through this delightful valley while, at the Henllan terminus, there are plenty of attractions to keep the whole family amused: woodland walks, crazy golf, the station tearooms, and a gift and souvenir shop.

LOCATOR MAP

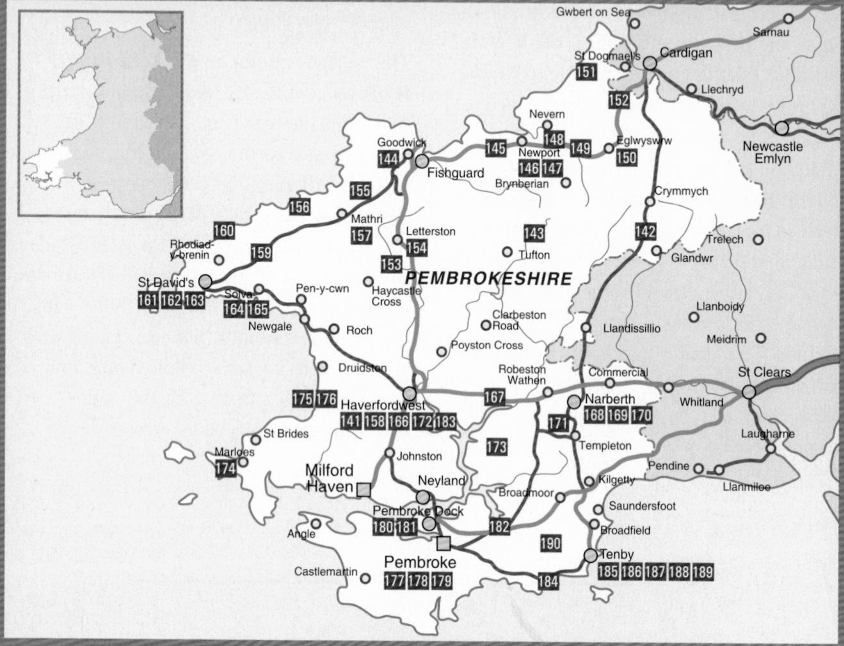

ADVERTISERS AND PLACES OF INTEREST

Accommodation, Food and Drink

141 | The Woof Guide - Pembrokeshire Coastal Cottages, Haverfordwest *pg 233*
143 | The Post Office Bistro & Bar, Rosebush *pg 235*
146 | Morawelan Waterfront Café, Bar & Restaurant, Newport *pg 239*
147 | Y Mochyn Drwg Restaurant, Newport *pg 240*
150 | Dyfed Shires & Leisure Farm, Eglwyswrw *pg 242*
151 | Coach House Trading, St Dogmaels *pg 243*
152 | Croft Farm & Celtic Cottages, Croft *pg 244*
153 | Stone Hall Hotel & Restaurant, Welsh Hook *pg 247*
154 | Indigo Brown, Letterston, Haverfordwest *pg 247*
155 | Clover Cottage, St Nicholas, Castlemorris *pg 248*
156 | Oriel-y-Felin Gallery & Tearoom, Trefin *pg 249*
158 | Pembrokeshire Coastal Cottages, Haverfordwest *pg 250*
159 | Crug-Glas Country House, Abereiddy *pg 251*
160 | Porthiddy Farm Holiday Cottages, Berea *pg 252*
161 | Sampler Tea Room & Museum, St David's *pg 253*
162 | The Waterings, St David's *pg 253*
163 | Oriel y Parc Landscape Gallery, St David's *pg 255*
164 | Aelwyd B & B, Solva *pg 256*
165 | Solva Woollen Mill, Solva *pg 257*
167 | Clerkenhill Farm Adventure Park, Slebech *pg 260*
171 | Narbeth Holidays, Molleston, Narbeth *pg 263*
172 | Toddle Pembrokeshire - Pembrokeshire Coastal Cottages, Haverfordwest *pg 264*
173 | Cwm Deri Vineyard, Martletwy *pg 265*
174 | Albion House, Marloes, Haverfordwest *pg 267*
175 | Ocean Café, Bar & Restaurant, Broad Haven *pg 269*
177 | The Cornstore, Pembroke *pg 271*
180 | Borders Bed & Breakfast, Pembroke Dock *pg 274*
183 | Refreshology - Coastal Cottages, Haverfordwest *pg 276*
184 | Celtic Haven, Lydstep, Tenby *pg 277*
186 | Bay House Bed & Breakfast, Tenby *pg 281*
187 | Holiday Connections, Tenby *pg 282*

Activities

145 | Havard Stables, Dinas Cross, Newport *pg 238*
149 | Castell Henllys Iron Age Fort, Meline *pg 242*
150 | Dyfed Shires & Leisure Farm, Eglwyswrw *pg 242*
151 | Coach House Trading, St Dogmaels *pg 243*

historic building · museum and heritage · historic site · scenic attraction · flora and fauna

7 | Pembrokeshire

Pembrokeshire, which is known as Sir Benfro in Welsh, is home to Britain's only coastal national park – the Pembrokeshire Coast National Park. Visitors flock to this leading European holiday destination to see the spectacular grandeur and tranquil beauty of the countryside and walk some of the 186-mile coastal cliff top path. The coastal region is also a paradise for bird watchers. Incorporating one of the most fantastic stretches of natural beauty in Europe, the Pembrokeshire Coast National Park begins (or ends) on the south-facing shoreline near

Tenby. Running right around the ruggedly beautiful southwestern tip of Wales, around St Brides Bay and up along the north facing coast almost to Cardigan, the Park also includes quiet fishing villages, the huge cliffs at Castlemartin, sweeping golden beaches and small, often busy harbours.

Although not strictly on the coast, the labyrinthine Cleddau river system also lies within the Park's boundaries and here there are delightful little villages such as Cresswell and Carew, as well as the superb sheltered harbour of Milford Haven.

📷 stories and anecdotes 🐿 famous people 🎨 art and craft 🚲 entertainment and sport 🥾 walks

Offshore there are various islands, including Grassholm, Ramsey, Skokholm and Skomer, which have changed little since they were named by Viking invaders.

Many are now bird and wildlife sanctuaries of international importance. Grassholm is home to thousands of gannets, Skokholm has Manx shearwaters, Skomer has shearwaters and puffins. In addition, Ramsey harbours such species as choughs and the red-legged crow, and is also the resting place of many Welsh saints. One island, Caldey has, for over 1,500 years, been the home of a religious community that continues today to live a quiet and austere life. Between their devotions, the monks of Caldey scrape a living from the land and are famous for their range of perfumes and toiletries inspired by the island's wild flowers. Pembrokeshire is the home of the corgi, which was brought to the notice of the Kennel Club by Captain Jack Howell. He presented Princess Elizabeth with her first corgi, and the rest, as they say, is history.

In Pembrokeshire you will also find the Preseli Hills, sometimes known as the Preseli Mountains, though in fact the highest point, Foel Cymcerwyn, is only 1,759 feet high. Though the range of hills is inland, it forms part of the Pembrokeshire Coast National Park, which takes a swing to the east to form a bulge before rejoining the coast near Cardigan. It is excellent walking country. Also it was from here that the bluestones for the inner circle of Stonehenge were quarried.

There is one place in Pembrokeshire that is sacred to all Welsh people - the city of St David's. City status was officially granted in 1994, though in truth, people had looked on it as a city long before that, thanks to its cathedral. It is near here that the country's patron saint, St David (Dewi Sant), was born, and it was in what was then called Rose Vale that he founded a monastery that later became St Davids Cathedral. In 589 AD he died, and his bones lie in the Cathedral to this day.

below Goodwick, where they formally surrendered to Lord Cawdor just two days after landing. Jemima Nicholas, who is said to have captured 12 Frenchmen single-handedly, became famous as the General of the Red Army. She died in 1832 and is buried in the **Parish Church of St Mary**. Though there has been a church here for centuries, the present church dates from 1857.

The Last Invasion Embroidered Tapestry, which was created in 1997 to mark the bicentenary of this bizarre event, hangs in a purpose-built gallery located in the Town Hall. Designed by Elizabeth Cramp RWS and worked by more than 70 embroiderers, the 100-foot long tapestry is in the style of the famous Bayeux Tapestry and depicts scenes from the invasion.

GOODWICK
1 mile W of Fishguard off the A487

🏛 Oceanlab   🌿 Manorowen Garden

This once-small fishing village is now effectively the base for Fishguard harbour, which was built between 1894 and 1906 by the Fishguard and Rosslare Railways and Harbours Company to provide a sea link between southwest Wales and Ireland. Still offering a much-used ferry service today, Goodwick is older than it first appears. The settlement was known to ancient inhabitants as Gwlad hud a Lledrith – the Land of Mystery and Enchantment. The surrounding countryside certainly lives up to this name, although the tales told by James Wade, one of Pembrokeshire's best known storytellers, are rather far-fetched, but nonetheless delightful.

PINK CORSAGE

Celtic House, Main Street, Goodwick,
Pembrokeshire SA64 0BN
Tel: 01348 871900
Mobile: 07885 203030
e-mail: info@pinkcorsage.co.uk
website: www.pinkcorsage.co.uk

This unique shop & studio where the owner Alison designs and hand crafts inspirational bespoke silk floral bouquets, corsages, table decorations, wrist corsages and fascinators. Alison offers a one-to-one floral design service providing a real alternative for your wedding bouquet designed and created in Wales. Alison specialises in decorative accessories, such as beading, crystals & feathers. Her skills mean that she can create the most creative and bespoke designs any bride could wish for. Silk flowers can offer a real alternative to fresh flowers...

Our range of corsages, buttonholes and fascinators can be designed to match your outfit, wrist corsages for the prom or just a special party!

In addition to the flowers there is a range of expressive and thoughtful gifts, wedding accessories which compliment Alison's style of floral designs, including garters, keepsake boxes, wedding cake toppers even comical Bride & Groom toilet roll! All the flowers and gifts are available to buy online from the web site.

For 2009, Alison is introducing relaxed creative flower courses from her Victorian town house in the picturesque coastal town of Goodwick with four star B & B accommodation available. The courses include creating bouquets, corsages and table decorations, working with silk flowers, beading and wiring techniques.

📖 stories and anecdotes   🦅 famous people   🎨 art and craft   🎭 entertainment and sport   🚶 walks

On one occasion Wade, who died in 1887, recounted that, while he was fishing on Goodwick beach, a great carrion crow swooped out of the sky and carried him, in its beak, across the sea to Ireland. On reaching land, the crow dropped Wade and he landed in a cannon where he spent the night. As he was waking the next morning, the cannon was fired and Wade was rocketed across St George's Channel and he landed beside his fishing rod in the exact spot from which he had been plucked!

The **Oceanlab** has hands-on exhibitions about marine life, and displays explaining how marine creatures defend themselves from predators. There is also a dolphin buzzer, a feel box and a food chain puzzle. Just a mile to the south of Goodwick lies **Manorowen Garden**, an interesting walled garden which

has an historic gazebo. The garden was also involved in the French invasion of the 18th century, with a skirmish taking place between Colonel William Tate's invading army and the local militia.

DINAS
3½ miles NE of Fishguard on the A487

🌱 Dinas Island   🌱 Dinas Head

The village is situated at the base of **Dinas Island,** which is, in fact, a promontory that culminates in the cliffs of **Dinas Head**, which are 463 feet high. Now no longer a true island, the land was given this name because at the end of the Ice Age it was indeed separated from the mainland. In the care of the National Trust, the headland is an important nesting site for sea birds, and grey and Atlantic seals can often be seen swimming offshore.

HAVARD STABLES

Dinas Cross, Newport, Pembrokeshire SA42 0SR
Tel: 01348 811452

Picturesque hillsides, quiet bridleways, open countryside, fresh Welsh country air, friendly riding horses. If you love any of these then you'll love a day at **Havard Stables**. Hannah Havard opened her family home as a riding establishment 7 years ago and has gained a wealth of experience in developing the skills of both the capable rider and the enthusiastic novice. You'll find staff are caring and friendly, in and out of the saddle! The school offers riding instruction/trekking.

Hannah's aim is to get people out and enjoying the Welsh countryside but with the added advantage of being on the back of a horse.

Just outside the quaint village of Dinas Cross in beautiful Pembrokeshire, Havard Stables is perfectly sited to offer all types of horse riding. Lessons are available in the enclosed sand school or escorted treks into the hills, where you can enjoy beautiful uninterrupted views. The horses are all well trained with happy expressions; they are safe, well mannered and enjoyable to ride on hacks or in the schooling arena. Pony rides are available for small children minimum age beeing 4 years thay last for half an hour. Longer rides are offered for older children and adults. Also pony days are a great day for children to lurn and have fun around ponies.

🏠 historic building 🏛 museum and heritage 🏚 historic site 🍃 scenic attraction 🌱 flora and fauna

MORAWELAN WATERFRONT CAFÉ, BAR & RESTAURANT

The Parrog, Newport,
Pembrokeshire SA42 0RW
Tel: 01235 820565
email:carreg@morawelon.fsnet.co.uk

Morawelan Waterfront Café, Bar & Restaurant has been owned and run by the Watts family for many generations and is currently in the capable hands of the mother-and-son team of Christine and Richard Watts.

Their café occupies a superb position overlooking Newport Bay, a wonderful spot from which to watch the sun go down. The menu features an excellent choice of freshly prepared, mostly local produce - dishes such as baked crab, hot buttered lobster, Welsh lamb cutlets, freshly prepared salads, and more. On Sundays, traditional roasts are served. To complement your meal, choose from the extensive selection stocked in the fully licensed bar. There are 50 seats inside or you may prefer to sit on the terraces surrounded by the sea and the Presili Hills. Morawelan is open from 5pm to 11pm, but closed throughout November.

Newport Parrog was once a lively sea port. This settlement predates the town below which it nestles but to which it has now long joined. Shipbuilding, fishing, slate quarrying, coastal trading and lime burning were important in the past. Parrog has an attractive coastal character, with impressive vertical slate sea walling and older buildings along the shore-relict warehouses and limekilns-standing today as reminders of its maritime, industrial and commercial past.

MORAWELON CAMPING & CARAVAN SITE

Newport, Pembrokeshire SA42 0RW
Tel: 01239 820565

Located behind Morawelon Café/Restaurant, the **Morawelon Caravan Site** is just a short distance from Newport Beach. The caravan site is very well-equipped, including showers, toilets, hot and cold basins, washing facilities, electric hook-up points and a covered area for barbecues. The site is ideal is ideally located as a base for exploring the many attractions of Pembrokeshire. For insurance reasons, the site is only open for eight months of the year.

Newport itself is an attractive, bustling coastal town between Fishguard and Cardigan on the A487. It boasts both a Norman castle and church, both of which stand proudly above the small medieval town clinging to the slopes of Carn Ingli mountain. Ancient streets and pathways lead directly to the river.

NEWPORT

6½ miles E of Fishguard on the A487

🏛 Lords' Castle 　 🏛 Carreg Coetan Arthur

As its name would suggest, Newport was once an important port. It had a brisk wool trade until the time of the great plague, when trade was diverted to Fishguard. Newport was also the capital of the Marcher Lordship of Cemaes - the only one not to have been abolished by Henry VIII – and the **Lords' Castle**, which was built in the 13th century, and has now been incorporated into a mansion house (not open to the public).

Today, this is a pretty little seaside town with a fine beach that still retains the charm of its fishing port. An excellent place from which to explore the Preseli Hills to the south. Just to the north of the town is **Carreg Coetan Arthur**, a collapsed burial chamber that reputedly held the remains of King Arthur.

NEVERN

8 miles E of Fishguard on the B4582

🏛 Parish Church of St Brynach 　 🏛 Nevern Castle

🏛 Mynydd Carn Ingli 　 🏛 St Brynach's Cross

🏛 Mounting Block

The village of Nevern's most interesting features can be found at the **Parish Church of St Brynach**, which is dedicated to the 5th century Irish saint whose cell was on nearby **Mynydd Carn Ingli** - (the Mount of Angels). Inside the church are two carved stones: the Maglocunus Stone, dating from the 5th century, commemorates Maglocunus, the son of Clutor, and it bears both Latin and Ogham inscriptions, and the Cross Stone, which bears a Viking cross and dates

Y MOCHYN DRWG RESTAURANT

Market Street, Newport,
Pembrokeshire SA42 0PH
Tel: 01239 820807
e-mail: info@ymochyndrwg.co.uk
website: www.ymochyndrwg.co.uk

Y Mochyn Drwg (Welsh for The Naughty Pig) is a small family run restaurant in Pembrokeshire, where chef Alastair Vaan and his wife Louise provide a personal and informal dining experience. The food is firmly rooted in Pembrokeshire, Welsh and British seasonal supply, using no imported fresh produce beyond the occasional citrus, onions and carrots.

Alastair has a self-professed passion for food and spends hours searching out the highest quality local produce to use in his exciting dishes. Locally and ethically sourced foods such as rare breed meats, artisan cheese, fresh local seafood and much more form the building blocks for the rapidly changing short menus, which are accompanied by an interesting European wine list.

Uncomplicated flavours, traditional foundations and modern technique come together at Y Mochyn Drwg to create an original and mouth-watering cuisine. Each course is beautifully cooked and exquisitely presented, examples might include smoked mackerel and leek tartlet to start, followed by braised blade and roasted sirloin of Longhorn beef, thyme and mustard carrots and dumplings and finishing with chocolate fondant with gorse flower ice cream.

Y Mochyn Drwg also runs events and food courses throughout the year, please contact the restaurant for details.

🏛 historic building 🏛 museum and heritage 🏛 historic site 🔱 scenic attraction 🌱 flora and fauna

PENBANC FABRICS

Plasyffynon, Felindre Farchog, Pembrokeshire SA41 3XB
Tel/Fax: 01239 820568

Twenty-five years of serving the local community has established an unbeatable reputation for quality, service and value for money at **Penbanc Fabrics**. The number of repeat visitors to Annie Washbrook's unique enterprise on the A487 Fishguard-Cardigan road is testimony to the success of this friendly family-run business, and the words has spread to the many holidaymakers who pass this way to discover the scenic and historic attractions of the coast and countryside. The place itself is a real delight: behind a farmhouse in a beautiful rural setting old farm buildings have been converted to house four large interconnecting rooms. To pass beyond the creeper-framed entrance is to enter an Aladdin's Cave of fabrics, an amazing choice that covers cotton, silk, denim, viscose, patchwork, bridal material, curtain fabrics and much more, covering all the brands you can think of and many more you can't, to take away or to have made up into curtains, chair covers or other soft furnishings. Six girls are kept busy working on the orders, and Annie can put customers in touch with designers for special orders. If you're looking for a fabric, any fabric, Annie is pretty sure you'll find it in this quaint, cosy, friendly place, which is open from 10am to 6pm on

from the 10th century. Outside in the churchyard, near the entrance to the church, stands one of the finest Celtic crosses in Wales - **St Brynach's Cross**. Dating from the 10th or 11th century, the cross stands some 13 feet tall and, according to tradition, the first cuckoo to be heard each year in Pembrokeshire sings from the top of the cross on St Brynach's Day (7 April). In the road outside the chruch can be seen the **Mounting Block**, used as a 'leg up' when riders were mounting their horses. It is one of only two left in Pembrokeshire.

To the northwest of the village are the remains of **Nevern Castle**, which was originally a local chieftain's fortress until, in around 1100, the Marcher Lord of Cemaes, Robert Martyn, built a motte and bailey castle on the site. The castle came into the hands of Rhys ap Gryffydd at the end of the 12th century and he added the stone castle, parts of which can still be seen today among the overgrown ruins.

EGLWYSWRW

11½ miles E of Fishguard on the A487

⛪ Parish Church of St Cristiolus

🏚 Castell Henllys

To the west of the village lies **Castell Henllys** (see panel opposite), an Iron Age settlement that is still being excavated by archaeologists. While the dig is continuing throughout the summer months, visitors to this late prehistoric site can also see the thatched roundhouses and outbuildings created to give as true an insight as possible into the lives of Iron Age man. Events throughout the season help to portray the wide spectrum of Celtic culture, from storytelling and craft demonstrations to the celebration of ancient festivals.

📖 stories and anecdotes 👤 famous people 🎨 art and craft 🎭 entertainment and sport 🚶 walks

CASTELL HENLLYS IRON AGE FORT

Meline, Crymych, Pembrokeshire SA41 3UT
Tel/Fax: 01239 891319
e-mail: enquiries@castellhenllys.com
website: www.castellhenllys.com

Castell Henllys Iron Age Fort is a unique, multi-award-winning visitor attraction set amid the spectacular scenery of the Pembrokeshire Coast National Park. In this glorious setting visitors can explore a defended hilltop fort to learn how people lived here 2000 years ago. The Castell Henllys roundhouses that are at the heart of the site are the only ones in the UK that have been rebuilt in exactly the same spot as the original Iron Age dwellings.

Archaeologists uncovered the old foundations and other information to enable the site owner, Pembrokeshire Coast National Park Authority, to reconstruct the fortress much as it would have appeared 2000 years ago, using the ground plan and applying basic principles – the necessary interior heights, the slope of the roof – to come as close as possible to the original Chieftain's House, Granary, Smithy, Old Roundhouse and Earthwatch, the last named after the foundation that helped to rebuild it.

Other attractions on this extraordinary site include the Exhibition Centre, ramparts, trails and some amazing talking sculptures. Signposted off the A487 between Newport and Cardigan, Castell Henllys is open from 10am to 5pm, April to October and 11am to 3pm, November to March.

DYFED SHIRES & LEISURE PARK

Carnhuan, Eglwyswrw, Cardigan, North Pembrokeshire, Wales SA41 3SY
Tel: 01239 891288
website: www.leisurefarm.co.uk

Meet some real Welsh farming characters at Wales' most well known Shire horse farm, home of the Dyfed Shires. **Dyfed Shires & Leisure Park** is a working farm that is also a family attraction, and with 11,000 square feet of undercover amusements it is great in all weathers. As well as the beautiful Shire horses you can enjoy an abundance of traditional farm animals. There are activities and fun for everyone, children can bottle feed baby animals or enjoy a horse and cart ride around the farm. Watch the Shires get dressed while listening to a fascinating insight into the animals. Witness the horses' splendid harness - a spectacle you would only see on the most special of occasions. Tractor rides, novelty train rides, 9 hole crazy golf and bumper boats are also available. Indoors there is a soft play area for children and a lovely carousel roundabout. You can also enjoy the indoor sand shed with toy diggers. Refreshments are available in the café or there is an indoor picnic area. And for those interested in the history of farming an 80 page booklet is available for purchase from the farm gift shop. Dogs on lead are welcome at the farm.

🏨 historic building 🏛 museum and heritage 🏚 historic site ⌬ scenic attraction 🌱 flora and fauna

The name of the village refers to St Eirw, a minor female saint who was said to have been buried in a small chapel that stood in Elizabethan times next to the persent **Parish Church of St Cristiolus**.

ST DOGMAELS

1 mile W of Cardigan on the B4546

- 🏚 St Dogmael's Abbey & the Coach House
- 🏚 The Mill 🐚 Poppit Sands

Situated on the western banks of the mouth of the River Teifi, it was here that the Lord of the Manor, Robert fitz Martyn, and his wife Maud Peverel, founded **St Dogmael's Abbey** in the 12th century for the monks of the Tironensian order brought over from Tiron in France. The restored **Coach House**, now the Abbey's visitor centre, displays a collection of early Christian standing stones associated with the site. Other stonework on display consists of monuments and architectural fragments from the Abbey using reconstructed cloister arches. Adjacent to the abbey ruins is a church that features an inscribed Sagranus stone whose markings and Latin inscriptions provided the key to deciphering the ancient Goidelic language. Close to the abbey is **The Mill** (Y Felin), a water-powered flour mill. To the west of the village is the **Poppit Sands**, a beautiful Blue Flag beach, and one of the most popular in the area.

CILGERRAN

15 miles NE of Fishguard off the A487

- 🏚 Cilgerran Castle 🐦 Welsh Wildlife Centre
- 🏚 Parish Church of St Llawdogg 🛶 Coracle Centre
- 🎭 Princess Nest 🐉 Sir William Edmond Logan

The remains of **Cilgerran Castle**, one the most picturesque in Wales, sits on a rocky promontory overlooking the River Teifi. A

COACH HOUSE TRADING

The Coach House, St. Dogmaels, Pembrokeshire SA43 3DX
Tel: 01239 615389
website: www.welshabbey.org.uk

The Coach House heritage centre in St Dogmaels is home to historical and geographical information on St Doegmaels Abbey. The heritage centre opened in 2008. It is built in an old coach house with a modern extension and incorporates both historical interpretation of the village and surrounding area and a cafe. The centre provides an interpretation facility with models and displays and an internationally important collection of inscribed Christian stones dating from early Celtic times between the 7th & 10th century and which pre-date The Abbey.

The Abbey nestles in a pastoral bowl of open fields divided by a small stream which comes tumbling down from a steep and narrow valley on its short, frantic journey to join the Teifi River. The site takes its name from Dogmael, one of the early Christian saints whose influence continued to be felt in this area until the coming of the Normans. The abbey itself was a Norman foundation but there are strong indications that it lay on or near the ancient pre-Conquest church of Llandudoch.

The centre provides educational facilities for schools, colleges and archaeological researchers. It also provides a venue for St Dogmaels History Society, workshops by local artists and rolling exhibitions of arts, crafts, local history and natural history.

🎭 stories and anecdotes 🐉 famous people 🎨 art and craft 🎭 entertainment and sport 🚶 walks

CROFT FARM & CELTIC COTTAGES

Croft, nr Cardigan, Pembrokeshire SA43 3NT
Tel: 01239 615179
e-mail: info@croft-holiday-cottages.co.uk
website: www.croft-holiday-cottages.co.uk

Visitors to **Croft Farm** can forget the bustle of everyday life and relax and recharge their batteries in the most wonderful surroundings. The collection of charming cottages and traditional stone farm buildings is located in colourful gardens in glorious North Pembrokeshire country, close to the spectacular scenery and the beaches of the Pembrokeshire and Ceredigion coasts.

The self-catering accommodation occupies three sides of the former farm courtyard, with the friendly owners Andrew and Sylvie Gow in their home on the fourth side. The eight letting properties, sleeping from 2 to 7, are individual in their charm and a character, but all provide everything needed for a go-as-you-please holiday. When Andrew and Sylvie took over here in 1988 three of the properties had already been converted, and they converted the rest in 1990. The names give an idea of the nature of each: the Farmhouse in a wing of the original farmstead; the Barn; the Cartwheel and above it the Hayloft; the Stable; the Dairy; the Granary; and (not so obvious!) Talar Aur.

Some cottages have private gardens with some areas of the gardens open to all. All the cottages have access to private patios, with barbecues and alfresco eating areas. Dogs are allowed, by arrangement, in all the properties except the Farmhouse and Talar Aur. Wi-fi internet access is available, and guests on arrival will find fresh flowers, a welcome hospitality tray and a flask of Welsh mead.

Croft Farm offers much more than delightful accommodation. Amenities available for all guests include an indoor heated swimming pool (one-to-one swimming lessons can be arranged), a spa pool, sauna, gym, and therapeutic massage and beauty treatment in their own cottage. This is very much a place for all the family, and children will spend many a happy, busy hour in the playground or meeting the farm animals, including horses, pigs, rabbits and chickens.

The gardens and the amenities at the farm will easily occupy the day, but the nearby countryside and coast provide an almost endless list of attractions; notable among theses are the historic town of Cardigan, Cardigan Island, The Pembrokeshire Coast Path, Ceibur Bay, Poppit Sands, Whitesands, Mwnt National Trust, the National Wool Museum, Cilgerran Castle and the Welsh Wildlife Centre.

Cilgerran Castle

the castle walls. One of the first major tourist attractions in Wales – in the 18th and 19th century it was fashionable to take a river excursion to the ruins from Cardigan - today, these romantic ruins still provide inspiration to artists, as they have done for centuries, and both JMW Turner and Richard Wilson are known to have visited here. Tourist signs lead from the point where the A478, A484 and A487 meet to the **Welsh Wildlife Centre**, an excellent place for spotting birds and animals, wild flowers and butterflies. Footpaths pass through woodland, reed beds, meadows, marsh and riverside, providing the chance to see a vast variety of wildlife in different habitats. More than 130 species of birds have been recorded, and more than 20 mammals, including otter, red deer, voles, badgers and bats. The River Teifi is one of the few rivers in Britain where fishing from coracles can still be seen. The **Coracle Centre** in Cilgerran tells the history of the town and its river down the centuries.

tranquil site today, this land was once hotly disputed territory and the castle's defences reflect this – there are almost sheer drops on two sides of the building, while the 13th-century twin round towers and curtain walls protect the flank away from the cliff. The building of the castle is thought to have begun around 1093, but it was strengthened by Gerald de Windsor, to whom it was granted by Henry I. Thereafter it changed hands many times, being partially sacked by Rhys ap Gryffydd in 1164, retaken by the Earl of Pembroke in 1204 and finally falling to Llywelyn the Great in 1233.

The castle is forever associated with the legend of **Princess Nest**, the Welsh Helen of Troy, who, in 1109, was abducted by the besotted Owain, son of the Prince of Powys. Nest's husband, Gerald of Pembroke, escaped by slithering down a chute through

In the churchyard of the **Parish Church of St Llawdogg** is the grave of **Sir William Edmond Logan** (1798–1875,) who was born in Montreal of Scottish parents, and became director of the Geological Survey of Canada. He produced the first geological survey of South Wales, and Canada's highest mountain, Mount Logan, is named after him.

LLANFAIR-NANT-GWYN
12½ miles E of Fishguard on the B4332

🌿 Bro-Meigan Gardens

Bro-Meigan Gardens, to the east of the village, is a delightful place to spend a few hours meandering through the carefully designed gardens. With panoramic views over the Preseli Hills, the backdrop to the gardens, visitors to Bro-Meigan will see an incredible

🎭 stories and anecdotes 🐦 famous people 🎨 art and craft 🎵 entertainment and sport 🚶 walks

range of plants from all over the world, all grown from seed. While enjoying the superb horticultural displays, visitors can also rest at the gardens' traditional tearooms housed in a 300-year-old barn, enjoying homemade cakes and scones served on bone china.

LLANGOLMAN
11½ miles SE of Fishguard off the B4313

🏛 Penrhos Cottage   ⚒ The Slate Workshop

Slate has been quarried in this area for centuries and, housed in a renovated 18th-century corn mill, **The Slate Workshop** is a place where the art of handcrafting quality Welsh slate items continues. A wide range of articles are made here, including high quality plaques, sundials, clocks and objets d'art, and many illustrate the great skill required to work and carve the slate. To the south of the village lies another interesting building, **Penrhos Cottage**, which is one of the few lasting examples of an 'overnight' house. If a man, with the help of his friends, could build a dwelling between sunset and sunrise, he was entitled to all the land that lay within, literally, a stone's throw from the door. This particular 'overnight' house dates from the 19th century and still contains the original furnishings.

LLANWNDA
4 miles NW of Fishguard off the A487

🏛 Parish Church of St Gwyndaf

🏚 St Gwyndaf Stones

The **Parish Church of St Gwyndaf** is Victorian, though there has been a church here for centuries. The **St Gwyndaf Stones** are a series of early Christian carved stones now incorporated into the churchyard wall. Giraldus Cambrances (Gerald the Welshman), the 12th-century historian and writer, was rector of the church at one time (see also Manorbier and St Davids).

STRUMBLE HEAD
3 miles W of Fishguard off the A487

🏚 Good Hope

⚘ Carregwastad Head

This huge headland, with its lighthouse warning ships off the cliffs on the approach to Fishguard harbour, offers some spectacular coastal scenery as well as an outlook over the great sweep of Cardigan Bay. Just to the east lies **Carregwastad Head**, a remote headland that was the landing place of the ill-fated French invasion of Britain in the 18th century. Also to the east is **Good Hope** (National Trust), a traditional farmed landscape with an unusually wide variety of plant life.

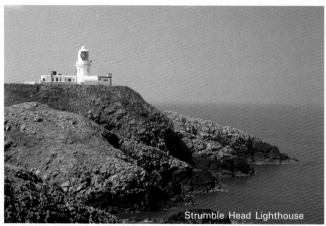
Strumble Head Lighthouse

🏛 historic building 🏛 museum and heritage 🏚 historic site ⚘ scenic attraction 🌿 flora and fauna

STONE HALL HOTEL & RESTAURANT

Welsh Hook, Haverfordwest,
Pembrokeshire SA62 5NS
Tel: 01348 840212
Fax: 01348 840815
website: www.stonehall-mansion.co.uk

Set in 10 acres of beautiful garden and mature woodland, in the heart of tranquil North Pembrokeshire, Stone Hall is one of areas prettiest and historic country houses.

The 600 year old Manor house has slate flagstones, rough hewn beams and great open fireplaces. 17th and 18th century extensions added fine wood panelling and decorative ceilings. All have been sensitively restored and beautifully furnished. With just four stylish bedrooms, ensuring a peaceful and comfortable night's sleep... Stone Hall is one of the hidden little gems of West Wales.

Wake to an orchestra of birdsong, the smell of freshly baked croissants and sizzling Welsh bacon. Spend the day exploring the Pembrokeshire coast or St Davids cathedral city... and return to an excellent dinner, prepared from fresh local ingredients, cooked with care and served in style, with old fashioned courtesy and individual attention- the epitome of country living

indigo brown

Swmbarch House, Letterston,
Pembrokeshire SA62 5UE
Tel: 01348 840177
e-mail: info@indigobrown.co.uk
website: www.indigobrown.co.uk

Indigo brown Creative Holidays, provide high quality residential painting courses for artists of all abilities, in some of the most beautiful and stunning landscape, Wales has to offer. Maggie Brown, an accomplished artist and teacher, and her husband Andrew, the resident chef, take clients to the unique and only Coastal National Park in Britain; 186 miles of awe inspiring sea views. The Preseli Hills and the numerous unspoilt valleys and estuaries are also on the agenda to draw and paint, before returning to delicious home cooking at Swmbarch House.

The property, an old farmhouse, has 'Visit Wales' four star grading. It has been beautifully extended by Andrew and Maggie, and offers 3 luxury en-suite double/ twin bedrooms, decorated to the highest standard. The courses are held in a large, spacious studio, over looking a charming garden with long views over the countryside. For those partners and friends who wish to follow other pursuits, Pembrokeshire offers any amount of exciting and interesting activities, all within easy distance. Swmbarch House is conveniently located in a quiet rural location between Letterston and Welsh Hook, minutes from Haverfordwest, Fishguard and the Coast.

🎞 stories and anecdotes 🐚 famous people ⚘ art and craft 🎭 entertainment and sport 🎿 walks

CASTLE MORRIS
7 miles SW of Fishguard off the A487

🏚 Castle Morris   🏚 Melin Tregwynt

Situated on the southern bank of the River Cleddau are the scant remains of **Castle Morris** itself. It was once a motte and bailey fortification, though the motte itself (the conically shaped hill on which the Norman castle stood) has long since disappeared. The bailey, or courtyard, still survives. The castle was an outpost of the much grander castle at St David's, but was soon abandoned, and there is no evidence that the timber castle was ever replaced by a more permanent stone one.

Melin Tregwynt was built in the 18th century as a corn mill, and was the mill for the nearby Tregwynt Estate. It later became a fulling, or 'pandy' mill, where hammers (driven by water) beat the finished cloth to soften it.

PORTHGAIN
10 miles SW of Fishguard off the A487

🏚 Brickworks

As well as being a natural beauty spot, the sheltered harbour at Porthgain ('Chisel Harbour') has added interest, as the harbourside is dominated by the shell of the 19th-century **Brickworks**. This monument to the village's industrial heritage stands close to remnants from Porthgain's heyday as a slate and granite exporting port. Many buildings, as far afield as London and Liverpool, have Porthgain granite in their construction. Nowadays, it is difficult to imagine the hectic scenes on the quayside a century ago when the harbour was packed with boats queuing for their cargoes of stone and brick needed for Britain's building boom. The harbour's unique personality has led it to being used as a location by film-makers.

CLOVER COTTAGE

Trellys-y-Cnwc, St Nicholas, Castlemorris, Pembrokeshire
Tel: 01348 891347
e-mail: sue@holidaypembrokeshire.com
website: www.holidaypembrokeshire.com

Clover Cottage is a spacious and comfortable self-catering barn conversion on a working farm with spectacular views of the Irish sea and Pembrokeshire coastline. The centrally-heated four-bedroomed cottage sleeps six (plus a cot) and has a sunny lounge, fully equipped kitchen, 3 first-floor bedrooms, a bathroom with bath and overhead shower. There is a single bedroom on the ground floor with an ensuite w/c and hand basin. It stands close to the village of St. Nicholas, a short drive from Castlemorris. The location and facilities make Clover Cottage an ideal choice for a quiet break in delightful surroundings, or a base from which to discover thte scenic attractions of the region. There is alwasy plenty going on around the farm, where the Gates family keep some 170 cattle, rear calves and grow cereals. Children will have a great time meeting the farm animals including chickens, cats, dogs and horses. The Pembrokeshire Coast National Park is almost on the doorstep and the coastal path offers spectacular scenery, wild flowers in profusion and is a paradise for birdwatchers and walkers and those just wanting to relax on the beaches.

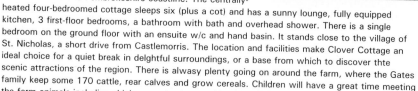

🏚 historic building 🏛 museum and heritage 🏚 historic site 🌿 scenic attraction 🌱 flora and fauna

ORIEL-Y-FELIN GALLERY & TEAROOM

15 Fford-y-felin, Trefin, nr St Davids,
Pembrokeshire SA62 5AX
Tel: 01348 837500
e-mail: gallery@oriel-felin.com
website: www.oriel-y-felin.com

Set in the delightful village of Trefin on the Pembrokeshire Coastal Path, the **Oriel-y-Felin Gallery & Tearoom** has been described as "a jewel in the artistic landscape".

Amongst the accomplished artists showcased here is St. Davids artist Pauline Beynon, noted for her atmospheric works of the wonderful St. Davids peninsula. The gallery is the only one in Pembrokeshire displaying her work. An example of other notable painters regularly exhibiting here include Susie Grindey, Howard Birchmore, Clive Burnell and Peter Cronin. Alongside is a constantly changing selection of carefully chosen ceramics, glass, bronzes, stainless steel and jewellery by makers such as Lawson Rudge, Andrew Bull, Martin Andrews, Michael Turner and Sarah Vernon to name but a few!

As you walk in to the gallery, you are met with a range of visual delights which overflow in to the tearoom where you can relax and savour the freshly prepared food, specialising in local Pembrokeshire produce at its best. Alongside the acclaimed colourful salads are tasty homemade soups, superb Welsh Black beef, local crab (when the weather allows the boats out!) ,great puddings and superb local clotted cream teas! Angela's home made lemonade and an extensive range of loose-leaf teas and excellent coffees ensure you can spoil yourself whilst savouring the artistic delights around you.

Owner Angela Samuel and her business partner Pauline Beynon have always strived to give their visitors a warm welcome, so were thrilled to have been awarded the Les Routiers British Cafe of the Year, thus proving they offer high standards in both Food and Art!

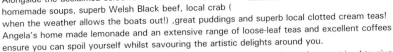

🎬 stories and anecdotes 🐾 famous people 🎨 art and craft 🎭 entertainment and sport 🚶 walks

CHRIS NEALE

Rhoslanog Fawr, Mathri, Pembrokeshire SA62 5HG
Tel: 01348 837570
e-mail: c.neale.1@virgin.net
website: www.chrisneale.info

Chris Neale has a passion for the land, coast and vernacular architecture, which provides his main inspiration. He works in pastels and watercolours and sources his images from a love for Wales and it's culture, from sketches, photographs and his imagination - but above all from 'being there'.

The influence of man is evident in many of his pictures as is Chris's understanding of the geography of the land. In his studio gallery signposted just off the A487 (Fishguard - St Davids) Chris shows his original landscape paintings and limited edition prints (also available in several other Welsh galleries). The prints, each in an edition of 500, are sold rolled (by post) or mounted.

The studio gallery is open from 11am to 3pm on Thursdays but is often open at other times, phone first if you wish to be sure. For directions please visit the website.

🏛 historic building 🏛 museum and heritage 🏛 historic site ⚜ scenic attraction 🌿 flora and fauna

CRUG-GLAS COUNTRY HOUSE

Abereiddy, nr St David's,
Pembrokeshire SA62 6XX
Tel: 01348 831302
e-mail: janet@crugglas.plus.com
website: www.crugglas.co.uk

Crug-Glas Country House is a luxuriously appointed house on a mixed working farm of about 600 acres, raising beef cattle, dairy cows and cereals – a traditional family farm working alongside nature. It stands a mile inland from the coast at the very end of the St David's Peninsula; the house and grounds command spectacular views over open countryside, with the sea in the distance, and the sun going down behind Penberi Rocks has inspired many artists down the years.

The guest accommodation provided by owner Janet Evans is of the highest standard, with en suite facilities for all the rooms and the little extras that make for a memorable stay – the number of repeat bookings is testimony to the quality of the product offered. Top of the range is the honeymoon suite, but all offer the very best in terms of peace, style and comfort, and the beautiful lawns and mature trees that surround the house ensure an atmosphere of total peace and relaxation. The drawing room is well supplied with the daily papers, videos and books, some of which record the history of the building and the farm and the families who owned it. The estate was mentioned in the Black Book of St David's as existing in the 12th century and it was owned by the Church for many centuries until being sold into private hands in the early 1900s.

A splendid cooked-to-order breakfast starts the day at Crug-Glas, and an evening meal is served every evening in the elegant restaurant. The head chef and his team seek out the finest and freshest local produce for the daily changing menu, which features such dishes as prawns in an aromatic sauce of tomatoes, cream and spices, served with pasta; salmon with a shellfish sauce; fillet of pork stuffed with apricots, onions, herbs served with an apricot brandy and cream sauce; and rack of lamb with a honey and mustard glaze. Quality wines and impeccable service complement the excellent cooking.

Crug-Glas is the perfect base for touring Pembrokeshire. The charming little city of St David's is just three miles away, the beach and the coast path are two miles away at Abereiddy, and the whole area is rich in scenic and historic appeal. The house is situated just off the A487 Fishguard-St David's road two miles south of Croes-goch. If coming from St David's take the first left after Carnhedryn.

🎭 stories and anecdotes 🐾 famous people ✍ art and craft 🎵 entertainment and sport 🚶 walks

PORTHIDDY FARM HOLIDAY COTTAGES

Porthiddy Farm West, Berea, Haverfordwest, Pembrokeshire SA62 6DR
Tel: 01348 831004 Fax: 01348 837588
e-mail: m.pike@porthiddy.com website: www.porthiddy.com

Porthiddy Farm Holiday Cottages above Abereiddy Beach, off the A487 northeast of St David's, is the perfect place for an active holiday by the sea or in the countryside, discovering the geology and the wildlife, exploring the Pembrokeshire Coast and the National Park – or just relaxing in serenely beautiful surroundings. Resident-owner Mrs Pike, who greets visitors with a welcome-pack that includes home-made cakes or biscuits, has two cottages that are available throughout the year. Bwthyn Hir is a long, roomy single-storey cottage for four. The open-plan living/dining area, with wooden floors, stone walls and sloping ceilings, is divided by an antique-pine partition into a sitting area with TV and DVD/Video player and a well-fitted kitchen. There are two bedrooms (one double, the other with two single beds, both overlooking the garden) and a large bathroom with bath and separate shower. Ty Canol is a light, roomy cottage for four or five guests, set on two floors. The large kitchen combines traditional elements with a comprehensive range of modern equipment; and also downstairs are a comfortable sitting room and a bathroom with bath and shower. Oak stairs lead up to two attractive bedrooms (one with a double and a single bed, the other with two single beds) and a separate room with shower and WC. Both are entered from the seaward side, where there is ample parking space and a small shed for bikes and surfboards.

ST DAVID'S

16 miles SW of Fishguard off the A487

🏛 St David's Cathedral   🏛 Bishop's Palace

🏛 Lifeboat Station   🏛 St Elvis

🐾 Ramsey Island   🏛 St Non's Chapel

🏛 St Non's Well   🐚 St Justinian's

To Welsh people everywhere, St David's is a special place. Named after Wales' patron saint, St David's is the smallest and the oldest cathedral settlement in Britain. It was here, in the 6th century, that St David founded a religious order and, on this site in 1176, the magnificent **St David's Cathedral** was completed. Situated in a deep hollow below the streets, so that not even its square tower can be seen above the rooftops, the cathedral contains several treasures that include saintly bones, believed to be those of St Caradog. The undoubted highlight of the cathedral's interior is the oak roof, which displays wonderful ornate carvings by 15th century craftsmen. In 1120, Pope Calixtus II decreed that two pilgrimages to St David's were equivalent to one to Rome and successive monarchs, from William the Conqueror to Queen Elizabeth II, have worshipped here. The Queen has a special seat reserved for her in the cathedral and it was from here that Maundy Money was distributed for the first time in Wales. Within the cloisters is the Refectory, where locally sourced food is available.

Adjacent to the cathedral, in the same grassy hollow, lie the ruins of the **Bishop's Palace**, a once imposing building that, even though now in a ruined state, still conveys the wealth and influence of the Church in medieval times. Most of the Palace's

🏛 historic building 🏛 museum and heritage 🏛 historic site 🐚 scenic attraction 🐾 flora and fauna

THE SAMPLER TEA ROOM & MUSEUM

17 Nun Street, St Davids, Pembrokeshire SA62 6NS
Tel: 01437 720757 e-mail: tea@sampler-tearoom.co.uk
website: www.sampler-tearoom.co.uk

In the centre of St Davids at the heart of the Pembrokeshire Coast National Park, awaits for you, an experience both unique and evocative. Unique, because owners Chris and Jill have created a traditional tearoom with sights and feel of a bygone era-and evocative, as they take you back in time amidst collections of Victorian Samplers and memorabilia. The peaceful and calming atmosphere of The Sampler Tearoom, with its cosy open fire and walls crammed with antique samplers,is the ideal place where you can enjoy that quintessential of experiences, 'afternoon tea'.

There are currently about 50 antique samplers displayed, the oldest is from 1728 by Martha Mottershead ranging through to one worked during air raids in 1940 by Nevarte Kurk. Visit the cellar for the WWII Home Front experience and other displays including '2000 years of British history from the River Thames', 'Pembrokeshire shipwrecks', 'Fossils','Pembrokeshire in the War' and more.

Chris and Jill have owned The Sampler for the past 11 years, Jill bakes every morning ensuring freshly made scones and cakes, whilst Chris is the museum 'curator'. They have very high standards, which perpetuate through the business. Nearly all the food is homemade on the premises –even the jam- with fruit picked from their own garden.

THE WATERINGS

Anchor Drive, High Street, St David's,
Pembrokeshire SA62 6QH
Tel/Fax: 01437 720876
e-mail: enquiries@waterings.co.uk
website: www.waterings.co.uk

The Waterings is a splendid Bed & Breakfast establishment in a quiet location close to the Pembrokeshire and the National Park Visitor centre and a short walk from the heart of St David's. Spacious, well-appointed accommodation, all on one level, comprises four family-size rooms and a double, set around an attractive sheltered courtyard. All rooms have en suite bath and shower, central heating, TV and hospitality tray, and the landscaped grounds include a croquet lawn, picnic area, barbecue facility and ample off-road parking.

Guests are warmly welcomed by hosts David, Sandra and William Chant, who are always ready with help and advice on local places of interest – these are many and varied, from coast and countryside walks and views, boat trips, birdwatching and a wide range of sporting activities. No children under 5 or pets. The B&B's name comes from a sheltered cove on Ramsey Island, one of the few deepwater havens on the peninsula, where sailing ships would anchor overnight and take on fresh water.

construction was overseen by Bishop Henry de Gower in the mid 14th century, and he spared no expense in creating this lavish residence, which he felt befitted a leader of both church and state. There were two complete sets of state rooms at the palace set around a courtyard. De Gower used one for his private business and the other for ceremonial entertaining. The palace fell into disrepair in the 16th century after the incumbent bishop stripped the roof of its lead in order to pay for his five daughters' dowries.

Unlike other national saints of the United Kingdom, we know something about David, thanks to biographies written in the 11th century by a man called Rhygyfarch, though what he wrote may be no more than a hagiography. Giraldus Cumbrances (see also Manorbier and Llawnda) also wrote a book in the 12th century about David's travels throughout Wales. He was born near what is now the city of St David's, his father being Sandde, grandson of the king of Ceredigion and his mother being Non, a lady 'of noble birth', who is also said to have been a niece of King Arthur. She dedicated herself to the religious life, but caught the eye of Sandde. He could not be denied, after they were married non fell pregnant. David was born in March 1st, which is celebrated to this day as St David's Day. He was canonised in 1120 AD by Pope Callactus II.

He was said to be a gentle person who ate only bread and herbs and drank only water, though he was well-built and muscular. Not only did he travel through Wales, he also visited southwest England, Cornwall and Brittany. Along with two companions, he once went on a pilgrimage to Jerusalem. One curious fact is that he was baptised at Solva, a few miles southeast of the city, by his cousin, a man called **St Elvis**. Because of this, some people have tried to claim that Elvis Presley was descended from Welsh stock (see also Solva), and that Presley is a corruption of Preseli, as the Preseli Hills are close by.

St David is a central figure in one of the many legends concerning how the leek came to be adopted as the national emblem of Wales. The legend states that just before a battle against the Saxons he advised the Britons to wear a leek in their caps to distinguish them from the enemy. On St David's Day, the traditional national day of the Welsh, Welsh people all over the world wear the leek, or the other national emblem, the daffodil. The Welsh words for leek and daffodil are the same

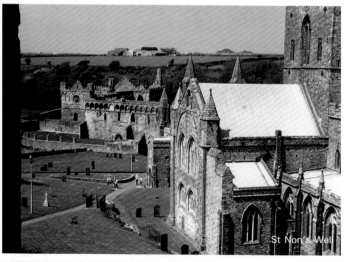

St Non's Well

(cenhinen means leek, cenhinen pedr means daffodil), which could explain why both are national emblems.

In August 2002, St David's hosted the National Eisteddfod, one of the highlights of which was the induction of the Archbishop-designate of Canterbury, Dr Rowan Williams, into the Gorsedd of Bards, a historic order of Druids. The ceremony was held in a circle of standing stones fashioned, like the stones at Stonehenge, from Pembrokeshire rock. The ceremony involved the singing of Welsh Christian hymns and the Welsh National Anthem, the reading of a citation by the Arch-Druid and the wielding of a giant ceremonial sword – a burdensome task entrusted to Druid Ray Gravell, a former Welsh rugby international. Dr Williams is the third Archbishop to be a member of the Gorsedd.

Speaking Welsh is a prerequisite for consideration for nomination, with one exception – the Queen.

Just outside the city, in a stunningly beautiful spot overlooking the sea, are **St Non's Well** and the ruins of **St Non's Chapel**, thought to be built on the actual site of David's birth. The bay is named after St David's mother and legend has it that he was born during a great storm in around 520 AD. The waters of St Non's Well are said to have special powers for healing eye diseases and it was much visited during the Middle Ages by pilgrims.

Another coastal beauty spot, which is also steeped in legend, is **St Justinian's**, a rock-bound harbour that is home to the St David's **Lifeboat Station**, which is open for visits between 10am and 4pm. Justinian was a 6th century hermit who retreated across to

---

🎞 stories and anecdotes 🐟 famous people 🎨 art and craft 🎭 entertainment and sport 🚶 walks

Ramsey Island, a short distance offshore, to devote himself to God. A strict disciplinarian, he must have been too severe with his followers as they eventually rebelled and cut off his head! Justinian is then said to have walked across the waters of Ramsey Sound, back to the mainland, with his head in his arms. Ramsey is a Norse name, a legacy of the time when this part of the coast was terrorised by Viking invaders. Today, the island is an RSPB reserve, and home to an abundance of wildlife. Boat trips round the island offer visitors the chance to observe the numerous sea birds and the colonies of grey seals.

SOLVA

16 miles SW of Fishguard on the A487

🏛 St Elvis's Cromlech   🔎 Solva Woollen Mill

Situated at the end of a long inlet and well protected from the sometimes stormy waters of St Bride's Bay, Solva harbour is one of the most sheltered in Wales. Green hills roll down to the quayside and this picturesque view was the last sight of Wales for many 19th century emigrants who sailed from Solva to America for 10 shillings - the price of a one way ticket. Now no longer such a busy port, Solva is a charming old seafaring village that boasts a good range of craft shops. **Solva Woollen Mill**, in the beautiful valley of the River Solfach, has been in continuous production since it opened in 1907. It now specialises in carpets and rugs, and visitors can usually see weaving in progress.

Some distance from Solva is the delightfully named St Elvis' Farm, where St David is supposed to have been baptised by his cousin St Elvis of Munster. There is also a Neolithic

---

AELWYD B&B

2 Maes Y Forwen, Solva, Pembrokeshire SA62 6TR
Tel: 01437 721806
e-mail: julia@aelwyd.com
website: www.aelwyd.com

This superb 4-star B&B is situated in Solva on the South West coast of Wales. Situated at the top of the village, it has superb views over St.Brides Bay and the surrounding countryside.

Aelwyd offers both Bed & Breakfast and self-catering options. The Griffiths family's hospitality is unrivalled. The house is bilingual as Julia is leaning to speak Welsh from her husband John. Julia moved to Solva 20 years ago and has a great love for the area and all its natural beauty. She enjoys welcoming people from all over the world to stay.

The accommodation is tastefully decorated and luxuriously furnished. There are two double/twin bedrooms, one with ensuite facilities and the other with an adjoining lounge with single bed and a large dedicated bathroom. Within the property there is a fully equipped self-catering apartment covering two floors.

A short walk away from the harbour and local shops, pubs, restaurants and art galleries and not far from Pembrokeshire's famous coastal path. Aelwyd is perfect for those looking for a peaceful place to relax.

🏛 historic building 🏛 museum and heritage 🏛 historic site 🔎 scenic attraction 🌿 flora and fauna

SOLVA WOOLLEN MILL

Middle Mill, Solva SA62 6XD
Tel: 01437 721112
e-mail: enquiries@solvawoollenmill.co.uk
website: www.solvawoollenmill.co.uk

Solva, once a busy and important port, is now a charming seafaring village with a beautiful natural harbour. The main legacy of the past is undoubtedly **Solva Woollen Mill**, a hidden jewel nestling in the beautiful valley of the River Solfach.

In 1900 there were 26 woollen mills in Pembrokeshire, now Solva Mill is one of only two remaining. It was purpose built in 1907 by Tom Griffiths, who moved the mill from its original location in St Davids to harness more power for the waterwheel. Throughout its history Solva Mill has always been busy, supplying local demand as farmers brought their fleeces to be turned into hand woven woollen goods as well as attracting visitors from further afield - the Rt Hon Sir Ramsey McDonald had a suit woven from Middle Mill tweed.

The mill, in continuous production since 1907, has a long established reputation for the production of high quality woollen products. Having only been owned by 2 families in 100 years Tom Grime now runs it with his wife Anna and they are the only woollen mill in Wales now specialising in flat weave carpets and floor rugs. Combining simplicity with durability, using natural fibres to weave classic designs with a contemporary twist creating a stylish Welsh accent for any room.

Solva Mill also offers a bespoke service for customers who would prefer to have flooring woven to suit their individual colours and style. Prince Charles and Camilla visited the mill in 2008 after commissioning rugs for their welsh home. The mill has also created reproduction historic carpeting for stately homes in the UK and USA. Designer Vanessa Arbuthnott has a range of rugs woven here to compliment her fabrics all of which can be seen at the mill.

The mill shop has a large range of rugs, carpets and throws, stylish Harris Tweed handbags, welsh tapestry bedspreads, jewellery and much more from local craftsmen.

There's plenty more to see at Solva Mill, including the original 10ft overshot water wheel fully restored in 2007. Visitors can walk around the weaving shed or relax beside the waterwheel and enjoy views along the valley. The waterwheel tearoom offers locally baked cakes.

Open all year round, 5 days a week, Monday - Friday 9.30 – 5.30pm and also Saturday 9.30 – 5.30pm and Sunday 2pm – 5.30pm from the end of July until September.

stories and anecdotes   famous people   art and craft   entertainment and sport   walks

burial chamber called **St Elvis' Cromlech** (see also St David's). Near to it used to stand St Elvis' Church.

Haverfordwest

🏠 Haverfordwest Castle

🏠 Parish Church of St Martin

🏠 Priory Church of St Thomas the Martyr

🎭 Landsker   🏠 Parish Church of St Mary

🏛 Haverford Town Museum

This old county town, with its pleasant rural surroundings, lies on the banks of the labyrinthine Cleddau river system and is more or less in the centre of Pembrokeshire. Lining the steep streets of this hilly town there can be found some fine Georgian buildings that date back to the days when Haverfordwest,

even though it is several miles inland, was a prosperous port trading largely with Bristol and Ireland. Its name means ford used by bucks, and the town is known locally as "Harford".

However, the town predates this trading boom by several centuries and its unusual name is a legacy of Viking raids. Set on a hill overlooking the River Cleddau is the striking landmark of **Haverfordwest Castle**, which was built around 1120 by the Englishman Gilbert de Clare, Earl of Pembroke. The town grew up around the fortress, and during the 12th and 13th centuries it saw various inhabitants including Henry II and Edward I, who gave it to his wife, Queen Eleanor. Throughout its history it was held continuously by the English, but by the late 16th century had become a ruin. During the

Civil War it was hastily rebuilt, and, for a while, was held by Royalists. A story is told of how the garrison mistook a herd of cows for Parliamentary soldiers, so hastily abandoned the castle. General Laugharne then took it in 1645 without a shot being fired. He ransacked the place, and today the former governor's residence is home to the **Haverford Town Museum**, which houses the oldest letterbox in Wales, dating to 1857.

The **Priory Church of St Thomas the Martyr**, founded by Augustinian Canons in the early 13th century, can be found by the Western Cleddau river. Excavations of the priory land have revealed that there were gardens here in the cloister and also between the priory buildings and the river. The riverside gardens, which were laid out in the mid 15th century, provide a rare example of the sort of garden that is often seen in medieval manuscripts and the narrow raised beds have been replanted with plant species appropriate to the period.

The **Parish Church of St Martin**, the oldest in town, dates from rebuilding in the 14th century. The west window is perpendicular, and there is a priest's room over the porch. The **Parish Church of St Mary** is the town's other church, and has one of the best collections of monumental brasses in Pembrokeshire. Its panelled Tudor roof, is reckoned to be the finest in Wales.

Close by is a strange, ghostly border that cannot be seen. Known locally as the **Landsker** (or land scar) it divides the English speaking 'little England beyond Wales' of south Pembrokeshire from the Welsh speaking north. This abrupt division of the county can be traced back to early medieval times when Norman invasions into these parts paved the way for Anglo Saxon and Flemish immigrants.

A line of castles was built from Amroth right across to Roch and, although the Landsker is an invisible border, its significance has been profound in the past. It was unthinkable that a marriage should take place between a man and a woman from different sides of the line even though they may have lived only a short distance apart.

The Landsker borderlands feature delightful countryside and fascinating villages and hamlets with a rich heritage and many stories to tell. The actor Christian Bale, was born in Haverfordwest, as was Gwen John, sister of fellow artist Augustus John. She and her brother were brought up in the town. Graham McPherson (also known as Suggs), the lead singer with the group Madness, attended school in Haverfordwest.

Around Haverfordwest

SCOLTON
4½ miles NE of Haverfordwest on the B4329

🏠 Scolton Manor House   🌳 Visitor Centre

🏛 Pembrokeshire's County Museum

The early Victorian **Scolton Manor House**, which dates from around 1840, along with its grounds is, today, a museum and country park that makes an interesting, and enjoyable visit. The house, stable block and exhibition hall, as **Pembrokeshire's County Museum**, features a number of displays that illustrate the history of this southwest region of Wales. While the past is concentrated on here, at the award-winning **Visitor Centre** there is an exhibition that looks to the future and, in particular, green issues and the wildlife of the surrounding park. The country park itself has lovely landscaped grounds, nature trails, picnic areas and a play area.

🎬 stories and anecdotes   🦜 famous people   🎨 art and craft   🎭 entertainment and sport   🥾 walks

LLYS-Y-FRAN

7½ miles NE of Haverfordwest off the B4329

 Llys-y-fran Reservoir

The impressive dam built to form **Llys-y-fran Reservoir** in the 1960s has been constructed in sympathy with the surrounding countryside and, when it was officially opened in 1972 by Princess Margaret, the reservoir was able to meet the growing needs of the county's population and of the oil refineries at Milford Haven. Surrounded by a glorious country park, which lies in the shadow of the Preseli Hills to the north, there is a seven-mile perimeter path around the reservoir that provides an opportunity to see some of the local inhabitants, including foxes, badgers, mink, squirrels and otters. The fishing is some of the best in Wales, with the waters regularly stocked with rainbow trout and with a steady population of brown trout. Anglers can fish from boats or from the banks.

CANASTON BRIDGE

7 miles E of Haverfordwest on the A40

Blackpool Mill   Oakwood

To the south of the village can be found two very different attractions. **Blackpool Mill**, beside the Eastern Cleddau river, dates from the early 19th century and it is one of the finest examples of a water-powered mill in Britain. Further south and hidden among trees lies **Oakwood**, Wales' premier theme park that is home to Europe's longest watercoaster, biggest wooden rollercoaster and largest skycoaster. As well as the outdoor rides there is an all-weather complex with a multitude of games, puzzles and rides. An area called Playtown is aimed at younger children.

CLERKENHILL FARM ADVENTURE PARK

Slebech, Haverfordwest,
Pembrokeshire SA62 4PE
Tel: 01437 751227
website: www.clerkenhill.co.uk

Clerkenhill Adventure Park is located on the A40 five miles east of Haverfordwest, on the northern edge of one section of the Pembrokeshire Coast National Park. A working cattle farm all year round, it opens up from Easter and throughout the summer as an adventure park that offers an exciting day out for the young and the young at heart. Visitors can explore adventure trails through working farmland and spooky woodland, swing in the tress like Tarzan, meet the farm animals and spot rare creatures in the wildlife ponds. A large play area with swings and slides and a 'petting zoo' is guaranteed to keep the younger ones busy and happy.

Farmhouse teas, cakes, sandwiches and soft drinks can be enjoyed inside or out – a great way to recharge the batteries for more adventure. On a ten-acre site beside the farm is a unique and addictive attraction in the shape of an 18-basket frizbee course, played like golf, with fairways from 14 to 90 metres and lots of hazards.

JELLYEGG

Units 9 & 10, The Old School, Station Road,
Narberth, Pembrokeshire SA67 7DU
Tel: 01834 860797
e-mail: info@jellyegg.com
website: www.jellyegg.com

Karen Bannister is responsible for two very different and very interesting retail outlets close to each other in the heart of Narberth. In the Old School, **Jellyegg** is the largest stockist of the renowned Crocs shoes – cheerful, quirky, bright, bold and known for their legendary comfort. Crocs started in 2002 with the clog-style beach shoe and the Cayman, and the range has expanded year by year. The original designs are still popular, but they have been joined by dozens of shoes and sandals and flip-flops and boots for adults and children, for work and play. Crocs also produce T-shirts, caps and accessories including knee pads, kneelers, shoe polish, straps and bracelets, and the Jibbitz range allows Croc-wearers to personalise their shoes with a wide variety of decorations and jewels. Associated ranges include Fat Boy bean bags for people and pets, Built NY tote bags, bottle holders and baby accessories, Little Mismatched clothes, Dig & Sit beach chairs and Envirosax eco-friendly shopping bags. Jellyegg is open from 9 to 5.30 Monday to Saturday. Everything in all the ranges can be viewed and ordered online.

JELLYEGG GALLERY

The Old Town Hall, High Street, Narberth,
Pembrokeshire SA67 7AR
Tel: 01834 860061
e-mail: info@jellyegg.com
website: www.jellyegg.com

A five-minute walk from the 'Croc Shop Jellyegg', the Old Town Hall is home to the **Jellyegg Gallery and Gift Shop**. It provides a relaxed, bright, accessible setting for affordable original paintings and open and limited edition prints both traditional and contemporary by local, national and international artists. These include Annabel Greenhalgh, John Knapp-Fisher, Valerie Davide, Sue McDonagh, Gillian McDonald and Dorian Spencer Davies. Also on display are ceramics, tableware, soft furnishings, rugs and throws, framed pictures and prints, photo frames and a varied selection of other lifestyle items and gift ideas. The Gallery and Gift Shop are open from 9.30 to 5.30 Monday to Saturday.

[f] stories and anecdotes 🐦 famous people 🎨 art and craft 🎭 entertainment and sport 🚶 walks

NARBERTH
9½ miles E of Haverfordwest on the A478

🏛 Narberth Castle   🏛 Narberth Museum

Narberth Castle

This small old town, sited on a steep hill, is said to have been the legendary court of Pwyll, Prince of Dyfed. It is, however, a historical fact that Narberth grew up around its early Dark Ages' castle and that the town was burnt down by Norsemen in 994 AD. **Narberth Castle**, in the southern part of the town, is one successor to the original fortification here; built in the 11th century, it was destroyed by the Welsh in 1115. Today, only a few fragments still stand of the castle rebuilt in 1264 by Sir Andrew Perrot and dismantled following the Civil War.

The **Narberth Museum** (formerly the Wilson Museum) has displays and exhibits on the social history of the town. It was founded

FABRIC HOUSE, SIXHIGHSTREET
6 High Street, Narberth, Pembrokeshire SA67 7AR
Tel: 01834 861063

Fabric House, Sixhighstreet is a fascinating and colourful shop selling a wide range of gorgeous homeware, gifts, fashion and accessories at prices that are realistic and affordable. Here you can browse to your heart's content knowing that the friendly, knowledgeable staff will offer all the advice and help that you might need. Lovely canteens of cutlery, dinner sets, curtains, bed linen, plate racks - they're all here, and more. There are many famous names to choose from, from Burleigh blue and white ware, silverware by Culinary Concepts of London and fabrics and wallpaper by Sanderson, Harlequin and Romo among others. You may even spy the odd gorgeous piece of occasional furniture...such as a painted bedside cabinet or a French style dressing table. Our style will suit either country or city living.

Accessories range from exquisite jewellery to attractive scarves. Why not buy one of the delightful Woodwick candles or pamper yourself with a 'Heaven Scent' bathroom product? Upstairs you will find a huge range of contemporary women's and menswear, which adds to the attractiveness of the place and nestled in the back of the shop is a delightful childrens room, full of gifts for newborns. Childrens clothes are also stocked from babygrows by Organics for Kids, our ever popular Fair Trade brushed cotton pj's, to a wider selection of organic clothes from 'Frugi'.

The place is owned and managed by Jenny Thomas who strives to stock British made products where possible. She has a wealth of experience in homewares and giftwares, and is always willing to share that experience with you as you buy a gift for yourself or a loved one. So call in, and be prepared to be delighted.

🏛 historic building 🏛 museum and heritage 🏛 historic site 🌄 scenic attraction 🌱 flora and fauna

NARBERTH HOLIDAYS

Grove Gate, Molleston, Narberth, Pembrokeshire SA67 8BX
Tel: 01834 860427
e-mail: info@narberthholidays.co.uk
website: www.narberthholidays.co.uk

A self-catering holiday to remember is the promise of **Narberth Holidays**, located a mile south of Narberth in the Landsker Borderlands of South Pembrokeshire. Highgrove is a luxuriously appointed rural property, a brand new bungalow standing in attractive countryside off the A478 Tenby road, a ten-minute drive from the coastline and its excellent beaches. From its elevated position it commands superb views across the Preseli Hills and provides a perfect base for touring, discovering the local wildlife and history, relaxing on the beaches....or just resting and recharging the batteries in the peaceful, civilised surroundings.

The four guest bedrooms, sleeping up to seven (plus a cot for a baby), are decorated and furnished to a commendably high standard. The house has two bathrooms (one of them a wet room), a luxurious kitchen/dining/sitting room with leather sofas and patio doors leading to a terrace; French doors open from the lounge onto an attractive lawn. This is wonderful walking and cycling country, with 100 miles of cycle paths; a path runs from near the house through the woods onto the Knights way, which links a number of places with historical connections to the Knights Templar and the knights Hospitallers. There are also many family attractions nearby, including Folly Farm Park and Oakwood Theme Park.

in 1982 when Desmond Wilson, managing director of a local wine merchants, donated the building, a former bonded store.

THE RHOS
3½ miles SE of Haverfordwest off the A40

🏰 Picton Castle 🌱 Woodland Garden

East of the Cleddau toll bridge lies the tidal estuary formed by the confluence of the Western and Eastern Cleddau rivers, into which also flow the Rivers Cresswell and Carew. Beside the river banks are some of the Pembrokeshire Coast National Park's most beautiful treasures. However, this area is so often overlooked by visitors that it has become known as the Secret Waterway.

The Rhos, the only village in the ancient parish of Slebach, overlooks the Eastern Cleddau and here, close to the river, lies **Picton Castle**, the historic home of the Philipps

family, still lived in by the direct descendants of Sir John Wogan, who had the castle built in the 13th century. The family, over the centuries, has had its ups and downs. They were awarded their coat-of-arms by Richard the Lionheart following their exploits during the Crusades, and they supported Parliament during the Civil War. In the 18th century, they took on prominent roles in the economic, educational and social life of Wales. Although the principal rooms were remodelled in the mid 18th century, some medieval features remain. In the 1790s, the 1st Lord Milford added the wing that now includes the superb dining room and drawing room.

The castle is also home to an art gallery with a permanent exhibition of paintings by Graham Sutherland. Outside, the gardens are equally impressive and include a walled garden with fish pond, rosebeds, culinary and medicinal herbs and herbaceous borders. In the extensive **Woodland Garden** there is a fine collection of woodland shrubs in among the ancient oaks, beeches, redwoods and other mature trees.

MARTLETWY

6 miles SE of Haverfordwest off the A4075

🏛 Parish Church of St Marcellus

🌿 Cwm Deri Vineyard

Cwm Deri Vineyard (see panel on page 263), to the south of Martletwy and set in the Valley of the Oaks, is the ideal place to see vines growing from spring through to the autumn harvest. At the vineyard shop visitors can purchase estate-grown vintage wines, fruit wines and liqueurs. Wine tastings, of course, are always very popular and, for younger members of the family, the vineyard is home

to some rescued donkeys plus a teddy bears' hideaway. The **Parish Church of St Marcellus** dates from a rebuilding of 1848–1850, though the chancel arch is thought to be 13th century and the south porch to be 16th century.

MILFORD HAVEN

6½ miles SW of Haverfordwest on the A40

🏛 Parish Church of St Katharine

🏛 Hubberston Priory   Milford Haven Museum

As well as being the name of the town, Milford Haven is also the name of the huge natural harbour here. Described by Nelson as "the finest port in Christendom", the harbour offers some of the best shelter in the world to large ships, as it is some 10 miles long by up to two miles broad. Norsemen used the harbour, as did both

🏛 historic building 🏛 museum and heritage 🏚 historic site 🌊 scenic attraction 🌿 flora and fauna

CWM DERI VINEYARD

Martletwy, Pembrokeshire SA67 8AP
Tel: 01834 891274 Fax: 01834 891464
e-mail: enquiries@cwm-deri.co.uk
website: www.cwm-deri.co.uk

Vineyard Walk - Restaurant
Wine Tasting - Holiday Cottage
Pets' Corner - Caravan Club
Licensed for Civil Ceremonies

These and others are among the reasons for visiting **Cwm Deri Vineyard**, which provides an interesting and enjoyable day out for all ages – or a weekend or longer break. Cwm Deri is a working smallholding that first opened to the public in 1992, since when it has become one of the major visitor attractions in the region, offering the very best of Welsh produce - wines, liqueurs, mead, beers, ciders, whisky, preserves, cheese, cakes, ice creams etc.

A chance to stroll through a vineyard in the UK's climate is a rare delight, a delight enhanced by doing it surrounded by the beauty of the Pembrokeshire National Park. Visitors can enjoy a tasting of Cwm Deri's wines and liqueurs, either in the shop and restaurant, or outside on the patio and terrace looking out over the vineyard, the animals and beyond to the National Park.

The shop sells the whole range of their products, and the staff will make up attractive gift packs to give as presents. The shop also sells a variety of delicacies and crafts sourced from the area around the vineyard. The whole Cwm Deri range can be ordered via the website. The café is a lovely spot for

enjoying a glass of wine, a tea or coffee or afternoon tea, while the children happily occupy themselves in the Pets' Corner with its pygmy goats, sheep, chickens, rabbits and guinea pigs. For something more substantial, the stunning conservatory restaurant beckons with a range of home-cooked food for a leisurely lunch, including popular roasts on Sunday. The restaurant is open on Friday and Saturday evenings for a memorable fine dining experience (bookings are required for Sunday lunch and evening meals).

Just 500 yards from the vineyard, in the rural village of Martletwy, Alpha Cottage is available to rent. Dating from 1896 and completely renovated in 2007, the cottage sleeps six in three double rooms, with the features of a character house complemented by up-to-date comfort and amenity. Cwm Deri also has an adult-members-only Caravan Club CL providing a tranquil retreat for five touring caravans. *WTB 4 Star Graded.*

stories and anecdotes ⚑ famous people ✿ art and craft ✐ entertainment and sport ⚶ walks

Henry II and King John, who set sail from here to conquer Ireland. However, it was Sir William Hamilton (husband of Lord Nelson's Lady Emma) who, having inherited two nearby manors, saw the potential of the haven as a major harbour. Hamilton was in Naples as an Envoy Extraordinary, so he appointed his nephew RF Greville to establish the town around the harbour. Greville contracted a Frenchman, J-L Barrallier, to lay out the town and dockyard in a square pattern that can still be seen today Although the docks, completed in 1888, failed to attract the hoped for larger ships, the Neyland trawler fleet moved here and, by the beginning of the 20th century, Milford Haven had become one of the country's leading fishing ports. During both World Wars, the Haven was busy with Atlantic convoys, but after 1945 there was a decline, and trawling also began to disappear. However, since the 1960s Milford Haven has developed as a major oil port and is still used by the leading oil companies.

Aptly housed in a former whale oil warehouse that dates from 1797, the **Milford Haven Museum** at the Old Custom House has a range of displays that follow the fortunes of the town and dockyard including hands-on exhibits tracing the town's history from a Quaker whaling port to a premier oil terminal. A seal hospital is located on the quayside opposite the museum. The tomb of Sir William Hamilton can be seen in the graveyard of the **Parish Church of St Katharine** (on which work started in 1802), while inside the church are a bible and prayer book presented by Lord Nelson.

Hubberston Priory once stood to the west of the town. It was founded in 1170 as a Benedictine house, but was dissolved by Henry VIII. Only scant remains are left.

SANDY HAVEN
8 miles W of Haverfordwest off the B4327

The sheltered creek in this lovely village has been described as truly idyllic and, particularly at low tide in the spring and autumn, many birds can be seen feeding here. The picturesque banks of the creek are heavily clad with trees and a path from the village provides walkers with an excellent view of the entrance to Milford Haven harbour.

ST ISHMAEL'S
9 miles SW of Haverfordwest off the B4327

🏠 Parish Church of St Ishmael   🏛 Long Stone

This small village, known locally as "Tish", sits on the Marloes and Dale Peninsula and is named after a colleague of the 6th century St Teilo. Close by is evidence of early inhabitants of the area as, on the village outskirts, lies a motte that is Norman if not earlier while, just half a mile away, is the **Long Stone**, the tallest standing stone in the Pembrokeshire Coast National Park. During the 14th century, Sir Rhys ap Thomas of Carew Castle is said to have promised Richard III that if Henry Tudor passed through Pembroke it would be by riding over his body. When Henry landed at Mill Bay, to salve his conscience, Sir Rhys lay under Mullock Bridge (between St Ishmael's and Marloes) as Henry rode over the river he then rode quickly to Carew Castle to welcome Henry.

The **Parish Church of St Ishmael**, hidden in Monk Valley is very picturesque. It has a double bellcote and was built in Victorian times on a site that is much older. There is a walk from the church to Monk Haven beach.

DALE
11 miles SW of Haverfordwest off the B4327

🏛 Dale Study Centre   🔌 St Ann's Head

A delightful little sailing and watersports

centre, Dale lays claim to being one of the windiest places in Britain, as gusts have been known to exceed 100 miles an hour. However, on the other side of the climatic coin, Dale is also one of the sunniest places in the country with an annual average of 1,800 hours a year - or five hours a day. To the south of the village, on the southern tip of the peninsula, is **St Ann's Head**, where a lighthouse and coastguard station keep a close watch over the dangerous rocky shores at the entrance to Milford Haven. The **Dale Study Centre** at Dale Fort is an excellent place to learn about the ecology and wildlife of the local coastline.

MARLOES
11 miles SW of Haverfordwest off the B4327

- Wooltrack Point
- Gateholm Island
- Skomer Island
- Skokholm Island

This inland village, on the road to **Wooltack**

Point, has a sandy bay to the southwest with **Gateholm Island** at its western extremity. Only a true island at high tide, the name comes from the Norse for Goat Island, and there are traces here of a possible monastic settlement.

Right up until the end of the 19th century, the ancient custom of hunting the wren, which was supposed to embody the evils of winter, was followed throughout Wales. In Pembrokeshire, the hunting took place on Twelfth Night, and the captured bird would be placed in a carved and beribboned 'wren house' and paraded around the village by men singing of the hunt. A particularly fine example of a wren house from Marloes can be found in the Welsh Folk Museum, at St Fagans, near Cardiff.

Close by, at Martin's Haven, boats leave for **Skomer Island** and **Skokholm Island**.

ALBION HOUSE

Marloes, Haverfordwest, Pembrokeshire SA62 3AZ
Tel: 01646 636365
email: albionhouse@yahoo.co.uk
website: www.bedandbreakfastmarloes.co.uk

Once a village of lobster fisherman, the pretty village of Marloes has tremendous sea views and is perfect for those who enjoy the crisp country air. The **Albion House** is a new house, providing accommodation in a beautiful setting.

There are 3 bedrooms available here, 1 double, family and single. Both the double and family room are complete with ensuite bathrooms and the single bedroom has its own private bathroom suite. The bedrooms are comfortable and include everything that you may require on a short getaway.

The prices vary from £25-£30 per person, per night and include a full cooked or continental breakfast, which is served between 8 and 9am.

Albion House is the perfect place to stay if you are interested in walking and exploring new places. Pembrokeshire's natural coastal path is the only true national park in Britain. It covers 240 sq miles of beautiful landscapes and beaches, making your time here very much worthwhile.

In the evenings it is recommended to visit the Lobster Pot in the village as being the local pub, there is always great entertainment on offer.

stories and anecdotes   famous people   art and craft   entertainment and sport   walks

Broad Haven

Distance: *3.8 miles (6.1 kilometres)*
Typical time: *120 mins*
Height gain: *160 metres*
Map: *Explorer OL36*
Walk: *www.walkingworld.com ID:2157*
Contributor: *Pat Roberts*

ACCESS INFORMATION:

Parking is in the large carpark at the north of the Broad Haven beach, near the Youth Hostel. There are toilets there, and there is a charge in the summer months.

DESCRIPTION:

Woodland is rather scarce in Pembrokeshire, so this circular walk is quite unusual. The outward route is up through Haroldston Woods, while the return is along the coast path. Note the unusual names of the rocks in this part of the coast path, Haroldston Chins, Settling Nose, and Sleek Stone.

FEATURES:

Sea, Toilets, Wildlife, Birds, Flowers, Great Views, Butterflies, Woodland

WALK DIRECTIONS:

1 | Where ever you are parked in the car park, head for the Youth Hostel and the old Visitor Centre building. Take the signed "Wood Walk" towards the Life Boat Station. Pass to the right of the boat house and continue towards the bushes.

2 | Pass a footpath into the caravan park, and come to a junction of pathways. To the right and the left are paths connected to the caravan site, we swing sharp right through a kissing gate to walk with the stream on the left. Keep to this good made-up track as it wanders through the trees, always gaining height. Look out for the birds, flowers and butterflies.

3 | At this point one finger points left and up, while our route bears right. Just after this point is a seat on the right, the view now rather cut short with trees. Continue to rise on a good

track, passing Timberlands, a holiday park of timber chalets.

4 | The path leaves the trees as it approaches a chapel. At the finger post go left to pass through a gate onto the road. Here right to walk past the chapel. Straight on at a junction and slowly gain a little more height.

5 | Take the first turn left, signed Druids haven. Pass a cattle grid, and when the road turns sharp right, look over the hedge on the left to see a track running in the field parallel to the road. This is an ancient trade route known as the Welsh Way. It runs from St. Ishmaels to Whitesands Bay. Carry on along this road for about 300 metres, to reach another cattle grid and parking for a few cars.

6 | Turn left into the carpark, and follow the path down towards Haroldstone Chins and the coast path.

7 | Left along the coast path. This is a particularly lovely part of the coast path, dramatic scenery and the usual crop of wild flowers. Keep with it down to Broad Haven. On reaching the road turn right to walk along the top of the beach.

8 | As soon as the road crosses the stream, take this opening on the left to walk back up, past the toilets to the carpark.

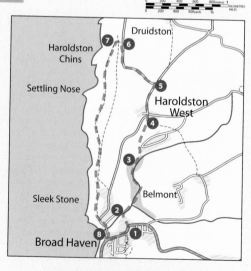

Skomer Island National Nature Reserve and Skokholm and Grassholm provide some of the best and most spectacular bird watching anywhere in Britain.

NOLTON HAVEN

6½ miles W of Haverfordwest off the A487

The village sits at the centre of St Brides Bay and the coastline here has steep, undulating cliffs and sandy beaches, which have remained completely unspoilt despite being within easy reach of Haverfordwest and Milford Haven. As part of the Pembrokeshire Coast National Park, the coastline is rich in outstanding natural beauty, with a wide variety of natural amenities available to the holidaymaker, including various short and

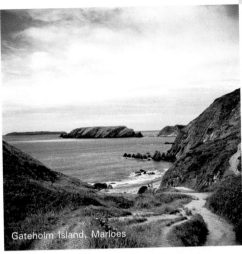

Gateholm Island, Marloes

longer distance footpaths from where an abundance of wildlife, sea birds and wild flowers can be seen. This area is a Mecca for

OCEAN CAFÉ, BAR & RESTAURANT

Broad Haven, Pembrokeshire SA62 3JG
Tel: 01437 781882
e-mail: info@oceancafebarandrestaurant.co.uk
website: www.oceancafebarandrestaurant.co.uk

In February 2009 Mostyn and Kay Davis took the helm at the **Ocean Café, Bar & Restaurant** on the seafront at Broad Haven, a coastal village on the St Brides Bay Heritage Coast. They moved to this popular dining bar to fulfil a desire to combine running a business with living by the sea, and their background as hosts in a free house makes has quickly made them many new friends. In the daytime the bright, modern corner premises are particularly popular with families, while in the evening the grown-up clientele create a lively, buzzy atmosphere in the three separate eating/drinking areas. The cooking is a major reason for the popularity of the place, and the main menu makes excellent use of local produce in cooked-to-order dishes that range from whitebait and garlic mushrooms to chicken with a barbecue sauce, beef madras, Pembrokeshire steak & Guinness pie and, for vegetarians, chestnut mushroom & leek crumble. Seafood lovers can push the boast out with 'The Ocean', a plate of oak-smoked haddock, cod fillet and juicy prawns in a rich, creamy sauce.

The Ocean stands directly opposite the beach, a popular spot for swimming and sunbathing in the summer and for bracing walks in the winter.

stories and anecdotes 🐦 famous people 🎨 art and craft 🎭 entertainment and sport 🚶 walks

THE BOATHOUSE GALLERY

St Bride's Road, Little Haven,
Pembrokeshire SA62 3UN
Tel: 01437 781910 Fax: 01437 781775
e-mail: shirley@the-boathouse-gallery.co.uk
website: www.the-boathouse-gallery.co.uk

Shirley and Ian Norman are passionate about their work and about the lovely part of the world where they live, and they combine the two passions at **The Boathouse Gallery**. It stands in the sunny seaside village of Little Haven, south of Broad Haven on the Pembrokeshire Coast Path. Little Haven's superb sandy beach has inspired many painters and photographers, and the coast and countryside are the inspiration behind Shirley and Ian's work. Shirley's original watercolours and giclée reproductions are shown here, along with her "Calligraphic Cards" – greeting cards using apt and humorous quotations. Driftwood is Ian's medium : he turns the wood into lamps, mirrors and "Nauticals" – quotations burnt into the driftwood. Each piece is unique, showing the diverse effects of the elements on the wood. New displays for 2009 are a range of reclaimed oak furniture and a selection of beautiful hand-crafted jewellery. The Gallery, which is located a short walk from the main car park, is open April to October from 11 to 4 (closed Mondays except School and Bank Holidays).

walkers, bird watchers, surfers, swimmers and sailors.

ROCH
5½ miles W of Haverfordwest off the A487

🏠 Roch Castle   👁 Adam de la Roche

Found on a rocky outcrop overlooking the village and the surrounding plain, are the remains of **Roch Castle**, which was originally built in the 13th century by the feudal Lord of Roch, **Adam de la Roche**. A local story tells that de la Roche was told by a witch that he would be killed by a snake, but that if he could pass a year in safety, then he need never fear the prophecy. Accordingly, de la Roche had the castle built in such a way as to be out of reach of any snake and so the fortress was constructed on this particularly well-defended site. His year free from snakes began and de la Roche moved into the top floor of the castle and remained there, in constant fear, for a year. The very last night of his self-enforced

imprisonment was bitterly cold and someone sent a basket of firewood to the castle to help Adam pass the night in comfort. The basket was taken to his room and, as de la Roche was putting the logs on the fire, an adder crawled out from among the logs and bit him. The next morning, Adam de la Roche was found dead in front of his hearth.

Pembroke

🏠 Pembroke Castle   🏛 Museum of the Home
🏠 Parish Church of St Nicholas and St John
🏠 Monkton Priory

This historic town, with its long and unbroken line of well-preserved medieval town walls, is dominated by the mighty fortress of **Pembroke Castle**. It was founded in the 11th century by the Montgomerys, who established the first timber castle on a rocky crag above the River Cleddau. The later stone

THE CORNSTORE

Quayside Café and Interior Furnishings, North Quay, Pembroke, Pembrokeshire SA71 4NU
Tel: 01646 684290
e-mail: info@vintage-interiors.net
website: www.vintage-interiors.net

THE CORNSTORE and CUSTOMS HOUSE CAFÉ sit in the shadow of PEMBROKE CASTLE amongst the individual shops of PEMBROKE'S NORTH QUAY.

This former eighteenth century warehouse, which is listed for its' historic and architectural importance, still enjoys a commercial role retailing inspirational items for self and home. It is one of the few physical reminders of Pembroke's influential maritime history and the quality of the buildings renovation has been recognised with a national award.

Many years ago you would have visited The Cornstore to purchase Coal, Ale, Grain or Potatoes. Today this three-storey building is bursting with sumptuous leather suites, occasional chairs and solid wood dining furniture. Cushions and throws are available in abundance, co-ordinating neatly with ranges of design-led unique lighting, mirrors and ceramics. Pembrokeshire Art is featured in-store alongside smaller gift items such as jewellery, leather handbags and silk scarves.

The Cornstore is proud to have been awarded the Pembrokeshire Produce Mark for the quality of its' fare. The Café is open Monday – Saturday for light lunches and snacks featuring daily specials, all made from fresh locally sourced Pembrokeshire produce. A selection of freshly brewed coffees and teas is always available and the cakes are 'simply to die for'. Meals can be eaten inside or taken onto the Quayside with stunning views of the Castle. It is advisable to book your table for lunch. There is ample free parking at the rear of the store.

stories and anecdotes ☙ famous people ♪ art and craft ✐ entertainment and sport � walks

THE BEACH HUT BOUTIQUE

28 Main Street, Pembroke,
Pembrokeshire SA71 4NP
Tel: 01646 682002
website: www.thebeachhutboutique.co.uk
blog: www.thebeachhutboutique.com

The Beach Hut Boutique *is a unique shopping experience. It is shopping as it should be – inspiring and original.*

Set in an old building typical of historic Pembroke The Beach Hut Boutique is light, spacious and welcoming. The shop is warm, contemporary and unpretentious. Its choc full of gorgeous must-have goodies, inspired by the seaside and many are sourced in Wales.

If you want to recapture the childhood memories of hanging out at a beach or to bring home the cutesy style of a beach hut, here you'll find handmade pieces designed to bring a little of the beach to your home (without the sand!).

The Beach Hut Boutique ethos is to provide lifestyle products where the emphasis is on craftsmanship and quality. It has an eclectic and sophisticated collection of things for every aspect of a relaxed coastal lifestyle, from ceramics to jewellery to photographs reminiscent of holidays spent in jolly, brightly coloured beach huts at the seaside in the 1950's.

Saltwater Taffy is an exclusive brand to the boutique bringing the outdoors in with a natural element for you décor; there are driftwood boats, hearts, chairs and wall art.

There is a fantastic range of canvasses; cushions, doorstops and throws made by a Swansea based artist, her style is quirky, fun and offers a refreshing take on embroidery. These are all pieces you can imagine living with.

Since opening in October 2007 The Beach Hut Boutique has gone from strength to strength, consequently tripling in size with a new gallery on the top floor. This is a beautiful space, flooded with light, with far reaching views over the town from the windows and original beams, just perfect for a gallery.

Of course not everyone can make the trip to Pembroke so The Beach Hut Boutique has extended its personal and friendly service to the internet. You can shop online and read the blog. Riley, a one-year-old Springer spaniel and store mascot promises to keep you updated on the new products as and when they arrive and what the staff have been up to.

THE ROOM – HOME ACCESSORIES & GIFT STORE

104 Main Street, Pembroke, Pembrokeshire SA71 4HN
Tel: 01646 686106   e-mail: theroom@tesco.net

The historic walled town of Pembroke has much of interest to the visitor, including the Castle, the Priory, the Museum of the Home and the Parish Church of St. Nicholas & St. John. It also has a number of interesting shops, one of the most interesting being The Room – Home Accessories & Gift Store. The store's Victorian façade and large window displays catching the eye of passers-by at the Eastern end of Pembroke's main street. The displays are the work of owner Sandra Senior, whose eye for attractive and unusual things extends throughout the 3 rooms of the shop. Each room is filled with all manner of beautiful things for the home, lifestyle and lovely gifts and treats. The constantly changing range includes bathroom fragrances & accessories, candles & holders, jewellery, bags and purses, scarves, glassware and pottery, clocks, paintings, prints and picture frames, greeting cards, soft toys, garden furniture and seasonal items. Sandra's lovely shop is open 10.00am to 5.30pm Monday to Saturday.

castle was built between 1189 and 1225. In 1457, Henry VII was born in the castle.

Found opposite the castle, at Westgate Hill, is the charming **Museum of the Home,** which houses a unique collection of household utensils, appliances, and toys and games that span three centuries. Also on display are Welsh costumes from the 19th century.

Just half a mile from the castle, and across Monkton Pill, stood **Monkton Priory,** founded in 1098 by Arnulf de Montgomery for Benedictine monks. It was given to St Albans in 1473. The priory church, now the **Parish Church of St Nicholas and St John,** with its long narrow barrel-vaulted nave and monastic chancel, was rearranged in the 14th century and, after lying in ruins for many years, was restored again in the late 19th century.

Around Pembroke

PEMBROKE DOCK
1½ miles NW of Pembroke on the A477

Once an important naval dockyard, Pembroke Dock sits on the southern shore of the Cleddau, at the point where modern development ends and the gentler hinterland of the river system begins. At one time the town relied on its naval dockyard for employment and 263 Royal Navy vessels were built here between 1814 and its closure in 1926. Also built here were the royal yachts *Victoria and Albert I, II* and *III.*

In 1930, the site was taken over by the Royal Air Force, and became the home of Squadron 210, which consisted of flying boats. It grew to become the largest flying boat base in the world, its most famous

[] stories and anecdotes famous people art and craft entertainment and sport walks

BORDERS BED & BREAKFAST

25 Park Street, Pembroke Dock,
Pembrokeshire SA72 6JG
Tel: 01646 689089
website: www.bandbwiththeborders.co.uk

A warm welcome is guaranteed from wonderful hosts Sue and Leigh Border at their inviting Victorian home at Pembroke Dock. **Borders Bed & Breakfast** stands just north of the B4322 close to the Irish ferry terminal and a short walk from the Pembrokeshire Coastal Path, with access to many miles of glorious coastal scenery.

Whether you are travelling with a partner or friend, you will find comfort aplenty in the three bright bedrooms. Each have TV, tea/coffee tray, radio, CD player, radio-alarm clock, hairdryer and wireless broadband internet connection. An iron and board are available, and a cot, high chair and stair gate can be also be provided on request. Cycles and motorcycles can be stored in a lock-up garage on the premises.

Sue prepares a super breakfast to start the day, and she will cook a 2/3-course evening meal by arrangement, packed lunches or make up a supper tray for late arrivals. Guests can enjoy TV, music or conversation in the sitting room or socialise over a glass of wine in the flower-filled barbecue area. The owners can arrange to collect or deliver guests from or to the ferry terminal or the bus or coach station.

PEMBROKESHIRE STAINED GLASS LTD

Units 11 & 12, Pier Road, Hobbs Point, Pembroke Dock,
Pembrokeshire SA72 6TR
Tel: 01646 621333   e-mail: cbale@clara.co.uk

Discover the beauty of stained glass at **Pembrokeshire Stained Glass Ltd**, situated at Hobbs Point in Pembroke Dock, close to the town of Pembroke itself. This ancient and time consuming craft is being carried out here at their workshops. Using traditional methods to produce individual works of art, they can create leaded lights for doors, windows and conservatories, mirrors and sun catchers .

Repairs and restoration of stained glass windows, leaded lights and all aspects of ecclesiastical are undertaken by experienced craftsmen. The company has carried out many projects within Wales, including Castlemartin, Ferryside and a spectacular, complete rose window in Porthcawl.

Treat yourself to a small souvenir of your visit to Wales by taking away a special piece of leaded glass. You can choose from a selection of handcrafted mirrors and suncatchers available at the workshop, or be inspired and commission a larger piece of work.

Call in and see for yourself, but to avoid any disappointment, please phone before you visit to confirm opening times. (Credit card facilities are unavailable).

🏭 historic building 🏛 museum and heritage 🏚 historic site 🐿 scenic attraction 🌿 flora and fauna

aircraft being the Short Sunderland. It supported air crews from not only the UK, but also from Canada, Australia and New Zealand. So important was the base that it was continually bombed in 1940, with over 200 houses in thr town being destroyed. The air base closed in 1959.

UPTON
3 miles NE of Pembroke off the A477

🐦 Upton Castle Gardens

Set in a secluded valley running down to the River Carew, **Upton Castle Gardens** have three raised formal terraces that drop down from the medieval castle. Along with the rose gardens and herbaceous borders, there are 40 acres of wooded grounds containing some 250 species of trees and shrubs. There's also a medieval chapel from which the walled garden can be seen.

CAREW
4 miles E of Pembroke on the A4075

🏰 Carew Castle   🏰 Carew Cheritan Control Tower

🏯 Carew Tidal Mill   🏚 Celtic Cross

Located on the shores of the tidal mill pond, **Carew Castle** and the **Tidal Mill** (see panel below) are one of the Pembrokeshire Coast National Park's most popular visitor attractions. As well as the castle and the mill, the Carew site also incorporates a causeway, a medieval bridge and an 11th century **Celtic Cross** that is one of the best examples of its kind in Wales.

CAREW CASTLE & TIDAL MILL
Carew, nr Tenby, Pembrokeshire SA70 8SL
Tel/Fax: 01646 651782
e-mail: enquiries@carewcastle.com
website: www.carewcastle.com

On the shores of the 23-acre tidal mill pond, **Carew Castle** is one of the few buildings of its kind to show the development from Norman fortification (it was built between 1280 and 1310) to Elizabethan manor. (The site is considerably older, as archaeological excavations have found remains that could go back some 3,000 years). Visitors can explore the winding stairs, massive towers, lofty halls, rooms and passages. Tread in the footsteps of servants, craftsmen, priests, soldiers and the nobility down the centuries. The Castle has witnessed many notable events, including the last Great Tournament, which was held in 1507 and was attended by 600 nobles. During the summer numerous events are staged, including drama, environmental and ecological tours, holiday activities and education programmes.

The **Tidal Mill**, built around 1800 on the site of an earlier mill, is the only restored tidal mill in Wales and still retains its original machinery. Visitors touring the four-storey building can learn about all aspects of the milling process. The Castle and Tidal Mill are open daily from April to October – phone for out-of-season times. Guided tours take place daily at 2.30, and self-guided and audio tours at any time. The site also incorporates a causeway, a medieval bridge and a superb 11th century Celtic Cross.

📖 stories and anecdotes 🐦 famous people ✏️ art and craft 🎭 entertainment and sport 🥾 walks

The **Carew Cheritan Control Tower** is on a World War II airfield near the village, and has been restored by a group of enthusiasts. It is sometimes open to the public in summer, usually at weekends.

MANORBIER

5½ miles SE of Pembroke off the A4139

🏚 Manorbier Castle

Manorbier is charmingly situated at the head of a valley that reaches down to the shore in a beautiful bay with a safe bathing beach. The village's name is thought to have been derived from Maenor Pyr (Manor of Pyr) and Pyr is believed to have been the first Celtic abbot of Caldey who lived in the 5th century.

Overlooking the bay of the same name, **Manorbier Castle** was founded by Odo de Barri in 1095, when he built a wooden hall

within a defensive structure. However, it was his son William who began building the stone fortification in the early 12th century.

Famous for being the birthplace, in 1146, of Giraldus Cambrenses (Gerald of Wales), a monk and chronicler who wrote the first account of life in medieval Wales, the castle was described by him as being "the pleasantest spot in Wales" (see also St David's and Llanwnda).

Today, life-size wax figures placed at various points, including the impressive great hall, the turrets and the chapel, bring the history of this ancient building to life as atmospheric music captures the castle's spirit. The castle gardens were laid out by JR Cobb in the late 19th century, and there is also a late Victorian cottage with appropriate herbaceous borders lining the castle walls.

🏚 historic building 🏛 museum and heritage 🏚 historic site 🝔 scenic attraction 🌿 flora and fauna

CELTIC HAVEN

Lydstep, Tenby, Pembrokeshire SA70 7SG
Tel: 01834 870000
e-mail: welcome@celtichaven.com
website: www.celtichaven.co.uk

Escape! Relax! Unwind! Explore!
At a Magical Location

Celtic Haven is part of a new generation of luxury self-catering holiday cottages, but located in an area steeped in history. With parts dating back 800 years, the 5-star resort occupies the land which was the estate of Lord St. David and is like a jewel in the beautiful crown of the Pembrokeshire Coast National Park.

Situated on the coastal path, Celtic Haven over-looks the monastic island of Caldey and the Atlantic Coast and is in close proximity to over a dozen sandy beaches and many historic sites. Staying at Celtic Haven for a few days or a week you are surrounded by the natural beauty of the Pembrokeshire coastline.

Celtic Haven's Elemis Premier Spa is the only Elemis Premier Spa in West Wales and offers over 80 blissful treatments and holistic therapies, making The Spa at Celtic Haven a true haven of tranquility.

Use of the Leisure Centre facilities is included with the cost of your stay - 2 all weather tennis courts, nine-hole headland golf course, indoor golf simulator, indoor heated swimming pool, bubble room hot-tub, sauna and fitness suite.

The stylish Waves bar & restaurant has a lovely view and offers a wide range of meals ranging from light snacks to substantial lunches and elegant dinners.

Guests seeking a traditional cottage experience may stay in one of the sixteen 12th century buildings in the older part of Celtic Haven. From The Parlour, a cosy romantic cottage for two, to the Manor House, sleeping twelve guests in six bedrooms, each cottage has been tastefully converted and retains its original beamed ceilings, exposed A- frames and studded floors.

Alternatively, for those looking for a more modern approach, Celtic Haven includes a newer raised courtyard of ten properties with breathtaking views over Lydstep Bay and Caldey Island.

All the properties are equipped to a 5 star standard with CD Stereo, TV Video/DVD, full central heating, dishwasher, microwave and washing machine.

Guests return to Celtic Haven time and time again for many reasons, not least of which is for the people – all the staff live locally and the reservation team are the same people who you will meet at the Welcome Centre upon your arrival. They are familiar with each of the properties and are well-versed in local knowledge, so whether it's a recommendation on where to go for dinner, what castle to see, the best local town for shopping, how to book a fishing trip or how to get to Dylan Thomas' Laugharne, someone will be on hand to offer friendly advice and personalized service.

**To check availability or request a brochure, call 01834 870000 or
email welcome@celtichaven.com**

📖 stories and anecdotes 🦜 famous people 🎨 art and craft 🎭 entertainment and sport 🚶 walks

LAMPHEY BISHOP'S PALACE
1½ miles SE of Pembroke on the A4139

🏛 Bishop's Palace

🏛 Parish Church of St Faith and St Tyfai

Just northwest of the village, in the 13th century, the medieval bishops of St David's built the magnificent **Bishop's Palace** as a retreat from the affairs of Church and State. Though improved over a period of 200 years, the major building work was undertaken by the dynamic Bishop Henry de Gower between 1328 and 1347 and he was responsible for the splendid great hall. Although now in ruins, this is a peaceful and tranquil site where successive bishops were able to live the life of country gentlemen among the estate's orchards, vegetable gardens and rolling parkland. The **Parish Church of St Faith and St Tyfai** has a fine late 14th/early 15th century tower and one of the best Norman fonts in the county.

HODGESTON
3 miles E of Pembroke on the B4584

🏛 Parish Church of Hodgeston

The **Parish Church of Hodgeston** has a 14th-century chancel built by Bishop Gower of St Davids and a fine Norman font. Its tower is early medieval, and close to the chancel are the stairs to a former rood loft. It is one of the few churches in Wales without a dedication to a saint (though it did have at one time), and is owned by the Friends of Friendless Churches.

ST GOVAN'S HEAD
5 miles S of Pembroke off the B4319

🏛 St Govan's Chapel

The cliff scenery is at its most spectacular at St Govan's Head, where the tiny, **St Govan's Chapel** huddles among the rocks almost at sea level. It is thought to have been built in the 11th century, though some experts say it may go back to the 6th century. Accessible by climbing down approximately 74 stone steps, the chapel was built on the site of a holy well that once attracted pilgrims who believed the well's waters to have miraculous healing powers. There is a legend that says that the number of steps cannot be accurately counted, and indeed people who try usually come up with different answers. However, there is a simple explanation. The steps have been cut irregularly, so some of them are 'half steps' which many people fail to count.

Inside is a vertical cleft in the

St Govan's Chapel

rock which, according to legend, first opened so that St Govan could hide inside and escape his enemies. Closing behind him, the rock did not reopen until the danger had passed. Accordingly, a wish made while standing in the cleft and facing the rock will come true provided the person making the wish does not change his or her mind before turning round. Although many miracles have been credited to St Govan he remains a mysterious and little known man. Some believe him to have been a disciple of St David while others claim that he was a thief who, having miraculously found the hiding place, became a convert. St Govan is also thought by some to have been a woman named Cofen - the wife of a 5th century chief - who became a recluse.

BOSHERSTON
4½ miles SW of Pembroke off the B4319

- Parish Church of St Michael and All Angels
- Stackpole Gardens

The **Parish Church of St Michael and All Angels** dates from the 13th century and later, and replaced an even earlier church that stood on the site. The font is medieval, and there is a 14th century tomb in the south transept, thought to be that of a Duchess of Buckingham. There is an old preaching cross in the churchyard. The building was restored in 1855 by the then Earl of Cawder, who owned the nearby Stackpole estate. To the east of the village and occupying part of estate, are **Stackpole Gardens**, which were landscaped in the 18th century. Romantic in style and containing some interesting and well-engineered water features, including an eight arched bridge, these are intriguing gardens to explore and, although the original manor house has gone, the 19th century terraces, woodland garden and summer house remain,

along with a grotto, an ice house and three walled gardens.

Tenby

- Tenby Castle
- Tudor Merchant's House
- Lifeboat Station
- Five Arches
- Parish Church of St Mary
- Tenby Museum
- South Parade
- Robert Recorde
- Silent World Aquarium and Reptile Collection

Tenby's Welsh name, Dinbych y Pysgod, means Little fort of the fishes and certainly its most photographed scene is the pretty harbour with its pastel-coloured Georgian houses. However, the whole place is a real delight, prompting many eulogies such as this from the artist Augustus John: "You may travel the world over, but you will find nothing more beautiful: it is so restful, so colourful and so unspoilt." The town still retains its charming medieval character together with the crooked lanes that are enclosed within its surprisingly well-preserved 13th-century town walls. On one particular stretch, **South Parade**, the walls are still at their full height, and the two tiers of arrow slits are very much visible. The **Five Arches**, a fortified gateway on the walls, is perhaps the most famous feature. Unfortunately, the same is not true for **Tenby Castle**, the scant remains of which can be found on a small headland. However, the ruins are well worth a visit for the spectacular views out across Carmarthen Bay and along the Pembrokeshire coast. A statue to Prince Albert can also be found on the headland, along with **Tenby Museum** (see panel opposite), which was founded in 1878, and is the oldest independent museum in Wales. As well as having archaeological and historical material relating to the area, the museum has a

stories and anecdotes famous people art and craft entertainment and sport walks

Tenby Harbour

TENBY MUSEUM & ART GALLERY

Castle Hill, Tenby, Pembrokeshire SA70 7BP
Tel/Fax: 01834 842809
e-mail: info@tenbymuseum.org.uk
website: www.tenbymuseum.org.uk

'To Visit, To See, To Learn, To Do,
To Enjoy, To Remember'

Tenby Museum & Art Gallery is run by an experienced
team with an impressive accumulated knowledge of the
town's and the region's history, geology and archaeology.
The oldest independently run museum in Wales, it has
been serving the community since 1878, when it was
founded by a self-appointed committee of local retired
professional gentlemen including amateur naturalists and
archaeologists, with the primary aim of displaying local
collections of natural history, geology and archaeology.
The three floors tell a local story that starts in prehistoric
times and follows through to modern times, with special
exhibitions on topics such as Tenby Harbour and the local
lifeboats. There are two art galleries: the Wilfred Harrison

Gallery features artists with local connections, including Augustus and Gwen John, David Jones
and John Piper, while the New Gallery hosts changing exhibitions throughout the year. Other
activities at Tenby Museum include a family history research facility, a year-round programme of
educational events, talks and workshops, a gift shop and a small cafeteria.

🏚 historic building 🏛 museum and heritage 🏚 historic site 🏝 scenic attraction �${}$ flora and fauna

PEMBROKESHIRE

BAY HOUSE BED & BREAKFAST

5 Picton Road, Tenby, Pembrokeshire SA70 7DP
Tel: 01834 849015
e-mail: info@tenbybandb.co.uk website: www.tenbybandb.co.uk

Everything you could wish for in this 'Five Star', luxury bed and breakfast in the heart of Tenby! Bay House is perfectly situated close to both the esplanade on South beach and to the town, with it's many individual shops and restaurants.

A Victorian townhouse lovingly restored to it's former glory with three spacious and privately situated en suite bedrooms decorated to a very high standard, combining traditional with a contemporary twist. Comfort is a priority with king-size beds and crisp white linen, bathrobes, fluffy towels and quality toiletries. TVs with DVD and ipod players (a good choice of DVDs are available). You will find beverages, fruit and biscuits, as well as fresh milk and chilled water.

A generous home-cooked breakfast will set you up for the day ahead. Bay House uses the finest local ingredients that can be found. Award winning Bethesda bacon and sausage or you can try the homemade vegetarian Glamorgan sausages, made to a traditional recipe with leeks and Welsh cheese. Fresh fruit, organic yoghurt and croissants are also available to ensure all tastes are catered for! Good food, comfortable rooms and an easy going, relaxed atmosphere ensures guests return time and again.

Tudor Merchants House, Tenby

fascinating maritime section and an impressive art gallery.

Close to the quay lies the **Tudor Merchant's House** (NT), a relic of Tenby's prosperous sea-faring days and a fine example of a comfortable townhouse of the late 15th century. Narrow and built with three storeys, the house has been furnished to re-create the atmosphere and environment in which a wealthy Tudor family would have lived. With a Flemish chimney, early floral frescoes on some of the interior walls, and a small herb garden outside, there is plenty at the house to evoke life around 600 years ago. The large and lavish **Parish Church of St Mary** is another testament to the town's illustrious maritime past. The tower was built in the early 14th century, and served as a place of sanctuary and a lookout point in times of trouble. The

stories and anecdotes famous people art and craft entertainment and sport walks

HOLIDAY CONNECTIONS

Holiday House, Warren Street, Tenby,
Pembrokeshire SA70 7JS
Tel: 01834 842444   Fax: 01834 845775
e-mail: enquiries@holiday-connections.co.uk
website: www.holiday-connections.co.uk

Holiday Connections are a small but very friendly agency
dedicated to assisting you find your perfect holiday
accommodation in and around Tenby and Saundersfoot,
Pembrokeshire, west Wales. Holiday Connections have many properties,
including self catering accommodation in west Wales, as well as
wonderful farmhouses and cottages in semi rural/rural areas which offer
a most peaceful and relaxing atmosphere.

   West Wales is full of exciting places to explore and experience. The
Pembrokeshire Coast National Park is laden with some of the most
beautiful, award winning beaches, secret coves and stunning scenery.
Children love the clean seas, acres of sand and marvel at the rock-pools
whilst the peaceful, countryside locations could not be more
picturesque. It's no surprise that this areas are a firm favourite with
holidaymakers and if you can't find what you're perfect base, then just
pick up the telephone and talk to one of the members of staff at Holiday Connections who will be
happy to speak to you through your requirements and suggest a possible suitable property for you.
Alternatively you log on to their website and browse the numerous properties, with photographs.

THE JAZZ

2 White Lion Street, Tenby, Pembrokeshire SA70 7ES
Tel: 01834 842253
e-mail: marilynmgr@aol.com

Tenby is a delightful little town with a pretty harbour,
historic buildings and town walls that date back to the 13th
century. Among the many landmark buildings, pride of place
for many is the sunny blue-painted sweet shop called **The
Jazz**. Opened in the 1930s in the old part of town, and for
many years owned and run by Will and Marilyn Gardner,
this wonderful shop has served generations of local
children, families and holidaymakers with an amazing array
of sweets and chocolates. The shelves are filled with more
than 100 old-style jars containing all the old favourites and
many more besides. There are sherbet lemons, wine gums,

acid drops, herbal tablets, Lyons fruit salads, aniseed balls,
Everton mints, Paynes Army & Navy drops....They also sell
a range of sugar-free sweets, including fruit drops,
strawberries & cream, Welsh mints – even sugar-free barley sugar! Will has contacts throughout
the confectionery world and his suppliers source sweets you'd be hard pressed to find elsewhere.
As well as the sweets sold loose from the jar – in old-fashioned paper bags if you like, or gift-
wrapped to give as presents The Jazz stocks a wide range of popular sweets and chocolates in
bags and bars and boxes. It also sells general supplies, including basic groceries like bread, tea and
coffee, soft drinks, newspapers and magazines. If you're sweet on sweets, The Jazz is definitely

FOUR SEASONS

Upper Park Road, Tenby, Pembrokeshire SA70 7LT
Tel/Fax: 01634 842540
e-mail: hugh4seasons@googlemail.com

Hugh Scale and his family not only own and run the **Four Seasons** farm shop, but also a fruit and vegetable shop just outside the castle and a florist's in Upper Frog Street. The farm shop, which is ideally located just outside Saundersfoot offers a fantastic selection beef, lamb, pork, poultry and game, all sourced from local suppliers. You'll also find a wonderful choice of cooked meats, pork pies, local cheeses, coleslaw, pastas, olive, biscuits and much more. There's even locally made fudge and sweets.

At the florist's shop, expert staff are on hand to create beautiful hand made arrangements to suit any occasion - birthdays, congratulations, anniversaries, thank you, new arrivals, "I love you", "Sorry" and more.

To complement the flowers, the shop stocks a wide range of gifts which can also be delivered your door. A full wedding service is also available with staff on hand to guide and assist you from the moment you choose your flowers right up until the big day.

tower is topped by a small spire, which itself is over 500 years old. The whole thing is 152 feet high. The chancel is 13th century as well, and its barrel roof has over 75 carved bosses. A wall plaque commemorates the 16th-century mathematician and alchemist **Robert Recorde** (1510–1558), who invented the equals sign (=). After a distinguished career in London, he eventually died a pauper in King's Bench Prison, Southwark.

Perhaps of more interest to younger visitors to the town is the **Silent World Aquarium and Reptile Collection** housed in an attractive 19th-century chapel. In these interesting, if somewhat unusual, surroundings there is a wide range of exotic fish, amphibians and invertebrates on display, as well as fish and other creatures that live around the shores of Pembrokeshire. Upstairs are the reptiles, and here visitors can see a fascinating collection of snakes and lizards

from around the world. Gifts for all ages, some made by local craftsmen, are on sale in the shop, where grown-ups can enjoy coffee, tea and a snack while the youngsters play with toys, draw, do a brass rubbing or try one of the quizzes. It is open all year. In 2006, Tenby's **Lifeboat Station**, which can be visited daily, was the first to receive the new Tamar class slipway-launched lifeboat, the *Haydn Miller*.

Around Tenby

ST FLORENCE

4 miles W of Tenby off the B4318

🏛 Parish Church of St Florence

🏛 Flemish Chimneys

🐦 Manor House Wildlife and Leisure Park

A small and quiet village located on the border

GRANDIFLORA PLANT & GARDEN CENTRE

St Florence, Tenby, Pembrokeshire SA70 8LP
Tel: 01834 871500
e-mail: rogerorliz@grandiflora.co.uk
website: www.grandiflora.co.uk

Just above St Florence, a short drive west of Tenby, Liz and Roger Hainsworth own and run one of the very few specialist semi-matured plant centres in the land. On display at **Grandiflora Plant & Garden Centre** are thousands of containerised British trees and shrubs, and plants up to 25 feet tall and 100 years old help customers achieve instant landscapes at any time of the year. They include palms, bamboos, Mediterranean, coastal, jungle exotic and unusual plants, as well as a wide range of smaller plants, with bedding plants and made-up hanging baskets in the spring.

The garden shop is packed with gardening aids and accessories and a selection of unusual garden-themed gift ideas. Tree and plant hire is available for functions, events and films, and the owners and staff offer a full advisory, delivery and planting service throughout South Wales. Next to the Centre is the very popular **Bramleys Tea Room** (Tel: 01834 871778), serving morning coffee, light snacks, lunches, cakes, desserts and cream teas. A fine choice of home-cooked local produce runs from soups and pies to meat and vegetarian sausages, Sunday roasts and monthly themed evenings. The Centre is open seven days a week from 10 to 5 (10 to 4 November to January).

of the National Park, St Florence is noted for its **Parish Church of St Florence**, which is Norman. Inside the church is a memorial to Robert Ferrar, Protestant Bishop of St David's, who suffered a martyr's death in Carmarthen in 1555 at the instigation of Mary Tudor. To the northeast of the village lies **Manor House Wildlife and Leisure Park**, where the original village manor house provides the perfect backdrop for the park's collection of birds, animals, fish and reptiles. Snake handling, bottle feeding and animal handling sessions all take place undercover in the Close Encounters Barn, while the wooded grounds and formal gardens are ideal places for both exploration and picnics.

Up until the early 19th century, the River Ritec was tidal as far as the village at high tide,

and it had a small port. You can still see the stone where the boats tied up. The so-called **Flemish Chimneys** attached to some 16th and 17th-century cottages in the village are reminders of the Flemish immigrants to the area, though in truth, they predate their coming.

SAUNDERSFOOT

2½ miles NE of Tenby on the B4316

🌱 Stammers Gardens

This picture, postcard fishing village is centred around its harbour, which, during the summer months, is packed with colourful pleasure craft. The harbour was constructed in the 1820s primarily for the export of anthracite, which was mined a short distance away then brought to the quay by tramway. Today,

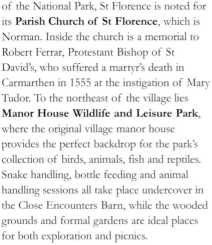

however, the industry has all but ceased and this resort, which has an attractive sandy beach, is probably one of the busiest watersports centres in South Wales. In the heart of the resort is a lovely surprise in the shape of **Stammers Gardens**, eight carefully developed acres with shrubberies, ponds, woodland and a bog garden.

AMROTH
4½ miles NE of Tenby off the A477

🌱 Colby Woodland Garden

Lying at the southeastern-most point of the Pembrokeshire Coast National Park, this quiet village has a lovely beach overlooking Carmarthen Bay. As well as the delightful surroundings, the village is home to the enchanting **Colby Woodland Garden**, an eight-acre area of woodland set round a Nash-style house in a secluded valley that is home to one of the finest collections of

rhododendrons and azaleas in Wales. Carpets of bluebells follow the displays of daffodils in the spring and there is a mass of colour during the summer when the hydrangeas flower, before the garden is taken over by the rich colours of autumn. The garden is part of the National Trust's Colby Estate, which takes its name from John Colby, a 19th-century industrialist.

CALDEY ISLAND
2½ miles S of Tenby off the A4139

🏛 Caldey Abbey   🏛 St Illtyd's Church
🏛 Old Priory   🏛 St David's Parish Church

This peaceful and tranquil island, which along with its sister island of St Margaret's, lies just a short distance off the coast of Tenby, has been the home of monks for some 1,500 years.

As well as **Caldey Abbey**, a modern working monastery that is home to a community of 20 monks of the Reformed Cistercian Order, there are the remains of a 13th-century monastery, which was also founded by the Cistercians. **St Illtyd's Church** (still a consecrated Roman Catholic church), along with the **Old Priory** ruins, can be visited, and a small museum tells the history of this beautiful island. **St David's Parish Church** is Norman, though some of its foundations may date back to the 7th century. There are some fine, modern stained-glass windows within it.

Today's monks live their lives according to the austere Rule of St Benedict, which necessitates them attending seven services a day - the first beginning at 3.15am.

Caldey Island

LOCATOR MAP

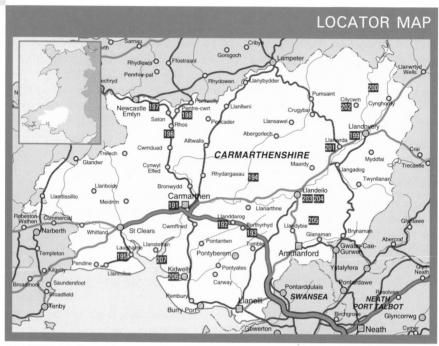

ADVERTISERS AND PLACES OF INTEREST

🏠 historic building 🏛 museum and heritage 🏚 historic site 🐚 scenic attraction 🌱 flora and fauna

8 | Carmarthenshire

Carmarthenshire has a wealth of interesting places and superb countryside to enchant the visitor. There are coastal strongholds at Laugharne and Kidwelly, abbey ruins at Talley and Whitland, and the famous rugby and industrial centre of Llanelli. Covering some 1,000 square miles, the county also has beautiful clean beaches, seaside towns and villages and rural idylls. A place of myths and legends, Carmarthenshire has remained essentially Welsh in most aspects.

The coastline, which is over 50 miles long, includes the award-winning Pembrey Country Park and beach, once the site of a munitions factory, and Pendine, whose long stretch of sand saw many land speed world records established. Of the seaside villages, Laugharne is certainly the most famous, due mainly to the fact that it is the place where Dylan Thomas lived for the last years of his short life. But the village does not rely solely on its literary links, as it also has one of the country's most handsome castles and offers wonderful views over the estuary of the River Taf.

Inland lies Carmarthen, the county town, whose origins date from Roman times. The town is a centre for the agricultural communities of West Wales, and to the east is an area associated with the legends and mysteries of Merlin the magician. Also in this part of Carmarthenshire is one of the country's most recent important projects - the National Botanic Garden of Wales. Dedicated to conservation, horticulture, science and education, and boasting the largest single-span glasshouse in the world, this is one of the country's newest gardens, while close by lies Aberglasney, one of the oldest, first mentioned in 1477. Evidence of the Roman occupation of Carmarthenshire is most striking at the Dolaucothi Goldmines, to the northwest of Llandovery. At Cenarth, visitors can see salmon fishermen on the River Teifi still using the coracle, a tiny round boat whose origins are lost in the mists of time. A fascinating museum tells the story of these distinctive little craft.

National Botanic Garden of Wales, Llanarthne

Carmarthen

🏛 Carmarthen Castle   🏛 Guildhall

🏛 Trinity College   🏛 Parish Church of St Peter

🏚 Caer Mari Unum   🏛 Carmarthen Heritage Centre

🏚 Merlin's Hill   🏚 Picton Monument

🐾 Oriel Myrddin

One of the oldest Roman towns in Wales, Carmarthen (or Caerfyrddin in Welsh) is now the county town of Carmarthenshire and lies at the centre of the West Wales agricultural community. The name means "fort of Myrddyin", and some people have linked this Myrddyin with Merlin the Magician. One particular story associated with the town has, thankfully, so far turned out not to be true. Carmarthen's inhabitants are eternally grateful that, when Merlin's Oak was removed during a road widening scheme, the town remained unharmed, and the prophecy, "When Merlin's Oak shall tumble down, then shall fall Carmarthen town" was not realised. According to another tradition, the magician is said still to live in a cave on **Merlin's Hill** (Bryn Myrddin) just outside Carmarthen where he is kept in perpetual enchantment by Vivien, the lady to whom he taught all his spells.

At the site of **Caer Mari Unum** (built about 75 AD), the most westerly Roman fort in Britain, the remains of the amphitheatre can still be seen, and the Roman town walls were known to have been visible in the 12th century. However, the historic old part of Carmarthen grew up around **Carmarthen Castle**, which was originally built around 1109 by Henry I. Overlooking the River Tywi, little remains of the castle today except the early 15th-century gatehouse. The **Guildhall**, which was built in 1767 to replace the hall of 1583, is

in Nott Square – named after Major General Sir William Nott, victor of the First Afghan War in the 1840s and a native of Carmarthen.

The town's Victorian Old Art College has, since 1991, been the home of **Oriel Myrddin**, a contemporary craft gallery and regional art venue. Focusing on the present and the future, the work of some of the most innovative and interesting craftspeople in Wales is displayed here and, in the retail area, there is a wide range of crafts for purchase. By contrast, housed in a new development on the banks of the River Tywi, is the **Carmarthen Heritage Centre**, which, through displays, multi-media and video presentations, tells the story of the town from the time of the Roman occupation

Merlin's Oak, Carmarthen

RAINBOW

10 Lammas Street, Carmarthen,
Dyfed SA31 3AD
Tel: 01267 230499

Tired of chain stores? Want clothes that look and make you look good and feel special? **Rainbow**, situated in the historic town centre of Carmarthen, has a large selection of quirky designs and quality collections that are affordable and wearable, with just the right amount of fashion detail for the discerning woman of today. At Rainbow as well as clothes and accessories for women, you can also buy home furnishings and accessories.

Welcoming, knowledgeable staff will ensure your shopping experience at Rainbow is an enjoyable one. Owner, Wendy Jones has succeeded in vision of a special personal service shop, where the customer is put first. She enjoys helping you to co-ordinate a look for your lifestyle and with a range of shoes and beautiful costume jewellery to compliment your outfit, you will be sure to look and feel stunning.

---

in 75 AD through to the present day.

Carmarthen is home to **Trinity College**, which, since 2005, has been part of the University of Wales. After Lampeter, it is the second oldest higher education institution in the country. It was originally a teacher training college, but has now widened its curriculum.

The Ivy Bush Royal Hotel in Carmarthen has notable literary connections. A stained-glass window and stone circle commemorate the 1819 eisteddfod, when Iolo Morganwg introduced the Gorsedd (society of bards) to the eisteddfod (see also St David's). The essayist and dramatist Sir Richard Steele stayed at the Ivy Bush in the later years of his life. Steele is best known for his periodical essays and for his collaboration with Joseph Addison. Educated, like Addison, at Charterhouse and Oxford, Steele published his first work in 1701, when he

was 28. It had the far from catchy title of *The Christian Hero: An argument proving that no principles but those of religion are sufficient to make a great man.* Steele had two wealthy wives and several children. Bad health and pressing debts forced him to move to Wales, and he died in Carmarthen in 1729. A brass plaque on the wall of the **Parish Church of St Peter** commemorates him. This church, which dates back to the 12th century, has many interesting features, including an organ thought to have been built in the reign of George III for Windsor Palace, and the impressive tomb of Sir Rhys ap Thomas, who led an army to fight for Henry Tudor at the Battle of Bosworth Field, where Richard III was killed and Henry crowned as King Henry VII on the battlefield.

The **Picton Monument** at the west end of the town commemorates Sir Thomas Picton

---

🎦 stories and anecdotes 🐦 famous people ✒ art and craft ✍ entertainment and sport 🚶 walks

(1758–1815), who was killed at the Battle of Waterloo. He had the rank of Lieutenant General, and was the Member of Parliament for Pembroke. His body lies in St George's Church, Hanover Square, London.

Carmarthen has a thriving food market, where one of the local specialities on sale is Carmarthen ham, which is air-dried, sliced and eaten raw, like the Spanish Serrano ham.

Gwili Steam Railway, Bronwydd

Around Carmarthen

BRONWYDD
2 miles N of Carmarthen on the A484

🏛 Gwili Steam Railway

From Bronwydd Arms Station (just off the A484 Carmarthen to Cardigan road) the **Gwili Steam Railway** offers visitors the opportunity to step back in time and take a short steam train journey through the Gwili Valley on part of the old Great Western Railway line connecting Carmarthen to Aberystwyth. This line originally opened in 1860 and, although it finally closed in 1973, it has been run by volunteers since the late 1970s. Trains run on timetabled days between April and October and in December. The station has a souvenir shop and sells hot and cold refreshments. Visitors can enjoy the train journey through a beautiful wooded valley, and the other end of the line, Llwyfan Cerrig, is the perfect place for a picnic by the river. Unusually, the village takes its name from an

inn that once stood here, the Bronwydd Arms. A plaque now marks the spot.

DREFACH
12 miles N of Carmarthen off the A484

🏛 National Woollen Museum

🏛 Woollen Mill Trail

Many of the water-driven mills of this area still continue to produce flour and distinctive woollen goods, and this important part of the region's industrial heritage is explored in the **National Woollen Museum**. One of the most traditional and rural industries, the processes involved in the spinning, weaving and dyeing of wool are explained here, and there are also demonstrations of cloth-making and dyeing carried out on 19th-century machinery. As well as trying their hand at spinning, visitors can stroll around the sites of the old woollen mills in the village, which still produce flannel cloth and tweeds, and follow all or part of the **Woollen Mill Trail** through the scenic Teifi Valley. There are 24 miles of waymarked trails from the museum, the longer ones taking in the seven so-called flannel villages.

PONTARSAIS

5 miles N of Carmarthen on the A485

🖎 Gwili Pottery

The village is best known as the home of **Gwili Pottery**. To the west of the village lies Llanpumpsaint, whose name literally means "the church, or enclosure, of the five saints". The five saints are Ceitho, Celynen, Gwyn, Gwyno and Grynnaro, who all lived in the 6th century, and were all brothers from the semi-royal Cunedda family. However, the present parish church is dedicated to just one saint – St Celynyn.

ABERGWILI

1½ miles E of Carmarthen off the A40

🏛 Carmarthenshire County Museum

🏛 Merlin's Hill Centre

Carmarthenshire County Museum occupies a lovely old house that was a palace of the bishop of St David's up until 1974, and visitors can still see the bishop's peaceful private chapel. Concentrating on

Carmarthenshire's past, the museum's displays range from Roman gold through to Welsh furniture, and there is also a reconstruction of a school room. The palace's grounds, too, are open to the public, and the delightful parkland is ideal for a stroll and a picnic.

Found on land that has been farmed for over 2,000 years, the **Merlin's Hill Centre** at Alltyfyrddin Farm explains the history and legends of the surrounding area and its connections with Merlin the Magician. As well as listening out for the wizard's wailings – he is supposed to be imprisoned under an Iron Age hill fort on the farm – visitors can also explore this dairy farm and learn about farming, past and present.

LLANARTHNE

7½ miles E of Carmarthen on the B4300

🏛 Paxton's Tower   🏛 Parish Church of St David

🏛 Caercastell Cross

🌱 National Botanic Garden of Wales

To the southwest of the village lies **Paxton's Tower**, designed by SP Cockerell and built in the early 19th century on the Middleton estate for William Paxton, who dedicated it to Lord Nelson. Constructed so that it could be seen from the main house, it affords panoramic views from the tower over the estate and the Tywi valley. The **Parish Church of St David** dates mainly from the 13th century, though the base of the tower may be earlier. In the porch can be seen the **Caercastell Cross**, which dates from the 10th or 11th

Paxton's Tower, Llanarthne

🖪 stories and anecdotes 🐦 famous people 🖎 art and craft 🖋 entertainment and sport 🚶 walks

FFERM COEDHIRION B&B

Llanddarog, Carmarthenshire SA32 8BQ
Tel: 01267 275666
e-mail: welshfarmhouse@hotmail.co.uk
website: www.welshfarm.co.uk

Selwyn, Daphne and Tomos Evans offer a choice of award winning accommodation at **Ffern Coedhirion**, their farm at Llanddarog, a village on the B4310, off the main A48 a short drive east of Carmarthen. For Bed & Breakfast guests they have well-appointed rooms with en suite facilities, television and hot beverage tray with a real Welsh breakfast included in the tariff.

For self-catering guests there's a choice of single, double or twin-bedded rooms in a number of stone cottages with living/dining rooms, kitchens, bath/shower rooms and access to gardens and patios.

The third option is a small caravan park that's open in spring and summer. It is available for tourers, camper vans and tents with a small duck-pond and surrounding woodland. Hook-ups and water are available on site as well as a nearby shower block, with hot showers, toilets and washing facilities. In the surrounding fields visitors can observe Welsh Black cattle, Texel and

THE EQUINE SHOP

Cwrt-y-Draeneg, Porthyrhyd, Carmarthen,
Carmarthenshire SA32 8PG
Tel: 01267 275586
website: www.theequineshop.co.uk

The owners of the Equine Shop are proud to be the largest specialist equestrian retailer in West Wales. Carrying a good selection of new and used saddles, offering a bespoke English leather saddle service including fitting and reflocking. Jane Johnson and Carol Jones have a straightforward aim to provide the best selection of quality and competitively priced horse and rider equipment, welcoming their customers to a friendly, relaxed environment, listening to their customers needs, and providing a customer service rarely seen today.

At The Equine Shop you will find a comprehensive selection of horse and rider equipment including: clothing, safety wear, a large selection of rugs, boots, hats, body protectors, stable wear, outdoor clothing, English leather bridles, saddles and plenty of gift ideas. Favourite brands including: Caldene, Totti, Equimins, Global Herbs, Woof Wear, John Whitaker, Thorowgood, E Jeffries, Loveson, Bucas, Belstane, Legacy, Toggi and Champion are always in stock. Country clothing including shooting jackets & tweeds are soon to be introduced.The Equine Shop also offers a full equine laundry, reproofing and repair service for rugs. Large car park, with plenty of turning space for trailers/horseboxes.

Open: Monday to Saturday 10am - 5pm. The Equine Shop is situated approximately 6 miles east of Carmarthen, just off the A48, exit and follow signs for National Botanic Garden.

National Botanic Garden of Wales, Llanarthne

Middle Ages. Tribute is also paid to the Welsh botanist Alfred Russel Wallace, whose theories of natural selection paralleled those of Charles Darwin. However, this is also very much a garden of the future and, in the Energy Zone, there is a biomass furnace using salvaged or coppiced wood for heating the site, and the Living Machine sewage treatment system.

DRYSLWYN
8½ miles E of Carmarthe on the B4300

🏰 Dryslwyn Castle

By the side of the River Tywi lie the remains of **Dryslwyn Castle**, built on the hill by one of Lord Rhys' descendants in the mid 13th century. An ideal location for a stronghold, the castle throughout its life suffered several savage attacks that contributed to its present ruined condition.

PANTGLAS HOME FARM

Llanfynydd Road, Llanfynydd, Carmarthen SA32 7BZ
Tel/Fax: 01558 668214
e-mail: janetwatkins@pantglasfarm.fsbusiness.co.uk
website: www.pantglasfarmholidays.co.uk

Set in unspoilt Carmarthenshire countryside, close to the stunning beauty of the Black Mountains, **Pantglas Home Farm** offers the choice of a 5-star self-catering holiday or you can stay on a bed & breakfast basis. The spacious ivy clad holiday cottage, built in traditional Welsh stone, adjoins the farmhouse of a working dairy and sheep farm, and provides a lovely location in which to relax and retreat.

The cottage is set in ½ an acre of a country cottage garden with ample parking for three cars, and a patio area to sit and relax or enjoy a barbecue. Inside, the spacious lounge has an original oak beam, log burner, TV, DVD and freeview tuner. An oak-beamed archway separates the lounge from the dining room with its oak dining table, six chairs and a Welsh dresser. The kitchen is fully equipped with microwave, dishwasher, fridge and electric cooker. The cottage sleeps 5 people, plus a child, in two large bedrooms - 1 double and 1 family room with 3 single beds.

For those of you who like a hands-on holiday, feel free to join in with the feeding of the calves, experience the milking of the dairy herd and help collect the eggs from around the farmyard!

🎭 stories and anecdotes 🐦 famous people 🎨 art and craft 🎵 entertainment and sport 🚶 walks

LLANGATHEN

11 miles E of Carmarthen off the A40

🏛 Parish Church of St Cathen

🌿 Aberglasney

The village is home to **Aberglasney**, one of the oldest and most interesting gardens in the country. The first recorded description of Aberglasney House and Gardens was made by the bard Lewis Glyn Cothi in 1477 when he wrote of "a white painted court, built of dressed stone, surrounded by nine gardens of orchards, vineyards and large oak trees". At a later date, at the beginning of the 17th century, the estate was sold to the Bishop of St David's, and it was Bishop Anthony Rudd who improved both the house and gardens in a manner befitting a bishop's palace. At the heart of the nine acres is a unique and fully restored Elizabethan/Jacobean cloister garden and a parapet walk, the only surviving example in the UK.

The **Parish Church of St Cathen** is medieval, worth visiting to see the tomb of Bishop Anthony Rudd, who became Bishop of St David's in 1594 and died in 1615. It is in the south aisle, and dates to the early 17th century.

GOLDEN GROVE

11 miles E of Carmarthen off the B4300

🌿 Gelli Aur Country Park

To the east of the village lies **Gelli Aur Country Park** (Gelli Aur means 'golden grove') on part of the estate of the ancestral home of the Vaughan family. Containing remnants of a 17th-century deer park (where the deer still roam), the landscaped parkland was laid out in the 18th century, and the country park includes a Victorian arboretum planted by Lord Cawdor. Other attractions

include nature trails, a new adventure playground and a cafeteria. The original mansion, now part of an agricultural college, was the work of the architect Joseph Wyatville.

LLANSTEFFAN

7 miles SW of Carmarthen on the B4312

🏛 Llansteffan Castle   🏛 St Anthony's Well

🏛 Parish Church of St Ystyffan

This village, near the mouth of the River Tywi, is dominated by the ruins of **Llansteffan Castle** on a headland above the estuary. The successor to an earlier defensive earthwork, the castle dates from the 12th century, and the main remaining feature is the impressive gateway dating from 1280. To the southwest of the castle lies **St Anthony's Well**, the waters of which were thought to have medicinal properties. The **Parish Church of St Ystyffan** dates from the 13th century and later. In 1170 AD the church was given to the Knights Hospitaller by the local lord of the manor, Geoffrey de Marmoin.

Llansteffan, along with Ferryside, its neighbour across the river mouth, is a paradise for walkers as well as sailors, and the waymarked walks around the estuary take in some truly breathtaking coastal scenery. The promontory of Wharley Point, in particular, affords stunning views across the Taf and Tywi estuaries to Carmarthen Bay.

LAUGHARNE

9 miles SW of Carmarthen on the A4066

🏛 Laugharne Castle   🏛 The Boathouse

🏛 Parish Church of St Martin

This pretty rural town of Georgian houses on the estuary of the River Taf is home to one of

THE STABLE DOOR WINE & TAPAS BAR

Market Lane, Laugharne,
Carmarthenshire SA33 4SB
Tel: 01994 427777

The Stable Door Wine & Tapas Bar enjoys a wonderfully atmospheric location behind the clock tower and up a pretty cobbled lane off the main street of the town where Dylan Thomas spent most of the last years of his life. It is owned and run by Wendy joy, who trained at Pru Leith's School of Food & Wine and for a while ran a restaurant and catering company in London. She thus brings a wealth of experience to the Stable Door, which is recommended in the 2009 *Good Food Guide* and has earned a bronze *Eating Out in Wales* award. The recent refurbishment of the restaurant includes a gallery which houses paintings and photographs, both old and new, of Laugharne. Many of the works are by local artists.

The sturdy stone walls of the original stables, the intimate lighting and the many interesting decorative touches make a splendid backdrop to an evening here. When the weather is fine the garden, with a conservatory overlooking both the garden and Laugharne Castle, is a quiet, pleasant alternative spot for a drink and snack or meal. The menu makes excellent use of fresh local produce in a wide variety of tapas-style dishes, with influences from Wales and the Orient as well as Spain. Typical choices might include nachos, halloumi kebabs, sticky chicken wings, meatballs, chorizo, white anchovies, sardines and Thai salmon kebabs, and there's a tempting selection of desserts and ice creams to round things off. An excellent choice of wines, with many New World bottles, can be enjoyed on their own or with a meal, and there's an extensive list of coffees and teas.

The Stable Door Wine & Tapas Bar is open from 6.30pm Thursday, Friday and Saturday; from 12.30pm on Sundaysfor a traditional lunch with roasts and also lunchtimes in high season, Xmas Day and Bank Holidays.

Dylan Thomas' Boathouse, Laugharne

the country's most handsome castles. Originally an earth and timber fortress, **Laugharne Castle** was built in stone around the 13th century and, although much of the fortification still remains, it is the transformations undertaken by Sir John Perrot in the 16th century that make this a particularly special site. Granted Laugharne by Queen Elizabeth I, Perrot, an illegitimate son of Henry VIII, turned the castle into a comfortable mansion that, after seeing action in the Civil War, declined into the ruins seen today.

However, romantic though the castle ruins are, this is not all Laugharne Castle has to offer, as the garden has been splendidly restored. Both the castle ruins and the superb surroundings have provided inspiration for artists over the centuries and, in particular, they are the subject of a dramatic watercolour by JMW Turner.

stories and anecdotes famous people art and craft entertainment and sport walks

Laugharne

Distance: *3.5 miles (5.6 kilometres)*
Typical time: *240 mins*
Height gain: *180 metres*
Map: *Explorer 177*
Walk: *www.walkingworld.com ID:2718*
Contributor: *Pat Roberts*

ACCESS INFORMATION:

There is a large free car park next to the castle.
There is only a small sign for it but there is plenty
of space. Toilets are up the road on the right as you
leave the car park, opposite the doctor's surgery.

DESCRIPTION:

Laugharne was the home of the poet Dylan
Thomas and this walk visits many of the places
made famous by him. There is plenty of
information in the village itself and there are
information boards at the places of note.

FEATURES:

Sea, Pub, Toilets, Church, Castle, Wildlife, Birds,
Flowers, Great Views, Butterflies, Cafe, Woodland

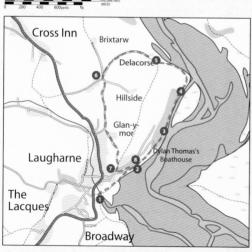

WALK DIRECTIONS:

1 | From the car park walk over the footbridge and
follow the path under the castle.

2 | Take this track l ft, signed to the Boathouse, and
over rocks at first before climbing steps to a tarmac
track. Right and soon come to the garage used by
Dylan as his writing Shed. After about 45 metres
see the Boathouse down on the right, there are
steps down to it should you wish to visit it.
Continue, cross over a road and on into the trees.

3 | There is a track own to the right but we keep to
the upper main track to reach a stile.

4 | Over the stile an follow the obvious track fairly
near the right hedge. Through some trees into the
next field and on to another stile behind a large tree
trunk.

5 | Over the double s ile and head for the
farmhouse. Over another stile and round to the left
of the farmhouse to continue up the drive. It is
quite a long drive with a gate (usually open) at the
top, here it is joined from the right by another
driveway to go forward for 20 metres to a road.

6 | At the road go left. The road soon swings
right and continues to lose height. At the end of
a wall look for a metal Kissing gate into the
churchyard. The old graves are particularly
interesting. Go to the front of the church
and up steps over a footbridge into the
new part. Left and up to reach another
kissing gate halfway across the top hedge.
Dylan Thomas' Grave is in the centre of
the new grave yard and is a large white
cross. Through the gate and turn right to
follow this old bridleway to the road.

7 | Reach the road at the entrance to a
caravan park. Cross the road and follow a
footway signed "The Boat House" until
reaching a white building with double black
doors.

8 | Right to walk bac down the steps and
path we ascended on the outward route.
Walk on round below the castle to the car
park.

Writers, too, have found this an inspiring place and both Dylan Thomas, who wrote in a gazebo in the grounds, and Richard Hughes, author of *A High Wind in Jamaica*, are associated with Laugharne Castle. This coastal town is today a shrine to its most famous resident, Dylan Thomas, who spent the last four years of his life living at **The Boathouse** set in a cliff overlooking the Taf estuary. Discovering this small out-of-the-way place in the 1940s, Thomas famously "got off the bus and forgot to get on again", and it was while in Laugharne that he wrote some of his best works, including *Under Milk Wood*, a day in the life of his imaginary village of Llareggub (read the name backwards to find why it has this odd name). Thomas, notoriously prone to destructive drinking sprees, died in The White Horse Bar in New York in 1953, at only 39 years of age. The Boathouse is now a heritage centre dedicated to the writer and, as well as the fascinating memorabilia on display here, there is also an interpretation centre, bookshop and tea room.

The **Parish Church of St Martin**, in the churchyard of which Thomas is buried, contains a replica of the plaque to his memory that can be seen in Poets' Corner, Westminster Abbey. The church itself dates mainly to the 13th century, and has a magnificent reredos and a carving of St Martin of Tours.

PENDINE
13½ miles SW of Carmarthen on the A4066

Museum of Speed

The vast, seven-mile-long expanse of sand which makes Pendine a popular place with families, was used in the 1920s by Sir Malcolm Campbell and others for attempting land speed records. In 1924, Sir Malcolm broke the World Motor Flying Kilometre Record here by averaging 146 miles per hour. He later raised that to 174mph, and went on to achieve speeds in excess of 300mph on the salt flats at Bonneville, Utah. In 1927, while attempting to beat Sir Malcolm's record, Welshman JG Parry Thomas was decapitated in an accident on the beach, and his car, Babs, lay buried in the sand before being unearthed in 1969 and restored by Owen Wyn Owen, a lecturer from Bangor. Babs can now be seen in all its gleaming glory at the **Museum of Speed**, which explores the history of this stretch of sand where so many records were broken. However, not all the speed attempts involved land vehicles, as it was from these sands in 1933 that the intrepid aviatrix Amy Johnson and her husband Jim Mollinson set off on a de Havilland Dragon Rapide for a non-stop flight across the Atlantic. In 2004, all vehicles were banned from the beach because of possible bombs buried on it, as at one time it was owned by the MOD.

The **Parish Church of St Margaret**, with its saddleback tower, has a cast iron gravestone in its churchyard. The building largely dates from the 14th century, though it was restored in Victorian times. No one knows which St Margaret the church is dedicated to, so one of the windows features three of them - St Margaret of Antioch, St Margaret of Scotland and the shadowy local saint St Margaret Marloes. As the lord of the manor at the time of the dedication, Sir Guy de Bryan, claimed descent from St Margaret of Scotland, she is the likeliest candidate.

ST CLEARS
8½ miles SW of Carmarthen on the A40

Parish Church of St Mary Magdalene

This small market town was the site of the defeat of Owain Glyndwr by Pembrokeshire's army in 1406. Later, in the 1840s, St Clears was involved in more trouble when it featured in the Rebecca Riots (see also Rhayader) during which the rioters destroyed toll gates. All that remains of St Clears Castle is its motte. It was founded in the 11th century, but we know little about its early history.

The large **Parish Church of St Mary Magdalene** had its origins in a Clunaic priory established here in the 12th century. It was a daughter house of St Martin des Champs in Paris, but supported only two or three monks at a time. As an 'alien' (ie foreign) priory, it was always viewed with suspicion, especially when England was at war with France. So much so that it was finally dissolved in 1414.

Whitland Abbey

WHITLAND

13 miles W of Carmarthen on the B4328

🏛 Whitland Abbey

🏛 Hywel Dda Centre

This small market town and centre of the dairy industry is historically important as the meeting place of the assembly convened by Hywel Dda in the 10th century. Born towards the end of the 9th century, Dda made a pilgrimage to Rome in 928 AD and, some 14 years later, he was ruler of most of Wales. Summoning representatives from each part of Wales to Whitland, Dda laid down a legal system that became known for its wisdom and justice, and which remained in force in Wales up until the Act of Union with England in 1536. This system and its instigator are remembered at the Prince of Wales Design award-winning building, the **Hywel Dda**

Centre. Here, too, is a memorial in the form of six gardens representing the six separate divisions of the law: Society and Status; Crime; and Tort; Women, Contract; the King; and Property.

Just north of the town lie the remains of the once great **Whitland Abbey**, which was founded in 1140 by Bernard, the first Norman Bishop of St David's. It moved to its present position in 1151 and, at one time, was the premier Cistercian house in Wales.

LLANBOIDY

12 miles NW of Carmarthen off the A40

🏛 Welsh Chocolate Farm   🏛 Llanboidy Cheeses

In old stone farm buildings to the north of the village is a chocoholic's dream – the **Welsh Chocolate Farm**, where chocolates of all shapes, sizes and flavours are made. As well as watching chocolate-making demonstrations and touring the factory to see just how the chocolate is produced, visitors can buy gifts and treats for family and friends (and selves) at the farm shop, which has the largest selection of chocolates in Wales. And, as this is rich dairy country, there are also farmhouse cheeses and other dairy delights for sale along

---

🏛 historic building 🏛 museum and heritage 🏛 historic site 🕭 scenic attraction 🌱 flora and fauna

TIPI HOLIDAYS

Larkhill, Cwmduad, Carmarthenshire SA33 6AT
Tel: 01559 371581
e-mail: contact@larkhilltipis.co.uk
website: www.larkhilltipis.co.uk

In quiet countryside off the A484 Carmarthen-New Castle Emlyn road, **Tipi Holidays** provide a relaxed alternative holiday in Native Indian-style tents (tipis, tepees) far from the hustle and bustle of city life. The tipis are set in 4 acres of private woodland with pathways, a stone circle and a wild flower meadow. The tents are very snug and comfortable, with futons, sheepskin rugs and log fires. Shared facilities include toilets and a washing area with showers. It's a unique pleasure to watch the stars by firelight in the evening and to

with a wide range of hand-roasted coffee beans prepared daily. Don't even try to resist the homemade fudge! Another gastronomic treat is in store at **Llanboidy Cheeses**, made since 1985 on Cilowen Uchaf farm by Sue Jones from local organic milk. She took the gold medal for cheeses in 2001.

CENARTH

16 miles NW of Carmarthen on the A484

- 🏛 Salmon Leap Museum 🏛 Cenarth Mill
- 🏛 Old Smithy 🏛 National Coracle Centre
- ⌣ Salmon Leap Waterfalls

This ancient village, first mentioned by Giraldus Cambrenses (see also St David's and

Manorbier) in the late 12th century when he passed through on his journey with Archbishop Baldwin to drum up support for the Crusades, has for centuries been a centre for coracle fishermen. Situated on the banks of the River Teifi, famous for its **Salmon Leap Waterfalls**, and the accompanying **Salmon Leap Museum**, the conservation village is home to **Cenarth Mill**. Dating from the 18th century, the watermill, which has two pairs of stones (one for barley, the other for oats) is powered by the river close to the salmon leap. Now restored and producing wholemeal flour, the mill complex also houses the **National Coracle Centre**, where visitors can see a unique collection of these ancient boats from around the world. Dating back to the Ice Age, these little round boats, once covered in skins, are still used for salmon fishing, and at the Centre visitors can see demonstrations of coracles at work. The **Old Smithy** can be found within an 18th-century blacksmith's workshop that still has some of the old tools used by a blacksmith. There is also a craft shop.

River Teifi, Cenarth

🎞 stories and anecdotes 🐦 famous people 🎨 art and craft 🎭 entertainment and sport 🚶 walks

CRYNGAE COTTAGES

Cryngae, nr Drefach Felindre,
Carmarthenshire SA44 5YW
Tel: 01559 370234
e-mail: cryngae@btinternet.com
website: www.cryngaecottages.co.uk

Peace and tranquillity are assured at **Cryngae Cottages**, a true rural retreat set in 74 acres in the beautiful Teifi Valley. The owners offer a very high standard of comfort in three luxurious cottages skilfully converted from stone barns to retain some of the best original features while adding contemporary twists. Cinnamon, set in a pretty courtyard garden, sleeps four guests, while its neighbour Tamarind and Poppy (with a little garden and decking) each sleep two, and all are provided with everything needed for a relaxed, go-as-you-please holiday, including a fully fitted kitchen and TV with DVD/CD player.

The countryside views are glorious, the area is a haven for wildlife, and walkers have instant access to many miles of local footpaths. The village shop, pub and Post Office are a short walk away, and Cryngae has a mile of its own fishing on the Nant Bargoed river. Nearby attractions include the National Wool Museum at Drefach, the Teifi Valley Heritage Railway and Old Gilgwyn Gardens, and the coast is an easy 20-minute drive away.

NEWCASTLE EMLYN

14 miles NW of Carmarthen on the A484

🏛 Newcastle Emlyn Castle

🌿 Old Cilgwyn Gardens

In Newcastle Emlyn, the first printing press in Wales was set up by Isaac Carter in 1718. The town grew up around **Newcastle Emlyn Castle**, which was built in 1240 by Maredudd ap Rhys beside the River Teifi. Like that of many other castles in Wales, Newcastle Emlyn's turbulent history is in some ways confirmed by the present condition of this now ruined fortress, as it changed hands several times until it was destroyed during the Glyndwr rebellion in the early 1400s. Having fallen into disrepair, the castle was granted to Sir Rhys ap Thomas by Henry VII in the late 15th century, and became a country residence

before being all but demolished during the Civil War for harbouring Royalist sympathisers. On the B4571, a mile north of Newcastle Emlyn, lie **Old Cilgwyn Gardens**. This is a 14-acre mixed garden set in 900 acres of parkland that includes a 53-acre Site of Special Scientific Interest. It contains the site of the last duel fought in Wales.

Llandovery

🏛 Llandovery Castle

🏛 Parish Church of St Mary on the Hill

🏛 Dolauhirion Bridge   🏚 Twm Sion Catl's Cave

🏛 Llandovery Heritage Centre

🏥 Physicians of Myddfai   🐦 Rhys Pritchard

As it is situated at the confluence of the Rivers Bran, Gwennol and Tywi, Llandovery's

---

🏛 historic building 🏛 museum and heritage 🏚 historic site 🌿 scenic attraction 🐦 flora and fauna

MAKEPEACE CABINETMAKING

Derw Mill, Pentre-cwrt, Llandysil,
Carmarthenshire SA44 5DB
Tel: 01559 362322 Fax: 01559 363627
e-mail: enquiry@makepeace.furniture.com
website: www.makepeacefurniture.com

'Individual Kitchens for True Individuals'

Makepeace Cabinetmaking are specialists in high-quality, bespoke fitted and free-standing kitchen and other furniture. Over more than 20 years the business has increased its reputation and seen its clientele grow throughout the United Kingdom and far beyond. Environmental awareness is a watchword, and the beautiful hardwoods used by Makepeace are sourced from sustainable forests around the world, with FSC certified hardwood only used. The oils for the wax finishes contain no polluting chemicals, thus ensuring the natural look, the hardwearing qualities and the beautiful appearance that owners can be really proud of. From initial consultation to final installation, clients can look forward to friendly, personal service from designers and craftsmen who offer a combination of quality, style and unbeatable value for money.

Kitchens are the first speciality, and the firm offers many style options: contemporary and traditional using Oak, Maple. Walnut and Ash in particular.

The Makepeace effect does not stop at kitchens, as they also design and make

furniture of the very highest quality for every room in the house, including study, bedroom, bathroom and freestanding furniture, for example Welsh dressers, settles and tables.

Makepeace Cabinetmaking is located in a late-19th century wool mill set in attractive grounds with woods and a stream. The premises are divided into a number of areas for each stage of production, from the timber store to the machinery area, the assembly room, the spray shop and the showroom. Pentre-cwrt lies by the A484 north of Carmarthen and east of Newcastle Emlyn. Opening hours are 9am to 5.30pm Monday to Friday, otherwise by appointment.The team's superior craftsmanship and quality can also be seen at the Royal Welsh Show at the Glamorgan Hall, Built Wells – the 2009 date is 20 to 23 July.

Our aim is to provide you with fine furniture for life

🎭 stories and anecdotes 🐦 famous people 🎨 art and craft 🎟 entertainment and sport 🚶 walks

Welsh name, Llanymddyfri (meaning the church amid the waters), seems particularly apt. Evidence suggests that the area around Llandovery has been important since Roman times. **Rhys Pritchard**, known as a preacher and the author of the collection of verses *The Welshman's Candle*, lived here in the 17th century, as did the renowned Methodist poet and hymn writer William Williams in the 18th century (see also Llanwrtyd Wells).

Llandovery Castle, the remains of which overlook the cattle market, was the most easterly Norman castle within Carmarthenshire, constructed in 1116 by Richard Fitzpons, only to be captured and destroyed some 42 years later. Although it was repaired in the late 12th century by Henry II, the castle was left to decay after 1403 and only the tumbledown remains are visible today. Within the ruins is a monument to Llewelyn

ap Gruffydd Fychan of Ceao who, in 1401, was executed for refusing to betray Owyn Glyndwr.

Visiting in the 19th century, the author George Borrow called Landover "the pleasantest little town in which I have halted". The history of this town, which delighted many people before and since George Borrow, is told at the **Llandovery Heritage Centre** where the legends surrounding the hero Twm Sion Cati - the Welsh Robin Hood - and the local **Physicians of Myddfai** are also explored. The legend concerning the physicians is that a lady appeared one day from a lake in the Black Mountain. A local farmer's son fell in love with her and she agreed to marry him on condition that he did not hit her three times without cause. Over the years he had given her three light taps for what he thought was poor behaviour and sure enough she returned to the

---

BRAMBLES

38 High Street, Llandovery,
Carmarthenshire SA20 0DD
Tel: 01550 720534

There can be few more delightful places to browse and buy than **Brambles**, which stands on the High Street in Llandovery. Mary Dunkley, who previously ran an antiques business in Heathfield, Sussex, came here in 2006, since when she has been filling her shop with an amazing variety of antiques, collectables, curios, giftware and things that put the finishing touches to a home.

Every inch of space is given over to a fascinating selection of items large and small: jewellery, selected pieces of furniture, china and glass, mugs and jugs, lamps, rugs, cushions, pillows, books on all kinds of eclectic subjects, dolls and dolls houses, baskets in all shapes and sizes......Mary is constantly on the lookout for interesting items, so every visit is certain to reveal new delights.

Usual shop hours are 11 to 4 Monday to Saturday, but it's best to phone before setting out on a visit.

🏛 historic building 🏛 museum and heritage 🏛 historic site 🍃 scenic attraction 🌱 flora and fauna

lake. But before disappearing she passed on her herbal healing secrets to her three sons, who became the first of the famous Physicians of Myddfai, a line of healers who practised from the 12th to the 18th centuries. A recent venture among a group of farmers in Myddfai (a short drive south of Llandovery) was bringing together this age-old legend and the growing modern interest in the properties of herbs. The **Parish Church of St Mary on the Hill** was built within the ramparts of a Roman fort that once stood in the town, and some Roman tiles can be seen in the walls of the church. Also of note are the barrel-vaulted chancel and tie-beam roof.

The attractive **Dolauhirion Bridge** spanning the River Tywi was built in 1173 by William Edwards. North of Llandovery, near

Rhandir-mwyn, is all that remains of **Twm Sion Cati's Cave**, the hideout of the 16th century Robin Hood of Wales. A poet whose youthful escapades earned him the title, Twn Sion later curtailed his activities and settled down after marrying the heiress of Ystradffin and even became a magistrate. He died in 1620.

Around Llandovery

CILYCWM
3½ miles N of Llandovery off the A483

🏛 Capel Bwlchyrhiw

🏛 Parish Church of St Michael

The village's **Capel Bwlchyrhiw** is said to have been the first meeting place of

---

THE ROYAL OAK INN

Rhandirmwyn, nr Llandovery, Carmarthenshire SA20 0NY
Tel: 01550 760201
e-mail: iwanttostay@theroyaloakinn.co.uk
website: www.theroyaloakinn.co.uk

Enjoying stunning views over the beautiful Towy Valley, The Royal Oak Inn was built in 1850 as a Hunting Lodge and it still retains many of the original features. Full of charm and character, it has a warm and welcoming atmosphere all year round. The bar features a quarry-tiled floor and large stone open fire. Owners, Christopher & Rachel, take great pride in the selection and quality of the real ales and cask ciders. The Royal Oak has featured in the Good Beer Guide for the past 22 years. During the summer months, you'll find up to 6 different brews on tap, as well as and an extensive range of whiskeys.

A wide selection of locally sourced meals are available from the dining menu with the house steaks being a speciality. The dining room can seat up to 40 guests and the huge wood burner set in another stone fireplace completes the homely atmosphere. The bar menu also offers great value food and children's meals. All meals are served every day from noon until 2pm, and from 6.30pm to 9.30pm (7pm to 9.30pm on Sunday).

The cosy accommodation comprises of 1 en suite family room, 1 en suite double and 1 en suite twin all with stunning views over the Towy Valley. There are also 2 singles with a shared bathroom and Rachel cooks a full breakfast from locally sourced food every morning to overnight guests.

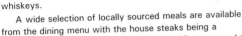

📖 stories and anecdotes 🐦 famous people 🎨 art and craft 🎭 entertainment and sport 🥾 walks

MOUNT PLEASANT FARM

Llanwrda, Carmarthenshire SA19 8AN
Tel/Fax: 01550 777537
e-mail: rivarevivaluk@aol.com

When Sue and Nick Thompson bought **Mount Pleasant Farm** some twenty years ago it was in desperate need of some tender loving care. Indeed, it needed total renovation and some rebuilding, a huge task which took some 18 months of hard work before they finally moved in. Sue is an interior decorator by profession and it is her expertise that has turned the 250-year-old stone-built farmhouse into a charming country house. Outside, sheep graze in the surrounding fields and there are exhilarating views of the Black Mountain. Inside, every room (including the spacious sitting room) and each guest bedroom has been furnished and decorated with imagination and flair - the whole place is a delight. The 3 beautifully appointed guest bedrooms include two with a 6ft 3in bed, en suite facilities and stunning views. At Mount Pleasant Farm food is very important and Sue is a great cook, using only the best of local products.

A full English breakfast is included in the tariff and evening meals can be arranged if notified at the time of booking.

🏚 historic building 🏛 museum and heritage 🏚 historic site 🏞 scenic attraction 🌱 flora and fauna

NEUADD FAWR ARMS

Cilycwm, Llandovery, Carmarthenshire SA20 0ST
Tel: 01550 721644   website: www.neuadd-cilycwm.co.uk

Two properties in the same ownership face each other in the village of m, a small farming community four miles north of Llandovery. The **Neuadd Fawr Arms** is a warm, friendly inn at the social heart of the village. It's a great place for a pint, with regularly changing beers from S A Brains (the Rev James is a great favourite) and local micro-breweries.

Owners Eddie and Bunty Morgan and their staff have built a strong following with their bar and restaurant food, which highlights fresh local produce in dishes that cater for both traditional and more cosmopolitan tastes. And for visitors touring this lovely quiet part of the world the inn has two family-size en suite bedrooms. Alternative accommodation is provided across the road, where a three-bedroom bungalow offers excellent self-catering facilities, along with stabling for up to three horses and a post and rail paddock.

This is great riding country, with numerous bridle paths all around and the slopes of Mynydd Mallaen nearby, and it's equally appealing to walkers and anyone who enjoys fresh country air and the great outdoors.

Methodists in Wales. The **Parish Church of St Michael** dates from the early 14th century, and the nave has delightful wall paintings.

LLANGADOG

5 miles SW of Llandovery on the A4069

🏰 Llangadog Castle   🏛 Carn Coch

🎭 Bethlehem

This small town in the Vale of Towy was once home to **Llangadog Castle**, although all that remains today is a mound, as it was destroyed by its owners in 1277 rather than let it fall into the hands of the English. A few miles to the southwest lies **Carn Coch**, the largest hill fort in Wales, whose earthworks and stone ramparts cover some 15 acres. Also southwest of the town is the village is **Bethlehem**. Thousands of people from all over the world send cards to the Post Office here at Christmas time to be

franked and sent on elsewhere, a practise that is known locally as 'franking sense'.

TRAPP

12 miles SW of Llandovery off the A483

🏰 Carreg Cennen Castle

🎨 Trapp Arts and Crafts Centre

Situated on the top of a precipitous limestone crag on the Black Mountain, and with a vertical drop to the River Cennen below, **Carreg Cennen Castle**, to the east of Trapp, enjoys one of the most spectacular locations of any Welsh castle. Although the present castle dates from the late 13th or early 14th century, there was undoubtedly a fortress here before that; some attribute a castle here to Urien, a knight of Arthur's Round Table. Despite its origins being shrouded in obscurity, the castle is known to have been

🎭 stories and anecdotes 🐿 famous people 🎨 art and craft 🎿 entertainment and sport 🚶 walks

hotly fought over. Carreg Cennen fell to Owain Glyndwr's Welsh insurgents and, during the War of the Roses, it became a base for bandit Lancastrians. Taken on behalf of the Yorkists in 1462, the fortress was dismantled on the orders of Edward IV, leaving the romantic ruins seen today. A visit is well worth the effort to enjoy the impressive views and to appreciate what a daunting task attacking the castle must have been. There is only one way up – a steep, grassy hill protected by a complicated system of defences.

One local legend tells of a narrow underground tunnel that leads from the castle to a wishing well where visitors used to throw corks into the water to make their dreams come true. The well's waters were also thought to have special powers, particularly in curing eye and ear complaints. Trapp itself has a connection with water as the village is the source of Brecon Carreg mineral water. In the converted barns of Llwyndewi Farm is **Trapp Arts and Crafts Centre**, which specialises in Welsh crafts. The shop stocks an interesting range of quality items including stained glass,

lovespoons, pottery and jewellery, and the art gallery on the first floor shows the work of local artists. Demonstrations and exhibitions run throughout the summer months, and the centre has a coffee shop.

LLANDEILO
11½ miles SW of Llandovery on the A483

🏛 Tywi Bridge   🏛 Parish Church of St Teilo

🏛 Dinefwr Castle   ♧ Dinefwr Park

The former ancient capital of West Wales, Llandeilo's hilltop position shows off to best advantage this pretty little market town. Pastel coloured Georgian houses line the main road, which curves elegantly up from the **Tywi Bridge** (its central span is said to be the longest in Wales) to the Victorian **Parish Church of St Teilo**, which was designed by the well-known architect Sir Giles Gilbert Scott. St Teilo lived in the 6th century, and was a companion of St David. He founded a monastery at Llandeilo, where he later died, on the site where the church now stands. It is best known for producing the beautiful *Gospel of St Teilo*, one of Wales' best-known manuscripts. It was later known as the *Lichfield Gospels* and Book of St Chad. Serving the rich agricultural land that surrounds it, Llandeilo was one of the original founders of the Welsh Rugby Union.

To the west of the town lies **Dinefwr Castle**, the ancient seat of the Princes of Deheubarth, one of the three ancient kingdoms of Wales. The fortress was built on the site of an Iron Age fort,

Carreg Cennen Castle, Trapp

🏛 historic building 🏛 museum and heritage 🏛 historic site ♧ scenic attraction ⚘ flora and fauna

N WALL JEWELLERS & BEAUTY SALON

127 Rhosman Street, Llandeilo,
Carmarthenshire SA19 6EN
Tel: 01558 822237 (Jeweller) 01558 823123 (Salon)
e-mail: nwall@nwall.co.uk
website: www.nwall.co.uk or www.bodybeautiful-salon.co.uk

In a mid-Victorian building which have retained many original features, Mr and Mrs Wall offer two very different specialist enterprises. **N Wall Jewellers** remains a traditional jewellers with a specialised repair work shop and modern computerised engraving service. The shop stocks a wide range of silver and gold jewellery, pearls and Casino and Timex watches. Recently Nick has introduced outdoor clothing by Sprayway and walking boots by Karrimor and has a wide range of cameras, Luger Binoculars and items for those wishing to enjoy the beautiful countryside. The shop is open daily from 9am to 5pm with half day closing on Thursdays.

'Inner Health & Outer Beauty'

Body Beautiful Beauty Salon is situated above N.Wall Jewellers and specialises in Collin of Paris Facial and Body Treatments. The comprehensive range of beauty services includes Aromatherapy, waxing, electrolysis and manicures. Open daily from Tuesday to Saturday.

J H COOPER

4 Carmarthen Street, Llandeilo,
Carmarthenshire SA19 6AE
Tel: 01558 823463
e-mail: jhcooper@btconnect.com

For many years **J H Cooper Family Butcher** has been providing the local area with the very best beef, lamb, poultry and game. Owner Julian Cooper and his staff are proud of the traditional qualities they bring to their profession, combining the finest meat (most of it locally reared or sourced) with friendly service and excellent value for money at their long-established shop. As well as the cuts and joints and poultry the shop sells its own home-cured bacon, Barbary ducks, home-made faggots and game both furred and feathered.

The shop, which is readily identified by its cheerful red canopy, is located in one of Llandeilo's many little side streets in Smithfield House gives its name to one of the many varieties of sausages made on the premises: the Smithfield Sausage is made with pork, leek, ginger and rosemary. Spit-roast chickens and delicatessen items including cooked and cured meats, cheeses (mostly Welsh) and olives make J H Cooper an ideal stop-off for self-catering holidaymakers to stock up. Shop hours are 8 to 5.30 Monday, Tuesday, Wednesday and Friday, 8 to 1 Thursday and 8 to 4.30 Saturday.

📖 stories and anecdotes 🐦 famous people 🎨 art and craft 🎭 entertainment and sport 🚶 walks

DINEFWR RIDING CENTRE

Llandyfan, Ammanford, Carmarthenshire SA182UD
Tel: 01269 850042
email dinefwrriding@btconnect.com

The countryside hereabouts, on the western edge of the Black Mountain area, is ideal for walking, cycling, touring and getting in touch with nature. And, of course, it's also popular for horseriding, and for riders of all abilities the **Dinefwr Riding Centre** is the place to head for. The Jenner family run the Centre alongside their working farm and offer the best in riding tuition for ages from five years upwards and under 14 st., from novices to experienced with a range of horses and ponies from quiet first timers to advanced dressage and jumping horses. All Instructors are fully qualified BHS Instructors with the Centre having full B.H.S. Approval status.

The facilities at the Centre include a large Indoor school, full set of Show Jumps , training paddocks, cross country course (weather permitting) and over 150 acres of farmland to ride over. They also boast an Equi-Simulator – a mechanical horse which can walk, trot and canter to help develop balance and confidence before getting on a real horse!

and legend has it that Merlin's grave is in the area. Overlooking the River Tywi, the first stone castle here is believed to have been built by Rhys ap Gryffydd in the 12th century and, seen as an important target, it was dismantled by Rhys Grug in 1220 to prevent Llywelyn from taking this strategic position. The castle ruins are surrounded by **Dinefwr Park** (NT). Extensive areas of parkland were landscaped by Capability Brown in 1775 and incorporated the medieval castle, house, gardens and ancient deer park into one breathtaking panorama. Footpaths through the parkland lead to the castle, bog wood and beech clumps and offer outstanding views of the Tywi valley. The site is one of international importance for wintering birds, including white-fronted geese, curlews and lapwings. There is a small herd of white cattle.

TALLEY

8½ miles W of Llandovery on the B4302

🏛 Talley Abbey　　🏛 Parish Church of St Michael

This village, with its backdrop of rolling hills, takes its name from Tal-y-llychau, meaning head of the lakes. Between two lakes lies **Talley Abbey**, founded in the late 12th century by Rhys ap Gryffyd, and the only Welsh outpost of the austere Premonstratensian canons who, ejected by the Cistercians in the early 13th century, had appealed to the Archbishop of Canterbury and were granted their own religious rights in 1208. Of the few remains to have survived, an immense tower still overshadows the peaceful abbey lawns. The nearby 18th-century **Parish Church of St Michael** is something of an oddity: it was built with no

🏛 historic building 🏛 museum and heritage 🏛 historic site 🌣 scenic attraction �￬ flora and fauna

aisle and its interior was entirely taken up with box pews.

CRUGYBAR
7 miles NW of Llandovery on the B4302

🏛 Felin Newydd

Just to the northeast of the village, and nestling in the beautiful foothills of the Cambrian Mountains, lies **Felin Newydd**, a 200-year-old working watermill believed to have been constructed on the site of a grist mill used by Roman soldiers working on the nearby gold mines. Restored in the 1980s, when fascinating graffiti on the mill walls linked the building with 19th-century Welsh colonists of South America, the mill is now capable of grinding flour once more.

The land around the mill is quiet, unspoiled and ideal for discovering all manner of wild plant and animal life. Lucky visitors have been known to see red kite circling overhead although there are also more friendly ducks and chickens to amuse young children. A renovated byre has been converted into a cosy tearoom that also includes an interesting selection of local crafts for sale.

PUMSAINT
8 miles NW of Llandovery on the A482

🏛 Dolaucothi Goldmines

Near this hamlet, whose names means five saints, is the **Dolaucothi Goldmines** (NT), which date back some 2,000 years to a time when the open-cast gold workings were secured by the Roman army. Once a likely source of gold bullion for the Imperial mints of Lyons and Rome, the mines are still in a remarkable state of preservation despite being abandoned by the Romans in 140 AD. They were reopened for a short time between 1888 and the late 1930s. Visitors can see both the ancient and modern mine workings, including a number of the horizontal tunnels dug into the hillside for drainage and access. There is also the opportunity to try gold panning, to see an exhibition of vintage mining machinery and to tour the surrounding woodland on a waymarked trail. The site also has a shop selling Welsh Gold and a tearoom serving delicious home-cooked food.

Llanelli

🏛 Parish Church of St Elli

🏛 Llanelly House

🦚 National Wetlands Centre of Wales

🖼 Parc Howard Museum and Art Gallery

🌳 Millennium Coastal Park and Cycleway

Essentially an industrial town with tin-plating, steel, chemical and engineering works, Llanelli was named after the Celt, St Elli, to whom the **Parish Church of St Elli** is dedicated. It has two naves, one dating from Norman times and one built in the 15th century. The stained-glass windows commemorate the traditional industries of the town – iron making and mining. While heavy industry certainly put the town on the map, Llanelli is perhaps best known as the home of the Scarlets, one of the most famous rugby teams in Wales. The saucepan tipped rugby posts at Stradey Park and the Scarlets' anthem, Sospan Fach ('little saucepan'), are both reminders of Llanelli's industrial heritage. In Stepney Street, the Stepney Wheel was made in the early 20th century; this was an inflated spare tyre on a spokeless rim, to be fixed over a punctured wheel. In India, the term Stepney Wheel is still sometimes applied to any spare tyre. Housed in a former mansion set in a large civic park, **Parc Howard Museum and Art Gallery** has a collection of local paintings and 19th century Llanelli pottery as well as displays on the history of the town. However, Llanelli is not all industry and rugby as the town is home to one of the country's newest attractions, the **Millennium Coastal Park and Cycleway**. Providing all manner of leisure activities and peaceful wildlife havens, the park incorporates wetlands, gardens, woodlands, a golf course and both sailing and watersports. **Llanelly House**, built in 1714, opposite the church, is a good example of an early 18th-century house. The local council has purchased the property, and will be restoring it.

Le Bocage, Llanelli

To the east of Llanelli lies the **National Wetlands Centre of Wales**, which is one of the eight centres established by the Trust founded by Sir Peter Scott at Slimbridge in 1946. Also a haven for wild plant and animal life throughout the year, the centre's 200-acre saltmarsh is home to flocks of curlew, lapwing and redshank, which visitors can observe from secluded hides. The Discovery Centre has hands-on activities to help visitors learn about conservation.

Around Llanelli

PEMBREY

5 miles W of Llanelli on the A484

🍃 Pembrey Country Park   🍃 Cefn Sidan

This village lies on the flat lands which border

Carmarthen Bay to the east of Llanelli, and during World War II a Royal Ordnance Factory produced munitions for the Allied Forces here. At the factory's peak, in 1942, it covered some 500 acres and employed 3,000 people. It ceased production in 1965, and since then the land has been landscaped to produce **Pembrey Country Park**, which offers visitors an unusual mix of pine forests, sand dunes and beaches as well as a dry ski slope, a toboggan run, a miniature railway and an adventure playground. Pembrey Pines Trail is a four-mile walk through dunes and woodland, with splendid views. There's also a visitor centre, and to the east lies Pembrey Saltmarsh, a local nature reserve and a Site of Special Scientific Interest. The park also includes **Cefn Sidan**, a blue flag beach that is one of Europe's best and safest, and from which there are glorious views over the Gower coastline.

🏛 historic building 🏛 museum and heritage 🏛 historic site 🍃 scenic attraction 🌿 flora and fauna

KIDWELLY

7½ miles NW of Llanelli on the B4308

🏛 Parish Church of St Mary 🏛 Kidwelly Castle

🏛 Kidwelly Industrial Museum ▥ Gwenllian

This historic town, whose charter was granted by Henry I in the 12th century, boasts a 14th-century bridge over the River Gwendreath and the **Parish Church of St Mary**, originally built as the church of a Benedictine priory in 1320.

However, the most interesting and impressive building is undoubtedly the remarkably well-preserved Norman **Kidwelly Castle**, which stands on a steep bluff overlooking the river. The castle spans four centuries, but most of what remains today is attributed to Roger, Bishop of Salisbury, who founded the priory and died in 1139 AD and also . One of Wales' best kept secrets, Kidwelly Castle gives a fascinating insight into the evolution of a medieval castle into a domestic dwelling of more settled times.

For hundreds of years, the ghost of **Gwenllian**, daughter of the King of Gwynedd and the wife of the Prince of South Wales, was said to haunt the countryside around the castle. During an attack on in 1136 which Gwenllian led, she was decapitated and legend has it that her headless ghost was unable to find rest until a man searched the battlefield and returned her skull to her. Princess Gwenllian was certainly a warrior, and she was perhaps also a writer. Some have attributed parts of *The Mabinogion* to her, and if the attribution is correct, she would be Britain's earliest known woman writer.

On the outskirts of the town, marked by its 164foot redbrick chimney, lies the **Kidwelly Industrial Museum** - housed in an original tin-plate works dating from 1737. Here visitors have a unique opportunity to see how the plate

KIDWELLY B&B

62 Causeway Street, Kidwelly, Carmarthenshire SA17 4SU
Tel: 01554 890716
e-mail: kidwellybandb@yahoo.co.uk
website: www.stayinkidwelly.com

Nick and Gerri Tennant welcome guests to their Bed & Breakfast establishment in the centre of Kidwelly, a short walk from the Castle, St Mary's Church and the town's pubs, clubs and shops. Come and go when you want with your own key; a Blue Flag beach is just two miles away.

The first-floor accommodation at **Kidwelly B&B**, where everything has been renovated for 2009, comprises three double bedrooms and a twin-bedded room, all with en suite shower, underfloor heating, flat-screen TV, radio/alarm clock, luxury bath sheets and toiletries. Guests have the use of a comfortable lounge/dining room, where they are free to bring their own food. Other amenities include a drying room, storage for luggage and bikes and secure car parking.

The accommodation, which is open all year round, is separate from the owners' home, but Nick and Gerri are on hand with help and advice if needed, and they welcome arriving guests with tea or coffee and home-made cakes and biscuits. Kidwelly B&B is an eco-friendly establishment that has won a Green Dragon Stage II Award.

Kidwelly lies on the estuary of the River Gwendraeth between Llanelli and Carmarthen on the B4308, just off the main A484. It is also well connected by rail to Swansea and on to London Paddington, and guests travelling by train can arrange to be picked up at the station.

▥ stories and anecdotes 🐦 famous people 🎨 art and craft 🏌 entertainment and sport 🚶 walks

Kidwelly Castle

DOROTHY MORRIS FINE ART, SILK & CERAMICS

9 Eva Terrace, Ferryside, Carmarthenshire SA17 5TD
Tel: 01267 267652
The Mezzanine Gallery, The Stackpole Centre, Pembroke SA71 5DQ
Tel: 01646 661425
e-mail: dorothy-morris@hotmail.com website: www.talented-art.com

Dorothy Morris is a teacher and creator of unique pieces in a variety of crafts, specialising in and widely known for her original fine arts, silks and ceramics. In her studio she produces hand-made and decorated plates, sculptures, batik bags, scarves and textiles, along with original Fine Art paintings inspired mainly by the flowers and fauna and the diverse wildlife of the woods and lakes in the magical area surrounding her place of work.

Her Mezzanine Gallery is located in the Stackpole Centre in Pembroke, in the beautiful grounds of the National Trust's Home Park Estate. Dorothy also produces limited edition prints and photographs printed with giclée inks on high-quality paper. She has long been fascinated by the unique attractions of batik, which led her to explore the many other art forms and techniques she has mastered. For many years she has been a representative of the Batik Guild.

With a degree in textiles and an MA in Fine Art, Dorothy is a qualified teacher specialising in textiles and surface decoration, and she organises regular workshops and accredited classes for adults and children across all sectors of society. The Mezzanine gallery is open on summer Saturdays, otherwise by appointment.

🏛 historic building 🏛 museum and heritage 🏛 historic site 🌄 scenic attraction 🌿 flora and fauna

was made, as well as learning something of the county's industrial past. The museum contains Britain's sole surviving pack mill.

GORSLAS
9 miles N of Llanelli on the A476

🎞 Mynydd Mawr

🌳 Llyn Llech Owain Country Park

Legend tell us that on **Mynydd Mawr**, a mountain to the north of the village, there was a well that was long ago given to the shepherds by the fairies to water their flocks. The only condition of the gift was that the shepherds had to replace the well slab after they used it. This the shepherds did, and everything remained peaceful. Some time later, King Arthur had sent his knights out to seek the Holy Grail, and one of them, Sir Owen (Sir Gwain in the Arthurian legends) met and slew a pagan knight who lived near Gorslas. Weary and parched, he rested by the well, and both he and his horse drank from it. But so tired was he that he forgot to replace the slab over the well before falling

asleep, and when he wakened he found that the water had created a great lake at the foot of the mountain.

Not only that, shepherds were running towards him, angry that he had robbed them of good farmland. He had to think of something to tell them, so he calmly explained that he had created a great lake at the foot of the mountain, so that they need not longer climb it to get good, fresh water. Placated, the shepherds left him in peace. The lake of water that was left is known today as Llyn Llech Owain - the Lake of Owain's Stone Slab.

Today, **Llyn Llech Owain Country Park** includes the lake, as well as the peat bog which surrounds it, an area of largely coniferous woodland and dry heath. The lake and peat bog, designated a Site of Special Scientific Interest, are home to a variety of rare plants such as bogbean, round leafed sundew and royal fern. The park's visitor centre has an exhibition that describes both the history and the natural history of the park.

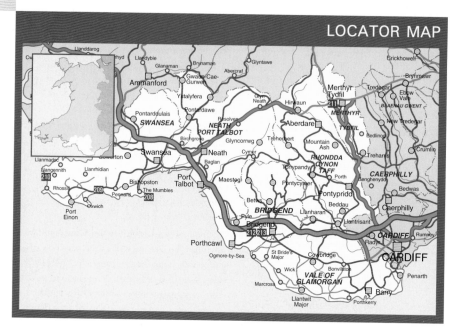

ADVERTISERS AND PLACES OF INTEREST

Accommodation, Food and Drink
209 | Maes Yr Haf Restaurant with Rooms, Parkmill,
Swansea   *pg 320*
210 | The King's Head, Llangennith, Gower   *pg 323*

Activities
212 | Health Diva, Bridgend   *pg 332*

Fashions
212 | Health Diva, Bridgend   *pg 332*

Giftware
208 | Cover To Cover, Mumbles, Swansea   *pg 319*

Specialist Food and Drink Shops
212 | Health Diva, Bridgend   *pg 332*
213 | Lou's Delicatessen, Bridgend   *pg 332*

Places of Interest
211 | Cyfarthfa Castle Museum & Art Gallery,
Methyr Tydfil   *pg 330*

🏛 historic building   🏛 museum and heritage   🏛 historic site   🐾 scenic attraction   🌿 flora and fauna

9 | The Gower Peninsula & Heritage Coast

The delightful city of Swansea, with a population of 226,000 (including its hinterland), is the second largest city in Wales, and marks the gateway to the southernmost bulge of Wales, the lovely Gower Peninsula, a region designated an Area of Outstanding Natural Beauty, much of it owned by the National Trust. The Gower's southern coastline is made up of a succession of sandy, sheltered bays, and along its whole coastline it is dotted with charming and relaxed seaside resorts.

This is also an area rich in natural beauty, with a long history that can be explored not only at the Gower Heritage Centre, but also through its various castles, religious sites and ancient monuments. The area has many small family farms that yield some of the finest produce in South Wales, with the Gower in particular being known for its cockles and its laverbread (edible seaweed).

Kenfig National Nature Reserve, Bridgend

The Vale of Glamorgan is characterised by gentle rolling hills, genteel towns, a coastline rich in heritage and history, pretty villages and rich farmland. This is where Norman warlords built their castles, and where, at Llantwit Major, one of the country's oldest seats of learning was founded.

Behind the coastal region lie the valleys of southwest Wales, which were known the world over for their coal mining and heavy industry. The best known is the Rhondda Valley, where only one mine survives from the numerous collieries that provided coal, not just for this country but many parts of the world. However, though mining has all but gone, the heritage remains. The towns and villages, where life revolved around the colliery, the chapel and the male voice choirs, survive. These famous choirs were formed mainly by coalmining and iron working communities of the South Wales valleys, and in the quarries of North Wales. Most of them welcome visitors dropping in on rehearsals as well as attending concerts.

In many cases, nature has reclaimed the hills and vales once scarred by the mining industry and, while pride in the industry remains, the various new country parks and nature reserves developed on the sites of the old mines are giving the area a new hope, and a new appeal.

Swansea

🏛 Swansea Castle   🏛 Parish Church of St Mary

🏛 Waterfront Museum

🏛 National Swansea Museum

🏛 Glynn Vivian Art Gallery

🏛 Egypt Centre   🌱 Clyne Gardens

🏛 Dylan Thomas Centre   🏚 Maritime Quarter

🌱 Plantasia Botanic Gardens

Swansea, the second city of Wales, was founded in the late 10th century by Sweyne Forkbeard, King of Denmark. Its English name means Sweyne's ey – ey being an inlet. **Swansea Castle**, which gained notoriety in the 18th century when the northern block became a debtors' prison, was first built by the Norman Henry de Newburgh in the late 11th century. However, it was all but destroyed by Owain Glyndwr in the early 1400s, when he ransacked the town that had grown up around the fortification.

As early as the 14th century, shipbuilding and coalmining were important industries in

Swansea Castle

the area and, by 1700, Swansea was the largest port in Wales. Smelters from Cornwall arrived here, attracted by the plentiful supply of coal, and copper works also flourished. Nelson's ships were covered in Swansea copper, and at one time, 90% of the country's copper was smelted here. In the heyday of the industry, other metals such as tin, lead, nickel and zinc were imported to the town for smelting and refining. In the 19th century Swansea became famouse for its porcelain.

Much of the traditional industry has disappeared now, and the old dock area has been transformed into a marina surrounded by stylish waterfront buildings. This **Maritime Quarter** is arguably the most impressive part of the town and is alive with cafés, pubs and restaurants. The **National Waterfront Museum** on Oystermouth Road has exhibits and displays from the early days of the port right through to the devastating bombing raids of World War II. There is plenty to see and learn at the museum.

The town is also home to the **Swansea Museum**, the oldest in Wales, but up to date, combining bygone Swansea history and culture with new exhibitions and events. Among the displays are Swansea porcelain, the Cabinet of Curiosities, a Welsh kitchen and the Mummy of Tem-Hor. More artefacts from Egypt can be seen at the **Egypt Centre**, where over 1,000 objects, from impressive painted coffins to everyday household items, can be seen that date back as far as 3500 BC. At the **Glynn Vivian Art Gallery** in Alexandra Road a broad spectrum of the visual arts is on display. Based on the bequest of Richard Glynn Vivian, the gallery houses an international collection of Swansea porcelain and various Old Masters, as well as numerous paintings and sculptures by 20th-century artists including Hepworth, Nicholas,

Marina, Swansea

from the Royal Horticultural Society. These 19th-century landscaped gardens were laid out by the Vivian family, who were also responsible for nearby Sketty Hall, a 19th-century version of an Italian parterre garden.

No mention of Swansea would be complete without referring to the town's most famous son, Dylan Thomas, who described it as viewed from his hillside home:

Ugly, lovely town crawling, sprawling, slummed, unplanned, jerry-villa'd, and smug-suburbed by the side of a long and splendid curving shore......

His former home on steep Cwmdonkin Drive in the Uplands district displays a blue plaque with the simple inscription, Dylan Thomas, Poet, 1914–53. Born in this house. The house can be viewed by appointment. Cwmdonkin Park, close to his home, was much loved by Thomas, whose poem *The Hunchback in the Park* was set there. The **Dylan Thomas Centre** in Somerset Place is dedicated to the poet's life and works, with the exhibitions featuring some of his original manuscripts, letters to friends and family and a moving American documentary about him. There are Dylan Thomas Trails to follow in the city centre, Uplands, Mumbles and Gower, and the annual Dylan Thomas Celebration attracts visitors from around the world.

The city was also the birthplace of other well know people. Sir Harry Secombe,

Nash, Ceri Richards and Augustus John.

The **Parish Church of St Mary** was founded in medieval times, though it was probably built on the site of a 6th-century monastery. The church was rebuilt in the 1890s when the 14th-century chancel and tower and the 18th-century nave were pulled down. However, this Victorian church was burnt down in February 1941 when it was bombed. Rebuilding continued until 1959.

At **Plantasia Botanic Gardens**, housed in the walled garden of Singleton Park, visitors can wander around a glass pyramid with three climatic zones – tropical, humid, arid – and 5,000 exotic plants. The hot house is also home to numerous exotic insects, fish and reptiles, such as leaf cutting ants, and there is a butterfly house where the various colourful species fly freely. **Clyne Gardens**, at Blackpill off the A4067 Mumbles road, are known in particular for their marvellous rhododendrons, including National Collections, their imposing magnolias and an extensive bog garden. In 2001, the rhododendrons captured 23 awards

Catherine Zeta Jones, Michael Heseltine, Rowan Williams (Archbishop of Canterbury) and the singer Bonnie Tyler were all born here.

If Dylan Thomas was Swansea's most famous son, its most famous dog was Jack (known as 'Swansea Jack'), a black retriever who lived in the city and died in 1937, aged seven. He was reputed to have saved 27 humans and two dogs from drowning and was awarded the canine Victoria Cross. In 2002, he was named "Dog of The Century".

Gower Peninsula

BISHOPSTON
3 mile SW of Swansea off the A4118

🌱 Bishopston Valley

The sheltered **Bishopston Valley** contains an extensive area of ancient woodland that supports a wide variety of plants and birds. A two-mile footpath leads along the valley from Kittle to Pwll Du.

MUMBLES
4½ miles SW of Swansea on the A4067

🏛 Oystermouth Castle

🏛 Parish Church of All Saints

🏛 Lovespoon Gallery   🏞 Langland Bay

🎦 Mumbles Passenger Railway

🦢 Thomas Bowdler

This charming Victorian resort grew up around the old fishing village of Oystermouth, which has its roots in Roman times, and where the Normans built a castle to defend their land. Now in ruins, **Oystermouth Castle** was built by William de Londres, and was later the home of the de Breos family. The gatehouse, chapel and great

hall all date from around the 13th and 14th century. Surrounded by small but beautiful grounds overlooking the bay, the ruins are now the scene of re-enactments that chart the history of the castle and, in particular, the siege of the fortress by Owain Glyndwr.

The village is now a popular sailing centre, with numerous pubs, a restored late-Victorian pier and, on the headland, a lighthouse guarding the entrance into Swansea harbour. The **Parish Church of All Saints** is built on ths site of a Roman villa, and originally dates from the 12th century, though it was restored in Victorian times. Inside there is a memorial to the famous Mumbles lifeboat, and in the churchyard is the grave of **Thomas Bowdler** (1754–1825), the literary censor, who published an expurgated edition of Shakespeare in 1818 and gave our language the word 'bowdlerise'. His *Family Shakespeare* omitted words and expressions that he considered could not be read aloud by a father to his family. Sex was out, but cruelty and violence remained largely unexpurgated. Bowdler died at Rhydding, near Swansea, in 1825, leaving a bowdlerised version of Gibbon's *Decline and Fall of the Roman Empire*.

An unusual attraction in Mumbles is the **Lovespoon Gallery**, where visitors will find an amazing variety of these unique love tokens. Lovespoons were traditionally carved from wood by young men and presented to their sweethearts as a token of their devotion. The custom dates back many centuries, but in these less romantic days the spoons are often bought simply as souvenirs of Wales.

The **Mumbles Passenger Railway** was the world's first, and ran from Mumbles north into Swansea. From 1807 to its closure in 1960, the five-mile line used horse, sail, steam, battery, petrol, diesel and electricity. On Bank

🏛 historic building   🏛 museum and heritage   🎦 historic site   🏞 scenic attraction   🌱 flora and fauna

COVER TO COVER

58 Newton Road, Mumbles, Swansea SA3 4BQ
Tel: 01792 366363
e-mail: sales@cover-to-cover.co.uk
website: www.cover-to-cover.co.uk

Opened in September 1999, **Cover to Cover** has become one of the most popular shops in the delightful Victorian seaside village of Mumbles, outside Swansea. An inviting bookshop where you can browse through quality fiction, an eclectic mix of non-fiction titles, plus a range of books on local, Swansea and Welsh interest.

The children's area is very popular with soft seats for little ones to settle and enjoy their books. The range stocked is excellent from Beatrix Potter to Harry Potter.

But Cover to Cover also sells an interesting selection of gifts, including leather wallets, bookmarks, key rings, journals, an award-winning fragrance range, photo frames, soft toys for children, and much more.

Holidays in the mid-Victorian period it was known to carry up to 40,000 passengers.

Beyond The Mumbles – the name is derived from the French *mamelles* meaning "breasts" and is a reference to the two islets of the promontory beyond Oystermouth – lies the lovely Gower Peninsula, designated an Area of Outstanding Natural Beauty. Gower's southern coast is made up of a succession of sandy, sheltered bays and the first of these, **Langland Bay**, is just around the headland from the village.

PARKMILL

8 miles SW of Swansea on the A4118

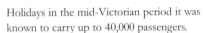

🏛 Pennard Castle   📷 Gower Heritage Centre

This village is home to the **Gower Heritage Centre**, which is itself centred around a historic water mill built in the 12th century by the powerful le Breos family, the Norman rulers of Gower. Originally constructed to supply flour for nearby **Pennard Castle**, now in ruins, this water mill is a rare survivor in Wales of a rural complex that would once have been found in most villages and hamlets. The Heritage Centre has displays on the history of this beautiful region along with a farming museum. Visitors can also tour the mill, where the restored machinery grinds flour on most days. Younger visitors to the centre can make friends with the farm animals and everyone will enjoy wandering around the craft units and workshops where a wheelwright, a potter, a blacksmith and a mason can be seen plying their trades.

The castle was originally built of wood in the 12th century by Henry de Beaumont, Earl of Warwick, when he became the lord of

MAES YR HAF RESTAURANT WITH ROOMS

Parkmill, Swansea SA3 2CH
Tel: 01792 371000
e-mail: enquiries@maes-yr-haf.com
website: www.maes-yr-haf.com

Since it was opened by David Kelly in the summer of 2007, **Maes yr Haf** has established itself as one of the finest places in the region for a meal or a holiday. For most of its life the 1940s property was a modest B&B house, sometime a shop and later a private residence, before being transformed into a top-class restaurant with rooms, a contemporary boutique hotel and restaurant in the heart of the lovely Gower Peninsula. It stands a short stroll from the beautiful Three Cliffs Bay and is centrally placed for the many other fine beaches of the South Gower coast.

In the restaurant, the emphasis is on the best-quality fresh produce and for most of what goes into accomplished head chef Christos Georgakis's kitchen that means Welsh – local meat, local fish and shellfish, local fruit and vegetables. Almost everything, from the bread to the pasta, the pastries and the ice cream, is made in house. The restaurant itself is highly individual and eye-catching in design, with extensive use of rosewood and sapele creating a warm, inviting feeling of luxury. The fixed-price lunch menu (served from 12 to 2.30) and the à la carte evening menu (7 to 9.30) tempts with dishes that combine top-quality ingredients with cooking that shows classic skills and contemporary flair. Typical

dishes might include laver- bread and home-cured bacon soufflé with a local cockle salad; grilled salsify with a poached egg, pink grapefruit hollandaise and a parmesan wafer; salmon with a leek & black pepper risotto and a crayfish bisque sauce; braised neck fillet of Welsh lamb; and, to finish, bread & butter pudding with an apricot glaze & Merlyn Welsh liqueur anglais. Local ales and cider, well-chosen wines, spirits and liqueurs and discreet, attentive service set the seal on a memorable meal. As well as lunch (roasts on Sunday) and dinner, Maes yr Haf is open for breakfast and afternoon tea/coffee with home-made bread and cakes and light meals. There's also a Ramblers Menu (12 to 7) with soup, sandwiches, pastries and hot and cold drinks, and residents can order a picnic pack for a day's sightseeing or a lazy day on the beach.

The accommodation comprises a selection of luxurious en suite doubles, each with a distinctive design by Hannah Davies of Salt Design, and all with large, super-comfortable beds and a range of hi-tech amenities. A hospitality tray is provided, but full room service is also available.

Gower. Later, it was rebuilt in stone, and the ruins you see today are from that period.

PENMAEN
7 miles SW of Swansea off the A4118

🏛 Parish Church of St John the Baptist

Tradition has it that a village, Stedwarlango, is buried here beneath the sand dunes. The National Trust owns an area that includes High Pennard, topped by a prehistoric hill fort, and Three Cliffs Bay, where there are old lime kilns, an ancient burial chamber and a pillow mound – an artificial warren used to farm rabbits. Cut into the rocks is Minchin Hole, a geological Site of Scientific Interest where evidence has been found of mammals and early man. The **Parish Church of St John the Baptist**, though it was heavily restored in Victorian times, has a wealth of memorial tablets.

OXWICH
11 miles SW of Swansea off the A4118

🏛 Parish Church of St Illtud 🏛 Oxwich Castle
🌀 Oxwich Point 🌿 Oxwich Nature Reserve

One of Gower's prettiest villages, Oxwich lies huddled along a lane at the western end of a superb three-mile-long beach. Once a small port exporting limestone, and also a haven for smugglers, Oxwich is today a marvellous holiday area with safe bathing, clean beaches, wind surfing and water skiing. The village has some picturesque cottages of the traditional Gower style which include one that was once occupied by John Wesley. The 13th-century **Parish Church of St Illtud**, half hidden by trees, is well worth seeking out as its ancient font is believed to have been brought here by St Illtud himself. There are several interesting carved tombs within the building, and the chancel ceiling was decorated in 1931 by a

scenic artist who worked at Sadler's Wells in London.

Just to the south of the village lies **Oxwich Castle**, a grand Tudor manor house built around a courtyard. Although this was probably the site of an earlier fortification, the splendid house was established by Sir Rice Mansel in the 1520s and added to by his son, Sir Edward Mansel, whose building work includes the Elizabethan long gallery. The Mansel family's time at this lavish mansion was short lived, and after they left in the 1630s the house fell into disrepair, although the southern wing was used as a farmhouse, and the southeast tower still survives to its full height of six storeys.

For walkers there are plenty of footpaths to explore and the walk to **Oxwich Point**, in particular, provides some magnificent views of the Gower Peninsula. Close to the beach lies part of the **Oxwich Nature Reserve**, home to many rare species of orchid as well as other plant life and a variety of birds.

KNELSTON
12½ miles SW of Swansea on the A4118

🏛 Parish Church of St David 🏛 Arthur's Stone

To the north of this attractive village lies **Arthur's Stone**, a large burial chamber capstone. Traditionally, this is said to be the pebble that King Arthur removed from his shoe while on his way to the Battle of Camlann in the 6th century. According to legend, Arthur threw it over his shoulder and the stone lies exactly where the pebble landed. Up until the 19th century, local girls would take part in a ritual here to discover whether their lovers were true or not. At midnight during the full moon, the girls would place a honey cake soaked in milk on the stone and then crawl under it three times. If their lovers were true, they would appear before them. The **Parish Church of St David** is 14th century, and has some interesting memorials within it. It was built by Henry de Gower, Bishop of St David's. It has a west tower with a saddleback roof that contains the oldest (and some say loudest) bell on the Gower Peninsula.

RHOSSILI
16 miles SW of Swansea on the B4247

🏛 Parish Church of St Mary   🏚 The Warren

🏞 Worm's Head   🏞 Rhossili Beach

This village, on the westernmost area of the Gower Peninsula, is thought to have been named after St Fili, who is said to have been the son of St Cenydd. The **Parish Church of St Mary**, which dates from the early 13th century, has a superb late Norman carved archway over the door. Inside is a memorial plaque to a Gower man, Edgar Evans, who is perhaps better known as Petty Officer Evans, who died on the ill-fated expedition to the Antarctic led by Captain Scott in 1912.

The original village, and its parish church dedicated to St Sili or Sulien, stood near the beach, and in the 13trh century was engulfed by the shifting sand dunes during a storm. It is said that the site, now called **The Warren**, was once a Celtic monastery founded by St Cynwal.

To the west of Rhossili lies **Worm's Head**, an island that is a National Nature Reserve. Reached by a causeway at low tide, there is public access to the island, but those making the crossing should take great care not to be cut off by the tide. Worm's Head marks the southern edge of Rhossili Bay, where **Rhossili Beach** can be reached by a steep downhill climb. At low tide, the remains of several wrecks can be seen, most notably the *Helvetia*, which was wrecked in 1887. The beach is very popular with fishermen, surfers and bathers.

LLANGENNITH
15 miles W of Swansea off the B4271

🏛 Parish Church of St Cenydd   🌱 Burry Holms

This quiet village is home to the largest church on the Gower Peninsula. The **Parish Church of St Cenydd** was built in the 12th century on the site of a monastery founded six centuries earlier by St Cenydd himself, which was later destroyed by Vikings. Inside, now mounted on a wall, is a curious gravestone thought to mark the resting place of the saint. He was born on the Gower Peninsula, and legend tells us he walked with a limp due to a withered leg. He was cast adrift in a basket on the Loughor estuary because of it, but was rescued by gulls and brought up by angels. To the west of the village, and marking the northern edge of Rhossili Bay,

Rhossili Bay

THE KING'S HEAD

Llangennith, Gower, Swansea SA13 1HX
Tel: 01792 386212 Fax: 01792 386477
e-mail: info@kingsheadgower.co.uk
website: www.kingsheadgower.co.uk

When the Stevens family took over the **King's Head** in 1988, it was what the name would suggest – a pub. They have transformed the long, low Welsh stone building opposite the ancient church into a fine inn. Rooms are new and separate from the pub in newly converted buildings offering top-class accommodation and excellent food. Comfort and luxury are the keynotes in the bedrooms, which feature restful, colour-co-ordinated décor and furnishings. The 27 rooms differ in size and design, but all have underfloor heating and sound-proofing, en suite bathroom with bath and power shower, wall-mounted wide-screen plasma TV, tea/coffee tray, alarm clock/radio and hairdryer. Some have wheelchair access, some have oversize baths, some command sea views, but all ensure an excellent night's sleep in this pleasant part of the world. Other amenities include ample car parking, lovely colourful borders and storage for surf boards – Llangennith is known as the surfing capital of The Gower, with a bay that stretches for three miles. The King's Head is an ideal base for exploring the lovely Gower Peninsula, much of which is a designated Area of Outstanding Natural Beauty, popular for walking, sailing, fishing, bird watching, painting, photography...or just sitting back and enjoying the views and the clean fresh air. The King's Head is also an excellent place for a meal, and in the restaurant an interesting menu and daily specials board offers a fine choice of dishes based as far as possible on Welsh produce (local farmers provide much of what goes into the kitchen). High-class pub-style dishes range from fish and shellfish specials to steak & kidney pie, pure Welsh lamb and beef, seasonal game, lasagne, chill and curries. There's always a choice for vegetarians, and children can choose from their own special menu.

And the King's Head remains what it once exclusively was – a delightful place for locals and visitors from further afield to meet for a chat and a drink. A wide choice of real ales heads the list of drinks served in the atmospheric bars, which features original beams holding up low ceilings, a black & amber tiled floor in the main bar, a huge oak beam sunk into the exposed brick over the fire and old photos with a nautical theme.

If coming from the M4, leave at J47 on to the A483 towards Swansea, then the A484 towards Llanelli. At the second roundabout take the B4295 through Gowerton to Llanrhidian then follow a minor road westward to Llangennith.

lies **Burry Holms**, another small island that can be reached via a causeway at low tide. On the island are the remains of an Iron Age earthwork and a monastic chapel dating from the Middle Ages.

LLANRHIDIAN

10½ miles W of Swansea on the B4295

🏛 Weobley Castle   🏛 Llanelen

🏛 Parish Church of St Illtyd

Close to the wild and lonely north coast of the Gower Peninsula, where some of the finest beaches in the country can be found, this village is also close to **Weobley Castle**. Dating from the early 14th century, and built by the de Bere family, Weobley is more a fortified manor house than a castle and stands today as one of the few surviving such houses in Wales. On an isolated site overlooking the eerie expanse of Llanrhidian Marsh, this house has been remarkably well preserved, and visitors can gain a real insight into the domestic arrangements of those days and, in particular, the owners' desire for comfort. In the late 15th century, the house came into the hands of Sir Rhys ap Thomas, an ally of Henry VII, and further improvements were made including the addition of a new porch and an upgrade of the accommodation in the private apartments. As well as seeing the interior of this impressive house, visitors can also view an exhibition on the Gower Peninsula - its history and other ancient monuments.

The **Parish Church of St Illtyd** is medieval, and has a fortified tower. It has strong links with the Knights of St John of Jerusalem, and in 1880 a curious carved stone was unearthed in the churchyard. Known as the Leper Stone, it is Irish in origin, and seems to show St Anthony and St Paul meeting in the desert.

Close to Llanrhidian is the site of the legendary lost village of **Llanelen**. During the reign of Edward VI in the mid 16th century, a ship ran aground in the Burry estuary, and the people of Lhanelen rescued the crew members and made them welcome. However, unknown to everyone, the crew were infected with the plague, and eventually the people either died or fled, abandoning the village. An archaeological dig between 1973 and 1985 uncovered foundations of simple cottages and what was thought to be the foundations of a church. Two memorial stones at the entrance to St Illtyd's Church commemorate the village.

LOUGHOR

6½ miles NW of Swansea on the A484

🏛 Loughor Castle

A strategic location on the mouth of the River Loughor gave this village prominence and

Loughor Castle

importance down the centuries. The Romans built their station of Leucarum here in the 1st century and, in the early 12th century, a Norman nobleman, Henry de Newburgh, built **Loughor Castle** on the edge of the Roman site. Unfortunately, all that is left of the stronghold, which protected the confluence of the Burry Inlet and the River Loughor, is the ruined 13th-century square tower.

Port Talbot

🏛 Baglan Bay Energy Park   🎞 Red Dogs of Morfa

Port Talbot grew out of a small community called Aberafan. Well known for its steel industry, it was named after the Talbot family, who were responsible for the development of the town's docks in the 19th century. Now called the Old Docks, this area saw significant expansion again in the 20th century when a new deep water harbour was opened by the Queen in 1970. Today, Port Talbot is home to factories and processing plants, and also to the solar centre of **Baglan Bay Energy Park**, which explains the history of the area and its power generating potential.

Coal mining has taken place in the area around Port Talbot for centuries, and during this time many superstitions have grown up. In 1890, the miners at Morfa Colliery reported seeing ghostly images in and around the colliery. They were said to be fierce hounds, which became known as the **Red Dogs of Morfa**. They would run through the streets with their appearance being accompanied by a sweet, rose-like scent which filled the mine shaft. Such were the number of eerie manifestations that on the morning of 10th March 1890, nearly half the morning shift failed to report for work. Later the same day,

there was an explosion at the colliery – 87 miners died in the disaster.

Around Port Talbot

NEATH
4 miles N of Port Talbot on the A465

🏛 Neath Abbey   🏛 Parish Church of St Illtyd

🏛 Neath Museum and Art Gallery   🌿 Neath Fair

While Neath's industrial history dates back to the late 16th century, when the first copper smelter in South Wales was built here by Cornishmen, the town has its origins in Roman times. Remains of Roman Nidum can still be seen close to the ruins of **Neath Abbey**, which was founded in the 13th century by Richard de Granville on land seized from the Welsh in around 1130. At first it was a daughter house of Sauvigny in France, but it later became Cistercian. It was a wealthy establishment, always wanting to expand its land holdings, and this led it into many disputes with Margam Abbey, to the southeast of Port Talbot (see also Margam). The buildings were converted into a mansion for Sir John Herbert in the 16th century and it was later used to house copper smelters. It was also de Granville who built Neath Castle, in the mid 12th century, around which the town grew and whose scant remains can be found near a town centre car park.

The **Parish Church of St Illtyd** was founded in the 6th century by the saint of the same name. Legend has it that this was where he used to come on retreat, and a wooden church was erected on the site. The present church is the result of a restoration of 1850, though there are still some Norman and Early English details – notably the font – to be seen. It was again restored in 2003.

🎞 stories and anecdotes   🕊 famous people   🎨 art and craft   🌿 entertainment and sport   🚶 walks

Housed in the Gwyn Hall in the centre of thr town, the **Neath Museum and Art Gallery** has permanent displays on the history of the town, including finds from the time of the Roman occupation, as well as regularly changing art and photographic exhibitions. The Museum has many hands-on activities, including grinding corn, using a Celtic loom and making a wattle fence.

Held each September, **Neath Fair** is the oldest such event in Wales, founded by Gilbert de Clare in 1280.

ABERDULAIS
6 miles NE of Port Talbot off the A4109

🐾 Aberdulais Falls

From as early as 1584, the power generated by the magnificent National Trust-owned **Aberdulais Falls** has been harnessed for a number of industries, including copper smelting and tin-plating. Today, the waterwheel, the largest currently in use for the generation of electricity, makes the Falls self-sufficient in environmentally friendly energy. The Turbine House provides access to a unique fish pass.

CRYNANT
9 miles NE of Port Talbot on the A4109

🏛 Cefn Coed Colliery Museum

In the beautiful Dulais Valley, **Cefn Coed Colliery Museum** provides a wonderful opportunity for visitors to discover what life was like for the miners who worked underground in some of the most difficult conditions experienced anywhere in the world. Through photographs, maps and other exhibits, the tradition and legacy of mining are brought to life. The museum also has a well-stocked souvenir and gift shop, with one of the best selections of genuine and

reproduction miner's lamps in the region. It is ideal for finding a special present from Wales.

CYNONVILLE
6 miles NE of Port Talbot on the A4107

🏛 South Wales Miners' Museum

🐾 Afan Forest Park

Virtually surrounding the village (to the north, west and south) lies the **Afan Forest Park**, a large area of woodland where there are trails for cycling, walking and pony trekking. At the Park's Countryside Centre an exhibition explains, with the aid of hands-on displays, the landscape and history of the Afan Valley. The **South Wales Miners' Museum**, also at the centre, illustrates the social history of the valleys' mining communities.

Cefn Coed Colliery Museum, Crynant

PONT-RHYD-Y-FEN

3½ miles NE of Port Talbot on the B4287

🐦 Richard Burton   🐦 Ivor Emmanuel

This mining village in the Afan Valley was the birthplace of the actor **Richard Burton** (1925 –1984), who was born Richard Walters Jenkins. He was the 12th of 13 children born into a Welsh-speaking family. His father was a coal miner and his mother died in childbirth two years after he was born. Consequently, he was brought up in Port Talbot by his much older sister. He was legally adopted by his schoolmaster at grammar school, Philip H Burton. It was also the birthplace, in 1927, of singer **Ivor Emmanuel**. Like Burton, he too had a tragic childhood, as his mother, father, sister and grandfather were killed when a German bomb fell on the village. He was a great friend of Richard Burton.

MARGAM

3 miles SE of Port Talbot on the A48

🏚 Margam Abbey   🏚 Parish Church of St Mary

🖼 Margam Stones Museum

🌳 Margam Country Park

To the southeast of the town lies **Margam Country Park**, surrounding a mansion built in the 1840s by the Talbot family. The land once belonged to **Margam Abbey**, a Cistercian house that was founded in 1147 by Robert, Earl of Gloucester (see also Neath). Following a violent revolt by the lay brothers, the abbey went on to become one of the wealthiest in Wales but, at the time of the Dissolution of the Monasteries, the estate passed on to Sir Rice Mansel, who built the first mansion here in 1537.

The park today boasts several buildings left by previous owners, including the **Parish**

Margam Abbey

🎞 stories and anecdotes   🐦 famous people   🎨 art and craft   🎬 entertainment and sport   🏃 walks

Church of St Mary, (the former abbey church, and all that remains of the abbey itself), a classical 18th-century orangery, recently restored monastic gardens, a unique fuchsia collection, and a restored Japanese garden from the 1920s. This huge recreational area – the park covers some 800 acres – also includes a visitor centre, waymarked trails, a deer park, bird of prey centre and the **Margam Stones Museum**, where visitors can see a collection of Roman, Celtic and Norman carved stones.

Pontypridd

🏛 Pontypridd Museum   🎵 Sir Geraint Evans

🎵 Stewart Burrows   🎵 Tom Jones

This friendly valley town is justly proud of its past, which is revealed in the **Pontypridd Museum** housed in an old Baptist chapel close to Pontypridd's historic stone bridge over the River Taff. As well as its industrial heritage, the town has a long tradition of music, and in the main park are two statues commemorating Evan and James, a father and son songwriting team who were responsible for composing the words and music for the Welsh National Anthem, *Land of my Fathers* (*Hen Wlad fy Nhadau*).

Perhaps better known to today's visitors, however, are the two opera stars **Sir Geraint Evans** (1922–1992) and **Stewart Burrows** (born 1933), who came from the same street in nearby Clifynydd. **Tom Jones** (born 1940), the international singing star, was born in Trefforest, a mile or so south east of the town. Just outside Pontypridd, at Fforest Uchaf Farm, Penycoedcae, is the Pit Pony Sanctuary, where visitors can meet more than 25 horses and ponies, including several retired

pit ponies. Also here are pit pony memorabilia and a reconstruction of a typical pony-powered Welsh drift coalmine.

Around Pontypridd

LLANTRISANT
4 miles SW of Pontypridd on the B4595

🏛 Parish Church of Saints Illtyd, Gwyno and Dyfod

🏛 Llantrisant Castle   🏛 Royal Mint Museum

🏛 Royal Mint   🎵 Dr William Price

The **Parish Church of Saints Illtyd, Gwyno and Dyfod** give the town its name – the enclosure, or church, of the three saints. It dates from 1246, with later additions and modifications. The east window, designed by Morris Burne Jones, is one of only three church windows that features a beardless Christ and, behind the altar in the Lady Chapel, is a curious stone known as the 'Resurrection Stone', thought to date from the 7th century. The church also has a baptistery where those being baptised can choose either a traditional baptism or full immersion. All that remains of 13th-century **Llantrisant Castle** is part of a round tower known as the Raven Tower. It was built in about 1250 by Richard de Clare, Lord of Glamorgan, to defend this area against the Welsh. It was probably to this castle, in 1326, that Edward II and Hugh Despenser were brought after falling into the hands of Queen Isabella.

Though some of the traditional heavy industry still remains, Llantrisant is best known nowadays for being the home of **The Royal Mint**, within a 38-acre site, which transferred here from Tower Hill, London, in 1967. It produces coins, not just for the United Kingdom, but for countries all over the world. At the **Royal Mint Museum** there

🏛 historic building   🏛 museum and heritage   🏛 historic site   🎵 scenic attraction   🎵 flora and fauna

is a permanent display of coins, medals, dies and drawings, along with a shop, café and a programme of events and exhibitions.

Standing in the town centre is a statue of a figure dressed in a fox skin headdress. This is the town's memorial to **Dr William Price**, an amazing and eccentric character who lived from 1800 to 1893. Espousing many causes, some of which scandalised straight-laced Victorian Britain, Price was a vegetarian who believed in free love, nudism and radical politics. His most famous deed took place in 1884, when he cremated his illegitimate son Iesu Grist (Jesus Christ), who had died in infancy. As a result of the controversy, and the ensuing court case, cremation became legal in Britain. To commemorate his centenary, the council constructed a heather garden that can be seen as one enters the town.

PORTH
3 miles E of Pontypridd on the A4058

🏛 Bacchetta's Italian Café Museum

The industrialised areas of South Wales attracted many Italian immigrants in the 1920s and 1930s. Many of them opened up cafés, and in Porth is the **Bacchetta's Italian Café Museum**, situated above the station café. Here you can see exhibits and artefacts connected with the cafés and the families who ran them.

TREHAFOD
1½ miles NW of Pontypridd off the A4058

🏛 Rhondda Heritage Park

In the Rhondda Valley alone, there were once 53 working mines in just 16 square miles but, although they have almost all gone, the traditions of coal mining live on. When the Lewis Merthyr Colliery closed in 1983, it re-opened as the **Rhondda Heritage Park**, a

fascinating place where former miners guide visitors around the restored buildings. As well as seeing the conditions in which the miners worked, and hearing stories from those whose families worked in the mines for generations, visitors can also see exhibitions on the role of women in a mining village, the dramatic history of the 1920s' strikes for a minimum wage and the tragedy of mining disasters. Between 1868 and 1919 in Rhondda one miner was killed every six hours and one injured every two minutes. The cultural and social history of a mining community, through brass bands, choirs and the chapel, is explored and visitors also have the opportunity to put on a hard hat and travel down the mine shaft in a cage.

ABERDARE
9 miles NW of Pontypridd on the A4233

🏛 Aberdare Museum

🏛 Tower Colliery Visitor Centre

🌳 Dare Valley Country Park   🦅 Griffith Rhys Jones

Situated at the northern end of the Cynon valley, Aberdare, like other valley towns, is famous for its strong music tradition - particularly male voice choirs. In Victoria Square is a statue of the baton waving choir conductor, **Griffith Rhys Jones** (1834-1897).

Aberdare Museum has many artefacts and photographs about the Cynon Valley, and in particular the 1984-85 miners' strike. Wales' last deep mine, the Tower Colliery, is now owned by the miners who work in it. Situated a few miles west of Aberdare, the **The Tower Colliery Visitor Centre** has photographs and displays about the mine and the life of its miners. The whole of the landscape of Aberdare was once shaped by coal mines and heavy industry, but with the closure of the mines the countryside is, through ambitious land reclamation and environmental improvement schemes, returning to its pre-industrial green and lush natural state. Just a short distance from the busy town centre is **Dare Valley Country Park**, which was opened in 1973 on former colliery land and where trails tell of the natural and industrial history of the area.

Merthyr Tydfil

🏠 Cyfarthfa Castle Museum and Art Gallery

🏠 Joseph Parry's Ironworker's Cottage

The main road in this area of Wales, the A645, acts as a dividing line. To the south are the historic valleys once dominated by coal mining and the iron and steel industries, while, to the north, lie the unspoilt southern uplands of the Brecon Beacons National Park. This rigidly observed divide is explained by geology, as the coal-bearing rocks of the valleys end here and give way to the limestone and old red sandstone rocks of the Brecon Beacons. The close proximity of the two different types of rock also explains the nature and growth of industry

in this particular area of South Wales as the iron smelting process required not just coal but also limestone. The iron ore was locally available too. These ingredients all came together in the most productive way at Merthyr Tydfil and this former iron and steel capital of the world was once the largest town in Wales. It took its name from the martyr St Tudful, the daughter of the Welsh chieftain Brychan (see also Brecon). She was martyred by the Irish for her Christian beliefs in 480 AD.

Described as "the most impressive monument of the Industrial Iron Age in Southern Wales", Cyfarthfa Castle is a grand mansion situated in beautiful and well laid out parkland. The castle was commissioned in the 1820s by the ironmaster William Crawshay, who constructed the grand house to overlook the family's ironworks, which at the time were the largest in the world. Today, this mansion is home to the **Cyfarthfa Castle Museum and Art Gallery** (see panel below), which not only covers the social and industrial history of Merthyr Tydfil and the surrounding area, but also has an extensive

Cyfarthfa Castle Museum & Art Gallery

Brecon Road, Merthyr Tydfil CF47 8RE
Tel/Fax: 01685 723112

Built in 1824, **Cyfarthfa Castle** is an impressive monument to the industrial revolution. Once a Regency mansion, it now houses a magnificent museum and art gallery. The basement atmospherically recalls over 3,000 years of history in this important Welsh town, whilst the restored upper floors are a grand setting for the srt displays and eclectic collections from the ancient world.

Cyfarthfa Castle is set in 160 acres of parkland containing formal gardens, sweeping lawns, a lake, children's play facilities, a model railway and much more.

The Castle and park are situated on the edge of the Brecon Beacons National Park and make a great day out. Open daily 1st April - 30th September 10am-5.30pm; 1st October - 31st March, Tuesday-Friday 10am-4pm and Weekend 12-4pm. Closed Mondays.

🏠 historic building   🏠 museum and heritage   🏛 historic site   🗘 scenic attraction   🌿 flora and fauna

collection of fine and decorative art. The parkland, too, is well worth exploring, and at the visitor centre information on the park's amenities and natural history can be found.

Joseph Parry's Ironworker's Cottage, in Chapel Row, provides a contrasting view of life in Merthyr Tydfil during its heyday. A superb example of a skilled ironworker's home, the cottage gives an interesting insight into the living conditions of those days. It was here that Joseph Parry, the 19th-century composer famous for writing the haunting hymn *Myfanwy*, was born; on the first floor is an exhibition of his life and work.

Another of the town's claims to fame lies in the political sphere: it was the first constituency in Britain to return a socialist Member of Parliament when, in 1900, Kier Hardie was elected to Westminster.

Around Merthyr Tydfil

PONTSTICILL
3 miles N of Merthyr Tydfil off the A465

🚂 Brecon Mountain Railway

From here the **Brecon Mountain Railway** travels a short, scenic route up to Pontsticill Reservoir in the Brecon Beacons National Park. The charming vintage steam trains follow the tracks of the old Merthyr Tydfil to Brecon line, which has been re-opened by railway enthusiasts.

ABERFAN
4 miles S of Merthyr Tydfil off the A4054

🚂 Memorial Gardens

This former mining village still carries about it a feeling of infinite sadness. On the morning of 21 October 1966 a great mountain of coal waste slid down onto the village, engulfing

Pantglas School and about 20 houses, killing 144 people, of which 116 were children. It was a disaster of international proportions. The then chairman of the National Coal Board, Alfred Robens, rather than visit the disaster site straight away, decided instead to attend a ceremony where he was installed as Chancellor of Surrey University. This, and his later insistence that the causes of the disaster had been hitherto unknown springs beneath the slag heap (when in fact they had been known about), blackened his name forever in Wales.

People come to the village nowadays, not as tourists, but as people who want to spend time reflecting in the **Memorial Gardens**, built on the site of the school

Bridgend

🏛 Newcastle Castle   🏛 Coity Castle
🏛 South Wales Police Museum

Known in Welsh as Pen-y-Bont Ar Ogwr (meaning "the crossing of the River Ogmore"), this bustling market town lies at the confluence of the Rivers Ogmore, Garw and Llynfi and it was once regarded as so vital a route that it had two castles, one on either side of the River Ogmore. The remains of 12th century **Newcastle Castle** lie on the west riverside while the more extensive ruins of 14th century **Coity Castle** stand guard on the other. Originally built by the Norman Payn de Turberville, and strengthened over the following three centuries, Coity Castle was finally abandoned in the late 16th century, having withstood a siege by Owain Glyndwr 150 years earlier.

Bridgend's distinction as a market town dates back as far as the early 16th century, and down the ages there have been tanneries, a woollen

HEALTH DIVA

18 Norton Street, Bridgend, Glamorgan, CF31 1DU
Tel: 01656 661441
e-mail: healthdiva@mac.com
website: www.healthdiva.co.uk

The Health Diva in Nolton Street Bridgend is a little haven of calm and tranquility, allowing you to explore the many lotions and potions. Vicky Perks (The Diva), with the support of her husband Darren, and Team Diva (Jennifer, Rachel and Laura) run this amazing little Health Shop, sharing their knowledge and helping you along on your life journey.

Natural Beauty Care is something we specialize in; The Diva knows it's not easy being beautiful, my public expects the best of me ... However I have a few beauty secrets that I am willing to share, because it's you, and I know you won't divulge my secrets!

The Diva prefers her bunnies in fields or made or chocolate, certainly not wearing her make up. The Diva only uses cruelty free beauty products, and demands high standards from the cosmetic companies she recommends: Organic Paraben free skin care made with love by companies such as Burt's Bees, Faith in Nature, Antipodes, Lavera, Green People, and Weleda.

Eating plenty of fresh fruits and vegetables, along with Viridian's Ultimate Beauty complex ensures I get my daily vitamins and minerals Eicosanoil added to my breakfast provides omega 3, 6, and 9 essential fats to moisturize my skin from the inside out.

LOU'S DELICATESSEN

38-40 Dunraven Place, Bridgend,
Mid-Glamorgan CF31 1JB
Tel: 01656 769199
website: www.lousdeli.co.uk

Since taking over here in 2008, owner Louise and cook Caroline have quickly built up a fantastic reputation for selling quality products at affordable prices. In a town-centre pedestrian street, with plenty of parking nearby, **Lou's Delicatessen** is a paradise for food-lovers, and serious foodies find it hard to walk past the mouth-watering window display. Louise and Caroline are passionate and enthusiastic about good food, either cooked on the premises or sourced from select producers, with the emphasis on Welsh goods. Caroline gets up at 6 in the morning to bake her super pies, including corned beef and chicken & ham, that are among the favourites in this outstanding deli. Other goodies include Welsh and Continental cheeses, specialist pasta, Emily's jams and pickles, Daffodil Cottage oat cakes, Laver Bread fudge, Italian olive oils, Welsh honey, Doves Farm award-winning bread, locally hand-made chocolates and the superb produce of Ogmore Farm and the Garlic Farm. Vegetarian and vegan options are available, and food allergies can be catered for. Lou's can supply hampers (including organic) either ready assembled from their wicker-basket range or to special order, and local bakers make lovely celebration cakes for birthdays, anniversaries, weddings and other special occasions.

Newcastle Castle, Bridgend

factory and local potteries in the area. However, for the past 250 years or so, Bridgend has been an agricultural market centre supporting the industrial towns in the valleys. In the South Wales Police HQ is the **South Wales Police Museum**, with displays, artefacts and photographs of policing in the area.

Around Bridgend

EWENNY
1 mile S of Bridgend on the B4265

🏛 Ewenny Priory   🏛 Parish Church of St Michael

🎨 Ewenny Pottery

This charming rural village is home to **Ewenny Priory**, whose church is now the **Parish Church of St Michael**. It was founded in 1141 by Maurice de Londres, the

son of William de Londres of Ogmore Castle. This is one of the finest fortified religious houses in Britain and, while its precinct walls, towers and gateways give the priory a military air, it is believed that they were built for reasons of prestige rather than defence. Close by lies 400-year-old **Ewenny Pottery**, said to be the oldest working pottery in Wales.

TONDU
3½ miles N of Bridgend on the A4063

🏛 Tondu Heritage Park

🌱 Parc Slip Nature Reserve

The nationally important Tondu Ironworks have now been incorporated into the **Tondu Heritage Park**, while the site of an old colliery and open cast coal workings have been developed into the **Parc Slip Nature Reserve**. The reserve's network of paths lead visitors through the various different wildlife habitats, such as grassland, woodland and wetland, where a wide variety of plants, birds and animals have made their homes.

BETWS
5 miles N of Bridgend off the A4063

🏛 Bryngarw House   🌿 Bryngarw Country Park

Just south of the village lies **Bryngarw Country Park**, which throughout the year presents a variety of enchanting landscapes including woodland, grassland, water features and formal gardens. A visitor centre provides information on the country park and on the many species of plants and birds to be found here. Perhaps the most interesting feature of the park is the exotic Japanese Garden, which was laid out in 1910 and where there are a series of interlinked ponds and an oriental tea garden pavilion, as well as superb azaleas, rhododendrons, magnolias and cherry trees.

The house at the centre of the estate, **Bryngarw House**, was built in 1834 by Morgan Popkin Treherne as a "small but elegant dwelling".

MAESTEG
8 miles N of Bridgend on the A4063

🏛 Tabor Chapel

This ancient market town was the centre of iron making in the 1820s, but the last great furnace was 'blown out' in 1886; one of the ironworks is now a sports centre. Maesteg was once linked to the coast at Porthcawl by a tramway, traces of which can be seen at Porthcawl. The **Tabor Chapel** in Maesteg was where *Land of My Fathers* was first sung in public in 1856. The Welsh words were written by Evan James, the music by his son James James. For 112 years, Talbot Street was the only alcohol-free high street in Britain, so covenanted in the will of the teetotal spinster after whom the street was named. In the summer of 2002, a restaurant challenged the covenant, and the magistrates ruled in his favour.

LLANGEINOR
5 miles N of Bridgend on the A4064

🏛 Parish Church of St Ceiwyr

This pretty village is home to the **Parish Church of St Ceiwyr**, built on the site of a 6th century monastic cell founded by St Ceindaughter of King Brychan, who gave his name to Breconshire. It has a fine 15th-century nave, a 16th-century tower and a Norman font.

HOEL-Y-CYW
4 miles NE of Bridgend off the B4280

🌄 Mynydd y Gaer

To the northeast of the village lies

Mynydd y Gaer, a wonderful 1,000-feet high viewpoint that provides spectacular views across the valleys to the north and the Bristol Channel to the south.

LLANTWIT MAJOR
8 miles SE of Bridgend off the B4265

🏛 Town Hall   🏛 Parish Church of St Illtyd
🏛 Llantwit Major Castle

This delightful town is perhaps the Vale of Glamorgan's most historic settlement. Its **Town Hall** is medieval, and still very much in use today. It was here, in 500 AD, that St Illtyd founded a church and school. One of the great Celtic saints who travelled in Britain, Ireland and Brittany, St Illtyd was a

Parish Church of St Lltyd, Llantwit Major

contemporary of both St David and St Patrick. Although little is known of him, he does feature in the book, *The Life of St Samson of Dol*, which was written around 100 years after his death. The church and school he founded here are believed to be the oldest learning centres in the country. The imposing **Parish Church of St Illtyd** seen today is a combination of two buildings, one an early Norman structure and the other dating from the late 13th century. Inside can be seen a fine collection of Celtic crosses, which includes St Illtyd's or St Samson's cross, found buried in the church grounds on top of two skeletons. **Llantwit Major Castle** – often referred to as the – "Old Place" – is in fact a ruined manor house at the centre of the town.

ST DONAT'S
7½ miles S of Bridgend off the B4265

🏰 St Donat's Castle   ⚓ Nash Point

🏰 Parish Church of St Donat

Close to the village lies **St Donat's Castle**, which was built in the 13th century. It came into the possession of the Stradling family through marriage in 1292, and they remained living there until 1738. A more recent owner was the American newspaper magnate William Randolph Hearst. Hearst, whose life was fictionalised in the classic Orson Welles film, *Citizen Kane*, spent huge sums of money restoring and furnishing this historic building, where he entertained film stars and other well known figures. To the west of the village lies **Nash Point** (see walk on page 336), a headland with two lighthouses and the remnants of an Iron Age fort. This area of the coast is overlooked by limestone cliffs which through wind erosion have begun to resemble giant building blocks. The present **Parish Church of St Donat** dates originally

from Norman times, but it has been much altered over the years. Within the Lady Chapel are tombs of members of the Stradling family.

SOUTHERNDOWN
4 miles S of Bridgend on the B4265

🏰 Dunraven Castle

🌿 Glamorgan Heritage Coast Centre

This popular holiday centre, overlooking Dunraven Bay, is home to the **Glamorgan Heritage Coast Centre**, which has displays and information about the 14-mile long stretch of wild and beautiful coastline, which begins in the west at Newton. The scant remains of **Dunraven Castle**, which is actually a 19th-century mansion can be seen. It was inhabited right up until the 1940s, but was partially demolished in 1963.

OGMORE
2½ miles S of Bridgend on the B4524

Lying at the mouth of the River Ogmore, this pretty village is close to a ford across the River Ewenny where the ruins of Ogmore Castle stand. It was built originally in timber in the early 12th century by William de Londres, and rebuilt in stone by his son Maurice. This was once the foremost stronghold in the area although all that can be seen today are the remains of a three-storey keep and the dry moat. The castle grounds are said to be haunted by a ghost known as Y Ladi Wen (The White Lady) who guards the treasure thought to be buried here. For its part, the River Ogmore is supposed to be haunted by the tormented spirits of misers who died without disclosing where they had hidden their riches. Legend has it that these spirits will be released from their misery only when their hoards are found and thrown into the river, downstream of the castle.

Nash Point

Distance: *2.8 miles (4.5 kilometres)*
Typical time: *75 mins*
Height gain: *90 metres*
Map: *Explorer 151*
Walk: *www.walkingworld.com ID:1893*
Contributor: *Peter Salenieks*

Marcross is approached along minor roads from the B4265 to the West of Llantwit Major. A private road leads from Marcross to the Car Park. Cars cost one pound per day in 2003 (50p after 5pm).

This walk will take about 75 minutes. The foreshore between Waypoints 3 and 4 is not accessible around high water.

Nash Point is a popular venue for outdoor activities such as walking, sea angling and birdwatching. This walk takes in part of the Glamorgan Heritage Coast, which was the first designated heritage coast in Britain,

together with points of archaeological and geological interest.

Starting at the entrance to the car park, where light refreshments are available in season, you walk up to reach the site of an Iron Age promontory fort. This is a Scheduled Ancient Monument. It is one of a series of promontory forts situated along the coast of the Vale of Glamorgan that were built between about 700 BC and the Roman invasion of Wales in 76 AD. Only a small remnant of the fort has survived centuries of erosion and undercutting of the cliffs.

There are fine views of cliffs, bays and coastal scenery. Children should be supervised closely, as the footpath is unfenced in places. The walk proceeds along the rocky foreshore to Nash Point. This offers a fresh perspective on the horizontally bedded rocks of the Lower Lias series that form the coastline. There is some unusual rock scenery, together with opportunities to explore the beach and rock pools.

Note that the foreshore between Waypoints 3 and 4 is not accessible around high water. Consult the local press for details of the tide times before you start and plan your day accordingly.

Sea, Toilets, Birds, Great Views, Cafe, Ancient Monument

1 | Follow the footpath down into Cwm Marcross, passing an interpretive sign. Cross Marcross Brook by a small, wooden footbridge and walk up the other side to reach the site of Nash Point Promontory Fort.

2 | Cross the dry-stone wall via a stile and continue north-west along the clifftop footpath. This leads over several more stiles before descending into Cwm Nash.

3 | Turn left (south-west) beside Nash Brook and walk along the foreshore to Nash Point (if the tide is high, then return along the clifftop footpath instead).

4 | Walk around Nash Point, crossing a series of rock pavements and a stony beach to reach the outflow of Marcross Brook.

5 | Join a footpath on the right (east) side of Marcross Brook and ascend towards the entrance to the car park.

6 | Walk from the head of the footpath to the café at Nash Point to complete the route.

Another story tells of the daughter of Maurice de Londres. It seems that the Norman knights regarded all the game in the area as theirs by right. The local population, however, had no other food but the abundant game, and took to poaching. Being caught poaching usually meant the death sentence, and after one such incident, Maurice's daughter intervened, saying that the Welsh should have an area of land where they could hunt. As it was her birthday, her father, as a birthday present, told her to walk in a circle until nightfall, returning to the same spot she started from. The land within that circle would be common land, and anyone could hunt there. Maurice's daughter duly set out, and by nightfall had marked out a vast expanse of land. Her father kept his word, and it is said that Southerndown Common, still in existence today, is that selfsame area of land.

A marked walk leads from the castle across meadows lying between the Ewenny and Ogmore rivers to Merthyr Mawr.

MERTHYR MAWR
2 miles SW of Bridgend off the A48

🏰 Candleston Castle 🏰 Dipping Bridge
🌿 Merthyr Mawr Warren

Situated down river from Bridgend, this delightful village of thatched cottages bordered by meadows and woodland lies on

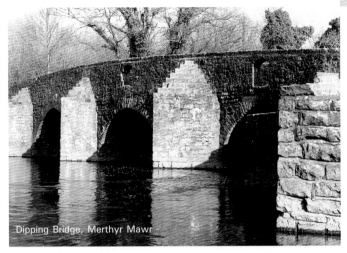
Dipping Bridge, Merthyr Mawr

the edge of **Merthyr Mawr Warren**, one of the largest areas of sand dunes in Europe. Now a Site of Special Scientific Interest, the dunes offer the perfect habitat for a wide variety of plants and animals.

Surrounded by the dune system are the remains of **Candleston Castle**, a 15th-century fortified manor house that was, until the 19th century, the home of the powerful Cantelupe family. Local children believe the house to be haunted but the biggest mystery of Candleston is the fate of the village of Treganllaw (meaning the town of a hundred hands) which is thought to have been engulfed by the dunes. Parts of *Lawrence of Arabia* were filmed here.

On the road approaching the village is the 15th-century **Dipping Bridge**, which has some interesting holes in its parapet through which in the past sheep were pushed into the river for their annual dip. An inn used to stand close to the bridge, where, it was claimed by locals, travellers were murdered for their money. This was dismissed as a far, fetched story until the inn was pulled down, and skeletons were dug up in the grounds.

NEWTON

4½ miles W of Bridgend off the A4106

Dating back to the 12th century, the village was founded as a 'new town', and by the 17th century was a thriving port from where grain and knitted stockings were exported. The imposing limestone Parish Church of St John the Baptist was originally built by the Sir Thomas de Sandfford family for the Knights of the Order of St John of Jerusalem in the late 12th or early 13th century, though some of what we see nowadays is 15th century. Thomas had obviously been on the Crusades, as he named his son and heir Jordan.

PORTHCAWL

6 miles W of Bridgend on the A4229

🏛 Porthcawl Museum   🏛 Lifeboat Station

🏛 Porthcawl Harbour

Porthcawl is one of the region's most popular resorts, with clean sandy beaches at Sandy Bay, Trecco Bay and the quieter Rest Bay, along with an amusement park that provides a wide variety of rides, from white knuckle roller coasters to more gentle carousels. This is also a haven for surfers, sailors and fishing enthusiasts, while the headlands above Rest Bay are the site of the famous Royal Porthcawl Golf Club.

The more dignified side of Porthcawl centres on the Edwardian promenade, a legacy of the prosperous days when this was a port exporting coal and iron. The history of the town can be discovered at **Porthcawl Museum** in John Street, where there is a fascinating collection of artefacts, costumes and memorabilia on display, while at **Porthcawl Harbour** there are still several

historic buildings that date from the heyday of this busy port. During the summer, two veteran steamships leave the harbour for trips along the Bristol Channel and across to Lundy Island. Down the years, the crews of Porthcawl's **Lifeboat Station** have earned 29 awards, including, in 2004, a Bronze Medal to the helmsman Aileen Jones, the first for a woman in 116 years. Crew member Simon Emms was awarded the Thanks of the Institution Inscribed on Vellum for the same rescue mission. In May 2009, the station, which can usually be visited daily, took delivery of the first of the new Atlantic 85 class boats, the *Rose of the Shires*.

KENFIG

6½ miles W of Bridgend off the B4283

🏰 Kenfig Castle   🏛 Kenfig Pool

🌿 Kenfig National Nature Reserve

This village was originally founded in the 12th century by Robert, Earl of Gloucester, who also built **Kenfig Castle**. However, some 300 years later, the sands of Kenfig Burrows had swamped the settlement and the medieval town lies buried in the dunes, although the remains of the castle keep are still visible. The settlement was actually a borough of some importance, with its own charter, town walls, a thriving High Street and a Guildhall. The legend of **Kenfig Pool** has it that on a quiet day when the water is clear, the houses of the buried town can be seen at the bottom of the lake and the bells of the old church can be heard ringing before a storm.

Today, this marvellous area of dunes to the northwest of the present village is the **Kenfig National Nature Reserve**. With over 600 species of flowering plants, including orchids, a freshwater lake and numerous birds, this is a haven for all naturalists as well as ramblers.

🏰 historic building 🏛 museum and heritage 🏛 historic site 🌊 scenic attraction 🌿 flora and fauna

Penarth & the Vale of Glamorgan

Penarth

Often described as the 'garden by the sea', Penarth (the name means cliff's head or bear's head in English) is a popular and unspoilt seaside resort which developed in Victorian and Edwardian times. Built for the wealthy industrialists of Cardiff's shipyards immediately to the south of the city, this once fashionable town has lost none of its late 19th and early 20th century elegance and style, typified by the splendidly restored pier, the promenade and the formal seaview gardens. If the town seems to have been lost in a time warp, a visit to the **Washington Gallery**, housed in an old cinema on Stanwell Road, will dispel this view through its exciting collection of modern and contemporary art.

In the early 1980s, a team of archaeologists uncovered the remains of a medieval village to the south of the town. It grew up around a manor house belonging to the Constantin family (some of the first Norman invaders in Wales) in the 12th

century. However, in the mid 14th century the Black Death reached the village, killing around one third of the population, and following a period of decline, it was left to decay. Today, **Comeston Medieval Village** is a tourist attraction, and several of the buildings have been reconstructed, allowing visitors, with the help of costumed characters, to gain a real insight into life in a medieval village in 1350 AD.

The village is in **Cosmeston Country Park**, an area of lakes, woodlands and meadows created from a disused limestone quarry. A peaceful and tranquil habitat for many birds and animals, with a wide range of plant life, the country park has a visitor centre, picnic areas and a café.

In 1897, **Lavernock Point**, to the southeast of the country park, was the site of Marconi's early experiments in radio transmission and the scene of the historic reception of the words, "Are you ready?", which were transmitted to Flat Holm, an island some three miles offshore. A tiny island with a

GOWER PENINSULA ND HERITAGE COAST

Comestone Medieval Village, Penarth

wealth of wildlife, Flat Holm also has a history that dates back to the Dark Ages, when it was used by monks as a retreat. Vikings, Anglo Saxons, smugglers and cholera victims are known to have sought refuge on the island, which was also fortified twice, once by the Victorians and again in World War II. Today, it is a Site of Special Scientific Interest, with a local nature reserve that is home to the largest colony of gulls in Wales.

Barry Island

Around Penarth

BARRY ISLAND
5 miles SW of Penarth on the A4055

🏛 Barry Island Railway Heritage Centre

🏛 Barry Castle   🏛 Cold Knap Roman Buildings

🌿 Welsh Hawking Centre

🌿 Barry Island Pleasure Park

Barry Island is not an island but a peninsula that faces the much larger town of Barry itself, whose natural, sheltered harbour has been used since Roman times. **Cold Knap Roman Buildings**, to the west of this seaside resort, are all that remains from those days. A popular place for holidaymakers for

generations, Barry Island offers its visitors all the traditional seaside resort trappings, from sandy beaches to a funfair, as well as views across the Bristol Channel to the Devon coast. The **Barry Island Railway Heritage Centre**, which had been closed, is due to re-open in September 2009 – call 01446 704868 to check. The **Barry Island Pleasure Park** has over 50 rides for kids of all ages, such as a log flume, a haunted mine, roller coaster and carousel. In the town of Barry itself, are the scant remains of **Barry Castle**, including a 14th-century gatehouse. To the north of the resort is the **Welsh Hawking Centre**, where 200 birds of prey have their homes and where there are regular flying demonstrations.

🏛 historic building   🏛 museum and heritage   🏛 historic site   🌿 scenic attraction   🌿 flora and fauna

COWBRIDGE

12½ miles W of Penarth off the A48

🏛 Parish Church of the Holy Cross   🏛 Town Walls

🏛 Cowbridge Museum

This handsome and prosperous town had its origins in a Roman settlement, which by the 4th century had grown into a small town. Recent archaeological digs have uncovered the remains of many Roman buildings, including a bath house. It has been the principal market town of the Vale of Glamorgan since medieval times, and is today noted for its quality shops, crafts and restaurants. The original Norman grid layout of the town is visible to this day, particularly in the mile-long main street, and Cowbridge's mid 14th-century **Town Walls** and gatehouse still stand. The large **Parish Church of the Holy Cross**, originally dedicated to St Mary, dates from around 1300. It has a fortified tower in which is a peal of 13 bells. The **Cowbridge Museum**, within the old town hall cells, has artefacts, photographs and displays on the history of the town. The work of local craftspeople can be seen at the Old Wool Barn Art & Craft Centre, which has studio workshops set around an attractive courtyard.

ST NICHOLAS

6 miles NW of Penarth on the A48

To the south of the village lie Dyffryn Gardens, which, as part of the Dyffryn estate, were landscaped in the 19th century. One of the finest surviving Thomas Mawson gardens in Britain, Dyffryn offers a series of broad sweeping lawns, Italianate terraces, a paved court, a physick garden and a rose garden, as well as a vine walk and arboretum. Perhaps the most impressive features are the Pompeian Garden and the Theatre Garden where open air plays and concerts are held.

ST HILARY

10 miles W of Penarth off the A48

🏛 Beaupre Castle

To the south of the village lies **Beaupre Castle**, which is in two parts. The earliest part, to the south, was built in about 1300 on one side of a small courtyard. In the 16th century the castle was owned by Sir Rice Mansell, who began building a new Tudor building on the north side, again round a court. The work was finished by William Bassett and his son Richard. The well-preserved outer gatehouse, with its exuberant carving, dates from this time.

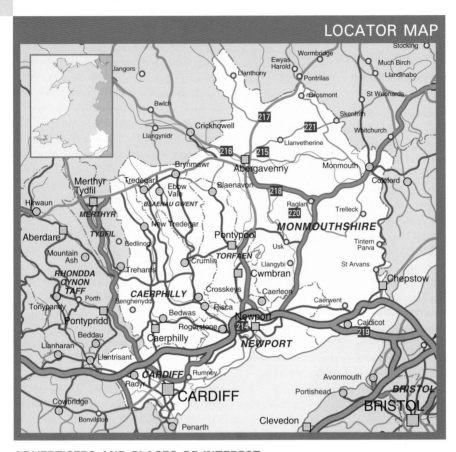

LOCATOR MAP

ADVERTISERS AND PLACES OF INTEREST

Accommodation, Food and Drink

215 | Werngochlyn Cottages, Llantilio Pertholey,
    nr Abergavenny   *pg 356*
216 | Pentre Court Country House, Abergavenny *pg 357*
217 | The Culinary Cottage, Pandy, Abergavenny *pg 358*
218 | The Charthouse, Llavihangel Gobion,
    Abergavenny   *pg 359*
220 | The Ship Inn, Raglan   *pg 368*
221 | 1861 Restaurant, Cross Ash, Abergavenny *pg 369*

Activities

214 | Busy Bees, Newport   *pg 349*
217 | The Culinary Cottage, Pandy, Abergavenny *pg 358*

Arts and Crafts

214 | Busy Bees, Newport   *pg 349*

Places of Interest

219 | Caldicot Castle, Caldicot   *pg 367*

🏚 historic building 🏛 museum and heritage 🏚 historic site 🝊 scenic attraction 🌿 flora and fauna

PENTRE COURT COUNTRY HOUSE

Brecon Road, Abergavenny, Monmouthshire, Wales NP7 7EW
Tel: 01873 853545
e-mail: judith@pentrecourt.com
website: www.pentrecourt.com

Nestled between seven hills right on the Welsh/English border, Abergavenny truly is a 'Gateway To Wales'. An ideal base for exploring the Brecon Beacons, Abergavenny has much to offer tourists - a blend of old and new, with activities and things to do to suit young and old alike. This ancient and welcoming town is the ideal centre for a truly wonderful, refreshing holiday, whether it be a short break at any time of the year or a longer leisurely stay.

And B&B accommodation doesn't come better than at **Pentre Court**. This small Georgian country house is beautifully set in 4 acres of well-wooded gardens and paddock through which runs the stream Nantiago. Adjacent to the house are footpaths to the River Usk and Sugar Loaf Mountain. It is an excellent base for fishing, sailing, golf, pony-trekking, hang-gliding and grass-skiing.

Accommodation includes en-suite bedrooms, central heating, a dining room and drawing room with open fire and colour TV. The drawing room provides a comfortable bright area for guests to mingle, watch television, read or plan the next day's excursions. In the garden is a heated swimming pool with diving board, changing room and sun terrace.

Meals include a typical British or Continental breakfast served in a dining room furnished with interesting antiques. Evening meals or dinner parties can be provided by prior arrangement and packed lunches and special dietary needs can be accommodated. All meals feature local produce wherever possible, and this area is famous for the quality of its produce. The Abergavenny Food Festival transforms this sleepy market town into a vibrant venue for the sampling of fine fare.

Within a short drive of Abergavenny are numerous castles, the most notable being Raglan, Chepstow and White Castle. Each one is set in a beautiful location and ideal for picnics. Only ten minutes away is the Big Pit at Blaenavon, a shaft coalmine dating back to the 1840s, and also an Ironworks dating back to the 1780s. There are extensive Roman remains at Caerleon, with a fine modern museum.

All in all, a stay at Pentre Court can fulfil all you holiday desires or simply feel like a break away from it all - you can almost feel time slowing down as you unwind and take in the fresh mountain air and some of the most picturesque landscape to be found in the UK.

stories and anecdotes 🕮 famous people 🎨 art and craft 🎭 entertainment and sport 🥾 walks

words mention many towns in southeast Wales, but the bells of Rhymney are called the "sad" ones.

ABERGAVENNY

8½ miles N of Pontypool on the A40

🏛 Parish Church of St Mary & Tithe Barn

🏛 Abergavenny Castle

🏛 Abergavenny Museum   🍃 Blorenge

Abergavenny has sometimes been called the gateway to South Wales, and is a particularly pleasant and thriving market town. It sits within the Usk Valley, with the Brecon Beacons National Park to the north. The town can trace its history back to the Roman fort of Gobbanium established here in either 57AD

or 58AD. In the early 12th century, the Norman knight Hameline de Balun built a castle here, and founded a priory. The **Parish Church of St Mary**, once the priory church, dates from the 14th century and later. Inside there are fine choir stalls and medieval altar tombs. The **Tithe Barn** of the church was started in the 12th century, extended in the 14th, enlarged again in the 17th, and refurbished in the 21st. It was officially opened by HRH Prince Charles in October 2008. It contains a Learning Space and Interpretation centre where visitors can learn about the Church and the town down through the centuries. Pride of place in the Tapestry Exhibition Area is the famed Abergavenny Tapestry, created over five years by 50 people.

THE CULINARY COTTAGE

Rose Cottage, Pandy, nr Abergavenny, Monmouthshire NP7 8DL
Tel: 01873 890125
e-mail: penelope@theculinarycottage.co.uk
website: www.theculinarycottage.co.uk

The exclusive hands-on **Culinary Cottage** cookery school and bed and breakfast offers the opportunity for participants to surprise themselves and impress their friends and family with their new cooking skills. The school is the brainchild of Penelope (Penny) Lewis, who spent years of cooking at the highest level at home and overseas for dignitaries, celebrities – even a private party for HM The Queen.

The premises and the area are both conducive to the atmosphere of calm and confidence in which the courses are run – a beautiful 150-year-old cottage in the shadow of the Black Mountains, in lovely walking country that's perfect for walking off a splendid meal or working up an appetite for the next! The friendly ambience and the expert individual attention makes cooking a pleasure, whatever the concerns, ambitions or skills level, and Penny is on hand to guide pupils effortlessly through each step. The courses range from 1 day to 5 days, from the first principles and the basics to advanced à la carte cooking, and covering such diverse topics as stress-free dinner parties, Aga cooking, eating al fresco, student survival and a three-day course devoted to seafood, salads and soufflés. Action-packed days start at 9am, ending with dinner at 7pm, and everything is provided, with tips and advice along the way and a portfolio of recipes to take away – and of course you get to eat everything prepared during the day. Four en suite guest bedrooms cater for students who wish to stay the night before (or during the course), meeting fellow students and Penny over an eve-of-course dinner.

THE CHARTHOUSE

Llanvihangel Gobion, Abergavenny,
Monmouthshire NP7 9AY
Tel: 01873 840414
e-mail: janedavies@waitrose.com
website: www.thecharthouse-bar-bistro.co.uk

Five miles from Abergavenny and nestling in the famous Usk Valley Jane Davies, who is as friendly a host as you could wish for, runs **The Charthouse**. Jane has given the place a nautical revamp since she took over last year. And what better theme than the inherent natural beauty of ocean scenes and the accompanying mystery and romantic appeal that it exudes. The Charthouse aims to provide customers with an all round enjoyable experience starting from when you arrive 'on board'. The bar is cream-panelled with brass portholes, there are models of ships on the windowsills and the walls are festooned with pictures of boats of every shape and size.

The Charthouse prides itself on its bistro menu; over which a great deal of attention and care has been taken, especially with regards to provenance (with the exception of their seafood, delivered daily from Cornwall, they use Welsh producers where possible). Despite the nautical theme, the menu incorporates a wider selection of food presenting you with a well-balanced selection. Their 28 day matured Welsh Black beef, tender and succulent is hard to beat - Jane considers traceability to be essential and the beef is sourced locally from farmers who take pride in their herd. The Charthouse fish pie takes you back to the nautical theme; the chef has prepared this dish with only the best ingredients fresh from the sea

as is the Cornish market traditional beer battered fish served with real homemade chips to compliment the flavour. The vegetables accompanying all dishes are fresh from the grower and prepared in a way that enhances their distinct flavours.

If you are a diner with a sweet tooth, the dessert section of the menu is possibly the one you most look forward to – and you won't be disappointed. The Charthouse understands that desserts tend to leave a lasting impression of the pub's overall food quality, therefore all desserts are home made straight from the 'Galley' and with choices including, rich chocolate and orange mousse, sticky toffee pudding with a butterscotch sauce or glacé nougatine – you will find it impossible to resist. The selection of Welsh hard and soft cheeses is a true example of the progress that has been made in Welsh cheese-making. The excellent flavours provide a final repast to what Jane hopes will be a truly pleasurable experience.

As with all food ingredients, The Charthouse relies on the seasons and consequently many of the items on the menu will be subject to availability and change to ensure you are presented with the best possible choice of dishes. Don't forget to check out the 'specials' board, which changes daily.

CARDIFF AND MONMOUTHSHIRE

Also in the Tithe Barn is a well-stocked Food Hall. In 1175, in the Norman **Abergavenny Castle**, the fearsome Norman lord, William de Braose, invited the Welsh lords to dine and then murdered the lot while they were disarmed at his table. Not very much remains, as King Charles I ordered it to be destroyed. Today, the rebuilt keep and hunting lodge of the castle are home to the **Abergavenny Museum** where exhibits from prehistoric times to the present day detail the history of the town and surrounding area. Displays include re-creations of a Victorian kitchen and a saddler's workshop. The castle and its grounds have been open to the public since 1881.

Abergavenny is a popular place during the summer. Surrounded by glorious countryside, it is a place from where all manner of activities, including walking, pony trekking and canal cruising, can be enjoyed. A little way south of town, the 1,834-feet **Blorenge** is a popular tourist spot. One of the car parks at its base is called Foxhunter. It was presented by Colonel Sir Harry Llewelyn in memory of his wonderful show jumper, which died in 1959 and is buried nearby.

LLANTHONY
19 miles N of Pontypool off the B4423

🏠 Llanthony Priory

In the beautiful Vale of Ewyas, also known as Llanthony Valley, **Llanthony Priory** was built on a spot that has links with the beginnings of Christianity in Wales, and in the 6th century was chosen by St David for a cell. The priory grew out of a hermitage founded by the Norman William de Lacy in the 11th century.

The beauty and tranquillity of the location have inspired many people. Eric Gill and Walter Savage Landor are among those who made their homes here. For many years the site was in a state of near decay, but the Welsh Office graded it as an Ancient Monument and so ensured its survival.

Monmouth

🏠 Monnow Bridge   🏠 Monmouth Castle

🏠 Round House   🏠 Great Castle House

🏠 Parish Church of St Mary   🏛 Castle Museum

🏛 Nelson Museum and Local History Centre

🏛 Regimental Museum   🏛 Naval Temple

🔱 The Kymin   🌱 King's Garden

🖋 Geoffrey of Monmouth   🖋 Charles Stuart Rolls

This prosperous and charming old market town grew up at the confluence of three rivers - the Wye, Monnow and Trothy - which are all noted for their fishing. The River Wye is crossed by a five-arched bridge built in 1617, but the Monnow boasts the most impressive of the town's bridges. **Monnow Bridge** is one

Monnow Bridge, Monmouth

of Monmouth's real gems, and its sturdy fortified gatehouse, dating from the 13th century, is the only one left of its kind in Britain. When work was undertaken some time ago on the bridge to strengthen it, the foundations of the previous wooden bridge, dating from about 1180, were discovered, directly under the present one. The gatehouse was not part of this new bridge, however; it was added in the early 14th century as part of the town's defences.

Long before the bridge was constructed, the Normans built **Monmouth Castle** here in around 1068. Later rebuilt by John of Gaunt in the late 1300s, the castle was the birthplace of his grandson, later Henry V, in 1387. Much later, in the 17th century, **Great Castle House** was built by the 3rd Marquess of Worcester from the ruins of the castle, and he lived here while his other homes, Badminton and Troy House, were being rebuilt. Today, the castle houses both the **Castle Museum** and the **Regimental Museum** where the histories of the castle and the Royal Monmouthshire Royal Engineers are explored. The **King's**

Garden is a re-creation of a small medieval courtyard garden, planted with herbs that would have been common around the time of Henry V.

Another interesting building in the town is the 14th-century **Parish Church of St Mary**, formerly a priory church, whose eight bells are said to have been recast from a peal that Henry V brought back from France after his victory at Agincourt. The story goes that as Henry was leaving Calais, the ringing of bells was heard and he was told that the French were celebrating his departure. He immediately turned back and took the bells to give as a present to his native town.

One of the graves in the churchyard is that of an obscure house-painter called John Renie, who died in 1832 at the age of 33. His headstone is an acrostic of 285 letters that reads, "Here lies John Renie". This epitaph can be read over and over again, upwards, downwards, backwards and forwards, and if doglegs and zigzags are also included, it is apparently possible to read "Here lies John Renie" in 45,760 different ways. The memorial also records the deaths of his two sons, one at the age of one year and nine months, the other at the age of 83. An earlier Monmouth man, **Geoffrey of Monmouth**, was the Prior at St Mary's before becoming Bishop of St Asaph in North Wales. It was probably in Monmouth that Geoffrey wrote his massive work, *A History of the Kings of Britain*, with its legends of

The Wye Valley, nr Monmouth

King Arthur and Merlin.

Also in the town is the **Nelson Museum and Local History Centre**, where a fascinating collection of material and artefacts about the great Admiral can be seen. This interesting collection of memorabilia was accumulated by Lady Llangattock, the mother of **Charles Stuart Rolls** of Rolls-Royce fame, who, while born in London, had his ancestral home nearby. The history of the town is illustrated in displays in the same building. The exploits of the Hon Charles Rolls in cars, balloons and aeroplanes are featured here; one of the most evocative pictures is of Rolls in the basket of his Midget balloon at Monmouth Gasworks in about 1908. Some five miles from the town is the Rolls estate where Charles grew up and developed an early interest in engineering and motoring that led to his forming the Rolls-Royce company. Charles died in an air accident in 1910 and his statue, along with a monument to Henry V, can be seen in the town's main Agincourt Square. He is buried in the churchyard of St Cadoc's, at Llangattock-vibon-Avel, not far from Monmouth.

Just to the west of the town, and practically on the border with England, lies **The Kymin**, a National Trust-owned hill overlooking the River Wye. From here there are spectacular views across the picturesque landscape. The **Round House**, also

found here, was erected by the Kymin Club in 1794. The members of this club were local worthies who liked to hold open-air lunch parties on the Kymin. They decided to construct a building so that they could picnic inside in bad weather, and the result is the Round House - round so that the views could be enjoyed from every part of the house. Offa's Dyke footpath (see Prestatyn) runs through the land. Nearby is the **Naval Temple**, opened in the early 19th century to commemorate the Battle of the Nile.

Around Monmouth

TRELLECK
4½ miles S of Monmouth on the B4293

🏠 Parish Church of St Nicholas   🏛 Harold's Stones

🏛 Preaching Cross   🏛 Tump Turret

🐎 Bertrand Russell

Trelleck's name means Three Stones and these large prehistoric monoliths can be found to the southwest of the village. For reasons unknown, they are called **Harold's Stones**.

Harold's Stones, Trelleck

🏠 historic building 🏛 museum and heritage 🏛 historic site 🗻 scenic attraction 🌿 flora and fauna

They do not represent all the historical interest here, as the **Parish Church of St Nicholas** is also worth visiting. It dates from the 13th and 14th century, and stands on the site of a church built in the 7th century and endowed by the ancient kings of Gwent. The **Preaching Cross** in the churchyard probably dates from that period. Close to the church a mound known as **Tump Turret**, which is all that remains of a Norman motte and bailey.

To the east of the village is the Virtuous Well, also called St Anne's Well. The water is full of iron, and it was once drunk as a curative. In medieval times, Trelleck was one of the most important towns in Wales, and a local field, where stone and masonry have been discovered, is said to mark the location of its main buildings.

The village was the birthplace of the philosopher **Bertrand Russell** (1872-1970). He was the grandson of the 1st Earl Russell.

TINTERN PARVA
7½ miles S of Monmouth off the A466

🏛 Tintern Abbey   🏛 Parish Church of St Mary

🏚 Old Station

This riverside village, which nestles among the wooded slopes of the lovely Wye Valley, is a very beautiful place, and the whole of the valley between Monmouth and Chepstow is designated an Area of Outstanding Natural Beauty. Here are found the enchanting ruins of **Tintern Abbey**, which lie beside the river. The abbey was founded by Cistercian monks in 1131, and largely rebuilt in the 13th century by Roger Bigod, the Lord of Chepstow Castle. The monks farmed the rich agricultural land as well as dedicating themselves to their rigorous regime of religious devotions right up until the time of the Dissolution. A rich and powerful abbey in its day, Tintern is now a majestic ruin with much delicate tracery and great soaring archways, in a glorious setting that has inspired painters and poets such as Turner and Wordsworth.

However, the abbey is not the only ruin in the vicinity. The ruins of the former **Parish Church of St Mary** lie close to the Beaufort Hotel, and originally served the parish of Chapel Hill, to the south of Tintern Parva. The church remained in use until 1972, but was burnt down in 1977.

A mile from the abbey, along the A466 Chepstow-Monmouth road, is the Victorian **Old Station**, which now acts as a visitor centre for the Wye Valley. Here, too, are a

River Wye, Tintern

Tintern Abbey

Distance: *3.1 miles (5.0 kilometres)*
Typical time: *95 mins*
Height gain: *185 metres*
Map: *Explorer OL14*
Walk: *www.walkingworld.com ID:213*
Contributor: *Peter Salenieks*

ACCESS INFORMATION:

The abbey is situated just off the A466 at the southern end of Tintern. The abbey car park is beside the River Wye (grid ref SO 532 001). Bus Service 69 connects Tintern with Chepstow and Monmouth. Contact Traveline for further details (0870-608-2608 or visit www.traveline.org.uk).

ADDITIONAL INFORMATION:

This walk will take about 95 minutes (at four kilometres per hour plus one minute per ten metres of ascent with no stops). It can be combined with a visit to Tintern Abbey. Contact the Information Centre on 01291-689251 to find out when the abbey is open. It is possible to make this into a longer circular walk by continuing south along Offa's Dyke Path from Waymark 12 towards Tidenham Chase, before descending west along a footpath that leads to a disused railway, which is followed back to Waymark 4.

DESCRIPTION:

Whilst Tintern is best known for its abbey, there is evidence of earlier settlements dating back to the Bronze Age. The name 'Tintern' is derived from Dyn Teryn (or King's Fort). It is where King Tewdrig chose to live as a hermit in the 6th Century, before defeating the Saxons in his final battle at nearby Pont y Saeson. The abbey was built on the ruins of Tewdrig's hermitage in 1131 and became the first Cistercian Abbey in Wales. It was rebuilt between 1270 and 1301 to reflect the growing wealth and power of the Cistercian

order and it continued to prosper until 1536, when King Henry VIII dissolved the abbey.

The opening of the Wye Valley Railway in the 1870s hastened the growth of Tintern and the Wye Valley as tourist attractions, prompting some restoration of the abbey ruins. Poets and artists, including Wordsworth and Turner, visited them. William Wordsworth first visited Tintern in 1793·and returned five years later, when he wrote the poem 'Lines composed a few miles above Tintern Abbey', saying that "no poem of mine was composed under circumstances more pleasant for me to remember than this".

This linear walk starts at Tintern Abbey and follows the western bank of the River Wye towards Tintern, where gifts, refreshments and accommodation are available. After crossing the river, wooded paths lead uphill to Offa's Dyke Path, which is followed to the Devil's Pulpit. This is a small limestone rock that juts from the cliffs. It looks down over Tintern Abbey from the hills beside Offa's Dyke on the eastern side of the River Wye. Local legend has it that the devil stood upon the Devil's Pulpit to preach to the monks below, tempting them to desert their order.

FEATURES:

River, Pub, Toilets, Church, Wildlife, Birds, Great Views, Cafe, Gift Shop, Tea Shop, Woodland.

WALK DIRECTIONS:

1 | Start at Tintern Abbey

2 | Follow the footpath along the western bank of the river. After the footpath turns inland towards Tintern, pass the Quay House on the left and continue along a minor road to reach a T-junction. There is a footpath sign directly ahead.

3 | Turn left (south) and walk a short distance along the minor road to a junction with the A466. Turn right (north-west) and walk along the pavement, passing a hotel on your left and an art

gallery and gift shop on your right. Continue until you reach a minor road junction on your right, which is just past the Abbey Mill Cafe.

4 | Walk north-east along the minor road towards the River Wye and cross the footbridge. Continue east along the footpath on the eastern side of the river, passing a footpath on the right (which leads to the riverbank). A footpath on the left

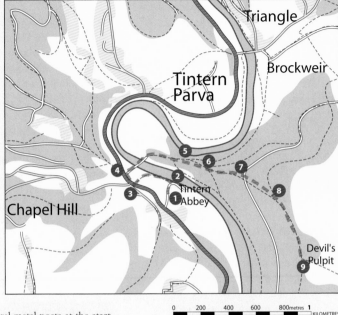

leads uphill, with several metal posts at the start. Follow the footpath uphill. Shortly after it levels off, there is a footpath junction beside a short section of stone wall on the left (north).

5 | Take the right-hand footpath and follow it for a short distance, until you reach another footpath junction marked by a wooden post with a footpath sign. Take the right-hand footpath and continue for a short distance to reach a footpath junction.

6 | Turn left and follow the footpath uphill, as it ascends the northern side of a narrow spur. As the gradient levels off, the footpath bears around to the right (south-east). A short flight of wooden steps can be seen on the left. Ascend the wooden steps to reach a track junction marked by a wooden post with a footpath sign. An antenna can be seen on the opposite side of the track. (It is also possible to ignore the steps and

continue along the footpath to reach the track at waymark 8. Turn right (south-east) and walk a short distance along the track to reach a footpath junction with a stone marker.

7 | Bear left at the junction and follow the footpath uphill to reach Offa's Dyke Path.

8 | Turn right (south) at the footpath sign and walk along Offa's Dyke Path until you reach a footpath junction and a sign at a right-hand bend.

9 | Continue west along Offa's Dyke Path from the footpath sign to reach the Devil's Pulpit at a left-hand bend. Tintern and the Wye Valley can be seen below through a clearing in the trees. Retrace your route back to the start.

countryside exhibition, a collection of signal boxes, a gift shop and a model railway.

CHEPSTOW

12½ miles S of Monmouth on the A48

🏛 Chepstow Castle   🏛 Parish Church of St Mary

🏛 Town Gate   🏛 Chepstow Museum

🏛 Port Wall

This splendid old market town, which lies on the border with England, takes its name from the Old English chepe stow, meaning market place. It occupies a strategic crossing on the River Wye between England and Wales, and looks across the river into England. Situated on a crag are the well-preserved ruins of **Chepstow Castle**, which William Fitzosbern, Earl of Hereford, began building in 1067 as a base for the Norman conquest of southeast Wales. Its importance can be judged from the fact that it was built of stone, when most Norman fortresses of the time were in motte and bailey form and built from earth and timber. The castle began life as a keep, and towers, walls, fortifications and gatehouses were added to prepare it for the Welsh wars, in which, as it happened, it played no part. It is open throughout the year.

A major exhibition within its walls, A Castle at War, relates its history, and a group of local people have come together to form the Chepstow Garrison; dressing up and re-enacting scenes from Chepstow's past, they have become a popular attraction for both local residents and tourists.

Built at the same time as the castle keep, and by the same William Fitzosbern, is the **Parish Church of St Mary**. It was the church of a former Benedictine priory that suffered considerable damage after the Dissolution of the Monasteries in 1536. It suffered further damage in 1701 when the massive central

tower collapsed. The vast three-storey original nave gives some idea of the grand scale on which it was built. The church contains some imposing and interesting monuments, including the Jacobean tomb of Margaret Cleyton with her two husbands and 12 children. This lady paid for the town's gatehouse to be rebuilt in 1609. Also entombed here is Henry Marten, friend of Oliver Cromwell and signatory to the death warrant of Charles I. Marten spent many years imprisoned in Chepstow Castle, in the tower that now bears his name. William Fitzosbern also founded the Abbey at Cormeilles in Normandy, a town with which Chepstow is now twinned.

Opposite the castle is **Chepstow Museum**, housed in an elegant 18th-century merchant's house, and here the rich and varied history of

Chepstow Town Gate

this border town is revealed. The museum has displays on the town's many industries, including shipbuilding, fishing and the wine trade. Chepstow was at one time an important centre for shipbuilding, and one of the many photographs in the exhibition shows the closing stages in the building of *War Genius* in National Shipyard No 1 in 1920. Ships were built well into the 1920s, and the tradition was revived during World War II with the construction of tank landing craft.

Throughout the town itself, the medieval street pattern is still much in evidence, along with surviving sections of the town wall, called the **Port Wall**, and the impressive **Town Gate**. But Chepstow is also a thriving modern town, and its attractions include an excellent racecourse offering both Flat and National Hunt racing; the highlight of the jumping season is the valuable and prestigious Welsh Grand National. The racecourse lies within the grounds of historic Piercefield Park. Piercefield Picturesque Walk was created in the 1750s by Valentine Morris the Younger, and follows the Wye river cliff up to the Eagle's Nest. Chepstow is at one

end of Offa's Dyke (see Prestatyn), the 8th-century defensive ditch and bank built by the King of Mercia. It is also the starting point for the long-distance Wye Valley and Gloucestershire Way walks.

CALDICOT
15 miles S of Monmouth on the B4245

🏰 Caldicot Castle

🏰 Parish Church of St Mary

Caldicot Castle (see panel below) dates from Norman times and was restored for use as a family house in the 1880s. It was originally built by Humphrey de Bohun on a much earlier fortified site in the early 13th century. Of particular note is the sturdy round keep and the gatehouse dating from the 14th century. The castle, which is set within a wooded country park, hosts occasional medieval banquets.

The **Parish Church of St Mary** dates originally from the 12th century, though it is now mainly from the 14th and 15th century. It was founded by Milo Fitzwalter on the site of an earlier church dedicated to St Bride.

Caldicot Castle

Church Road, Caldicot, Monmouthshire NP26 4HU
Tel: 01291 420241 Fax: 01291 435094
e-mail: caldicotcastle@monmouthshire.gov.uk
website: www.caldicotcastle.co.uk

Visit **Caldicot Castle** in its beautiful setting of tranquil gardens and a wooded country park. Founded by the Normans, developed in royal hands as a stronghold in the Middle Ages and restored as a Victorian family home, the castle has a romantic and colourful history. Find out more with an audio tour, explore the medieval towers and take in the breathtaking views from the battlements. Enjoy a leisurely game of chess or drafts, using giant playing pieces, visit the Children's Activity Station or relax in the gardens and grounds. Events take place throughout the season. Open Daily March to October.

📖 stories and anecdotes 🐿 famous people 🎨 art and craft ✎ entertainment and sport 🚶 walks

CAERWENT

14 miles SW of Monmouth off the A48

🏛 Parish Church of St Stephen   🏛 Venta Silurum

Close to the Wentwood Forest, this town - which is now more of a village - was the site of **Venta Silurum**, a walled Roman city built by the invaders for the local Celtic Silures tribe. Sections of the Roman defences still stand and are some of the best preserved in Britain, while inside the walls can be seen the remains of the forum basilica and the Romano-Celtic temple. Venta Silurum is thought to have been the largest centre of civilian population in Roman occupied Wales, and covered over 44 acres. It is yet another suggested site for King Arthur's Camelot.

Much of the present village is built of stone taken from the Roman site, including the **Parish Church of St Stephen**, which was constructed in medieval times.

RAGLAN

6½ miles SW of Monmouth off the A40

🏛 Raglan Castle   🏛 Clytha Castle

To the north of this village of shops and inns and a mix of old and modern buildings, lies **Raglan Castle**, one of the finest late medieval fortresses in Britain. Built towards the end of the Middle Ages, and thus in relatively peaceful times, the castle was also constructed with comfort in mind, and it represents wealth and social aspirations as much as military might. Started in 1435 by Sir

THE SHIP INN

8 High Street, Raglan, Monmouthshire NP15 2DY
Tel: 01291 690365

The Ship Inn is a delightful family run business, housed in a16th century stone built pub that combines all the best traditions of an 'olde worlde' inn with modern standards of service and great value for money. It has a fine reputation, both with locals and visitors, and there's plenty of entertainment on offer; a pool and games room, regular live music on weekends, open mic night on the last Tuesday of month and quiz night every first Thursday of the month.

The interior has bare stone walls, old beams and an open fireplace where a fire burns during the winter months. It sells a great range of drinks, from real ales to beers, wines, spirits (the alcoholic kind!) and soft drinks. And the food is outstanding. So much so that you are well advised to book in advance for evening meals and for Sunday lunch. All the produce used is sourced from a local farm shop, and master butcher Neil James, ensuring maximum freshness and flavour. The menu includes such favourites as steaks with all the trimmings, tasty cottage pie, chicken and mushroom pie, lasagne, curries, sliced ham, egg and chips and faggots served with peppered mash, onion gravy and peas.

Teas and fresh-ground coffees are also available, and within the outdoor courtyard are tables and chairs for eating and drinking al fresco during the warmer months. This is a pub that takes its customers seriously, and always offers a warm welcome to all including children and well behaved dogs.

🏛 historic building 🏛 museum and heritage 🏛 historic site 🍃 scenic attraction 🌿 flora and fauna

William ap Thomas, who fought at Agincourt, the building work was continued in the same lavish manner by the next owner, William Herbert, who was responsible for the addition of the formal state apartments and the magnificent gatehouse. Despite being more a palace than a fortress, Raglan Castle withstood one of the longest sieges of the Civil War. To the west lies **Clytha Castle**, a folly designed by John Nash for an owner of the Clytha Park estate in memory of his wife.

The village indirectly gives its name to the Raglan sleeve, which is joined to the main part of a pullover in a diagonal manner, from collarbone to armpit. It was named after Fitzroy James Henry Somerset, 1st Baron Raglan (1788-1855), who lost an arm at the Battle of Waterloo.

USK

11½ miles SW of Monmouth on the A472

🏰 Usk Castle   🏠 Parish Church of St Mary

🏠 Gwent Rural Life Museum

This delightful small town, which takes its name from the river on which it sits, was founded by the Romans in 75AD. Well known for its excellent local fishing - the River Usk is a fine salmon river - the town attracts fishermen from far and wide. Also noted for its floral displays and historic buildings, Usk is home to the **Gwent Rural Life Museum**, housed in several historic buildings, which tells the story of life in this Welsh border region from Victorian times up until the end of World War II. Among the many themes covered here are domestic and agricultural life exhibits ranging from hand tool

1861 RESTAURANT

Cross Ash, Abergavenny, South Wales NP7 8PB
Tel: 0845 388 1861
website: www.18-61.co.uk

The picturesque hamlet of Cross Ash, just outside Abergavenny, is home to a new gourmet cuisine experience. **1861** takes its name from its year of construction, but no longer looks its age following a serious sprucing-up by owners, Simon and Kate King. Inside has a subtle contemporary feel, while maintaining its original features, black-painted beams, white-washed walls and well-spaced tables, and is presided over by a small yet knowledgeable staff, with Kate managing the front of house.

Simon, owner and head chef, has worked in some of the country's top restaurants; fine dining is very much his forte. The kitchen teams technical skill with a knack for eye-catching presentation, delivers a modern British menu that doesn't disappoint.

Simon and Kate are fully committed to sourcing the finest of local ingredients and ensuring the provenance of those ingredients. A truly family affair their parents provide most of the vegetables and fruit used in the restaurant from nearby Penperlleni, their quest for the freshest ingredients serves to create an ever changing seasonal menu that is quickly providing them with a very positive recognition.

Not surprisingly, 1861 has become one of Abergavenny's hotspots, attracting customers with top class food, value for money and sharp service that manages to be both friendly and efficient.

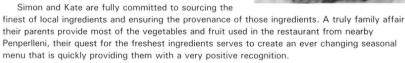

📖 stories and anecdotes 🦉 famous people 🎨 art and craft 🎭 entertainment and sport 🚶 walks

crafts to mechanisation.

Usk Castle was built in the early 12th century, and passed to and fro between the English and the Welsh. It was strengthened by Gilbert de Clare in the late 13th and early 14th century when he built the tower keep. De Clare was eventually killed at Bannockburn, and it then passed to Elizabeth de Burgh and eventually, the Mortimer family. The Duchy of Lancaster, which owned it next, allowed it to fall into decay.

The **Parish Church of St Mary** was formerly the church of a Benedictine priory for nuns founded in the 12th century, and has a 15th-century roodscreen.

LLANVETHERINE
9 miles NW of Monmouth on the B4521

🏛 White Castle

🏛 Parish Church of St James the Elder

To the south of the village lies one of the Three Castles, **White Castle**, which is so called because when it was built the masonry was rendered with gleaming white plaster, patches of which can still be seen. Starting life as a simple earthwork not long after the Norman Conquest, White Castle was rebuilt in stone during the late 12th and 13th century to provide, along with Skenfrith and Grosmont castles, a triangle of fortresses to control this strategic entry point into Wales. Situated in a beautiful and isolated place, the ruins are still able to conjure up the romance of the Middle Ages. Much later, during World War II, Hitler's deputy, Rudolf Hess, fed the swans on the castle's moat while held at a local mental hospital following his mysterious flight from Nazi Germany. The **Parish Church of St James the Elder** dates from the 14th century, though it was restored in 1872. The Arts and Crafts pulpit dates from 1900.

GROSMONT
9½ miles NW of Monmouth on the B4347

🏛 Grosmont Castle

🏛 Parish Church of St Nicholas

This village takes its name from the French, gros mont, meaning big hill; it is the site of **Grosmont Castle**, the most northerly of the Three Castles.

Now in ruins, Grosmont started life as a steep earthen mound but, after having been replaced by a stone fortification, it was unsuccessfully besieged by both Llywelyn the Great and Owain Glyndwr. During exploration of the ruins, an Arabic 'faience jar' was found here - undoubtedly a relic from the Crusades. The 13th-century **Parish Church of St Nicholas** has an octagonal tower surmounted by a spire. The nave has an unusual tomb - the stone carving of the recumbent knight above it was never finished.

SKENFRITH
5½ miles NW of Monmouth on the B4521

🏛 Skenfrith Castle   🏛 Parish Church of St Bridget

At this point the Monnow Valley forms something of a gap in the natural defences of the Welsh Marches and its was here that the Normans built **Skenfrith Castle** (NT), the last of the Three Castles - the others being White and Grosmont. Situated beside the river, Skenfrith Castle was built in the 13th century by Hubert de Burgh and is noted for its fine round tower keep and its well-preserved curtain wall. Once the troubled domain of medieval warlords, this border region is today peaceful and undisturbed. The **Parish Church of St Bridget** dates from the 13th century with later additions, and sits close to the River Monnow, where stand the remains of a medieval quay.

TOURIST INFORMATION CENTRES

ABERAERON

The Quay, Aberaeron SA46 0BT
Tel: 01545 570602
Fax: 01545 571534
e-mail: aberaerontic@ceredigion.gov.uk

ABERDULAIS (SEASONAL)

The National Trust, Aberdulais SA10 8EU
Tel: 01639 636674
Fax: 01639 645069
e-mail: aberdulaistic@nationaltrust.org.uk

ABERDYFI (SEASONAL)

The Wharf Gardens, Aberdyfi LL35 0ED
Tel: 01654 767321
Fax: 01654 767321
e-mail: tic.aberdyfi@eryri-npa.gov.uk

ABERGAVENNY

Swan Meadow, Monmouth Road,
Abergavenny NP7 5HL
Tel: 01873 853254
Fax: 01873 853254
e-mail: abergavennyic@breconbeacons.org

ABERYSTWYTH

Terrace Road, Aberystwyth SY23 2AG
Tel: 01970 612125
Fax: 01970 612125
e-mail: aberystwythtic@ceredigion.gov.uk

BALA (SEASONAL)

Pensarn Road, Bala LL23 7SR
Tel: 01678 521021
Fax: 01678 521021
e-mail: bala.tic@gwynedd.gov.uk

BANGOR (SEASONAL)

Town Hall, Deiniol Road, Bangor LL57 2RE
Tel: 01248 352786
Fax: 01248 352786
e-mail: bangor.tic@gwynedd.gov.uk

BARMOUTH

The Station, Station Road, Barmouth LL42 1LU
Tel: 01341 280787
Fax: 01341 280787
e-mail: barmouth.tic@gwynedd.gov.uk

BARRY (SEASONAL)

The Promenade, The Triangle, Barry CF62 5TQ
Tel: 01446 747171
Fax: 01446 747171
e-mail: barrytic@valeofglamorgan.gov.uk

BEDDGELERT (SEASONAL)

Canolfan Hebog, Beddgelert LL55 4YD
Tel: 01766 890615
Fax: 01766 890615
e-mail: tic.beddgelert@eryri-npa.gov.uk

BETWS Y COED (SEASONAL)

Royal Oak Stables, Betws y Coed LL24 0AH
Tel: 01690 710426
Fax: 01690 710665
e-mail: tic.byc@eryri-npa.gov.uk

BLAENAU (SEASONAL)

Unit 3, High Street, Blaenau LL41 3ES
Tel: 01766 830360
Fax: 01766 830360
e-mail: tic.blaenau@eryri-npa.gov.uk

BLAENAVON (SEASONAL)

Blaenavon World Heritage Centre, Church Road,
Blaenavon NP4 9AS
Tel: 01495 742333 Fax: 01495 742332
e-mail: blaenavon.tic@torfaen.gov.uk

BORTH (SEASONAL)

Cambrian Terrace, Borth SY24 5HY
Tel: 01970 871174
Fax: 01970 871365
e-mail: borthtic@ceredigion.gov.uk

BRECON

Cattle Market Car park, Brecon LD3 9DA
Tel: 01874 622485
Fax: 01874 625256
e-mail: brectic@powys.gov.uk

BRIDGEND

Bridgend Designer Outlet, The Derwen,
Bridgend CF32 9SU
Tel: 01656 654906
Fax: 01656 646523
e-mail: bridgendtic@bridgend.gov.uk

TOURIST INFORMATION CENTRES

CAERLEON
5 High Street, Caerleon NP18 1AE
Tel: 01633 422656
Fax: 01633 422656
e-mail: caerleon.tic@newport.gov.uk

CAERNARFON
Oriel Pendeitsh, Castle Street, Caernarfon LL55 1ES
Tel: 01286 672232
Fax: 01286 676476
e-mail: caernarfon.tic@gwynedd.gov.uk

CAERPHILLY
The Twyn, Caerphilly CF83 1JL
Tel: 029 2088 0011
Fax: 029 2086 0811
e-mail: tourism@caerphilly.gov.uk

CARDIFF
The Old Library, The Hayes, Cardiff CF10 1AH
Tel: 08701 211 258
Fax: 029 2023 2058
e-mail: visitor@cardiff.gov.uk

CARDIGAN
Theatr Mwldan, Bath House Road, Cardigan SA43 1JY
Tel: 01239 613230
Fax: 01239 614853
e-mail: cardigantic@ceredigion.gov.uk

CARMARTHEN
113 Lammas Street, Carmarthen SA31 3AQ
Tel: 01267 231557
Fax: 01267 221901
e-mail: carmarthentic@carmarthenshire.gov.uk

CHEPSTOW
Castle Car Park, Bridge Street, Chepstow NP16 5EY
Tel: 01291 623772
Fax: 01291 628004
e-mail: chepstow.tic@monmouthshire.gov.uk

CONWY
Castle Buildings, Conwy LL32 8LD
Tel: 01492 592248
Fax: 01492 573545
e-mail: conwytic@conwy.gov.uk

DOLGELLAU
Ty Meirion, Eldon Square, Dolgellau LL40 1PU
Tel: 01341 422888
Fax: 01341 422576
e-mail: tic.dolgellau@eryri-npa.gov.uk

FISHGUARD (SEASONAL)
Ocean Lab, The Parrog, Fishguard SA64 0DE
Tel: 01348 872037
Fax: 01348 872528
e-mail: fishguardharbour.tic@pembrokeshire.gov.uk

FISHGUARD (SEASONAL)
Town Hall, Market Square, Fishguard SA65 9HA
Tel: 01437 776636
Fax: 01384 875582
e-mail: fishguard.tic@pembrokeshire.gov.uk

HARLECH (SEASONAL)
Llys y Graig, High Street, Harlech LL46 2YE
Tel: 01766 780658
Fax: 01766 780658
e-mail: tic.harlech@eryri-npa.gov.uk

HAVERFORDWEST
Old Bridge, Haverfordwest SA61 2EZ
Tel: 01437 763110
Fax: 01437 767738
e-mail: haverfordwest.tic@pembrokeshire.gov.uk

HOLYHEAD
Stena Line, Terminal 1, Holyhead LL65 1DQ
Tel: 01407 762622
Fax: 01407 761462
e-mail: holyhead@nwtic.com

KNIGHTON
Offa's Dyke Centre, West Street, Knighton LD7 1EN
Tel: 01547 528753
Fax: 01547 529027
e-mail: oda@offasdyke.demon.co.uk

LLANBERIS (SEASONAL)
41b High Street, Llanberis LL55 4EU
Tel: 01286 870765
Fax: 01286 871924
e-mail: llanberis.tic@gwynedd.gov.uk

TOURIST INFORMATION CENTRES

LLANDOVERY

Heritage Centre, Kings Road, Llandovery SA20 0AW
Tel: 01550 720693
Fax: 01550 720693
e-mail: llandovery.ic@breconbeacons.org

LLANDUDNO

Library Building, Mostyn Street, Llandudno LL30 2RP
Tel: 01492 577577
Fax: 01492 577578
e-mail: llandudnotic@conwy.gov.uk

LLANELLI

Millennium Coastal Park Discovery Centre, North Dock,
Llanelli SA15 2LF
Tel: 01554 777744
Fax: 01554 757825
e-mail: DiscoveryCentre@carmarthenshire.gov.uk

LLANFAIRPWLLGWYNGYLL

Station Site, Llanfairpwllgwyngyll LL61 5UJ
Tel: 01248 713177
Fax: 01248 715711
e-mail: llanfairpwll@nwtic.com

LLANGOLLEN

Y Chapel, Castle Street, Llangollen LL20 8NU
Tel: 01978 860828
Fax: 01978 861563
e-mail: llangollen@nwtic.com

MERTHYR (SEASONAL)

14a Glebeland Street, Merthyr CF47 8AU
Tel: 01685 379884
Fax: 01685 379884
e-mail: tic@merthyr.gov.uk

MILFORD (SEASONAL)

94 Charles Street, Milford SA73 2HL
Tel: 01646 690866
Fax: 01646 690655
e-mail: milford.tic@pembrokeshire.gov.uk

MOLD

Library Museum & Art Gallery, Earl Road,
Mold CH7 1AP
Tel: 01352 759331
Fax: 01352 759331
e-mail: mold@nwtic.com

MONMOUTH

Market Hall, Priory Street, Monmouth NP25 3DY
Tel: 01600 713899
Fax: 01600 772794
e-mail: monmouth.tic@monmouthshire.gov.uk

MUMBLES

The Methodist Church, Mumbles Road,
Mumbles SA3 4BU
Tel: 01792 361302
Fax: 01792 363392
e-mail: info@mumblestic.co.uk

NEW QUAY(SEASONAL)

Church Street, New Quay SA45 9NZ
Tel: 01545 560865
Fax: 01545 561360
e-mail: newquaytic@ceredigion.gov.uk

NEWPORT

Museum & Art Gallery, John Frost Square,
Newport NP20 1PA
Tel: 01633 842962
Fax: 01633 222615
e-mail: newport.tic@newport.gov.uk

NEWPORT (SEASONAL)

2 Bank Cottages, Long Street, Newport SA42 0TN
Tel: 01239 820912
Fax: 01239 821258
e-mail: NewporfTIC@Pembrokeshirecoast.org.uk

OSWESTRY (SEASONAL)

Mile End Services, Oswestry SY11 4JA
Tel: 01691 662488
Fax: 01691 662883
e-mail: tic@oswestry-bc.gov.uk

TOURIST INFORMATION CENTRES

OSWESTRY (SEASONAL)
The Heritage Centre, 2 Church Terrace,
Oswestry SY11 2TE
Tel: 01691 662753
Fax: 01691 657811
e-mail: ot@oswestry-welshborders.org.uk

PEMBROKE (SEASONAL)
Visitor Centre, Commons Road, Pembroke SA71 4EA
Tel: 01437 776499
e-mail: pembroke.tic@pembrokeshire.gov.uk

PENARTH (SEASONAL)
Penarth Pier, The Esplanade, Penarth CF64 3AU
Tel: 029 2070 8849
e-mail: penarthtic@valeofglamorgan.gov.uk

PORTHCAWL (SEASONAL)
Old Police Station, John Street, Porthcawl CF36 3DT
Tel: 01656 786639
Fax: 01656 782387
e-mail: porthcawltic@bridgend.gov.uk

PORTHMADOG
High Street, Porthmadog LL49 9LD
Tel: 01766 512981
Fax: 01766 515312
e-mail: porthmadog.tic@gwynedd.gov.uk

PRESTEIGNE (SEASONAL)
The Judge's Lodging, Broad Street, Presteigne LD8 2AD
Tel: 01544 260650
Fax: 01544 260652
e-mail: presteignetic@powys.gov.uk

PWLLHELI
Min y Don, Station Square, Pwllheli LL53 5HG
Tel: 01758 613000
Fax: 01758 613000
e-mail: pwllheli.tic@gwynedd.gov.uk

RHYL
Rhyl Childrens Village, West Parade, Rhyl LL18 1HZ
Tel: 01745 355068
Fax: 01745 342255
e-mail: rhyl.tic@denbighshire.gov.uk

SAUNDERSFOOT (SEASONAL)
The Barbecue, Harbour Car Park,
Saundersfoot SA69 9HE
Tel: 01834 813672
Fax: 01834 813673
e-mail: saundersfoot.tic@pembrokeshire.gov.uk

ST DAVID'S (SEASONAL)
Visitor Centre, Oriel y Parc, St David's SA62 6NW
Tel: 01437 720392
e-mail: enquiries@stdavids.pembrokeshirecoast.org.uk

SWANSEA
Plymouth Street, Swansea SA1 3QG
Tel: 01792 468321
Fax: 01792 464602
e-mail: tourism@swansea.gov.uk

TENBY
Unit 2, The Gateway Complex, Tenby SA70 7LT
Tel: 01834 842402
Fax: 01834 845439
e-mail: tenby.tic@pembrokeshire.gov.uk

WELSHPOOL (SEASONAL)
The Vicarage Gardens Car Park, Church Street,
Welshpool SY21 7DD
Tel: 01938 552043
Fax: 01938 554038
e-mail: ticwelshpool@btconnect.com

WREXHAM
Lambpit Street, Wrexham LL11 1WN
Tel: 01978 292015
Fax: 01978 292467
e-mail: tic@wrexham.gov.uk

INDEX OF WALKS

Looking for more walks?

The walks in this book have been gleaned from Britain's largest online walking guide, to be found at *www.walkingworld.com*.

The site contains over 2000 walks from all over England, Scotland and Wales so there are plenty more to choose from in this book's region as well as further afield - ideal if you are taking a short break as you can plan your walks in advance. There are walks of every length and type to suit all tastes.

Want more detail for the walks in this book? Next to every walk in this book you will see a Walk ID. You can enter this ID number on Walkingworld's 'Find a Walk' page and you will be taken straight to the details of that walk.

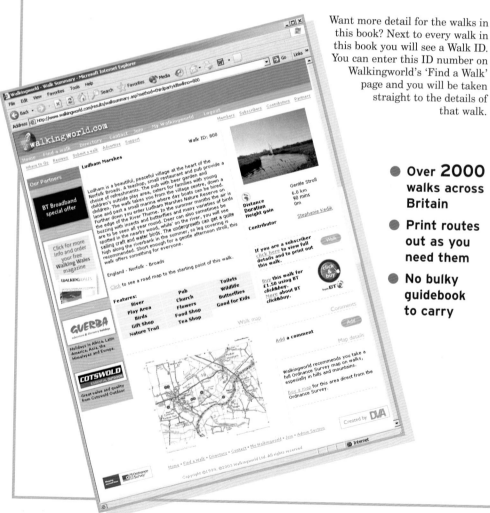

● Over **2000** walks across Britain

● Print routes out as you need them

● No bulky guidebook to carry

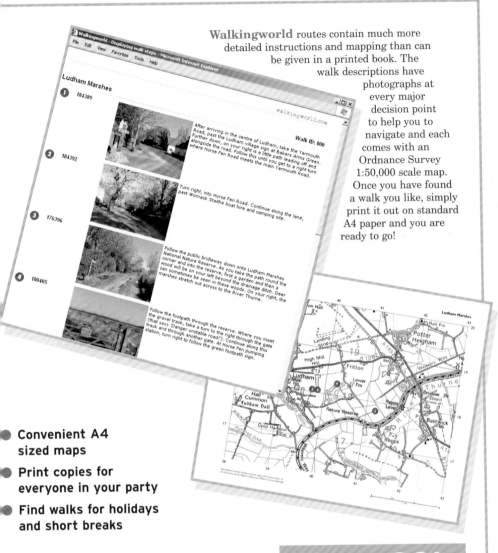

Walkingworld routes contain much more detailed instructions and mapping than can be given in a printed book. The walk descriptions have photographs at every major decision point to help you to navigate and each comes with an Ordnance Survey 1:50,000 scale map. Once you have found a walk you like, simply print it out on standard A4 paper and you are ready to go!

● **Convenient A4 sized maps**

● **Print copies for everyone in your party**

● **Find walks for holidays and short breaks**

A modest annual subscription gives you access to over 2000 walks, all in Walkingworld's easy to follow format. The database of walks is growing all the time and as a subscriber you gain access to new routes as soon as they are published.

Visit the Walkingworld website at *www.walkingworld.com*

ORDER FORM

To order any of our publications just fill in the payment details below and complete the order form. For orders of less than 4 copies please add £1 per book for postage and packing. Orders over 4 copies are P & P free.

Please Complete Either:

I enclose a cheque for £ [_____] made payable to Travel Publishing Ltd

Or:

CARD NO: [_____]   EXPIRY DATE: [_____]

SIGNATURE: [_____]

NAME: [_____]

ADDRESS: [_____]

TEL NO: [_____]

Please either send, telephone, fax or e-mail your order to:

Travel Publishing Ltd, Airport Business Centre, 10 Thornbury Road, Estover, Plymouth PL6 7PP
Tel: 01752 697280   Fax: 01752 697299   e-mail: info@travelpublishing.co.uk

	PRICE	QUANTITY		PRICE	QUANTITY
HIDDEN PLACES REGIONAL TITLES			**COUNTRY LIVING RURAL GUIDES**		
Cornwall	£8.99	....	East Anglia	£10.99	....
Devon	£8.99	....	Heart of England	£10.99	....
Dorset, Hants & Isle of Wight	£8.99	....	Ireland	£11.99	....
East Anglia	£8.99	....	North East of England	£10.99	....
Lake District & Cumbria	£8.99	....	North West of England	£10.99	....
Lancashire & Cheshire	£8.99	....	Scotland	£11.99	....
Northumberland & Durham	£8.99	....	South of England	£10.99	....
Peak District and Derbyshire	£8.99	....	South East of England	£10.99	....
Yorkshire	£8.99	....	Wales	£11.99	....
HIDDEN PLACES NATIONAL TITLES			West Country	£10.99	....
England	£11.99	....			
Ireland	£11.99	....			
Scotland	£11.99	....			
Wales	£11.99	....			
OTHER TITLES					
Off The Motorway	£11.99	....	**TOTAL QUANTITY**	[_____]	
Garden Centres and Nurseries of Britain	£11.99	....	**TOTAL VALUE**	[_____]	

READER REACTION FORM

The **Travel Publishing** *research team would like to receive readers' comments on any visitor attractions or places reviewed in the book and also recommendations for suitable entries to be included in the next edition. This will help ensure that the* **Country Living series of Rural Guides** *continues to provide its readers with useful information on the more interesting, unusual or unique features of each attraction or place ensuring that their visit to the local area is an enjoyable and stimulating experience. To provide your comments or recommendations would you please complete the forms below and overleaf as indicated and send to:*

The Research Department, Travel Publishing Ltd, Airport Business Centre, 10 Thornbury Road, Estover, Plymouth PL6 7PP

YOUR NAME:

YOUR ADDRESS:

YOUR TEL NO:

Please tick as appropriate: COMMENTS   RECOMMENDATION

ESTABLISHMENT:

ADDRESS:

TEL NO:

CONTACT NAME:

PLEASE COMPLETE FORM OVERLEAF

READER REACTION FORM

COMMENT OR REASON FOR RECOMMENDATION:

....

....

....

....

....

....

....

....

....

....

....

....

TOWNS, VILLAGES AND PLACES OF INTEREST

Shrinking Sam
and the
Rat

Sam came home from school.

He was eating a burger.

"That burger smells!" said Sam's

mum. "Please eat it outside!"

Sam went into the street and ate up his burger.

His mum looked out of the window. "I want you to do a little job for me," she said. "I have lost the key to my bike lock. Please look for it out there."

Sam knew what would happen next.
There was a great big *FLASH* and
he shrank!
This always happened when his
mum asked him to do a *little* job.
Now Sam was tiny!

NO.1
BURGER

BURGE

Sam looked around.

He saw Mum's key. It was next to the drain. He had to get it. Then he would grow to the right size again.

Suddenly Sam saw something.
It was an enormous rat!
The rat grabbed the key,
and jumped into the drain.

"Oh no!" said Sam.
Now he had to find the rat
to get the key.

Sam looked down the drain.
Suddenly, he fell in.
Down and down he fell.
At the bottom of the drain
was the rat.
It was trying to eat the key!

Sam was scared of the enormous rat.
Then he had an idea.

He said to the rat, "If you give me
that key, I'll give you something
really tasty. It's up in the street."

"Is this a trick?" said the rat.

"No way!" said Sam. "But I can't get out of here on my own."

"OK," said the rat. "Get on my back."

The rat took Sam and the key
back up to the street.

"Now give me the key," said Sam, "and you can have *that*!" He tapped the burger box. "Mmmmm," said the rat. "It smells good!"

Sam took the key and *FLASH* he was the right size again.

The rat looked in the burger box.

It was empty.

"It **was** a trick!" cried the rat.

The rat was so cross, it bit the box.

"Enjoy your meal!"
Sam said to the rat.
Then Sam took the key
inside to his mum.

Quiz

Text Detective

- How did Sam get out of the drain?
- What do you think Sam told his mum at the end of the story?

Word Detective

- Phonic Focus: Long vowels
  Page 6: Sound out the phonemes (sounds) in 'drain'. What long vowel can you hear?
- Page 5: Why is the word 'little' in italics?
- Page 7: Find a word meaning 'very large'.

Super Speller

Read these words:

ate   trying   I'll

Now try to spell them!

HA! HA! HA!

 Q What do you call a rat with lots of legs?

A A raterpillar!

17

Find out about

- The 'Great Plague' of 1665
- How fleas and rats spread the 'Great Plague' of 1665

Tricky words

- plague
- germs
- fever
- caused
- poison
- special
- caught
- weather

Introduce these tricky words and help the reader when they come across them later!

Text starter

Hundreds of years ago a terrible sickness called the 'Great Plague' came to England. In those days, no one knew what caused the plague and thousands of people died.

The Great Plague

Hundreds of years ago,
there was a terrible sickness
called the 'Great Plague'.
All over the world people died.
The sickness was spread by rats.

How Rats Spread the Plague

Rats had lots and lots of fleas.
The fleas were full of germs.
Some fleas jumped off the rats
and bit people!

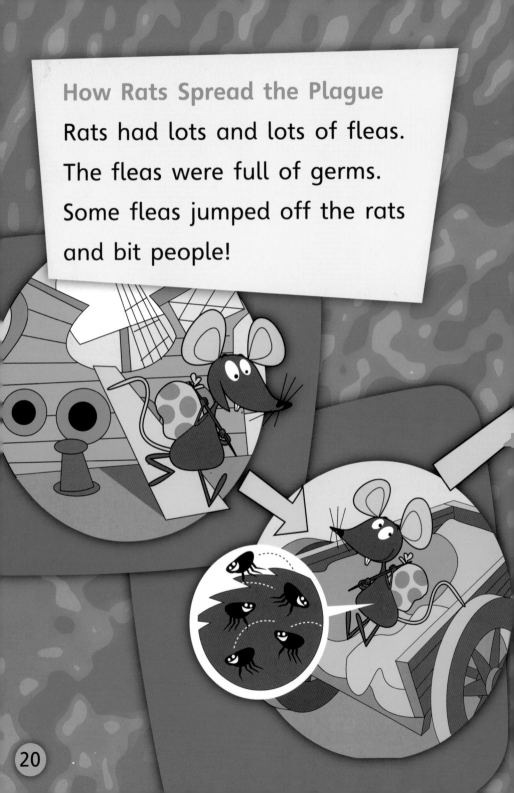

If a person was bitten by
a flea they got the germs too.
The germs were so bad, the
person died.

The Terrible Sickness

First the people got sick.
Then they got big lumps on
their bodies.
Soon they had a terrible fever.
In a few days they died.

People also caught the plague from other sick people!

GRAVEYARD
1 MILE

The plague spread fast.
In England, thousands of people
died each week!

What People Thought

People did not know what had caused the plague.

Some people thought that other people had caused the plague by putting poison in the water. This was not true.

Some people killed cats and dogs because they thought **they** had caused the plague.
This was not true.

What Doctors Did

Doctors did not know how to stop the plague. They thought special clothes would stop them catching the plague. This did not work.

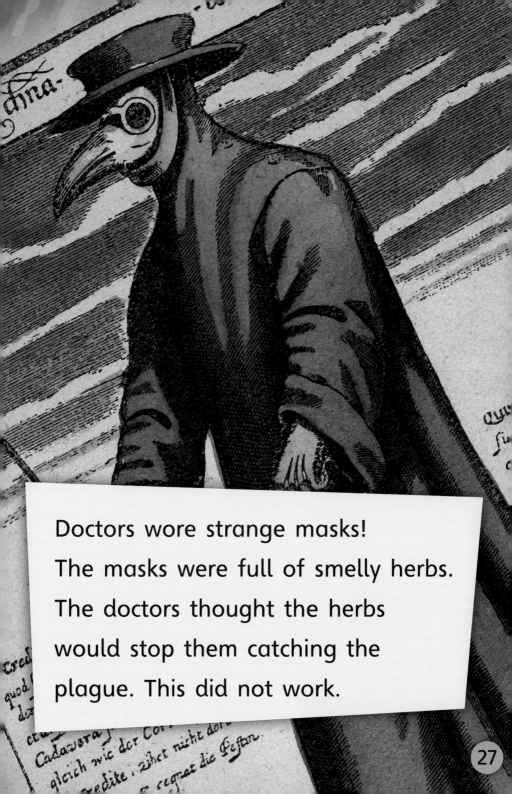

Doctors wore strange masks!
The masks were full of smelly herbs.
The doctors thought the herbs
would stop them catching the
plague. This did not work.

Catching the Plague

If a person caught the plague
they had to stay in their house.
So did all their family.
The door was marked
with a red cross.

Every day a man would come down
the street and call out,
"Bring out your dead!"
The dead bodies were put on a cart
and taken to be buried in huge pits.

The End of the Plague

In the end the plague went away.
The fleas died when the weather
was cold and so the sickness
did not spread any more.

Today doctors know how the plague was spread ...

... and they know how to stop it!

So the plague will not come back.

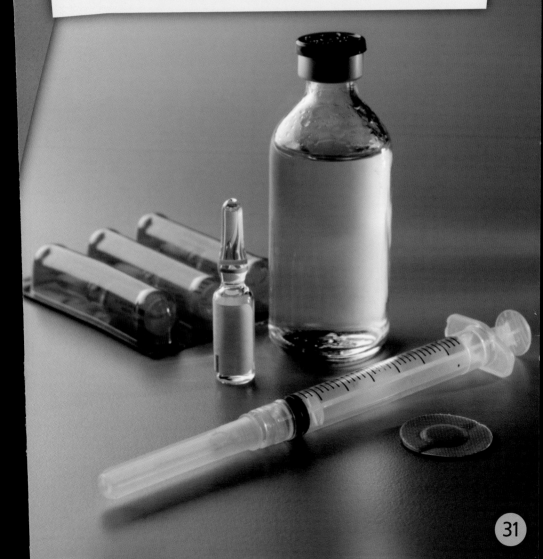

Quiz

Text Detective

- Why won't the plague come back?
- What is the most interesting fact you have learned from this book?

Word Detective

- **Phonic Focus:** Long vowels
  Page 19: Sound out the phonemes (sounds) in 'died'. What long vowel can you hear?
- Page 19: Find a word meaning 'awful'.
- Page 22: Why do the words 'The Terrible Sickness' have capital letters?

Super Speller

Read these words:

spread died years

Now try to spell them!

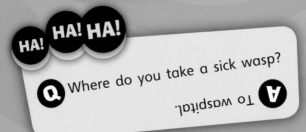

HA! HA! HA!

Q Where do you take a sick wasp?

A To waspital.